WISDOM FROM ALL MY TEACHERS

WISDOM FROM ALL MY TEACHERS

CHALLENGES AND INITIATIVES IN CONTEMPORARY TORAH EDUCATION

Edited by

Jeffrey Saks and Susan Handelman

ACADEMY FOR TORAH INITIATIVES AND DIRECTIONS

URIM PUBLICATIONS
Jerusalem • New York

Wisdom From All My Teachers:
Challenges and Initiatives in Contemporary Torah Education
Edited by Jeffrey Saks and Susan Handelman

Copyright © 2003 by ATID
Academy for Torah Initiatives and Directions, Jerusalem
First Edition
ISBN 965-7108-56-x

Urim Publications, P.O. Box 52287, Jerusalem 91521 Israel

ATID – The Academy for Torah Initiatives and Directions
9 HaNassi Street, Jerusalem 92188 Israel
Tel. 02-567-1719 Fax: 02-567-1723
www.atid.org

Lambda Publishers Inc.
3709 13th Avenue Brooklyn, New York 11218 USA
Tel: 718-972-5449 Fax: 718-972-6307
Email: mh@ejudaica.com

www.UrimPublications.com

עַל שְׁלשָׁה דְבָרִים הָעוֹלָם עוֹמֵד:
עַל הַתּוֹרָה וְעַל הָעֲבוֹדָה וְעַל גְּמִילוּת חֲסָדִים

This book, a product of ATID's pioneering work
under the leadership of our cherished friend,
Rabbi Chaim Brovender,
is dedicated in memory of our beloved parents

Joseph Straus ז"ל
יוסף שמואל בן בנימין ז"ל

Gwendolyn Straus ע"ה
גיננדל בת משה יעקב ע"ה

whose lives were consecrated to the advancement of
Torah u-Madda u-Medinah:
the study of our sacred Torah heritage,
the pursuit of higher education,
and the building of the State of Israel.
Their selfless example of leadership in the Jewish community
has inspired us to strive to emulate their legacy of love
for the entire Jewish people.

יהי רצון שיהיו מליצי יושר בעדנו ובעד כל בית ישראל

Zahava & Moshael Straus and Family
Joyce & Daniel Straus and Family
Adina & Jeffrey Rubin and Family
Bethia Straus & Paul Quintas and Family

CONTENTS

PREFACE

בן זומא אומר איזהו חכם הלומד מכל אדם שנאמר (תהלים קיט:צט) "מכל מלמדי השכלתי." – אבות פ"ד, מ"א

אמרו חכמי האומות כי היודע כל החכמות אם אינו אוהב החכמה אינו חכם אלא טיפש הוא אחר שאינו אוהב החכמה כי היא הדעת. אך האוהב אותה ומתאוה אליה אע"פ שאינו יודע כלום הרי זה נקרא חכם שעל כל פנים תשיג אל החכמה האמיתית "ודעת אלקים תמצא" (משלי ב:ה). ועל זה אמר בן זומא "איזהו חכם הלומד מכל אדם" שכל כך אוהב החכמה ומתאוה אליה ששואל לכל אדם ואף מי שאינו יודע כי אם דבר אחר [נ"א: אחד] ילמד ממנו ואז יצליח דרכו ואז ישכיל. ועל זה נקרא חכם שנאמר "מכל מלמדי השכלתי" שכן אמר דוד ע"ה שלמד מכל אדם ולא היה אומר זה אינו יודע כמוני כי מכלם למד והשכיל. משל לאדם שהפסיד כלי קטן והלא מכל אדם מבקש אותו: – פירוש רבינו יונה על אבות

Ben-Zoma says: Who is wise? One who learns from every person, as Scripture states (Ps. 119:99): **"From *all* my teachers I grew wise."**
— *Avot* 4:1.

The sages of the nations declared that if one were to know *all* wisdom, yet not *love* wisdom – such a person is not wise, but a fool, since he does not love wisdom, which is the knowledge. However, one who loves and hungers after wisdom, even were he to know nothing at all, is called "wise" – since inevitably he will acquire true wisdom "and attain knowledge of God" (Prov. 2:5). About this, Ben-Zoma said: "Who is Wise? One who learns from every person" – since he so greatly loves and hungers after wisdom that he seeks it from every person, even from someone who knows merely one thing. He will learn from that person, succeed, and become enlightened. For this trait he is called wise, as Scripture says, "From *all* my teachers I grew wise." Thus stated King David, who learned from all, never saying, "This one knows not as much as I" – but from *every* person he learned and gained insight. This is similar to one who loses a small item, and seeks it from each person.
— Rabbeinu Yonah on *Avot*

BEN ZOMA'S READING of the verse in *Tehillim* about the acquisition of wisdom – from which we have borrowed the title of our book – is a most appropriate epigraph for a collection of essays and reflections by teachers of Torah about the holy task they undertake. The best educators are themselves perennial students, and a true student is one who learns from all because he or she loves wisdom (the literal meaning of the Greek word "philosophy"). This idea is echoed in another well-known talmudic source: "Much Torah have I learned from my rabbis [and teachers], from my colleagues even more, but from my *students* most of all."[1]

Indeed, upon entering *yeshivot*, or other settings of traditional Torah study, one encounters a unique educational setting, one in which teachers don't teach and students don't study – rather, everyone *learns*. In addition to learning, however, educators must *also* teach. Much can be said about the relationship between learning and teaching and, as we know, Rambam counts these two components as one unified *mitzvah*.[2] It is no surprise, then, that one's students – and the need to teach them – serve as the greatest impetus to a teacher's ongoing acquisition of wisdom.

In this light, Rabbi Joseph B. Soloveitchik resolved an apparent contradiction in the *halakhah*.[3] On one hand, we are obligated to recite the blessing over Torah study (*birkat ha-Torah*) prior to any learning whatsoever. On the other hand, even though one does indeed fulfill the *mitzvah* of Torah study through mental contemplation alone (*hirhur*), no blessing is required.[4] The Rav explained that although silent and solitary study does constitute the learning component of *talmud Torah* (as defined by Rambam), it lacks the potential for the second component, namely, *teaching*. Torah study, in its fullest sense, is always dialogical – possessing the capability to educate others. Silent contemplation (*hirhur*), although a fulfillment of "You shall meditate on it [Torah] day and night" (Josh. 1:8), does not meet the criterion for requiring its own blessing, since it is impossible to teach others through *hirhur* alone.

---

[1] *Makkot* 10a; cf. version in *Ta`anit* 7a. On Maharal's discussion of Ben Zoma's principle, see Yael Wieselberg's essay in this volume.

[2] See his *Sefer ha-Mitzvot*, Positive Commandment #11, and the introduction to *Mishneh Torah, Hilkhot Talmud Torah* (as opposed to the opinion of *Behag* and *Semag*, e.g.).

[3] Cited by R. Mordecai (Morton) Green in *Ha-Darom* 64 (Elul 5755): 95. See also the opening discussion in R. Aharon Lichtenstein's essay in this volume.

[4] This question is based upon the *halakhah* as presented by the *Shulhan Arukh* in *Orah Hayyim* 47:4, from which the Vilna Gaon dissents in his *Bi'ur ha-Gra*.

In both the halakhic tradition and in pedagogical practice, learning and teaching are symbiotically connected. The teacher's own learning reaches its full potential when it is transmitted to students – and the teaching of those students forms the basis for the teacher's own wisdom.

This volume, an outgrowth of the work begun by the Academy for Torah Initiatives and Directions in Jewish Education (ATID), which is based in Jerusalem, offers reflections by leading Jewish educators from Israel and the Diaspora on our most pressing issues. ATID has been working since 1998 to create a broad community of Torah educators; our conviction is that the much-needed reforms in Jewish education will come through involving all those entrusted with this work: teachers and parents, administrators and lay leadership, formal and informal educators, academics and school personnel, students of *yeshivot* and of universities. We seek to bring all actively and intensely together in ATID to map out the future and create a new generation of educational decision-makers, designers, and practitioners. ATID's work, and this book by extension, seeks to be a forum in which the interplay between learning and teaching – in all of its complexity – can be activated and explored.

The twenty essays in this volume are both descriptive and prescriptive. The authors represent a remarkable cross-section of contemporary Torah educators: men and women; teachers with but a few years of experience side by side with the leading figures in Torah teaching. The issues they cover include the nature of the *mitzvah* of *talmud Torah* and its relation to the love and awe of God, and to personal moral development; the role of worldly wisdom in Torah education; the cultivation of the student's soul; the challenges of teaching students or adults who do not fit into the mold of the traditional curriculum; deliberations on the teaching of Talmud and *Tanakh* to this generation; the use of philosophy and *Aggadah* in the yeshivah curriculum; and the place of the Israel experience in shaping the religious personality.

By definition, a book is a static vehicle to convey a message and communicate ideas, yet we hope this volume will serve on one level as a snapshot of ATID's dynamic and rigorous effort to explore and translate those ideas into innovative practice. Furthermore, we believe that the body of thinking that stands behind the book has the potential to both enlighten and ennoble our work, and that it may serve as a springboard for the type of deliberation that will foster educational improvement in a variety of settings. In sum, our goal is for these essays to stimulate all who feel strongly about the future of Torah teaching. Regardless of your window on the world of Jewish education – be it from within home, school, or synagogue – we hope our book will provoke you to think more profoundly and act more sensitively toward the complexities and challenges that we face together as teachers of Torah in the contemporary world. It is our prayer that *Wisdom From All My Teachers* will aid the community of Jewish educators, parents, and policy-makers in our collective efforts on behalf of Jewish children and the Jewish people.

Finally, in the spirit of *Sukkah* 49b, may we all be reminded of the most sublime aim of learning:

> Rabbi Elazar said: What does it mean, "Her mouth is open with wisdom, and the Torah of kindness is on her tonge" (Prov. 31:26)? Is there a "Torah of kindness" and a Torah that is not of kindness?... Some explain, studying Torah in order to teach – this is Torah of kindness; studying Torah without the intention of teaching – this is Torah that is not of kindness.

Jeffrey Saks *and* Susan Handelman
Jerusalem
Erev Shavuot 5763
Hag Matan Torah

ACKNOWLEDGEMENTS

IT IS OUR PLEASANT duty to gratefully acknowledge the many friends and colleagues whose efforts have helped bring this volume to fruition. Uri Cohen, Yoel Finkelman, Anne Gordon, Simi Peters, and Joel B. Wolowelsky all lent editorial help and advice with various parts of the project, and Joel Linsider guided the manuscript through the final copy editing with precision and care. Tzvi Mauer, of Urim Publications, was unfailingly supportive from the very instant the idea for this book arose. We thank the talented array of Torah educators who agreed to take part in this project, as well as the various authors whose work graces these pages.

The support of the Straus, Rubin, and Quintas families enabled the publication of this volume, which serves as a monument to the memory of their late parents, Gwendolyn and Joseph Straus ז"ל. We are grateful for their partnership in this project, and in other initiatives undertaken by ATID on behalf of Torah education.

Publication of *Wisdom From All My Teachers* marks a significant achievement for ATID – both as an institution and as a collective of dedicated Jewish educators working in harmony to improve the state of Jewish education. Since our founding in 1998, we have been privileged to work with an outstanding cadre of young teachers and future educational lay leadership (from both Israel and the Diaspora). We are therefore particularly proud that a number of the essays in the volume began as work undertaken by the educators in our ATID Fellows program, and others by members of our faculty. We have benefited from the input and dedication of many colleagues, themselves outstanding Torah educators and trendsetters, in both the design and the execution of the ATID program, and we are particularly grateful for the ongoing commitment to our work of friends such as David Ebner, Beverly Gribetz, and Daniel Marom.

The visionary leadership of Rabbi Chaim Brovender, President of ATID, informs everything that we do as an institution. His dedication to Torah study as the formative component in helping a student navigate his or her own development as a thinking, religious soul is legendary. Publication of *Wisdom From All My Teachers* coincides with the thirty-sixth year of his involvement in Torah education in Israel, and we pray that he be blessed with many years of health, together with his wife Miriam, leading us in ATID to new heights of excellence, improving the state of Jewish education, and meriting in the continued teaching of *Torat Hashem Temimah*.

    – *The Editors*

My parents, Gail and Gene Saks, my first and most important teachers, have served as lifelong models of doing "right and good in the eyes of God" (Deut. 6:18). Their love and support, together with that of my in-laws, Sorie and Ed Goldstein, have enabled Ilana and me to build a home for our children dedicated to seeking wisdom from every person. Additionally, it has been my great privilege to direct ATID since its inception, and I am grateful to my colleagues and the ATID Fellows, who continue to make it a rewarding experience.

    – *J.N.S.*

Since making *aliyah* the number of my teachers has increased greatly. In addition to the many extraordinary *talmidei* and *talmidot hakhamim* to whom I am privileged to have access (and especially R. Marc Kujawsky), the people of *Medinat Yisrael* – in their infinite variety and abundant spirit in the face of the trauma and suffering of the past three years – each day teach me many precious lessons about life and what it means to be a Jew. My *havrutot* in Jerusalem over the years have been not only stimulating companions and teachers in the journey of endless discovery, consuming passion, and joy that is Torah study – they have also become my very dear friends. I would like to acknowledge and thank: Sara Aisenfeld Beyer, Ora Wiskind Elper, Bryna Yocheved Levy, Simi Peters, Gilla Ratzersdorfer Rosen, Esther Sha'anan, Yardena Cope-Yossef, and Avivah Gottleib Zornberg. And also the ATID Fellows whom I have taught for the past three years, and ATID staff with whom I have worked: you have become a treasured community of fellow teachers from whom I have gained great wisdom, support, pleasure, and inspiration.

    – *S.H.*

KNOWING VS. LEARNING:
WHICH TAKES PRECEDENCE?

NORMAN LAMM

EDUCATION IS THE LIFEBLOOD of Judaism. "The study of Torah out-weighs them all" (*Pe'ah* 1:1). There are several *mitzvot* that the Sages said "outweigh them all," but clearly Torah study has the greatest place of emi-nence in the hierarchy of Jewish values.[1] R. Hayyim of Volozhin taught in his *Nefesh ha-Hayyim* that it is not that Torah study is on one side, while all the other *mitzvot* are on the other side, and Torah study is weightier than the others. Rather, Torah study is the entity from which all others radiate. They are the part, of which Torah study is the whole.[2] This gives Torah study a completely different status. It is not something apart from *mitzvot*. It is the origin of all *mitzvot*.

The Sages asked, "Which is greater, *talmud* (study) or *ma'aseh* (action)?" They concluded, "Study is greater, since it leads to action" (*Kiddushin* 40b). One who does not know Torah cannot practice the *mitzvot* properly. That is why they said, "An ignoramus cannot be pious" (*Avot* 2:6). An ignoramus

---

[1] Not only R. Hayyim of Volozhin, who was the leading student of the Vilna Gaon, and therefore the ideological spokesman for the mitnagdic point of view, but even *hasidut* and *hasidim* agree with this. This is very much counter to the popular prejudice, that *hasidim* were all lower-class people or commoners, who were not sufficiently intel-lectually inclined to be *talmidei hakhamim*. That is a rather crass prejudice, as there were many distinguished Torah scholars from the hasidic world. A story about R. Avraham Bornstein (the Sochatchover Rebbe, author of the *Avnei Nezer*) is indicative of the value placed by *hasidim* on Torah study. When he was older, he became ill. The doctors commanded him to stay in bed, and added that he must not study Torah, because when he did study he would get so involved that he would exert himself, and it was liable to bring premature death. When they told him this, he replied that he was going to study anyway. They said, "Rebbe, it is a matter of life or death." He retorted, "If I learn Torah, then I will die. But if I do not learn Torah, I am going to die. I would rather die from learning Torah than from not learning Torah."

[2] R. Hayyim of Volozhin, *Nefesh ha-Hayyim* 4:29.

cannot know that which he needs to practice as a Jew. Torah knowledge has a clear place in the general structure of the values of Torah.

The question is: which is more important, Torah study or Torah knowledge? Clearly, Torah study (*limmud*) is exceedingly important, and so is Torah knowledge (*yedi'ah*). But is there more importance to learning as a process, or to knowing as a passive achievement?

If Torah knowledge is the totality and ultimate aim of Torah, then it might be possible sometime in the future to fulfill one's obligation of Torah study by purchasing a microchip that contains all 400 books of responsa from the Bar Ilan CD-ROM and implanting it in one's brain. One would have Torah knowledge. What more would one need? There are other shortcuts that technology might invent, by which one could achieve a great deal of knowledge without spending terribly much energy in acquiring that knowledge. So the question is: which will it be?[3]

Judaism vs. the Greeks

This question has certain clear philosophic underpinnings. It goes back to the days when Judaism was involved in a struggle with Hellenism and the teachings of Greek civilization. The Jewish struggle with the Greeks was not only a physical battle. We won that battle, so we celebrate Hanukkah.[4] But it was also a conflict in the world of ideas and values, and that has many consequences.

Scholars tell us that Plato, whose writings are the origin of so much of Western philosophical thought throughout the ages, posed an ontological question, that is, a question about the very nature of reality. He said that there was a difference between *being* and *becoming*. Becoming means development, constant growth, progress. Being means the aim, the end result. Greek thought, starting with Plato, said that being trumps becoming.[5] Being is the ideal, and becoming is just the means toward achieving that ideal. The end is the more important. The word "end" in English, like the word "*takhlit*" in Hebrew, has two meanings – it means the final item or part, and also means the purpose, as in "means and ends." Since the purpose is greater than what leads to it, being takes precedence over becoming. Ac-

---

[3] In the following analysis, I elaborate on the approach I previously developed in "Education in Israel and in the United States," *Ten Da'at* 8:1 (Spring 1995): 11–14.

[4] Actually, we may have lost part of the battle, because the question then was assimilation, and unfortunately assimilation is still very much a part of Jewish society.

[5] This appears, among other places, in the allegory of the cave. See Plato, *The Republic*, book VII: 518–19.

cordingly, the Greeks believed that knowledge is the ultimate goal because it is a state of being.

In his *Shemonah Perakim*,[6] Maimonides poses a similar question. Who is greater, he asks: the righteous person who was born with perfect character (*he-hasid ha-me'uleh*), or the one who struggles with his own evil inclination and overcomes it (*ha-kovesh et yitzro*)? Maimonides answers that the Greek philosophers taught us that the one who was born perfect is preferable, because a person who already has his perfection is the ideal for which we aim. This fits in beautifully with the Greek concept that being is superior to becoming. But, he continues, the Jewish sages prefer the one who is constantly involved in the struggle with his own self, with his own darker forces, and overcomes them. That is much more virtuous than the one who was effortlessly well behaved all along. Interestingly, Maimonides himself tries to reconcile the differences. In some ways he prefers the one who was born perfect; in others, the one who overcomes himself. But he concedes that the Jewish sages hold that the one who overcomes himself is greater than the one who was born perfect; the struggle is more precious than the prize.

We may, I believe, find precedent for this clash of ideas in the biblical narrative concerning the conflict between Yosef and Yehudah. Yosef is well behaved all along, a favorite or darling of his father. He is unselfconsciously a leader, and does the right thing almost all the time. (Even when we find a struggle, in Yosef's encounter with Potiphar's wife, it is one in which he ultimately does the right thing.) He seems to be much closer to the prototype who was born perfect. But Yehudah is different. At the same time that Yehudah is sold into slavery, starting a series of events that elevate him to become the viceroy of Egypt, we read, "At that time Yehudah descended" (Gen. 38:1). Yehudah becomes involved with a woman whom he takes to be a harlot, and she turns out to be his daughter-in-law. Also, he previously said, "What profit is there in killing our brother?" – we might as well sell him (Gen. 37:26–27). Yehudah appears as a man who is beset by less-than-noble impulses. When Tamar shows Yehudah that he is the owner of the tokens he gave her when he thought her a harlot, she asks him, "Recognize this?!" (Gen. 38:25). It is the same expression that the brothers – and probably Yehudah himself – had used when speaking to Ya'akov: "Recognize this? Is this your son's multicolored coat?" (Gen. 37:32). What is Yehudah's reaction? He sees the challenge and overcomes it. He says, "She is right and I am wrong" (Gen. 38:26). Later, he rises to

---

6 *Shemonah Perakim*, chap. 6.

the occasion when he confronts Yosef (whom he does not recognize as Yosef), and, in offering his own life instead of Benjamin's, he shows greatness. This explains why Ya'akov, on his deathbed, speaks lovingly of Yosef but of Yehudah says, "Yehudah is a lion's cub, my son, you ascended from prey (*teref*)" (Gen. 49:9). Rashi asks: what is "*teref*"? It is based on the words, "*Tarof toraf Yosef* – Yosef has surely been torn apart" (Gen. 37:33). Yehudah, who led Ya'akov to believe that Yosef had been torn apart by a wild beast, has risen above all that. Instead of "Yehudah descended," it is "you ascended." There is a great sense of growth in Yehudah. This is an example of the contrast between the one who was born perfect and the one who overcomes himself, with the one who overcomes himself taking precedence.

Judaism, then, adopts a worldview diametrically opposed to that of the Greeks and holds that becoming takes precedence over being. Accordingly, we believe that study is more important than knowledge. If knowledge is a state of being, studying is an act of becoming. As one studies, he keeps growing and growing. There is always movement toward the goal of knowledge. The process, the becoming, is what the studying is all about. In Judaism, the active process, the experience of learning, is valued more than passive knowledge. Torah study is greater than Torah knowledge, because becoming is greater than being. That is why, although a scholar of the Talmud is called a *hakham* (wise person), the term we usually use is *talmid hakham* (student of the wise). A *hakham* is one who knows; a *talmid hakham* is one who learns. Similarly, a *lamdan* (a master of Torah study) is not one who knows, but one who learns, in the same way that a *gazlan* (a thief) is not one who knows how to steal, but one who actually steals. The passion for learning is more important than knowing.[7]

---

[7] A personal anecdote may illustrate the point. I recall, as a young man, coming with high anxiety to the class of the late Rabbi Soloveitchik. He was extremely demanding. We would come into his class ready for intellectual battle – and we shriveled up. We would put our *Gemarot* in front of our faces and peek over them, so he would not recognize us and call on us. Unfortunately, he very often caught me. I remember once, when he had been developing a thesis for some time, he asked me, "Lamm, what does *Tosfos* say?" I was intimidated, so I repeated what he had said the previous day. I thought, "He is going to be pleasantly surprised." But he erupted like a volcano, and said to me, "I know what *I* am saying. I do not need you to tell me! What do *you* think?" His greatness as a teacher was that he wanted a student to learn to think along the lines of his method, but not simply repeat his conclusions parrot-like. He valued a student who challenged him over a student who passively received the information. As a matter of fact, he got so angry with me that he added, "They can sell you the Brooklyn Bridge! The problem is that you check your evil inclination outside the classroom door and come in with the good inclination. Next time, bring your evil inclination with you, and leave your good inclination outside!" He wanted a student to use his "evil

Practical Implications

This preference for the process explains what the Sages mean when they say (*Avot* 5:26), "According to the pain is the reward." What one is rewarded for is the pain involved in the process – the pain of studying, the pain of researching, the pain of thinking, the pain of solving conflicts, the pain of being confronted by one's own ignorance and struggling to overcome it. King Solomon says, "The one who adds knowledge adds pain" (Eccles. 1:18). Rabbi Menaham Mendel of Kotzk, one of my favorite sources of hasidic wisdom and wit (not in the humorous sense, but in the sense of intelligence), comments, "*krenken zolst du, aber lernen musst du*" – "Though you shall become sick, still you must learn!"[8] Torah is acquired through suffering; there is no easy way out. If a person wants to achieve anything in the life of Torah, he needs to invest his peace of mind, health, concentration and focus.[9] Five hundred years ago, one of the giants of Ashkenazic Jewry, R. Yisrael Isserlein (the author of *Terumat ha-Deshen*), wrote about some of his students who came from wealthy homes. They had a new invention that they brought into the *beit midrash*: a type of turntable. Instead of standing up and walking over to the shelf to get a book, they would place all their *Gemarot* and other volumes on the "lazy Susan." They were able to learn with greater ease. They had a shortcut. R. Isserlein comments as follows, "Those rich, pampered students ... are not acting properly. On the contrary! When someone seeks a book and gets it with great effort, because of that [effort] he will remember what he wants to learn."[10] If one invests pain and effort in learning something in the book, he will remember what he learned. If it comes easy, then easy come, easy go.[11]

---

inclination," his passion, in order to conquer a *Tosafot* and understand it properly. He valued the passion and process of study over knowledge, important as knowledge is. The "correct answer" is secondary to the effort to attain it. That was an experience that I have taken with me throughout my life.

[8] Cf. *Emet Mi-Kotzk Titzmah*, ed. Moshe Shenfeld (Benei Berak: Netzah, 1961), #584, commenting on Eccles. 1:18.

[9] See *Berakhot* 5a. Taking it one step further, the *Hazon Ish* writes in a letter, "It is my nature to view everything as difficult, and I hardly ever found anything easy." Everything in life is difficult. Nothing is easy. See R. Avraham Yishayahu Karelitz, *Kovetz Iggerot*, ed. S. Greineman (Benei Berak, 1955), vol. 2, #34 (pp. 44–45).

[10] R. Yosef ben Moshe, *Leket Yosher*, vol. 2, p. 39, citing R. Israel Isserlein.

[11] Another personal anecdote for which I beg the reader's indulgence: When I was a youngster, I needed to save pennies in order to buy a book. I find that what I learned from books I bought then remains with me much longer than what I learn from books I purchase by walking into a bookstore, and easily writing out a check. The investment

To my mind, the most amazing example of the traditional emphasis on study as opposed to knowledge comes to us from a rather arcane book. One of the most difficult, the most recondite, abstract, and abstruse parts of the Zoharic literature is the small volume, *Sifra de-Tzeni'uta*. The Gaon of Vilna wrote a commentary, equally difficult, on the *Sifra de-Tzeni'uta*. It was published with an introduction by the Gaon's student, R. Hayyim of Volozhin. There R. Hayyim records astounding biographical items about the Vilna Gaon. It is well known that the Gaon was already a great genius in his youth. But he also lived an exceedingly rich mystical life. Now R. Hayyim was no fantasy-spinning Hasidic rebbe; he was a sober Litvak, very careful, measured, and precise about what he said. Yet the Gaon told R. Hayyim that, from the time he was nine years old, he had had *aliyyot neshamah* (spiritual experiences) every night, which continued for about seventy years. He received mystical visitations from Ya'akov Avinu, from Moshe Rabbeinu, and of course from Eliyahu ha-Navi. One day the Gaon called R. Hayyim in and said, "Go see Zelmele.[12] Tell him that tonight he will have an angelic visitation of *maggidim*.[13] They will offer him solutions to all the problems that he is having in his Torah study. Tell him to chase them away, because any Torah knowledge which comes without the toil of Torah study is not worth it." The Gaon did not say they would offer false information. They

---

plays a major role. When I was about sixteen or seventeen, I was learning with my grandfather, R. Yehoshua Baumol, who was a great *posek* (halakhic expert). Somewhere in the beginning of *Pesahim*, *Tosafot* quotes a Rashi in *Yevamot*. I read it in – "Rashi explains" – and went on. My grandfather interrupted, "Wait a minute. What are you doing?" I said, "I'm reading the *Tosafot*." He asked, "But what is *Tosafot* saying?" I replied, "He's quoting a Rashi in *Yevamot*." He challenged, "Well, how do you know he is telling the truth? Maybe *Tosafot* is fooling you. Maybe he didn't read it correctly." My grandfather continued, "I want to tell you something: When it comes to *emunot ve-de'ot* (theology), you have to be a *ma'amin* (believer). When it comes to learning, you have to be an *apikores* (heretic)! One needs to challenge everyone, one needs to be a skeptic. If *Tosafot* claims that Rashi says so, get up – don't be lazy, learn that Rashi, and make sure *Tosafot* is telling the truth." As everyone knows in the world of scholarship, that is the way to genuine achievement. One needs a skeptical attitude, and that means investing a lot of energy and time.

12 Zelmele was the nickname of R. Shelomo Zalman, the younger brother of R. Hayyim. Zelmele died young, at the age of thirty-three. A contemporary of his maintained that had Zelmele lived to a ripe old age, he might have exceeded the Gaon of Vilna himself. See Y.L. Maimon, *Sarei ha-Me'ah* (Jerusalem: Mosad ha-Rav Kook, 1965), vol. 2, p. 131.

13 *Maggidim* refer, in this context, to a type of paranormal phenomenon in which the mystic has his own voice speak from within him without his conscious control. In the sixteenth century, R. Yosef Karo, the author of the *Shulhan Arukh*, would have a visitation from a *maggid* every Friday night. After eating and saying the Grace after Meals, he would put his head down and go into a type of trance, and the *maggid* would tell him Torah thoughts. R. Karo describes this in his book, *Maggid Meisharim*.

would offer correct information, but it should not be accepted. Any Torah knowledge that is easily acquired is simply not Torah; it has no spiritual or moral value. The value of one's Torah knowledge is directly proportionate to the energy, the suffering, and the hard experience of acquiring it. The more one has invested in becoming, the more will he achieve in the realm of being.

The dispute we have seen between Judaism and Hellenism has certain surprising results. When the Greeks spoke about education, they usually had in mind adults, not children. The only reason a child needed to learn was as preparation for being an adult. An indication of the Greeks' priorities appears in a Greek word which midrashic literature borrows: "*pedagogue*." The pedagogue was a teacher, but was usually a slave as well – a knowledgeable slave whom the master would use to teach his children. In Judaism, the relationship goes the other way around: the teacher is called a *rav*, a master. There is a very interesting counterpoint here. For the Greeks, the children's teacher was usually only a slave. In Judaism, the children's teacher is an important master. Interestingly, in Maimonides' *Hilkhot Talmud Torah*, the first three *halakhot* deal almost exclusively with the education of children. (For example: the father must teach the child; if the father is absent, who teaches the child?) Only in the fourth *halakhah* does Maimonides finally state that just as it is a *mitzvah* to teach children, so too it is a *mitzvah* to teach oneself. Learning by oneself as an adult is in a sense derivative of the requirement to teach one's children. For Judaism, teaching children becomes more important than teaching adults. Why? Although the end product is considered important, the process – the study – is much more important. Teaching demands more insistent and persistent effort than educating oneself. This explains why, generally, our priority is child education, as opposed to adult education.

To summarize, we have an encounter of two different worldviews, and the consequences thereof. The Greek worldview valued being over becoming, so it emphasized the end product, the knowledge acquired by adults. The Jewish worldview gives full value to Torah knowledge, without which one cannot perform *mitzvot*, but it ascribes greater value to Torah study, the process of acquiring that knowledge. Accordingly, Judaism emphasizes child education and the greatness of a teacher as a master, one who is responsible for educating the next generation.

The Struggle of Teaching

As I am somewhat involved in the field of education, I know that teachers are very often frustrated. There is a very high degree of burnout. It is not easy to be a teacher. Therefore, educators frequently fret. I have heard this from many teachers in elementary schools, in high schools, and even in universities. They complain that they put so much effort into teaching and yet they do not produce the desired results. They do not see the students getting as much as they should out of school. They feel frustrated by not being able to fulfill their educational goals. Both the quantity learned and the joys of learning are less than they ought to be. The struggle is often a very disheartening one.

Nevertheless, we who dedicate our careers and lives to educating the next generation need to remember this principle: the process is more important than the results. The very act of teaching, the struggle of challenging the students, is worthwhile even if it does not succeed in the way the teacher would like, and even if it appears to fall on deaf ears. Who is to say that as circumstances change and children's minds mature and expand, today's ignored lessons will not be recalled with nostalgia and verve? Our work remains sacred even when our labors seem in vain. Success should be measured not by our students' gain in knowledge but by their desire to learn more. That is the point of our craft, of our profession, of our call, of our commitment.

Two statements can illustrate the importance of the struggle. The first is by R. Shneur Zalman of Lyady, known as the *Ba'al ha-Tanya*. He addresses the struggle we all have, the eternal war between the evil inclination and the good inclination. It can be discouraging, because the evil inclination too often is the victor.[14] The *Ba'al ha-Tanya* writes, "A person must not let his heart sink or be depressed, even if this war continues for his whole lifetime. Perhaps it is for this that he was created, and this is his service [of God]."[15] The same holds true for any kind of worthy struggle in which we are engaged – whether it is the struggle between our base passions and our yearning for the good and the true and the sacred, or the struggle involved in teaching, or the struggle of maintaining one's balance in Judaism while confronting the secular world (a struggle in which all of us are engaged). It may be frustrating and it may be painful. Nevertheless, the *Ba'al ha-Tanya* advises, we must not lose heart, we must not complain, because it is not the achievement and the end, but the means, the very act of struggle to which the greatest virtue adheres.

---

[14] R. Yisrael Salanter once said that the evil inclination is compared to a fly. A person chases it away, and it comes right back again.

[15] R. Shneur Zalman of Lyady, *Likkutei Amarim (Tanya)*, chap. 27.

The Talmud states, "If someone tells you, 'I struggled but I did not reach my goal,' do not believe it" (*Megillah* 6b). R. Menahem Mendel of Kotzk comments, "The struggle itself is already an achievement of the goal." Even if one has not achieved what he wanted, as long as he struggles he has won. The final product is secondary. We must not believe the one who says "I did not reach my goal," because he does not realize that the goal is secondary. Rather, "I struggled and succeeded – believe him." We must believe that the attempt to achieve is what the Torah and the moral life are all about.

This is the relationship of knowing and learning. Without denying the crucial value of knowing, learning has primacy. It is the struggle that is the source of our heroism, our value, and our contribution.

HARBATZAT TORAH:
MOTIVES AND OBJECTIVES

Aharon Lichtenstein

At first glance, a discussion in this volume of the motives for *harbatzat Torah* – disseminating Torah – seems entirely superfluous. Is there any need to explain to Jewish educators, and those concerned with the holy enterprise of Torah education, the importance and critical nature of this endeavor? Yet, on second thought, there is no concern here of "carrying coals to Newcastle." Specifically because this topic is so fundamental and central, and since it can be formulated in a variety of ways, it is appropriate for this volume to host the presentation of one formulation.

We may open the discussion itself with a parallel between two elements of Torah study: studying and teaching. With regard to the first, a careful look at the text instituted by the Sages for the blessing recited over Torah study reveals that it relates to two principles. Every yeshivah student is aware of the precision required in the formulation of the text of blessings recited over the performance of *mitzvot*, when we define the nature and root of the *mitzvot*, and this is surely true of one of the most fundamental: Torah study.[1]

[An earlier, Hebrew version of this essay appeared in *Al Derekh ha-Avot*, ed. A. Bazak, S. Wygoda, and M. Munitz (Alon Shevut: Tevunot/Mikhlelet Herzog, 2001), pp. 15–31, published for the 30th anniversary of the Yaakov Herzog Teachers' Training College at Yeshivat Har Etzion. David Silverberg prepared this translation. After this essay was completed, a collection of Rabbi Lichtenstein's essays was published as *Leaves of Faith: The World of Jewish Learning* (Jersey City: Ktav, 2003). The interested reader is referred to that collection for further discussion of issues raised in this essay and in others in the present volume.]

[1] The very association of *birkat ha-Torah* to the general realm of *mitzvot* is subject to dispute. It is generally assumed that the *berakhot* recited on *mitzvot* originated from rabbinic enactment, whereas with regard to the source of *birkhot ha-Torah* the *rishonim* are in disagreement. Undoubtedly the most prominent among those who view this obligation as biblical in origin is Ramban, from whom it appears that *birkat ha-Torah* is an expression of praise and thanksgiving for the phenomenon, not a *berakhah* relating to a

Responding to the query, "What does one recite" over Torah study (i.e., which blessing), the Gemara (*Berakhot* 11b) presents a variety of formulations:

Rav Judah said in the name of Shemuel: "… who has sanctified us with His commandments and commanded us to engage (*la'asok*) in words of Torah."[2] Rabbi Yohanan ends with the following conclusion: "The Lord our God, make the words of Your Torah pleasant in our mouths and in the mouths of Your nation, the House of Israel, and we, our descendants, and the descendants of Your nation, the House of Israel, all of us, shall be people who know Your Name and engage in Your Torah. Blessed are You, O Lord, who teaches Torah to His nation, Israel." Rav Hamnuna said: "Who has chosen us from all the nations and has given us His Torah. Blessed are You, O Lord, giver of the Torah." Rav Hamnuna said: this is the greatest of the blessings; let us therefore say all of them [the aforementioned formulations].

We, of course, follow the Gemara's conclusion, but the *rishonim* argue as to its meaning. The Ba'al ha-Ma'or explains that the three different blessings relate to different areas of Torah: "They correspond to Torah, Mishnah, and Rabbi Yishmael's system of extrapolation through the thirteen principles [of halakhic exegesis]."[3] The Ra'avad objected to this approach:

Is not the entire concept of Torah a single concept? Why then is a blessing necessary for each [area]? Furthermore, if a blessing is required for each as

---

personal obligation; in Reb Hayyim's terminology, a type of *birkat ha-nehenin* (blessing recited before deriving benefit from food and the like) on the very concept of Torah. While this might lead one to conclude that it is futile to reflect on the essence of the *mitzvah* of Torah study by examining its blessing, I believe such an inquiry is, indeed, appropriate. Firstly, even if we would explain that this blessing does not constitute a *birkat ha-mitzvah* at all, it still features the standard text formulated by *Hazal*; we may assess the quality of one of the focal points in our lives by analyzing *Hazal*'s formulation in any context. Secondly, we may reasonably assume that the nature of *birkat ha-Torah* as a blessing expressing praise is limited to its biblically ordained aspect. Rabbinic enactment has added a further aspect, that of a *birkat ha-mitzvah*, precisely as the Sages' ordinance in this regard applies to *mitzvot* in general. For more on this topic, see the Hebrew version of this essay, pp. 15–16 and sources in notes 1–7.

[2] The Rif's version of the text reads, "with regard to words of Torah," rather than "to engage in words of Torah." This point obviously touches upon the general discussion among the *rishonim* centered around the Gemara in *Pesahim* 7b as to the principles governing the formulation of a *birkat ha-mitzvah* with the term, "*al-*" ("with regard to…") or "*le-*" ("to do such-and-such"). This issue lies beyond the scope of our discussion.

[3] Ba'al ha-Ma'or on the Rif, *Berakhot* 5b (in the Rif's glosses).

if they were three *mitzvot*, then one should bless and then read [from the corresponding area of Torah to which the given blessing relates]. Where do we find a composite *berakhah* for many *mitzvot*?!

He suggests two alternatives to the rejected explanation:

Rather, Rav Papa said [to recite all three] because he was in doubt as to which is the accepted one. The question has been asked on Rav Papa's comment: does one not utter a blessing in vain [by reciting all the different blessings suggested merely out of doubt]? For there is no doubt regarding Rav Hamnuna's blessing that it is the best of the [suggested] *berakhot*, and we fulfill our obligation through it in the synagogue! I say that since Rabbi Yohanan's *berakhot* include a request relevant to [all of] us, that we do not err in matters of Torah, we do not want to leave it out.[4]

According to both the Ba'al ha-Ma'or's explanation and the Ra'avad's conclusion, the multiple *berakhot* result from the multifaceted nature of Torah study, each facet being critical and significant, and not from a halakhic doubt. It seems that there remains room for further analysis, to continue in their direction, only by pointing to other elements – particularly with regard to the formulations of Shemuel and Rabbi Yohanan.[5] Our relationship to Torah study is a twofold one. We learn, on one level, in fulfillment of a divine imperative. Whatever the reason behind the *mitzvah* – be it to acquire guidance for *mitzvah* observance, for spiritual enrichment, to draw nearer to the Almighty, or, simply, *li-shemah*, to come in contact with the eternity of God's word, without gearing towards any other purpose – we lean over the *Humash* and Gemara in compliance with the divine command. The *berakhah* formulated by Rav Judah in the name of Shemuel is devoted to this perspective: "Who has sanctified us with His *mitzvot* and commanded us to involve ourselves in the words of Torah."

But despite our subjugation to Torah study by virtue of the obligation, we surely do not wish to feel content with this aspect. Certainly, we will delve into talmudic deliberations (*havayot de-Abaye ve-Rava*) even if, Heaven forbid, we find no interest in them, as a sort of continuation and perpetua-

---

[4] Ra`avad's *Hasaggot* on the Ba`al ha-Ma'or, ibid.

[5] The blending of different elements characterizes *halakhah*'s acceptance of a combination of differing liturgical texts in situations similar to ours. For example: "*zokher ha-berit ve-ne'eman bi-vrito ve-kayyam be-ma'amaro*" (Berakhot 59a); "*rov ha-hoda'ot ve-ha-Kel ha-hoda'ot*" (ibid., 59b); "*rofei kol basar u-mafli la`asot*" (ibid., 60b); "*ha-nifra le-Yisra'el mi-kol tzareihem ha-Kel ha-moshi`a*" (Megillah 21b); and the text of *modim de-rabbanan* (Sotah 40a). We should note, however, that in all these examples we deal with additional expressions within a single *berakhah*, not multiple *berakhot*.

tion of the suspension of Mount Sinai coercing us to accept the Torah. But our aspiration is to occupy ourselves in Torah out of an existential attachment, as we discover its inner light and experience its being "complete, restoring the soul," and as we become bound to it through bonds of love. *Hazal* (*Eruvin* 54b) went very far in expressing their love of Torah:

> Rabbi Shemuel bar Nahmani said: What does the verse mean, "A loving doe, a graceful mountain goat..." (*Mishlei* 5:19)? Why are the words of Torah likened to a doe? To teach you that just as a doe's womb is narrow and she is beloved to her mate each time just as at the first time, so are the words of Torah beloved on their students each time just as at the first time. "And a *graceful* mountain goat" – it draws the grace of its students. "Let her breasts satisfy you at all times" – why are the words of Torah likened to a breast? Just as whenever a baby handles the breast he finds milk in it, similarly, whenever a person engages in the words of Torah he finds flavor in them."

Love of Torah

Is the exultant student, when he reenacts daily his wedding night with the word of God, driven solely by the command? Is the one who engages in Torah, who nurses from the breasts of his Torah-parent, working out of a sense of obligation? Here the second aspect of our study is reflected, and to this aspect Rabbi Yohanan's *berakhah* is devoted: establishing the love of Torah, the aesthetic, sensual, experiential attachment to the Almighty's laws, "that are more desirable than gold, than fine gold; sweeter than honey, than drippings of the comb" (*Tehillim* 19:11). All this is, in part, a human undertaking. A person must strive towards the realization of "I will delight in Your commandments, which I love. I reach out for Your commandments, which I love; I study Your laws" (*Tehillim* 119:47–48). But he may also yearn for divine assistance for the realization of "Be infatuated with love for her always." This is the crux of Rabbi Yohanan's plea. It is not only, as the Ra'avad writes, "a request that we do not err in matters of Torah," but rather an appeal by the individual reciting the *berakhah* that he may earn the privilege of fortifying his learning simultaneously on the foundations of obligation and love. "*Ha'arev na Hashem Elokeinu*": Rashi explains, "May it be pleasant to us to occupy ourselves in them out of love."

This is true with regard to study and applies as well to teaching. Torah instruction, too, is based upon two foundations: obligation and love. *Hafatzat Torah*, spreading Torah – bringing it into public awareness and establishing it, explained and elucidated, in the public domain – is possible to do with other motives. But *harbatzat Torah* – implanting it, rather than merely supplying it; bequeathing it to students and granting them a portion in Torah – is driven by a combination of responsibility and emotional attachment.[6]

Melekhet Hashem

These two components subdivide further, each one independently, into several branches. First, the obligation is four-tiered: towards the Almighty, towards the Torah itself, towards "*Reb Yisra'el*" (the individual Jew) and towards *Kenesset Yisra'el*. As for the first, it is summed up in one expression used by *Hazal* in reference to teaching Torah: "*melekhet Hashem*" – God's work.[7] This expression appears in a verse in Yirmiyahu in a much different context. In a prophecy of fury describing the foreseen destruction of Moab, the prophet declares, "Give wings to Moab, for she must go hence, her towns shall become desolate, with no one living in them. Cursed be he who is slack in doing God's work! Cursed be he who withholds his sword from blood!" (*Yirmiyahu* 48:9–10). As Rashi explains, this verse speaks of "the work of the destruction of Moab, which is the mission of the Almighty." But in a daring fling, *Hazal* transferred the verse to an entirely different mission, as they depict David citing this verse to Joab's teacher, scolding him for having erred in his instruction of the section of *zakhor*. This is indeed codified – let us hear the severity of what is demanded of us! – by the Rambam (*Mishneh Torah, Hilkhot Talmud Torah* 2:3):

> A schoolteacher who abandons the children and leaves or who does some other activity with them or is lax in their study is included under, "Cursed be he who is slack in doing God's work." It is therefore proper to appoint only a God-fearing man who is skilled in reading and precision.

This terminology has several implications. Firstly, Torah instruction is the work in which the Almighty Himself engages. The Sages described Him as such in their formulation of the text for *birkhot ha-Torah*: "*ha-melammed Torah le-ammo Yisra'el*" – "Who teaches Torah to His nation, Israel." True, the Rambam, in a famous and characteristic responsum, inveighs against

---

[6] *Mo`ed Katan* 25a, *Bava Metzi`a* 85b, *Temurah* 16a all speak of *lerabetz*, employing the *pi`el* verb form, as opposed to *.leharbitz*, but its distinction from *hafatzah* (spreading) is identical.

[7] See *Bava Batra* 21b.

this conclusion of the blessing, viewing it as undermining the hegemony of free will:

> The *berakhah* is meant to conclude, *noten ha-Torah* [Giver of the Torah], for this concept [of its having been given to us] is what obligates us to study it. This is the concept of its having been given, and this is the intent of the *berakhah*: to request assistance in order to learn it. But one who concludes [the *berakhah*], *ha-melammed Torah* errs, for God does not teach it to us, but rather commanded us to learn it and study it. This is built on a fundamental precept of our faith, that the performance of the commandments – or their neglect – is in our hands, not forced upon us from God.[8]

In light of this protest, the Rambam adopted a different text for the *berakhah*, one which corresponds to that accepted by Rav Sa'adyah Gaon[9]: "*noten ha-Torah.*"

Generally, however – despite the testimony of *talmidei Rabbenu Yonah*: "With regard to *ha'arev*, there are places that conclude, *Barukh atah Hashem noten ha-Torah*"[10] – the text, "*ha-melammed Torah*" has been accepted as the standard conclusion.[11] And we need not wonder as to why. The Gemara (*Bekhorot* 29a) inquires as to the source of the prohibition against taking money to study or teach Torah. "Rav Judah said: The verse states, 'Behold, I [Moshe] have taught you [statutes and laws, as the Lord my God has commanded me' – *Devarim* 4:5] – just as I [studied] free of charge, so [must] you [study] free of charge." In other words, Moshe is to teach *Kenesset Yisra'el* in the same manner as the Almighty taught him. Thus, the process of the command is equated with the study, and the Giver of the Torah with its teacher. That which applied with regard to Moshe, applies as well to his nation.

---

[8] *Shut ha-Rambam*, ed. Blau, chapter 182, vol. 2, p. 333; see the editor's notes *ad loc.*

[9] See *Siddur Rav Sa`adyah Gaon*, ed. Assaf (Jerusalem, 5730), p. 358. We should note, however, that, unlike the accepted practice, Rav Sa`adyah Gaon's version places "*ha`arev na*" as the continuation of the *berakhah*, "*asher bahar banu.*"

[10] Glosses to the Rif, *Berakhot* 5b.

[11] Some controversy exists as to the Rambam's ruling in *Hilkhot Tefillah* 7:10. The *Haggahot Maimoniyot* comments: "But Rashi there explains that one concludes, *ha-melammed Torah le-ammo Yisra'el*," indicating that his text of the Rambam follows the ruling in the responsum; this is indeed how the text appears in the Venice edition. By contrast, in the Rome edition and those in widespread use today, the text reads, "*ha-melammed Torah le-ammo Yisra'el*," though Rabbi Kapach and Rabbi Rabinovitch adopted the text of the *Haggahot Maimoniyot*.

"Behold, I [Moshe] have taught you statutes and laws, as the Lord my God has commanded me" (*Devarim* 4:5). From this verse emerges a second aspect of the definition of Torah instruction as "God's work." The straightforward reading of the Gemara in *Nedarim* (37a) – "He commanded me, and I [commanded] you" – implies that "commanded me" relates to the content of the Torah, to the *mitzvot* in general, which Moshe heard from the Almighty. We may, however, suggest an alternate explanation, that "commanded me" modifies "I have taught," that the command was to teach. Indeed, this reading of the verse was adopted by the Rosh - "Just as I [studied] free of charge - He commanded me to teach you free of charge just as He taught me free of charge" - and the Ran - "Meaning, that He commanded me to teach free of charge";[12] and the ramifications are clear. But do we even require a precise analysis of the meaning of an isolated word to determine that teaching Torah is the work that the Almighty commanded to perform? There are explicit verses that cry out to this effect. Some, such as, "And now, write for yourselves the words of this song and teach it to the Israelites; place it in their mouths" (*Devarim* 31:19), were directed at the time specifically to the religious leaders, while others, such as, "And make them known to your children and to your children's children" (*Devarim* 4:9), and, "Impress them upon your children" (*Devarim* 6:7), were spoken even initially to the nation as a whole. "For without question," the Maharitz concludes, "Moshe was commanded by God to teach them at Sinai and after Sinai until they all knew the practical commandments, statutes, laws and prohibitions that they must observe, until it became a 'set table' before them."[13]

Moreover, the Rambam positioned the aspect of "*lelammed*" in the center of his treatment of the laws of Torah study. The first seven *halakhot* of his *Hilkhot Talmud Torah* deal with the details and parameters of the obligation to teach; only in the eighth does the Rambam discuss personal study: "Every man among Israel is obligated in Torah study... Even one with a wife and children must set aside time for Torah study by day and night, as it says, 'You shall engage in it day and night.'" Even more remarkable is *halakhah* 3: "One whose father did not teach him must teach himself once he possesses sufficient intelligence, as it says, 'You shall study them and learn to do them.'" The Rambam does not write that the individual must "learn," but rather "teach himself." This formulation requires some explanation; and the answer is self-evident. The *mitzvah* contains two components. The

---

[12] See their respective commentaries to *Nedarim*.

[13] Cited in *Shitah Mekubbetzet*, *Nedarim* 38a.

first is the study, the involvement in God's Word, in and of itself, irrespective of its contribution towards the shaping of the student's personality and his status as a servant of God or his development into a scholar. When the Rambam includes under the obligation discussed in *halakhah* 8 "a very aged man whose strength has diminished," he does not expect that this elderly man's involvement in Torah will have a revolutionary impact on his scholarly talents or religious level. The devotion to the task, the effort and dedication, the exertion rather than the result — these are the main features of this obligation.

A beautiful expression of this perspective emerges from a scenario described in the Gemara (*Shabbat* 30a) in the form of a dialogue between King David and the Almighty:

> R. Judah said in the name of Rav: What does it mean, "Tell me, O Lord, what my term is, what is the measure of my days; I would know how fleeting my life is" (*Tehillim* 39:5)? David said before the Almighty, "Master of the world, tell me, O Lord, what my term is." He said to him, "I have decreed that I will not disclose the term of any human being." "What is the measure of my days?" "I have decreed that I will not disclose the measure of a human being's days." "I would know how fleeting my life is" [Rashi: "On which day will I cease and be eliminated from the world?"]. He said to him, "You will die on *Shabbat*." "Let me die on Sunday." He said to him, "The time for your son Shelomo's reign has already arrived, and one reign cannot infringe upon another even a hairsbreadth." "Let me die on Friday." He said to him, "Better one day in Your courts than a thousand [anywhere else]" (*Tehillim* 84:11) — one day when you sit and involve yourself in Torah is better for Me than the thousand burnt-offerings that your son Shelomo will sacrifice before Me on the altar.

That single day, when David will have the opportunity to sit and study Torah on his deathbed, is not meant, presumably, to mold new qualities in his being. Nevertheless, an hour in service of God, which itself is more valuable than all of life in the next world, can avail itself at any time.

Teaching

The foregoing component of the obligation belongs to the strict "learning" aspect. A second aspect, however, exists as well, its essence rooted in teaching. Involvement in Torah constitutes — particularly during one's formative, younger years — a central instrument in the fashioning of one's Jewish spirit. It is meant to establish a person in our spiritual world — to confer a reservoir of Torah knowledge and scholarly talent, to implant the love and fear of God, to instill faith and knowledge of our ancestral heritage, to build a personality overflowing with loyalty and sense of obligation to a life of Torah and *mitzvot*. This creative effort, which is most certainly geared towards an end result, which requires arduous exertion and perspiration but strives for spiritual output, takes effect, first and foremost, in education within the family. The realization of its goals is latent within the imperative, "And impress them upon your children," whereby the learning serves as the key medium but the goal is the transmission of the tradition and the development of its recipients. This is what the Rambam explains, that one who did not have the privilege of a proper Torah education during childhood and has yet to reach an appropriate spiritual level, must, when he reaches maturity, not only fulfill the commandment of learning Torah for its own sake, but also "teach" – meaning, to mold – himself, and, as an autodidact, become simultaneously the builder and the one built, teacher and student.

This process is not limited to the teacher's offspring: "Not only one's son and grandson; there is rather a commandment for each and every scholar in Israel to teach all students even though they are not his children, as it says, 'Impress them upon your children.' Through tradition it is taught that 'your children' refers to your students, for students are called children, as it says, 'The children of the prophets left.'"[14] This, as stated, is the focus of the Rambam's introduction in his laws of Torah study, and it forms a natural transition to the third aspect of "God's work." *Harbatzat Torah* is an occupation that is performed not only following the Almighty's lead, imitating His conduct and obeying His order, but also for Him, as it were. One who teaches Torah furthers the realization of His will and serves to carry out Providence's plan. We may not inquire as to that which lies beyond our comprehension, and who will dare to explain the reason behind the creation of man and the universe. But even if the "why" is beyond our reach, we may, and perhaps must, delve into the teleological question of "for what purpose, and towards what end?" Obviously, this question extends well beyond the specific context of Torah study and even transcends the narrow focal point of *Kenesset Yisra'el*. Clearly, its answer may be the all-inclusive, universal formulation of the Ramban: "The intention behind all the commandments is that we believe in our God and acknowledge that He created us, and this is the intention behind creation. For we have no other reason for the original creation, and the Supreme Lord has no desire for the lower

---

[14] Rambam, *Hilkhot Talmud Torah* 1:2.

world other than that man will know and acknowledge that God created him. The intention behind the inspirational sound of prayers and the intention behind synagogues and the merit of public prayer is that people have a place to gather and acknowledge that God created them and brought them into existence, and that they publicize this and say before Him, 'We are Your creatures.'"[15] However, it is also clear that, with respect to implanting Torah, advancing the "need" for the Kingdom of Heaven is of supreme importance, either because it instills fear of Heaven, and thereby strengthens and deepens the preparedness to declare, "We are Your creatures," or because the knowledge of God, in and of itself, constitutes a sublime goal of Providence's plan, the eschatological crown jewel of which is, "The earth will be filled with knowledge of God, like water covers the sea" (*Yishayahu* 11:9).

In the expression of the "needs" and "longing" of the Almighty, and the adulation of disseminators of Torah as advancing them, there is undoubtedly an element of problematic impertinence. Nevertheless, even as it must be done with care, it has support. On the kabbalistic level, this element is quite common. For example, the Ramban, in a familiar passage, after rejecting Rashi's explanation of the conclusion of the section dealing with the daily *tamid* offering in *Parashat Tetzaveh* – "They shall know that I am the Lord their God who took them from the land of Egypt to reside in their midst; I am the Lord their God" (*Shemot* 29:46) – notes:

> But Rabbi Avraham [Ibn Ezra] said that [the verse means,] I took them from the land of Egypt only so that I may dwell in their midst, and this is what is meant, "You will serve God on this mountain," and he explained well. If so, then within this concept lies a great secret, because according to the simple approach to the matter, the *Shekhinah* in Israel serves a need of man, not a need of God. But the truth is that which is said, "Israel, that through you I am glorified"; "Here I will dwell for I have desired it"; and it is written, "I will remember the land."

But the concept may be understood as well in purely rationalistic terms. If, as a result of the series of exiles, "the Almighty has in His world only the four cubits of *halakhah*," then whoever disseminates Torah and raises its banner delineates, as it were, the portion of his Creator in the world.

In light of this, we should draw a clear distinction between *melekhet Hashem* (God's work) and the corresponding term, *melekhet shamayim* (the

---

[15] Ramban's commentary on the Torah, *Shemot* 13:2.

work of heaven). This expression appears in the Gemara with regard to the preparation of materials to serve as sacred objects. Rav Yosef, for example, taught, "Only the skins of permitted [kosher] animals are suitable for *melekhet shamayim*" (*Shabbat* 28b). That is, only these skins may be used for the boxes, parchment, and straps of *tefillin*. Similarly, Rabbi Ishmael warned Rabbi Meir, then a scribe's apprentice, "My son, exercise great care in your work, for your work is *melekhet shamayim*" (*Eruvin* 13a). Quite obviously, as these examples demonstrate, the description, "*melekhet shamayim*" also comes to glorify a certain activity and extol its value. Nevertheless, it remains very far, in both scope and intensity, from the array of qualities analyzed earlier. We speak here of a contribution towards the advancement of certain needs or interests, as it were, of the Almighty, by creating and shaping the necessary tools. The areas involved and the product, the importance of sacred objects — and certainly sacred bodies — notwithstanding, are relatively concentrated and relate to the means, as opposed to the ends. This is not the case, as we have seen, with regard to the concept of "*melekhet Hashem*," which, from differing perspectives, is linked to the Almighty Himself, and harnesses the One who disseminates Torah to His chariot.

Responsibilities to the Torah Itself

Aside from the connection to the Giver of the Torah, we have a responsibility to the Torah itself. Besides its role towards us, as a guide and source of truth, the Torah is, in its splendid isolation, a treasury of precious vessels. In it, as it were, the King of the world delights, both before creation: "I was with Him as a confidant, a source of delight every day, rejoicing before Him at all times" (*Mishlei* 8:30);[16] and in the wake of creation: "He [Moshe] said before Him: Master of the world, You have a precious treasure in which You delight every day; shall I flatter myself?" (*Shabbat* 89a).[17] *Kenesset Yisra'el* has exulted in it throughout its generations and dispersions, and it exalts and extols it in its poetry and *midrash*, song and praise, in the mouths of children and nursing babes as well as the mouths of the elderly and distinguished. It is the Torah whose presence within us, given our intense concern for its wondrous and sublime proliferation, obligates us, even if we hadn't accepted it. Would an art enthusiast refrain from rushing to save the Mona Lisa if it came under the threat of destruction? When dealing with the eternal Torah, all the more so.

---

[16] Based on the *Sifrei, Devarim, Ekev* 37, ed. Finkelstein, p. 70, offering the view that the "wisdom" spoken of in this chapter refers to the wisdom of the Torah.

[17] Compare with *Avodah Zarah* 3b.

We have, however, accepted it, and we accepted it as a delightful treasure. It was specifically this quality that prompted the ministering angels, in *Hazal*'s graphic description, to protest its transmission to those living in physical bodies: "They said before Him: this precious treasure that has been concealed with You for nine hundred and seventy-four generations before the world was created – You wish to give it to flesh and blood?" (*Shabbat* 88a). It was in this capacity that we accepted it, as both a gift and something for us to protect. In one sense, we acquired it; in a different sense, we are its guardians – and, presumably, given that we conduct our lives according to the Torah, we are like the *sho'el* (a borrower, as opposed to a renter), about whom the Talmud says all the benefit is his.

This responsibility of ours has several different aspects. First and foremost, there stands an obligation to protect the content of the Torah, its sanctity and purity; to resist efforts, from both within and without, to dilute, distort, and misconstrue. However, there is also the task of raising the Torah's banner, of striving to bring it to the center of the life of our nation and community, to ensure that it will not remain isolated in a corner. This objective is preceded, in part, by a certain quality of studying – study that is, at once, both static and dynamic, rooted in traditional sources with firm belief in them, yet at the same time linked to contemporary intellectual and social reality. Clearly, however, the motivation comes primarily from the task of teaching. The comprehensive, concentrated effort to disseminate God's word in every location is the only guaranteed way to raise its flag to a height commensurate with its value, to steer towards a situation where all the schoolchildren "from Dan to Be'er Sheva" acquire proficiency in the laws of ritual purity. In disseminating Torah, then, we are driven by our relationship to the Giver of the Torah and the Torah itself.

And, correspondingly, to those who have accepted the Torah. We have dealt heretofore with a responsibility to disseminate Torah from the viewpoint of "*bein adam la-Makom*" (our obligation to the Almighty), on two different levels. But aside from this, we are obliged at this point to move our discussion to the aspect of "*bein adam le-haveiro*" (one's obligation towards others). Recall that this aspect, too, splits into two subdivisions – towards *Reb Yisra'el* and towards *Kenesset Yisra'el*. In a general sense, the first – and perhaps both – involve *hesed*, an act of kindness. Indeed, *Hazal* (*Sukkah* 49b) pointed to this connection:

Rabbi Elazar said: What does it mean, "Her mouth is open with wisdom, and the Torah of kindness is on her tongue" (*Mishlei* 31:26)? Is there a "Torah of kindness" and a Torah that is not of kindness? ...Some explain, [studying] Torah in order to teach – this is Torah of kindness; [studying Torah] without the intention of teaching – this is Torah that is not of kindness.

It is noteworthy that this passage does not speak of actual teaching, but rather of the purpose behind one's study. The message conveyed is that already in the preliminary stages of academic preparation and training, determining the final goal lends a quality of *Torat hesed* – even before any concrete actualization of this goal. If this is the case regarding Torah that is learned, then it applies all the more so with regard to Torah that is taught.

In this context, it must be emphasized that we do not speak here merely of a coincidental meeting of two qualities under a single roof. A careful reading of the aforementioned talmudic passage suggests that the quality discussed adds a layer to the Torah, one which qualitatively changes its fundamental character. It seems to me that in this vein we may understand the conclusion of the discussion at the end of the first chapter of *Bava Kamma* (17a). The Talmud there assesses the relative values of study and performance. After first noting a contradiction between earlier sources in this regard, the Talmud distinguishes between studying and teaching. Rashi explains: "Studying for oneself – performance is preferable; but teaching others is preferable over performance."[18] It appears that here, too, the determining factor is not the cumulative effect of the two areas – study and performance – over the single area of study alone, but rather the very fact that learning itself receives added weight when its springs gush forth to the public.

From a more specific perspective, this issue relates to the concept of *arevut* (mutual responsibility). Colloquially, this term is used in reference to the national aspect of this concept. In its source in rabbinic literature, however, the dominant thread – albeit with regard to punishment more so than with regard to responsibility (though clearly these two issues are intertwined)—is, specifically, the personal element: "'They shall stumble over one another' (*Vayikra* 26:37) – each in the sin of his brother. This teaches that all of Israel are mutually responsible for one another" (*Shevu'ot* 39a). It is commonly understood that the most famous halakhic application of this principle is embodied in the rule of "*yatza motzi*," by which an individual who has already satisfied his requirement vis-à-vis a given recitation or

---

[18] *S.v.* "*lemigmar*." Although many commentators have different versions of the Gemara's text or explained it differently, they would not necessarily dispute the ruling that emerges from Rashi's approach.

reading may read or recite on behalf of those who have yet to fulfill their requirement. Despite the Mishnah's axiom that "Whoever is not obligated in a given matter cannot fulfill the obligation of the masses on their behalf" (*Rosh ha-Shanah* 3:8), one who has already satisfied his obligation may read on behalf of others, since *halakhah* deems his requirement as not yet completely fulfilled. This is indeed Rashi's explanation: "Even if he has fulfilled [his requirement], he nevertheless may fulfill the requirement for others, since all of Israel are responsible for one another with regard to *mitzvot*" (*Rosh ha-Shanah* 29a, s.v. "*af al pi*"). If Re'uven's responsibility towards Shimon establishes that he, Re'uven, has not completely satisfied his obligation with regard to a given *mitzvah* so long as Shimon has not performed his duty towards it, then this concept is most certainly valid regarding Re'uven's obligation to transmit to Shimon the messages of the Torah in all their parameters and instill within him a sense of obligation towards them.

The relationship between *harbatzat Torah* and *arevut* is emphasized in the Talmud's central treatment of the latter concept, in the context of the blessings and curses administered at Mount Gerizim and Mount Eval: "A blessing with respect to the community, a blessing with respect to the individual; a curse with respect to the community, a curse with respect to the individual. 'To study, to teach, to observe and to perform' – the result is twice four" (*Sotah* 37a). Rashi explains (*s.v. lilmod u-lelammed lishmor ve-la'asot*):

> All the *mitzvot* carry these four [elements]: "You shall study them"; "You shall observe, to perform"; and it is written, "You shall teach them to your children," etc. We thus have here four commandments with regard to every *mitzvah*, and for all four a curse and a blessing were administered on both the community and individual: "Blessed are those who study; cursed are those who do not study," and the same with regard to teaching, observing, and performing. Over each one there are four covenants: a covenant of blessing for the community, a covenant of blessing for the individual, a covenant of curse for the community, a covenant of curse for the individual.

We must internalize this message very well. This passage does not say that if one takes the *lulav* properly but refrains from instructing others in this regard, he has satisfactorily fulfilled the *mitzvah* of *lulav*, but lacks the fulfillment of teaching others. It rather states that the commandment of *lulav* itself consists of four elements. So long as one has not addressed them all, his fulfillment of this specific *mitzvah* is incomplete.

This notion is undoubtedly both a novel and powerful one; in any event, for a Jew who both senses and believes, the central message is clear even without it. A person who, on the one hand, feels deep concern for the welfare of others and, at the same time, is saturated with the belief in the assertion that a life of Torah and *mitzvot* are "for our own good" (*Devarim* 6:24); a person who feels obligated towards his fellow's progress on the one hand, and for whom, on the other, the declaration that "they are our lives and the length of our days" is not merely a habitual, routine recitation from the lips outward, but rather an expression of a deeply entrenched awareness – is it plausible that he would not take upon himself the mission of binding others to the world and yoke of Torah? In the context of the obligation to return a lost item to its owner, the famous dictate in the Mishnah reads: "A lost item of one's father and a lost item of one's rabbi – that of his rabbi takes precedence, for his father brought him to this world, whereas his rabbi, who taught him wisdom, brings him to life in the next world" (*Bava Metzi'a* 2:11). Correspondingly, then, if saving one's fellow is included under *hashavat aveidah* (the obligation to return a lost item) – "The loss of one's body – from where [do we derive an obligation to 'return' it]? The verse states, 'You shall return it to him' (*Devarim* 22:2)"[19] – then, in light of the Mishnah, all the more so does this *mitzvah* include "returning" the soul of another. If we bear in mind as well that this *mitzvah* requires not only the return of a lost item, but also preventing it from being lost – "If one saw floodwaters coming, he must erect a barrier before them; Rava says: 'for all your fellow's lost property' (*Devarim* 22:3), including the loss of land" (*Bava Metzi'a* 31a) – then the interpersonal aspect of *harbatzat Torah* becomes particularly evident.

Torah and National Formation

The realm of "between man and his fellow" has a national element, as well, and with regard to it there is a fourth obligation of *harbatzat Torah*. On one level, this touches upon our very identity as a nation. The conception and birth of *Kenesset Yisra'el* occurred in a spiritual melting pot. The nation entered the world without the standard national ingredients, without territory or sovereignty, by rallying around a lofty system of values and ideas. The preservation of its identity depends on the continuity of its attachment to that system. "Our nation is a nation," as Rav Sa'adyah Gaon established,

---

[19] *Sanhedrin* 73a. It is not clear to me whether by saving someone from drowning one fulfills the formal *mitzvah* of *hashavat aveidah*, returning a lost item to its owner, or if this *mitzvah* is limited to the loss of property, and the obligation of saving the body of another is established by logical deduction (through a *kal va-homer*).

"only in its Torah."[20] Ahad ha-Am correctly observed that more than Israel guarded the Sabbath, the Sabbath guarded Israel.[21] Thus, whoever strengthens this attachment bolsters our national identity.

Beyond the issue of identity, the connection to Torah determines the stature of *Kenesset Yisra'el* – towards itself, before the world at large, and in relation to the Almighty. Since long ago, extraordinarily, the element of distinction characterized our existence and awareness. Rabbi Judah's description in the *midrash* regarding Avraham – "The entire world is on one side, and he is on another"[22] – in explaining the appellation "*Avraham ha-Ivri*" ("*ever*" means "side") paved the way for the patriarch's descendants. "This is a people that dwells apart" – imbued with a sense of distinction and destiny, saturated with faith, a people that sees "And who is like Your people Israel, a singular nation on earth" as parallel to "You are one and Your Name is one." The foundation of both this singularity and this destiny is the Torah, in the dissemination of which we exert ourselves.

So are we perceived in the eyes of the other nations. Both our admirers and foes have seen in us, since time immemorial, a spiritual power, carriers of the banner of faith and wisdom embodied in the Torah. The Bible clearly testifies to this perception: "Observe them faithfully, for that will be proof of your wisdom and discernment to other peoples, who on hearing of all these laws will say: Surely, that great nation is a wise and discerning people" (*Devarim* 4:6). Our system of laws and statutes has not always earned the admiration of other peoples. But from a broader, long-term viewpoint, there is no doubt that the Torah is perceived as our major contribution to world culture. Promoting the yoke of Torah, then, amounts to promoting the glory of Israel.

However, our status among the nations is meaningless compared to our status vis-à-vis the Almighty.[23] On one level, our attachment to Torah has an impact on Providence. This is the central message of the descriptions of the blessings and curses in the Torah, the sections referred to as the *tokhehah*: "If you follow My laws and faithfully observe My commandments…" (*Vayikra* 26:3), as opposed to, God forbid, "If you reject My laws and spurn My rules…" (*Vayikra* 26:15). A Jew expresses this faith every day and night in the second section of the *Shema*, and it runs like a thread though

---

[20] *Emunot ve-De`ot*, 3.

[21] See *Kol Kitvei Ahad ha-Am* (Tel-Aviv: Dvir, 5707), p. 286.

[22] *Bereishit Rabbah (Lekh-Lekha), Parashah* 42:8; Vilna edition, p. 172.

[23] See Ramban, on *Devarim* 4:6, who explains that the importance of the gentiles' admiration lies in its impact upon *kiddush Hashem* (the sanctification of God's Name).

the world of the prophets. Even with all the care taken to avoid simplistic applications and lightheaded dogmatism, this principle constitutes a fundamental pillar of our world outlook.

However, the significance of our Torah level is not limited to the workings of Providence. On a more fundamental level, it determines the degree of the *Shekhinah*'s presence in our midst and our definition as God's people. Its presence itself is guaranteed: "For the Lord will not forsake His people; He will not abandon His very own" (*Tehillim* 94:14). *Hazal* refuted the claims of the dissidents who were skeptical in this regard. The Talmud relates: "A certain apostate[24] said to Rabbi Hanina, 'Now you are certainly impure, as it is written, "Her impurity clings to her skirts"' (*Eikhah* 1:9). [Rashi: 'You are certainly impure, and the *Shekhinah* does not reside among you in a state of impurity.'] He said to him, 'Come and see what it says about them: "... who dwells among them in the midst of their impurity" (*Vayikra* 16:16) – even when they are impure, the *Shekhinah* dwells among them'" (*Yoma* 57b–58a). The dispute among the *tanna'im* with regard to the dependence of our relationship to the Almighty on our conduct – ("'You are children of the Lord your God' [*Devarim* 14:1] – Rabbi Judah says: If you act like [His] children, you are [His] children; otherwise, you are not [His] children. Rabbi Meir says: In either event, you are children of the Lord your God, and it similarly says, 'The number of the people of Israel shall be like that of the sands of the sea' [*Hoshea* 2:1]"[25]) involves the nature of the relationship, but not its very existence. Nevertheless, even if disregarding Torah and *mitzvot* does not erase *Kenesset Yisra'el*'s identity as God's nation, it clearly dilutes it. As "the measure of good exceeds the measure of calamity," the dissemination of Torah deepens it and empowers it.

Motivations of Love

At the outset of our discussion we noted that *harbatzat Torah* has two main roots: a sense of obligation, and love. Until now we have dealt with the first and delineated its four types. We are now obliged to discuss the second, the motivation of love, which does not contradict the first but certainly differs from it. Scores of pens have been broken over the subject of

---

[24] This is the text in *Dikdukei Soferim*, and it stands to reason that this refers to a Christian. In our editions the text reads "*ha-hu tzeduki*" – a certain Sadducee.

[25] *Sifrei, Devarim, Re'eih* 96, ed. Finkelstein, p. 157. This debate is cited as well in *Kiddushin* 36a, but with two differences: the disputants cite different verses as proofs for their positions, and in place of "you are children" it says, "you are called children." However, the Gaon of Vilna, in his glosses, emends the text of the *Sifrei* to correspond to that of the Talmud.

love in general – its description, analysis, and breakdown – and a considerable portion of philosophical and literary work, particularly in Western culture, has been dedicated to it. It is not, of course, our concern here to conduct a comprehensive analysis of the concept itself, but it is worthwhile to enlist the help of several common definitions and distinctions relevant to our discussion.

In a word, love involves attachment or a longing for attachment. According to one version, such as prevalent romanticism, we speak of a connection founded upon a preexisting common denominator, on the one hand, and the desire, on the other, to deepen and strengthen that connection. According to another version, such as in Neoplatonic epistemology, we speak of a convergence, half mystical and half noetic, between a definitive predicate and its object. The nature of the love changes according to the identity of the beloved. The connection to an inanimate object or even to a living creature differs drastically from a mutual bond between two human beings. And, of course, from a religious perspective, man's love for God and God's love for man has an entirely singular status. However, as stated, everything is rooted in attachment.

But this root may produce differing, even contradictory, branches. One type is expressed through giving, through a powerful drive to shower all the goodness in the world on the beloved, with an expectation to provide all his needs and further his welfare. The paradigm of this model is the love of a parent for a child – the mother that gives her breast, the father that hovers and protects:

> This is analogous to one who was walking along the way and his son led the way before him. Bandits came to capture [the son] in front of [the father]; he took him from in front and placed him in the rear. The fox came to attack [the son] from behind, so [the father] placed him in the front. Bandits in front of him and a fox behind him! He took him and placed him on his shoulders, as it says, "And in the desert, where you saw how the Lord your God..." (*Devarim* 1:31).[26]

---

[26] *Mekhilta de-Rabbi Yishma'el - Mesikhta de-"ba-Hodesh," Yitro*, 2, ed. Horowitz-Rabin, pp. 207–208; see also Rashi on *Devarim* 32:11. On an entirely different level, we should note that the obligation to sacrifice one's life in situations of *yeihareig ve-al ya`avor* (the three sins that one may not commit even at the expense of his life) is derived from the imperative, "You shall love..." – see *Pesahim* 25a; Rambam, *Hilkhot Yesodei ha-Torah* 5:1; the Netziv, *Meishiv Davar* 1:44.

At times, the drive to give not only expresses love, but also serves as its basis. A mother nurses a child because she is already attached to him. But there may be a drive to bestow that also forms the *foundation* of the attachment. In this regard, there are two different traditions in Western culture. In the Greek world, including its various branches and evolutions, love is extended to those who are worthy. Only the beautiful earns love. By contrast, Christianity glorified unconditional love, which not only expects nothing in exchange in the future, but even has no basis in the present. According to Christianity, the ideal love is expressed specifically towards the unsightly and the leper, whose positive qualities do not arouse love; only the lover's desire to give and sacrifice pulls towards them.

A second type is characterized by the opposite quality: not giving, but acquisition; not sacrifice, but control. Out of a powerful attraction for the object of love, the lover desires him/her; he desires, in the extreme level, to consume and, on the more moderate level, to acquire. As opposed to the preceding type, this one is by essence egocentric, and if we would search for a model in the system of human relationships, the bond between man and woman would be far more appropriate than parenthood. This bond is characterized by the element of ownership – and, at times, the struggle for it – which is prone to express itself in competition and strife. For good reason, jealousy appears as the central motif in this system of male-female relationships; and despite the claims that are heard in contemporary polemics, it is bilateral. Medea and Cleopatra showed domination that falls short of neither Othello nor Monsieur Bovary. But whatever our conclusion with regard to this detail, there is undoubtedly a kind of love that strives for ownership, of which the plane of marriage is characteristic.

If we come, on the basis of this simple outline, to assess the nature of the love of Torah as a motive for its dissemination, it appears to me that we will conclude that it has two aspects. At the root of the matter lies the declaration of King David: "O how I love Your teaching! It is my study all day long" (*Tehillim* 119:97). This is reliable testimony to the individual's bond with Torah, his association with it, his betrothal or marriage to it, the intertwining of his soul with the Torah's. As a result, he immerses himself in its study from two opposite directions. He studies it out of a sense that he thereby furthers its interests, as it were; not that he is obligated towards it or to give to it, but rather because it is the breath of life and the life of our soul, and in his fervent love and reverence for it he will painstakingly study it and teach it in order to serve it. At the same time, he engages in its study from an entirely personal angle: "She is more precious than rubies, all of your goods cannot equal her" (*Mishlei* 3:15); and he, in and of himself, is intensely in love with it. Small wonder, then, that he will exert himself to purchase it, acquire it, and conquer it!

The duality of the lover who both sacrifices and masters is evident in the student but is expressed in the instructor, as well. On the one hand, he is prepared, to the extent that it becomes necessary, to sacrifice. True, his hope and wish is that this will not be necessary. He hopes that "to learn" and "to teach" will be simultaneously successful, for the joy of Torah creativity is interwoven with the furthering of the interests of one's beloved. But he is infused with dedication; as a true lover, he will even sacrifice his Torah ambitions, his spiritual yearnings, on its behalf.

An inspiring expression of this preparedness, alongside the existential complications involved therein, appears in an impressive piece from the writings of a spiritual giant whose life was tragically cut short, but not before he enriched the worlds of *halakhah* and Jewish thought. At the height of his efforts in promoting a teachers' seminary in Kovno, Rabbi Avraham Elya Kaplan *z"l* wrote the following to his wife:

> For example, here I was summoned together with my colleagues to the education department, this desolate, sorrowful department without its children… desolate without anyone thinking of helping it – and we are involved in improving the courses for teachers, that is, providing funds, first and foremost, for this purpose… We need at least ten thousand marks to begin construction; for maintenance afterwards there is hope in funding abroad – here you have intensive work that devours days upon days. Immediately thereafter comes the work of arranging the courses themselves and all the massive planning involved, such as accepting students, testing, arranging support, lectures, etc. However, out of all this abundance of work my soul hears a voice speaking: "And what about Torah? This Torah for which you worked throughout your youth, for which you expended all your thoughts and that became your source of life and delight – will you now leave it and abandon it? This is Torah, and this is its reward?" Indeed, it is true that even this work in the [seminary] courses is Torah from beginning to end – beginning with giving Torah to the youngsters standing on the threshold of life, and ending with giving Torah to the children who will study from their mouths in the days to come – but, when all is said and done, there is no place here for that broad, enlightened, grand and exalted profession that we call *lomdus*, that sensational excursion aboard the ship of thought over the waves of the Talmud and its commentaries. Indeed, one must be a totally righteous and pious individual to manage to sacrifice the

Torah itself on the altar of Torah, to separate oneself from the Torah in order to work on behalf of the Torah.[27]

The average disseminator of Torah lacks the personal talent and Torah capacity that would require his being a totally righteous and pious person to devote himself to the education of others at the expense of his personal study. But the basic dilemma and preparedness to sacrifice as required is indeed the lot shared by many.[28]

The love of Torah stimulates its dissemination from its other facet, as well, the aspect of "*she-lo li-shemah*" – "not for its own sake." There exists, of course, a dimension of acquisition and control in every form of teaching – from cracking and deciphering the material, through its organization and presentation, and until the gratification of teacher and student when their meeting is crowned with success. Clearly, though, the more we speak of teaching that combines, as one, material and values, and, what is more, that deals with matters of the most paramount concern, the sense of achievement and its significance increase.

Every topic that becomes clarified in a *shi'ur* turns into a focal point of spiritual force, in and from which inspiration is showered upon the student and internalized by the rabbi. Every teacher of Torah, even a beginner, can testify to the extent to which through his teaching the verse, "and Your Torah is in my inmost parts" (*Tehillim* 40:9) sees fulfillment, beyond that which occurs in relation to the Torah he studies individually. This entails both the acceptance of the Torah as devotion, and the acquisition of Torah as control.

Over the course of teaching, the love of Torah blends with the love of the student. On one level, teaching is entirely about giving. Immense efforts are invested in preparing and transmitting the material, and in the development of its recipients. Abundant energy and extraordinary patience are directed towards the giving over of Torah, towards the presentation of the ways to understand it and the inculcation of its messages. In this process, every rabbi, like Moshe in his time, works in the spirit of "the generous man is blessed" (*Mishlei* 22:9); in every *shi'ur*, a merging of inspiration occurs. "The teaching of Torah by a rabbi to a student," the Rav *zt"l* writes,

---

[27] *Be-Ikvot ha-Yir'ah* (Jerusalem: Mosad ha-Rav Kook, 5720), p. 200. The letter was written in 1920.

[28] My remarks throughout this concluding section are phrased in the masculine but should certainly be interpreted to refer equally to women who enter the field of Jewish education and undertake the task of Torah dissemination.

is a wondrous, metaphysical act of exposure of an impacting personality to an impacted personality. This exposure is also the attachment of rabbi and student. The student who understands the scholarship attaches himself to the wise. If he comprehends the rabbi's logic he becomes attached to the rabbi in the sense of the unity of scholar and scholarship. Latent in this principle is the secret of the Oral Law, that by its nature and essence has never reached objectification, even after it was written. *Torah she-be-al peh* (the Oral Law) means Torah that blends with one's personal uniqueness and becomes an inseparable part of the person. When it is transmitted, one's personal self is transmitted, as well.[29]

On the other hand, even with respect to his students, the teacher possesses – motivated, we hope, by idealistic factors, though also influenced by personal considerations – an ambition for acquisition and control. True, it ought to be balanced by an awareness of the student's status and his destiny as a developing spiritual entity, not merely as raw material being molded. But this sense has certainly earned its place. The educator is enchanted by the wonder of the young, pure soul that thirstily drinks his words, and he is stirred by the desire to multiply it. He fulfills the dictum of the Men of the Great Assembly (*Avot* 1:1), "educate many disciples" – not merely out of obedience to their command or out of responsibility for the Torah being learnt, but out of a desire to create and influence, to shed light and acquire. In a certain sense, "and from my students I have gained more than from them all" (*Ta'anit* 7a) is realized not only in their becoming the source of inspiration, but also with respect to the output achieved. "The souls they made in Haran" (*Bereishit* 12:5) should be read, "they acquired in Haran," for an artisan acquires ownership through the enhancement of the utensil [given to him for repair] – how much more so through the enhancement of a soul! Through dissemination of Torah, the teacher acquires both souls and the word of God. In fashioning centers of Torah, he expands his personal hegemony over both Torah and its embodiment. The love of control and the love of sacrifice together contribute towards the proliferation and glorification of Torah.

In conclusion, I return to my point of departure and the misgivings raised at the outset. From a certain perspective, this essay is undoubtedly both incomplete and superfluous. On the one hand, it is difficult to find anything novel in it. It seems that every detail concerning the value and

---

[29] "*U-Vikashtem mi-Sham*," in *Ish ha-Halakhah: Galuy ve-Nistar* (Jerusalem: WZO, 5739), p. 229.

centrality of Torah in the life of the individual and community is clear and simple to the knowledgeable. On the other hand, its claims may appear exaggerated: is every teacher guiding third-grade students through *Sefer Shemot*, or every rabbi who dazzles high school students with an elucidation of a *Tosefot*, motivated by the array of factors enumerated here, or does he realize all the goals described?

The answer is clear, and let us not foster any illusions. Nevertheless, it is important – perhaps critically important – to gather the motivations under a single heading and engender an integrated awareness of their relationship and cross-fertilization. This can both lend some encouragement and chart some direction; and in the world of education, direction is critical. Naturally, the efforts in that direction are slow, winding, and long-term, but the awareness ought to be constant, and it has the capacity to instill a spirit of mission, already from the early stages.

In cultivating this awareness, the Modern Orthodox world lags far behind the *haredi* (ultra-Orthodox) community. In the *heders* and *Talmud Torah* schools, the sight of a *melammed* (school teacher) adorned with a *kaplush* and wrapped in a *kapote*, who had spent many long years on the benches of the study hall, now practicing the pronunciation of Hebrew letters and vowels (*kawmetz-alef-aw...*) or reviewing the Mishnah of "*Arbah avot nezikin*" with his students, is very widespread. "This is because," the skeptics will respond, "they have no choice, as other professions are inaccessible to them"; and this is partially true. To no less an extent, however, this results from their viewing their work as blending into a long, broad landscape; because in the mischievous youngster the *melammed* perceives, powerfully, the Torah giant who, in characteristic hyperbole, he preaches into his young ears that he is capable of becoming. When a person feels that embedded in his *melekhet Hashem* is the guarantee of the eternity and redemption of Israel, teaching schoolchildren to read constitutes both a profession and a mission.

In the modern community, this motivation is less evident. On the one hand, on the ideological level, the thrust towards the realization of national and historical goals is presumably stronger than in the *haredi* camp (which distinguishes itself in its emphasis on personal spiritual development). Yet, the translation of the abstract outlook into the language of personal action is problematic indeed. If a Modern Orthodox yeshivah student is prepared to think of education as an occupation, he tends to hinge his involvement in this endeavor on the expectation that he will teach advanced classes. The hesitation lies, in part, in the ambition for an academic challenge, which only the advanced levels provide. But often it results as well from a disdain for inferior positions, from an inability or unwillingness to weave that which takes place in class within the broader, historical framework of values.

Commenting on Zekhariah's question, "Who scorns a day of small beginnings?" (4:10), Rabbi Elazar remarks: "Who caused the table of the righteous to be squandered in the future? Their smallness, that they did not believe in the Almighty" (*Sotah* 48b). This does not, of course, refer to skepticism, as we deal here with the righteous. Rather, we speak here of a mentality that undermines the importance of the awareness of God's Kingdom in all its power and scope, and thereby weakens the faith in "His glory fills the earth" (*Yishayahu* 6:3). We can assess the full significance of educational activity of *harbatzat Torah* if we see it as intertwined in a broad, complex system – though, needless to say, we may not disregard the beautiful moments in their own right. Thus, anything that can encourage and arouse thought on a broad scale, anything capable of contributing towards exaltation in this endeavor, is worthy of being expressed and heard.

While disseminating Torah in Haran, Avraham dealt, presumably, with many trifles; "He would inform," the Rambam describes, "to each and every individual in accordance with his capacity" (*Hilkhot Avodah Zarah* 1:3). But in this activity, too, he exposed the wonder of creation – which is expressed in all *harbatzat Torah*, not only in conversion, in its narrowest sense, as noted in the *midrash*:

> "And the souls they made in Haran" (*Bereishit* 12:5) – Rabbi Elazar bar Zimra said: if all creatures on earth would gather to create even a single mosquito they could not cast a soul therein; and the verse states, "the souls they made"? Rather, these are the converts that they converted. If, indeed, they converted them, why does it say "they made"? To teach that whoever brings an idolater and converts him is considered as having created him.[30]

This involvement, too, is included in Avraham's historic mission, for which he was rewarded: "For I have singled him out, for he will instruct his children and his posterity to keep the way of the Lord by doing what is just and right, in order that the Lord may bring about for Avraham what He has promised him" (*Bereishit* 18:19) – the way of the Lord, in which He, as it were, walks; the way of the Lord, regarding which He commanded; and the

---

[30] *Bereishit Rabbah (Lekh-Lekha)* 39:14; Vilna edition, p. 81.

way of the Lord, which progresses the building of the world and its establishment in accordance with His will.

TOWARDS AHAVAT HASHEM:
ART AND THE RELIGIOUS EXPERIENCE

CHAIM BROVENDER

IS THERE A PLACE for the serious study of fine arts in an Orthodox school, and, if so, what is its specific purpose within the context of the larger curricular goals of Jewish education? In attempting to clarify these questions, let us at first try to discover what the purpose or the value in the study of fine arts might be; if we find that there is indeed value, then we will try to understand what place it should be given in a Torah-based standard curriculum.[1]

We are aware that there are many subjects or skills that students may study beyond or outside of the school curriculum (often outside of the school building itself, often for practical reasons). In fact, it has been shown that there is a clear advantage to this use of extra-curricular studies. If the economic realities are such that the extra hours are available to the student (assuming that someone is able to pay for this luxury), then the results are often superior to conventional school-based learning. This advantage exposes one of the great problems of modern education – how do we encourage the student to apply himself as an individual while functioning within a collective?

While it might not be practical to teach everyone how to play the harp, for example, a student especially talented in harp playing will surely gain

---

[1] Clearly, there are significant practical and ideological differences among the various types of Jewish schools (even within the Orthodox community), as well as between those in Israel and the Diaspora, and these differences may ultimately affect some of the attitudes to the study of fine arts. In this essay I will try to achieve a consensus statement and not attempt to resolve the nuances as they affect the study of fine arts in the various schools. In fact, since most of us are unfortunately very distant from the subject of this discourse, I think that the finer distinctions will necessarily have to await further study.

from private hours of study. Those hours will usually be outside of the school structure and day and will be geared to the needs of the individual student, who will gain significantly by studying the harp privately.

In this essay, however, I am specifically asking a question about the standard curriculum, the one taught inside the school to all students. Should an Orthodox day school teach fine arts, include this material in its curriculum, and present this subject matter to all students? This would imply thereby that the study of such material is more than generally interesting or important for those few students with special talents. It indicates that in some way it is essential to the education of the particular Jew that the school and community are trying to develop.

For the sake of clarity, I will lay down the following postulates that I believe ought to be common to the Jewish schools considered in this essay. I focus on schools whose intention it is to produce students who are committed to and careful with the fulfillment of their *mitzvah* obligations and who are willing to accept that Torah study is a crucial part of life. In these schools the study of Torah should be presented as a unique value, and the student should be directed to maximize the time spent on the study of Torah. Therefore, one will necessarily conclude that while there are subjects or whole areas of study that are interesting and of value, they will occasionally have to be set aside because of the overriding demands of Torah study. Even schools that profess a certain parity between Torah study and secular studies recognize that the study of Torah severely limits the time available for the pursuit of other material. The question, restated to reflect these Torah-based schools, is: In a program or curriculum that sees itself obligated to teach math and science intensively, and give serious time to history and English, where could we possibly find the time for the study of fine arts? Such study can clearly be described as a luxury – practically and ideologically.

Jewish Nature of Fine Arts

Fine arts were not generally perceived as a Jewish subject and were not traditionally included as part of the Torah curriculum. They have not been included in the more recent additions to that curriculum (such as history, languages, math, etc). We are challenged to imagine or intuit what the Jewish "angle" might be that would justify the study of fine arts. It is equally difficult to envision the study of fine arts as a stepping-stone to riches or power (in most instances), unlike the salient promise of science or computers. Similarly, for those interested in exploring the nature of the Universe or benefiting mankind through technology, the arts do not seem to present the opportunities to probe these issues in the way that physics or mathematics offers. To justify taking valuable time from math or physics to study the nature of the enterprise called "art" can be hard to defend. Most important, the study of art does not seem to have any apparent value for the religious personality that Jewish schools ought to be trying to produce.[2] There does not seem to be a need for the student who wants to be well versed in Torah, be it in the narrow sense or even in the more modern, expanded view that includes general knowledge, to deal with the question of fine arts. Furthermore, there is no obvious advantage to the study of art for the person interested in his Jewishness or in touching his or her own spirituality.

It is my intention to develop a short theory of aesthetics that is integratable with the wider curriculum of contemporary Torah institutions. I would like to suggest that, in spite of the very real problems (both technical and ideological), the study of art might have serious redeeming features that make it worthy of consideration for the standard curriculum. In fact, the study of art may be valuable in developing the religious personality and enabling the student to enter into a dialogue with Heaven. In this regard it is important to note that I do not refer to the exceptional or gifted student who might be drawn to art for a variety of personal reasons. Rather, I am referring to the average student looking for ways to develop his or her own position regarding Torah, spirituality, and a personal involvement in that enterprise.

Fine Arts and the Standard Curriculum

First, let us review the commonly held positions on the purpose of fine arts in conventional curricula, which are generally arranged under four headings.[3]

The first position assumes that the student can be educated to derive "pleasure" from the encounter with the fine arts. There is no indication as to what determines the nature of the pleasure, or how we are to distinguish the pleasure of reflecting on a painting from, as an example, the pleasure of watching baseball. There is no doubt that baseball gives pleasure, and that many do participate in benefiting from that pleasure. As loyal fans will at-

---

[2] I am not considering the halakhic issues that might come to the fore in the study of fine arts. In this regard, see Aaron Kirschenbaum, "*Ha-Omanut be-Halakhah*," in *Ha-Yahadut ve-ha-Omanut*, ed. D. Cassuto (Ramat-Gan: Bar-Ilan, 1989), pp. 31–69 (inc. responses).

[3] These four commonly held positions are outlined in the Hebrew *Entziklopediah Hinukhit* (Jerusalem: Bialik, 1964), vol. 2, col. 4–5.

test, there is a certain amount of study that has to be engaged in to maximize the pleasure. We have to study the current and past statistics, reflecting player achievement, in order to increase the pleasure that can be derived from watching the event. In fact, it is difficult for me to explain why the pleasure of art is more important or more significant in any way than the pleasure of baseball.[4] Nor can I easily explain why the pleasure of art should be studied and developed in a school setting, while we are able to learn about the pleasures of baseball from our peers and elders in an informal setting. If there is some value to the study of art, surely it can be absorbed in the same *ad hoc* or informal way.

The second generally assumed purpose is to develop aesthetic refinement and to learn to distinguish the good from the bad in the plastic arts. Though one may not yet know what art is exactly, we can be certain that the distinctions of "good" and "bad" are important. It seems to me that the ability to make these distinctions can be developed from a wide array of activities and is not something limited to the study of art. Again, baseball (while not exactly the same as art) may also foster these qualities. But there must be some way to determine what the essential benefit in art might be in order to make any decisions about studying the material seriously. If we cannot determine what this benefit might be, baseball remains the better choice. It is important to remember that the study of baseball is conducted by most young people outside the school premises. They are able to create the necessary "curriculum" and become as expert as they wish without the intervention of schools or formal teaching. I can hardly imagine the effort that the system would have to expend to make the younger generation "fans" of the fine arts. For baseball, the fans are all there and the results seem to be very encouraging.

The third general assumption is that the study of art develops fine taste in work and in daily life. "Taste" is very much a matter of taste, and it is difficult to arrive at an objective definition in any sort of precise way. I imagine that baseball does not represent "good taste" to most people, but there is in fact an entire literature written about the game, and some if it is

---

[4] That difficulty, of course, echoes the famous statement, attributed by John Stuart Mill to Jeremy Bentham, that the "quality of pleasure being equal, push-pin [a game of the time] is as good as poetry." What Bentham actually said was "Prejudice apart, the game of push-pin is of equal value with the arts and sciences of music and poetry. If the game of push-pin furnish more pleasure, it is more valuable than either." Jeremy Bentham, "The Rationale of Reward," in vol. II of Bentham's *Works*, ed. Bowring (1843).

rather respectable.[5] Similarly, the plastic arts have taken baseball as a theme and produced items of passable taste.

What might be the purpose of this "good taste"? How is it useful in work and in daily life? What is the profit that a person of taste has over a person lacking that quality? What if, for the sake of argument, the person with "no taste" is also a great Torah scholar? How are we to evaluate him and his "lack of taste"? Finally, what is the place of pursuing the acquisition of good taste in a Torah-based school?

The final commonly assumed goal of an arts curriculum is a national one. In Israel this is often meant to expose the student to the remains of ancient art in our land, with the assumption that this will foster a connection between the student and our national history in *Eretz Yisra'el*. This goal might also be pursued in the Diaspora, especially in schools that teach that Israel should be the first national love of its students.[6] On this point baseball cannot compete. (I know I may be selling baseball short, but that is not my intention. I am aware that international competition often gives the fans a feeling of national pride.)

Art in the service of the national ethos is a modern position (as is the concept of "national ethos" itself). Even if architecture, for example, was often seen in the ancient world as an expression of the national ethos, only in modern times has art been seen as an efficient and effective way of educating the masses. The Soviet Union excelled in this effort. I recall that the first time I visited Moscow I could not help noticing the heroic statue of Yuri Gagarin (the first man in space) set up at the entrance to the city. Art in the service of the national ethos – I admit I thought it was in poor taste.

I can understand this position (though I don't sympathize with propaganda generally, nor with the use of art for narrow purposes), but I don't think it deals with any essential questions relating to art itself. Propaganda is an important topic, and art in the service of propaganda is certainly an option in certain situations. But in a religious school (even in the Diaspora), where love of the land of Israel is taught in many different ways and our history is seen as invariably connected with the land, it seems unnecessary to study the art of ancient Israel in order to make the point that we are connected to the land and are directed to love it. Similarly, using the art of modern-day Israel to engender positive feelings for the State seems forced,

---

[5] See, e.g., *The Faith of 50 Million: Baseball, Religion, and American Culture*, ed. C. Evans and W. Herzog (Louisville: Knox Press, 2002), and of course the various books by Roger Angell and George F. Will.

[6] Here there may be a special issue, worthy of considering – the use of art in achieving more general educational goals – but this is not the specific topic that concerns us.

and likely to prove ineffective in the long run.[7] These assumptions about the goals of art education do not address the specific issues of religious education. They do not help us in considering whether to set aside hours for the study of fine art in a situation where the hours available are limited. There is no attempt to determine the relative importance of such study, nor is it clear what reason there might be for undertaking such a program. Most lacking is a clearly articulated vision of what art contributes to the meta-goals of the Torah curriculum, or, for that matter, the religious personality. This being the case, I will attempt to put forth a preliminary vision, and try to answer these questions, in the hope that it may allow all entrusted with decision making for Jewish education to develop a more rigorous and so-phisticated approach to the use of the arts in our schools.

Toward a Torah-Based Philosophy of Art

Developing a Torah position on the study of art is difficult because there are no traditional sources that consider the question in a general way.[8] While some modern thinkers have touched briefly on the subject of art,[9] there is no systematic presentation that could enhance our ability to de-velop an educational position. We will have to develop an independent ap-proach to the study of art for the person in the Torah education system by considering sources that have serious implications for the study of art, though they do not directly refer to it.

In this regard, I think it is helpful to review several points made by Rambam in his discussions about the *mitzvah* of loving God (*ahavat Hashem*). In his introduction to *Mishneh Torah, Hilkhot Yesodei ha-Torah*, he enumerates the several *mitzvot* to be examined. The first three are intellec-tual (meaning that they do not seem to include a practical or active compo-nent) and demand acceptance of a certain opinion. Each of us is directed to believe that these principles are true, and we must assume each ought to be included in the basic curriculum. These principles are:

---

[7] A somewhat related, yet deeply more complex issue, is the use of art in Holocaust memorialization. See, e.g., C. Miriam Campanini-Fleer, "Holocaust Memorials: The Politics of Perception," *Tradition* 28:2 (Winter 1994): 19–33; and Erica Brown "'Turn-ing All the Past to Pain': Current Trends in the Memorialization of the Holocaust," *Torah U-Madda Journal* 9 (2000): 108–132, esp. pp 110–13.

[8] See Kirschenbaum, "*Ha-Omanut be-Halakhah*."

[9] For example, see Rav Kook's letter to the Betzalel School of Art in *Iggerot ha-Reiyah* (Jerusalem: Mosad ha-Rav Kook, 1962), vol. 1, #158. Cf. the famous passage in his introduction to *Shir ha-Shirim* in *Olat Reiyah* (Jerusalem: Mosad ha-Rav Kook, 1989), pp. 3–4.

1. To know that God exists.
2. To not entertain the notion that there is any other God beside Him.
3. To possess some notion of God's "oneness."

Additionally, the fourth and fifth *mitzvot*, although different from the first three in nature, are of special interest to this study:

4. To love God.
5. To fear God.

These last two *mitzvot* interest me because they seem at first not to concern intellectual or rational understanding, but to represent human emotions. Love and fear are inner feelings and cannot be defined or easily comprehended (unlike the first three *mitzvot*). The person who accepts God as a matter of faith understands that there is some commonality in this feeling. Love and fear, however, are subjective emotional positions, with different meanings for different people and therefore difficult to prove or define. It is not immediately understood how Rambam thinks he can legislate love, or demand love by the halakhic Jew, when that emotion cannot be objectified. Nevertheless, Rambam sets out to teach us the secret, and to show us the existence of actions that may *lead to* a greater appreciation and awareness of the love of God.

Later in *Hilkhot Yesodei ha-Torah*, Rambam takes up the challenge of defining the parameters of this obligation. He directs us to develop the quality of love for God, and to encourage actions that enhance this quality, just as we might encourage a person to develop a theory that helps him to assume other intellectual commitments (such as causality, on which see more below). He makes the following programmatic suggestion (*Hilkhot Yesodei ha-Torah* 2:1):

This God [whose nature is described earlier], honored and revered, it is our duty to love and fear Him; as it is said "You shall love the Lord your God" (Deut 6:5)…[10]

---

[10] There is an obvious anthropomorphic aspect to the directive. "Love" is something that we know about from our everyday relationships. Parents, siblings, and spouses teach us about love. But the connection of the love in the verse to the more general notion of devotion is not immediately clear. I mention this point because it represents the position of Rashi in his interpretation of the verse. Basing himself on the *midrash*, Rashi states:

"Love" [in Deut. 6:5] refers to assuming the mantle of the *mitzvot*, to accepting the yoke of the commandments. One who serves out of love cannot be compared to

In *Hilkhot Teshuvah* (10:2), in a discussion of serving God with love, Rambam continues his assessment of this emotion, and its relation to devotion to God, making a significant comparison to human romantic love:

> Whoever serves God with love, occupies himself with the study of Torah and fulfillment of *mitzvot* and walks in the paths of wisdom, impelled by no external motive whatsoever, moved neither by fear of calamity nor by the desire to obtain material benefits – such a person cleaves to the truth *because* it is true, and as a result happiness comes to him. This standard is very high indeed; not every Sage attained it. It was the standard of Abraham our father, who was called by God "my beloved," because he served only out of love. We are commanded by God, through Moses, to achieve this state, as it is said: "And you shall love the Lord your God" (Deut. 6:5). When one loves God with this kind of love, he will then be able to do all the *mitzvot* with love.

While there is a connection between the two passages, they certainly differ in how they present love. In *Hilkhot Yesodei ha-Torah*, the love referred to is a *mitzvah* act in and of itself. This means that everyone is obligated to achieve some minimum level of devotion (this in spite of the fact that a particular standard or set of halakhic parameters cannot be determined). There is a verse in the Torah that directs us all to love, and that verse has to be accepted and fulfilled. This is what the term *mitzvah* means – an obligation that devolves equally upon all the people.

In *Hilkhot Teshuvah*, however, Rambam has a different notion in mind. He states quite clearly that "whoever serves God out of love, occupies himself with the study of Torah and fulfillment of *mitzvot*." Here, Rambam presents love not as an obligation, but as a quality or emotion that enables all

---

one who serves out of fear. If you serve out of fear and find that you are overburdened by the master's demands, you will leave and go out in your own.

It seems obvious to Rashi that "love" implies unshakeable devotion. More than acceptance, we are directed to "cleave" to the *mitzvot*, to love God by doing his will, and to maintain that devotion even in difficult times. Rashi has changed the verse and its more obvious intention, love, and has depersonalized the sentiment, turning it into an act of devotion. There is a human activity that can be compared to the love of God, namely the love of the master. In both cases, love is expressed by a sense of duty and the willingness to suffer difficulty in doing that duty. According to Rashi, the metaphor (master-slave) helps us to understand the intention of the verse, such that its anthropomorphic content is no longer as offensive as it might be perceived in Rambam's rendering. There is no doubt that Rambam does not shy away from this very human emotion and uses it to describe the relationship between man and God.

other *mitzvot* to be made more significant. Further in *Hilkhot Teshuvah* (10:4) Rambam comments:

> The Sages said, "Lest you will say, 'I will study Torah in order that I may become rich, or that I may be called Rabbi, or that I may receive reward in the World to Come.' It is therefore written 'To love the Lord.' Whatever you do, do it only out of love."

It seems that the love Rambam refers to is that which makes the other *mitzvot* more significant. Torah study in itself might be a response to the divine will. Surely we study because we are directed to study! At the same time we study because it gives us the opportunity to have a profound relationship with God, and this relationship itself is called love. Regarding this love, Rambam says it is like the love of a man and a woman (*Hilkhot Teshuvah* 10:3). It is all consuming and it is romantic. This is the love that we try to achieve while studying Torah and doing the *mitzvot*.

Rambam has introduced us to two categories of love that the Jew must strive to attain, but they differ from each other in scope and nature.[11] That of *Hilkhot Yesodei ha-Torah* – stated as a normative obligation – stands on its own and is not connected to any other *mitzvah*, per se. It is the love that establishes our connection to God, and it is generated through looking carefully upon the created world and being inspired by the love indicated in its workings. When we notice God's love reflected in the workings of the world, our response will be greater love for the creator.

The love described in *Hilkhot Teshuvah* is of a different sort, and poses a different challenge. This love and devotion is integrally connected to the performance of every other *mitzvah*, especially the *mitzvah* of Torah study.[12] This kind of love is that which is "very exalted and comparable to the love of a man and a woman." Its source is in the relationship between God and humanity, expressed in His gift of the Torah and *mitzvot* – the essence of his will. For Rambam, this is the philosopher's love of the truth, and we are

---

[11] In *Sefer ha-Mitzvot* Rambam seems to unite these two distinct categories of love – see Positive Commandment #3 (and cf. *Sefer ha-Hinukh* #418). It seems, however, that the presentation is more significant in the *Mishneh Torah*.

[12] Though every *mitzvah* indicates God's love for His creation, Torah study opens the greatest aperture for returning that love. Torah study is about God's declared intention for His created man. If I study Torah diligently, I will discover more and more about this will, and I will be filled with love for the source of this goodness. See *Nefesh ha-Hayyim* 4:6 and *Tanya*, chap. 22.

directed to achieve this special and more esoteric love of God through his *mitzvot.*

Perhaps this distinction can be seen in another way. The love demanded in *Hilkhot Yesodei ha-Torah* is based on observation (science) and is achieved by looking into the created world, studying it, and finally standing before that creation in wonder. The second kind of love, in *Hilkhot Teshuvah,* is the philosopher's love – "the truth because it is true." While we are all directed to have the first kind of love (it is clearly a *mitzvah*), only some will achieve the second. We can all stand with wonder at the vision of creation, but only a few will be able to love the truth itself.

The Scientist's Love

Let us look more carefully at the first category of Maimonidean love, the love of the scientist, of the observer, and of the organizer of information about the created world. The world is a reflection of the Creator's concern for His creatures, and if we look into that world carefully through scientific observation, and organize the information as scientists do, we will certainly come to love its Creator.

Love develops within us as the result of our awareness that the world reflects mutual concern. If someone feeds us when we are hungry, then we will surely develop special feelings for the source of sustenance. If we are convinced that the offer (of food, for example) is unflinching and will always be available, then we are overcome with feelings of love. We are directed to love God. Rambam teaches us that if we understand our relationship properly, if we are the "scientists" of divine creation, then the love becomes simple and obvious.

Look into the world and note that God gives us constant, ongoing support. There are no prior conditions, and the world is always there to serve us. We have only to notice that there is sustenance on earth and to realize, by implication, that there is one overwhelming source of support in heaven. This analysis will generate the desired feelings and enable us to perform the *mitzvah* of loving God. Look more carefully and note the complexity of the world and the "extremes" to which the creator has gone in order to care for us. The more we know, the more our feelings of love are enhanced and strengthened. This is strongly expressed by Rambam elsewhere in *Hilkhot Yesodei ha-Torah* (2:2):

> And what is the way that will lead to the love and fear of Him? When a person contemplates His great and wondrous works and creatures and from them obtains a glimpse of His wisdom which is incomparable and infinite,

he will straightaway love, praise, and glorify Him, and exceedingly yearn and desire to know His great name; even as David said (Ps. 42:3): "My soul thirsts for God, the living God; O when will I come to appear before God?"

While it is true that *ahavat Hashem* seems difficult at first, there is nonetheless a democratic aspect to this *mitzvah* that enables all the Jews in the world to achieve this level of service. Apparently, everyone can stand in wonder at the world that God created for our good. Everyone can understand the love of a parent, which generates concern and support. Since every person can observe and reflect on his or her own state, just as a scientist might, we each can potentially achieve some aspect of the awareness that generates *ahavat Hashem*.

Rambam himself was a scientist, involved in observation and in deriving the correct inference from his observation. Further, he felt that if one developed this capacity for observation, one would certainly come to the conclusion that the relationship between God and the world is one of love. For Rambam, the study of science and serious observation of the world can only enhance the feelings of devotion of a religious person who accepts the first three principles of *Hilkhot Yesodei ha-Torah*. If you study science and you know how God's world is formulated, you are necessarily impressed by the complexity of creation and the concern of the divine for His creations — in general and, especially, for the least resilient, most dependent, and most aware of the creations, humanity. For Rambam, there is a simple relationship between science and religion, and that relationship produces the kind of awe that is a prerequisite for fulfilling the *mitzvah* of loving God.

The notion that Torah and worldly knowledge or science enhance each other is clearly present in Rambam's works. The created world was there to be observed, assessed, and analyzed, and, in turn, it could only enhance the believer in his convictions.[13] It is important to note that Rambam did not say that belief itself would be generated by science, only that science can enhance belief and make it more serious an endeavor for the practitioner. More correctly, Rambam thought that belief would be enhanced and strengthened by observing the created world in a scientific manner. It is true that belief in God may not have been a serious problem in Rambam's time, as people may have found believing in God an easier position to adopt than nonbelief. Nevertheless, to enhance and deepen belief, observing the world was absolutely necessary.

---

[13] See generally, *Guide of the Perplexed* III:25–28 and discussion below.

The Role of "Miracles" as an Introduction to Observation

Rambam recognized the importance of miracles in the world organized and directed by God. But he did not believe that miracles were the *source* of one's belief in God; rather, they enhanced it and gave it certain substance. This is demonstrated by the recounting of the Exodus miracles on Passover night – an obligation on the wise and simple alike.

In the context of our discussion, we might say that the miracles teach us how to observe the world around us and direct us to discover more about God's goodness. This, in turn, enables us to participate actively in the *mitzvah* of loving God. Science does not relate to miracles per se, but the fact that there *are* miracles prods us to study further and to investigate the realities of the physical world. The miracle enhances faith generally because it proves (or shocks us into realizing) that God is concerned with His creation. The miracle also demands study, thereby giving us entrée to the world of God's love, forcing us to take note of His role in the created world.

In the modern world, miracles have become problematic. After Britain emerged from the long war with France in 1815, a new world was established. On the one hand, Britain was a great power and premier economy in the new world order. On the other hand, there was great urban poverty and social dismay. All this in the face of severe challenges to faith and a new-found uncertainty about ideas that were previously unassailable. It was a time of contradiction. The prudery, which is synonymous with the Victorian age, paralleled a violent immoralism, as seen in the writings of the Decadents.

Against the background of this controversy, Thomas Carlyle, in his philosophical satire, *Sartor Resartus*, argues for a new mode of spirituality in an age of mechanism. He was looking for a way of bringing the people back to a truer form of religious devotion, but one appropriate for his time. In an often-quoted line he states, "Wonder is the basis of worship."[14]

In the six centuries from Rambam to Carlyle, there had been no change. Wonder – or, as I have tried to explain, the love of God – remained the basis of worship. Rambam knew that to develop this sense of wonder and to be able to see God's concern in the world, an opening was needed – some way of creating more direct access to a feeling of relationship (scientific knowledge having been much less developed than it is in our time). In earlier times, this was accomplished through the experience of miracles. The reason that we continue to tell the stories of the miracles of the escape

---

[14] *Sartor Resartus* (1883), book 1, chap. 10.

from Egypt, and are not content to tell only of the exalted change that the people experienced, is that we need the miracle and the memory of the miracle in order to enter the world of God's love for His people.

But miracles were problematic even in antiquity. In the first century B.C.E., Cicero, the Roman philosopher and man of letters, made a well-known denial of miracles:

> Nothing can happen without cause; nothing happens that cannot happen, and when what was capable of happening has happened, it may not be interpreted as a miracle. Consequently, there are no miracles. We therefore draw this conclusion: what was capable of happening is not a miracle.[15]

I am less concerned with the truth of the statement than with its possible influence. To say that everything must have a cause is an attractive position, because it enables us to study phenomena and to classify and organize the material of nature in a systematic manner. Alternatively, one might say that the scientist, because of his powers of observation and analysis, might develop an antipathy to the notion of miracles. Even if one believed in the possibility of a miracle, he would tend to try to find a "scientific" explanation for a particular occurrence and not be inclined to claim the rationale of "miracle."

As I have pointed out, miracles can often provide the student of Torah with the impetus necessary to concern himself with the workings of God's world and, especially, with the *mitzvah* of loving Him.

Rambam and Miracles

Rambam, though disagreeing with Cicero, believed that miracles were not essentially beyond understanding. He agreed that a kind of causality was at the bottom of all things and that that causality had to be investigated and appreciated. This is not the place to present a full discussion of Rambam's position on miracles, but it is important to remember that, for Rambam, miracles do not necessarily imply an abrogation of the laws of nature. His position is that all miracles are predetermined at the time of creation and do not indicate a change in God's wisdom or intentions. The miracle of the splitting of the sea does not imply a change in the nature of the water; rather, it came about because of an extraordinary (but natural) wind that affected how the water was deployed. The conclusion is that even miracles are subject to the study of nature. It is fair to ask how a particular

---

[15] Cicero, *De Divinatione* 2:28.

miracle was accomplished, since God works in accordance with the laws established at creation (divine will and wisdom).[16]

In sum, it appears that the difference between the position of Cicero and that of Rambam is narrow, a function of one's belief or faith in God. They agree that all things should make sense and can be understood as a reflection of the laws of nature. Rambam believes that there are unique events in history that can be explained as part of nature but that are, nonetheless, miraculous, either because of their infrequency or because there is independent substantiation (in the Torah) of their miraculous quality. For example, if the Torah indicates that the splitting of the Red Sea was a miracle, then it indeed is so, even though it can be explained as the result of a combination of natural events. The miracle is Heaven's way of reminding us that all observation should enhance our feeling about God's love.

Unfortunately, we live in a world in which miracles are no longer an effective prod to encourage the search for divine love. Rambam devalued the notion of miracle and rejected it as a primary sign of our relationship with God, but he saw the miracles related to us in the Torah as an entry point to understanding that the world reflects God's love for us. It is difficult for us today to recognize the miracle and to use it as a critical element in our own religious development. My instinctive feeling is that even when some people claim to be living in a miraculous world in which they are sure God is concerned about them, they often mean that the world is simply too complicated to assess. Instead of driving a person on to greater analysis and investigation of the created world, the use of miracles today is often a statement about the *inability* to investigate and to determine what is going on in a more precise manner. Instead of clarifying the miraculous nature of our existence, one becomes entrenched in a more limited position, where the designation "miracle" becomes a cover-up for a lack of general understanding and for serious confusion about one's position in the world of God's making.

There is another reason that the miracle can no longer be the basis for the development of serious *ahavat Hashem*, and that is our contemporary estrangement from the source of all goodness due to our perception of the rules of causality. In Cicero's time, it was quite clear (to him) that all things have a cause, leading him to believe that there could be no miracles. Rambam wanted to assume both positions and claimed that there were miracles,

---

[16] For Rambam's theory of miracles, see esp. *Guide* II:29, III:25 and III:32 and his commentary to *Avot* 5:5. See also Menachem Kellner, "Maimonides' Allegiances to Science and Judaism," *Torah U-Madda Journal* 7 (1997): 88–104.

but that they could be assessed on the same principles as other natural phenomena. In this way, he wanted to connect the possibility of miracle and analysis; true, the events could be understood and analyzed, but there also could be miracles. This satisfied the scientist who wanted to believe that ultimately God rules the world of his creation. Everything can be analyzed and understood, but the world belongs to God and operates with His wisdom.[17]

In modern times we are directed (by the Rambam) to believe in miracles, but also to believe that they can be explained by science and some acceptance of causality. As a result, the miracle, or the apparent miracle, is no longer a source of wonder, and it generates neither a love for God, nor a desire to reciprocate the miraculous event with that love. Instead, we are obsessed with the questions: How did that happen? What rules can explain this event? We are convinced that we can understand whatever happens, and we are further convinced that even if an event seems to contradict our perception or experience, we will shortly understand the principles or rules that govern it. We find it difficult to stand in awe and declare an event a miracle. We are confident that the seemingly miraculous event will soon be understood, as are all other events in our experience.[18]

For Rambam, miracles might be understood in some scientific way, but they remained indicators of God's love. As such, they were important for the continued religious development of man. Even though I might claim to understand the nuts and bolts of the miracle, that understanding need not devalue the "wonder" of the miracle. In our time, when faith in causality is virtually absolute, and we are convinced that we are able to precisely explain every phenomenon, the wonder in the miracle has disappeared. We are bereft of an entry-level experience into the world dominated by the *mitzvah* of loving of God.

There is, nevertheless, one great mystery we have discovered in modernity that Rambam was not aware of, but, unfortunately, even it has been unable to challenge our underlying denial of the miracle as an effective force for religious development. That has to do with Werner Heisenberg's formulation in 1927 of what has become known as the "uncertainty principle." According to this principle of quantum mechanics, it is impossible to simultaneously specify the position and momentum of a particle, such as an

---

[17] See the somewhat similar sentiment in Albert Einstein, "Science and Religion II," in *Out of My Later Years* (New York: Philosophical Library, 1956), pp. 22–28.

[18] For a discussion of one result of the Maimonidean de-emphasis on the miraculous, see David Berger, "Some Ironic Consequences of Maimonides' Rationalistic Messianism" (Hebrew), *Maimonidean Studies* 2 (1992): 1–8.

electron, with any precision. This implies something about the causal laws that exist in nature. In fact, it seems that causal laws cannot account for the behavior of these individual particles, and only the reactions of great groups of these electrons can be predicted, on the basis of statistical rules. The rules of causality have become approximate; it is no longer possible to know what the precise cause of any phenomenon is, and the world has, in theory, returned to a state of miracle and wonder. This uncertainty principle makes it necessary to reassess everything we see and experience as a new event, as a miracle.

Still, even uncertainty could not effect a change in modern skepticism, and it seems that as modern individuals we remain in the world of causality, avoiding the entry of the miraculous into our conscious. Even though many high school physics students can explain the principle of uncertainty, they have not changed their world view. They remain tied to a world of causality.[19]

Not only are students of this mind; some leading modern physicists have similarly refused to give up causality despite their understanding of uncertainty. Einstein reportedly posited that what was excluded by the uncertainty principle was not the fact of the causality principle in nature, but merely the precise knowledge of it. We do not know it, but it is there. For these scientists, causality continues to rule. Just as there are many physicists who can speak of uncertainty, there are also many who know that causality lives even within uncertainty.

Rambam's model has become ever more difficult. He thought that the vision of the miracle would enable us to see God's goodness in the world of creation; that the laws of nature and the understanding of those laws would enable us to appreciate the creation – but this does not usually seem to be the case now. In fact, we are not necessarily interested in the rules as a source of faith. Our great trust in the principle of causality and in the explanatory power of science makes it almost impossible for us to stand with wonder before any particular natural event we might encounter.

Science has robbed us of the simple feelings of wonder when we think about the events of the physical world we inhabit. We would like to take Carlyle's advice, we would especially like to follow the Rambam into a world of loving God, but this has become almost impossible for us.

---

[19] This is comparable to the continued use of Newtonian physics in our post-relativity world. We know that there is relativity, but we live and think in the world as described by Newton.

The question of love of God in our time can be restated: Is it possible to consider another point of entry for the religious personality who seeks to achieve some degree of wonder when gazing upon the world of creation? Is it possible to circumvent the causality developed by science and reestablish a sense of wonder when looking upon God's works?

Aesthetics and the Philosophy of Art

We seem to have a natural predilection for the aesthetic; we are drawn to the beautiful and repulsed by the horrible in nature – even though it is difficult to define the exact parameters of each. Let us imagine a confrontation with the Scottish highlands. Can anyone remain neutral? Would he not draw a deep breath and say, "that is surely beautiful" or perhaps insist that this is the wonder of God's creation? We can easily imagine that someone would find a particular sunset in a certain time and place remarkable. Astronauts are constantly commenting on the "beauty" and the "wonder" and the "vision" of creation. This is not the result of study or understanding, but a natural inclination with which we seem to be endowed.

It is true that the term "beautiful" can indicate a variety of things and lacks a clear or simple meaning. Almost everything can be seen as beautiful by someone, or as reflecting his or her particular point of view. But there are enough people who seem to be affected in a similar way by certain visions to make us think that "beautiful" is real and has been programmed into the human personality. It is possible that one of the reasons we are endowed with an innate sense of beauty is to enable us to stand with wonder and awe at the creation, or at least at those moments which, in an almost miraculous way, direct us to the beauty of the divine craft.

If we have been robbed of the miraculous moment, if we do not see anything in the workings of God's world other than the causal principle, if "uncertainty" does not create the option of awe, then perhaps we have to turn to beauty – the special quality of the creation which takes our breath away and leaves us enraptured with wonder. It may be that beauty and the aesthetic moment provide the only possible contemporary entrée to discovering God's love in the creation. The beautiful sunset is really there. The snow-capped mountains are really there – they inspire in us the notion that creation is perfect and appropriate for us and us alone. This feeling is often useful in *tefillah*, and it may be one of the reasons that the medieval kabbalists in Safed went out into nature to greet the Sabbath Queen.[20]

Difficult though it may be to define the subject of aesthetics, there is no doubt that we are impressed by "beauty" (or its opposite). But there is one further point. We are not simply given the gift of perceiving a beautiful landscape or moment; we are able as well to reproduce that beauty or moment in a variety of ways. The *ruah memallela*[21] enables man to practice his appreciation of aesthetics in creation in a number of ways. We are able, for example, to recreate the sunset, or the highlands of Scotland, by painting and reproducing God's world as art. Art (or poetry or music) becomes an interpretation of the aesthetic feeling within us. We take note of the sunset, deciding that it is a vision that has meaning and that leaves an impression, and we try to reproduce it as art.[22] Art as a human endeavor is an attempt to connect to that aspect of creation determined by the aesthetic consciousness to be beautiful.

Art represents the world of beauty (in the sense that it inspires wonder) but also necessarily interprets it. Art does not reproduce the feeling of awe that exists in the created world. Strictly speaking, that would not be possible, nor would there be any point in its being done. Art presents its own experience of the beauty of the creation as seen through the eyes of the artist, and, finally, through the eyes of the observer of the artist's work.

Art is about becoming part of the wondrous experience of gazing on beauty. The wonder of the world as created is sufficient; the enterprise of the artist is to restate it and to make it his or her own, in some way. If we learn to look at the work of art in the proper manner we should be able to connect to this human vision of beauty, which originates in God's created world but insists that beauty must ultimately be seen, reflected, or interpreted by the human view.

---

[20] This is not the time to discuss the use of the aesthetic moment in the performance of *mitzvot*. Suffice it to say for the present that the aesthetic moment seems to enhance our ability to achieve *kavvanah*.

[21] Although generally associated with humanity's unique capacity for verbal communication (see Onkelos to Gen. 2:7, and also Rashi there, s.v. *la-nefesh*), I am using this term as synonymous with man's "godly" spirit and general creative capacity – including music, arts, etc.

[22] This act of "reproduction" is clearly evident in classical – or "representational" – art, but is also true when the reproduction is more interpretative, such as in impressionism or, certainly, abstract art.

This can be understood from the opposite perspective. The literary critic Cleanth Brooks spoke of the "heresy of paraphrase."[23] In following an argument by the Italian critic and philosopher Benedetto Croce, Brooks posited that the meaning of a poem (or any work of art) consists in what is not translatable. The meaning of the poem is connected to the disposition of the words, their arrangement, and their rhythm. There is a sensory side to the poem as a work of art. You don't just read the poem; you experience it. To alter any of the above (by translation for example) is to produce *another* work, which may or may not have merit as art. A poem is like a sunset in that it is rooted in a sensory experience. But the poem uses special talents that are indigenous to the human being. Words, rhythm, order, and meaning are all things that give the poem its structure and produce aesthetic merit and the quality of wonder.

Looking at the divine sunset in nature encourages us to produce our own sunset; to use words, music, and the plastic arts to reproduce, and then to express in a personal way, the sunset that is God's gift of beauty. Further, the sunset we have produced, written of, or painted, becomes in itself an object of wonder and amazement. If it is true that for the believing person a sunset can be inspiring, if the natural beauty we encounter tells us that we are experiencing God's love and should reciprocate, then it may also be true that the representation of the beauty in nature through art grants us entrée into the special experience of God's love, seen through the prism of human creativity. This notion is expressed by Joseph Conrad in the preface to his 1897 novel *The Nigger of the Narcissus*:

> [The artist] speaks to our capacity for delight and wonder, to the sense of mystery surrounding our lives; to our sense of pity, and beauty, and pain; to the latent feeling of fellowship with all creation....[24]

To students of Torah it is clear that the capacity to speak and to clarify ideas using reason and words enables us to connect to God and His Torah in a unique manner. We experience the Torah's grandeur by engaging it with those talents that God has bestowed upon us. God has given us the Torah as an act of love, and we engage that love through study of it.

The significance of the relationship between study and love can be further extended. Creation itself is connected to the Torah. "God gazed into

---

[23] Cleanth Brooks, *The Well-Wrought Urn: Studies in the Structure of Poetry* (New York: Harcourt-Brace, 1947).

[24] Joseph Conrad, *The Nigger of the Narcissus* (New York, 1897; many reprints), p. xlviii.

the Torah and created the world"[25] is a notion that guides the student of the Torah. Through study, we gain information and expertise, both necessary to follow the demands of the Torah. But we are also involved in *hiddush* (new or novel interpretation), which can be explained as new understanding of the Torah's system and, by implication, clarification of God's love for his chosen creations.

Looking into the created world is available to all who have faith, in order to prod and develop that faith. Looking into the Torah is available to those who accept the Torah from the Creator of the world, to be used in determining the more refined nuances and facets of that love. Learning Torah is experiential in the sense that it enables one to stand with wonder before God's goodness, which has been bestowed upon the students of the Torah. And there is a democratic principle at work here. Everyone can study Torah, though it represents the greatest "crown" available to man. As Rambam states (*Hilkhot Talmud Torah* 3:1):

> The crown of Torah lies ready and is accessible to all of Israel, as it says (Deut. 33:4): "Moses commanded us the Torah, as the heritage of the [entire] congregation of Jacob" – anyone who wishes may come and take [this crown].

As educators, we are witness to the fact that not all students are affected equally by the opportunity to study Torah. Ideally, everyone who entered the paradise of Torah would find sure footing therein. But that is not the reality, and, whatever the reason, some of those who attempt to study are rejected by the enterprise. They do not find the study of Torah an entry-level experience into God's love for His creation. Tragically, some find it so oppressive that it stymies any pure religious thought or experience the student might have.

It has been suggested that there may be other ways to gain access to God's love. Some have suggested that it can take place in the social context of young people striving to express themselves religiously, and others think that a "Carlebach *minyan*" is the best option. I would like to propose that reconnecting to our human spirit, and standing in wonder at God's creation through the use of that spirit, may provide us a significant option. Not every student will find his or her way to God's love through the arts and with the understanding that the human capacity to render the created world in a special way is a gift that should be exploited; but for some it might

---

[25] *Zohar, Terumah* 161a-b.

provide the necessary spiritual moment in an essentially nonspiritual existence that would enable them to begin to consider and later to experience
God's love.

A Final Note: Artwork and an Explanation

Two specific paintings by the seventeenth century Dutch painter Johan-
nes Vermeer are significant to our discussion (as are many others, but
Vermeer's stand out in my mind). I refer to his paintings *The Geographer* and
The Astronomer.[26]

In *The Geographer* (fig. 1) we encounter the man who is trying to map the
world in which he lives. He deals with small matters, trying to orient the
small sections of our existence into a comprehensive whole, and the painting clearly depicts a moment of insight – the light streaming in draws our
attention to his eyes. He holds his cartographer's instrument in midair, as if
he has suddenly been caught by an idea, and, again, the window's light
shines on those hands for emphasis. Just as the window allows that light in,
it allows the geographer's gaze to escape the confines of the room – emphasizing his interest in the outside world. The globe is tucked away on a
shelf behind the geographer and is irrelevant to the enterprise of the map-
maker since it depicts the *entire* world – our man is interested in the details.
The picture on the wall behind the geographer is that of a sea chart – very
much part of the world in which he lives. *The Geographer* is a pictorial representation of "a man discovering a new fact about reality in a world wide
open to his inquiring mind."[27]

In contrast, in *The Astronomer* (fig. 2), the surveyor of the heavens holds
in his hand the globe with the constellations, indicating his yearning to be
part of the greater conception. The two paintings were clearly meant to go
together, yet the contrast is stark. Unlike the geographer – caught in mid-
action, gazing out of the window – the astronomer is at rest, contemplating
his celestial globe. On the wall behind him is the painting *Finding of Moses*.
This is one of the great moments of salvation in world history. The Jewish
people were saved because the child Moses was saved from the river (Exodus, chap. 2). Art historians have pointed out that the inclusion of this
"painting within a painting" was meant for allegorical purposes, reinforcing

---

[26] For more on Vermeer see the books by Arthur K. Wheelock, Jr., esp. his *Vermeer and the Art of Painting* (New Haven: Yale, 1995) and, most recently, Bryan Jay Wolf, *Vermeer and the Invention of Seeing* (Chicago: Univ. of Chicago, 2001).

[27] Dianne Durante, "Vermeer's *Geographer*," *AOB News* 9:2 (1999): 13. See also James Welu, "Vermeer's *Astronomer*," *Art Bulletin* 68:2 (1986): 263–67.

Fig. 1
The Geographer (c. 1668–69)
Johannes Vermeer
Oil on canvas, 53x46 cm.
Courtesy of Steadelsches Kunstinstitut
Frankfurt am Main, Germany

the artist's underlying meaning – God's divine providence in the finding of Moses, symbolizing that spiritual guidance in man's attempt to discover His world.[28]

We read these pictures as though they were a *midrash*. They introduce us to the two aspects of human wonder. The geographer tries to measure and describe the world in which he lives; the astronomer tries to understand things that go beyond and through them, to grasp our position in that greater world.[29] We understand salvation as being an act of God's love, enabling us to reciprocate that love.

Surely these ideas can be stated in language and are found in the words of *Hazal*. But not everyone can appreciate the wonder in the world through the word, and not everyone can appreciate the love that is expressed in creation through the use of language.

Vermeer enables us to look upon these notions through an amazing representation of reality. For those who make the effort, the interpretation is greatly enhanced by the work of art itself. It gives us the opportunity to stand with wonder before the idea, to be able to find ways of connecting to the Creator through the beauty of the represented creation. It is hard to ignore the ability of the artist to present an idea through his art, and it is impossible not to draw a deep breath when confronting these works.

I have attempted in broad strokes to articulate the promise of art as an alternate avenue to achieving *ahavat Hashem* in Torah education. I do not pretend that there are any easy solutions. We are well served to remember Conrad's concluding warning:

Art is long and life is short, and success is very far off. And thus, doubtful of strength to travel so far, we talk a little about the aim – the aim of art, which, like life itself, is inspiring, difficult – obscured by mists. It is not in the clear logic of a triumphant conclusion; it is not in the unveiling of one of those heartless secrets which are called the Laws of Nature. It is not less great, but only more difficult. To arrest, for the space of a breath, the hands

---

[28] See Wheelock, *Vermeer and the Art of Painting*, pp. 161–62. Vermeer used the *Finding of Moses* in the background of another painting, *Lady Writing a Letter with Her Maid* (National Gallery of Ireland, Dublin), in which that scene is reproduced more fully and on a larger scale.

[29] Two outstanding works by the historian Daniel J. Boorstin detail these different poles of human creativity. See his *The Discoverers: A History of Man's Search to Know Himself and His World* (New York: Random House, 1983), and *The Creators: A History of Heroes of the Imagination* (New York: Random House, 1992).

Fig. 2

The Astronomer (1668)

Johannes Vermeer
Oil on canvas, 50x45 cm.
Courtesy of Le Louvre

Paris, France

busy about the work of the earth, and compel men entranced by the sight of distant goals to glance for a moment at the surrounding vision of form and colour, of sunshine and shadows; to make them pause for a look, for a sigh, for a smile – such is the aim, difficult and evanescent, and reserved only for a very few to achieve. But sometimes, by the deserving and the fortunate, even that task is accomplished. And when it is accomplished – behold! – all the truth of life is there: a moment of vision, a sigh, a smile – and the return to an eternal rest.[30]

The way to love of God has many paths; art is surely one of them.

---

[30] Conrad, *The Nigger of the Narcissus*, pp. l–li.

THE MANUFACTURE OF SULPHUROUS ACID: ON WISDOM AS A CATALYST IN TORAH STUDY

SHALOM CARMY

"Like the merchant's ships, from far she brings her bread" (Prov. 31:14) —
the words of Torah are poor in one place and rich in another place.
(Yerushalmi Rosh ha-Shanah 3:5)

I am a part of all that I have met;
Yet all experience is an arch wherethro'
Gleams that untravell'd world whose margin fades
For ever and for ever when I move.
(Tennyson, "Ulysses")

AN EMINENT PHYSICIST was once consulted by a group of rabbis. One of them came directly to the point. "About electricity, Professor," he asked: "Is there fire in the wire?" And then he waited for a straightforward answer.

When most people consider interaction between worldly knowledge and the study of Torah, it is encounters like this that they envisage. A specific body of secular knowledge is deployed, in a tangible way, in order to reach a specific conclusion in the study of Torah. The physicist's job is to tell us where the electric current dwells, and the botanist identifies the fruits and vegetables to which the laws of *berakhot* or *zera'im* are applied. Such inquiry is not limited to the natural sciences. In order to understand certain *halakhot* pertaining to business practices it may be necessary to know the details of medieval or early modern contracts. Documents and artifacts of the Ancient Near East may supply relevant information about biblical vocabulary or poetic form. One thinks of the conclusions of natural science or a body of historical and philological data.

Scholarly training is valuable both as a means to broader understanding and as an end in itself. In general, however, the study of the humanities does not yield this kind of clear-cut, incontrovertible benefit. The skeptic therefore argues that studying general history or literature or philosophy does not contribute to our knowledge of Torah. Those of us who have gained insight, and not only information, from our general studies have difficulty demonstrating what it is exactly that we have gained. In this essay I will not add to the literature arguing for the value of the humanities in the study and internalization of Torah. I assume that most readers agree that knowing how people lived and imagined and thought in the past enables us to study Torah and to experience our own creative relationship with *devar Hashem* and with *mitzvat Hashem* more vigorously and effectively, quite apart from the technical corpus of information contained in these disciplines. I shall concentrate on concrete, everyday illustrations of the interplay between the liberal arts, in this wider sense, and the life of Torah. My hope is to reveal aspects of that interaction that are neglected in more abstract treatments. The final sections concern the place of such interaction in the work of the contemporary Torah educator.

To begin, we must return to the distinction between the search for wisdom or humanistic insight and the academic enterprise, narrowly defined. Scholarship, in its purest form, seeks to accumulate knowledge, thus aspiring to the status of science. It either proposes general theories about matters significant to the study of Torah, or claims to arrive at the truth about particular propositions relevant to Torah. Many of us, whose initial attitude is the popular one sketched above, reinforced by exposure to the ideals of scholarship at some point in our education, try to assimilate humanistic insight to the scientific-scholarly model. One outcome is the impoverishment of insight and creativity, when the imitation of scholarly method prevents more imaginative approaches (and I am ignoring, for now, the secularist biases to which academic orthodoxies are prone). The alternative danger is the pretense that undisciplined approaches, rooted in arbitrariness, are equivalent to approaches sensitive to the demands of scholarly rigor. The excesses of *darshanut* (homiletics) often seek corroboration, nowadays, in the whimsicality of the more blustering and self-assured reader-reception ideologies. If, to paraphrase Kant's aphorism, scholarship without imagination is empty, then imagination that disdains the questions and evidence of scholarship is little more than fantasy.

The most memorable scholarship, of course, is more than amassing accurate data. It partakes in the rich life of the imagination; and, as already noted, creative thinkers care a great deal about pertinent scholarship. Nonetheless, the orientations differ, and teachers and would-be thinkers alike should recognize the characteristics of each. So before offering examples and general observations on their place within our educational framework, we ought to adumbrate some of the overall contrasts between scholarly method in its ideal – that is to say, professionally pure – form and the kind of humanistic insight I call wisdom.

First, ordinary scholarly production takes place within a rigidly defined disciplinary matrix. Humanistic insight, like the acquisition of wisdom in everyday life, is often marked by serendipity. We are surprised by insights that neither we, nor others, could have predicted.

Second, ordinary scholarly production can usually be boiled down to a finite number of steps. At its worst, this degenerates into a kind of "painting by the numbers," in which information is amassed without any conception of why it should be of interest to anyone. One may work out an algorithm for wisdom, accumulating note cards or reading randomly and then waiting for insight to strike, but such effort is a necessary rather than a sufficient condition for an intellectual breakthrough.

Third, the elements in productive scholarly research cannot be deleted from the final record. The record can be abridged or relegated to footnotes, but whatever is pertinent must be reported to the scholarly community; the personal aspects are not pertinent features of the enterprise. A scholarly theory or discovery can often be formulated without reference to its intellectual and imaginative genesis. An insight in Torah, like a scientific discovery, should be able to stand on its own, independent of the subjective factors that brought it to consciousness. In that respect, scholarly Torah presentations resemble scholarship, and differ in style from humanistic insight.

Fourth, wisdom is inseparable from the personal quest and achievement of the creative individual. In principle, the results of scholarship should be regarded as true or adequate regardless of the traits of the person who presents them. For the study of Torah and for the type of humanistic insight we are discussing, as in real life, whether an insight has been earned, both spiritually and intellectually, is crucial in determining its validity and its value.

Fifth, the appropriation of Torah, like the wisdom of the humanities, is incomplete if it does not affect the way the recipient thinks and lives. No such claim is attached to scholarly attainments.

Sixth, failure can be an important element in both scholarly research and the search for wisdom. For the ordinary scholar, the failure of a project, or a negative result, indicates a wrong path to be avoided next time. For the student of Torah, failure is more than a mere matter of trial and error. The talmudic teaching that one does not fully grasp Torah matters unless one has "stumbled" in one's pursuit appeals to a midrashic move according to which "stumbling block" (*makhshelah*) is a way of referring to Torah (*Gittin* 43a). For the searcher after wisdom, as well, the exposure of faulty assumptions and confused intuitions is an integral part of the self-knowledge that paves the way to truth.

Finally, because the search for wisdom requires unrelenting examination of one's motives and presuppositions, along with those of one's culture, to become wise, to gain insight, is also to come face to face with one's own foolishness. Often our study of culture – what human beings (including ourselves) have thought, imagined and done – provides the Archimedean lever that pries us loose from error and silliness. Self-understanding is not afraid of analogies and insights that the self-important academician may regard as frivolous. To this anxiety the thinker can only respond: "It is Torah, and we need to learn it" (see *Berakhot* 62a).

Our list begins with questions of intellectual procedure and method and moves on to spiritual matters: how study affects the personality of students and teachers. The two categories are not always separate, even as historical investigation is not always hermetically sealed off from theological and existential truth. The overall distinctions are nevertheless useful: keeping them in mind may spare you unnecessary confusion. The examples below show some aspects of the interplay between various facets of our concerns. They will presume an ideal commitment of time and intellect on the part of the educator. I will allow myself passing comments about the problems of translating the ideal into reality prior to confronting these obstacles and opportunities head on in the closing section.

II
Jewish Thought and Free Will
R. Eliyahu Dessler is well known for his theory of limited free will.[1] I will note one aspect of his teaching: the notion that we do not know the self as it truly is. R. Dessler posits a first-person awareness, in which we are free, and another perspective, in which actions are completely covered by scientific determinism. The approach, and even the language, indicates R. Dessler's indebtedness to Kant's Third Antinomy, which maintains the im-

---

[1] See, e.g., R. Dessler's "Treatise on Choice: Part I" in *Mikhtav me-Eliyahu*, vol. 1 (Benei Berak, 1964), pp. 111–116. I discussed the intricacies of his views in a paper presented to the 2002 Orthodox Forum, forthcoming as "Use It or Lose It: On the Moral Imagination of Free Will," in *Judaism, Science, and Moral Responsibility*, ed. David Shatz and Yitzhak Berger.

possibility of rationally demonstrating either the existence or non-existence of uncaused events, and his view that the human self is "noumenal," not the object of perception. The rudiments of Kant's philosophy were familiar to the Eastern European rabbinic elite. Thus, the historical connection between Kantian and Desslerian ideas can be assumed. It is legitimate to explain some of the similarities between them as a result of this connection, and also to pay special attention to the areas where they diverge. Ignorance of the history of Western philosophy would therefore diminish one's ability to understand what R. Dessler is doing.

Frequently, we cannot locate such an exact point of contact. Even if we doubted R. Dessler's acquaintance with Kant, we would want to know something about the intellectual milieu in which R. Dessler formulated his theories: What is he trying to justify? Whom is he trying to confute? What data, what arguments, and what rhetorical and analytic tools are available to him? Scholarship can improve the accuracy of our speculations, and save us from fantastic blunders, but it cannot exempt us from the responsibility of entering imaginatively into the mind of the thinker and his original audience.

The goal of philosophy is not merely antiquarian. In the end, we care not only what a thinker meant, but, more importantly, why his arguments succeed or fail; if the latter, why a serious thinker might have been led astray, or what profound truth he may have been struggling to express, and whether better arguments can be constructed. To examine R. Dessler in this way would necessitate a broader backdrop than his own intellectual biography or even that of his age. We would want a synoptic and analytic insight into the vast array of problems, ranging from metaphysics to epistemology to ethics and theology, impinging upon the question of free will.

This is the prototypical situation in the study of Jewish philosophy, and it is equally so in other Torah pursuits. The encounter with R. Dessler could thus either draw upon, or open into, a variety of confrontations with the history of philosophy, with philosophical analysis, history of ideas, even social history and psychology. It is, of course, impossible to study all things simultaneously. The more knowledge and insight we gain, the better we understand how hard it is to communicate a balanced and lucid outlook to those for whose education we are responsible. You can probably bone up overnight on the relevant comparisons between R. Dessler and Kant, like an undergraduate cramming for a final. But the larger questions cannot be taken by storm; they take a lifetime to sink into your bones. Inevitably, therefore, the daunting program I have just outlined demands patience and persistence and sustained passion. The insight gained cannot be communicated transparently in a neatly packaged lesson, not least because the patience and the persistence and the sustained passion are at the heart of what the teacher must give over.

Auden and the Missing *Nun*

We have just looked at an area where understanding of Torah and engagement in humanistic culture are virtually inseparable. Here is a case where information about modern English poetry is directly relevant to the study of *Tanakh*, albeit in a manner that is totally extraneous to the deeper meaning of the biblical text.

Psalm 145 (widely known as "*Ashrei*" after the verses that preface it in liturgical usage) is an alphabetical acrostic. The verse corresponding to the letter *nun* is missing. The simple explanation is that the acrostic scheme is sometimes adhered to irregularly.[2] R. Yohanan (*Berakhot* 4b), however, proposed that the absent verse referred to *nefilah* (falling) and was omitted in order to avoid its negative associations. The following verse (15), which states that God supports those who fall, confirms the hypothesis that we have here a euphemistic elision. In this harmonious psalm, the calamity from which God rescues one is indicated by its noticeable omission.

How seriously can one take this interpretation at the *peshat* (simple meaning) level? Is it likely that the author of a twenty-two-line poem would deliberately breach the poetic form of the composition in order to make a subtle point that is likely to be lost on the casual reader? Is R. Yohanan not reading an idea into the text that has no purchase on the text?

This issue was far from my mind the day I read W.H. Auden's "Atlantis." The poem, comprising seven twelve-line stanzas, which exhibit a complicated pattern of rhyme and meter, describes the effort and resourcefulness required to reach the mythical island of Atlantis. The voyage culminates in a scene where the traveler, having overcome many ordeals, collapses: "With all Atlantis shining/ Below you yet you cannot/ Descend." At this precise point in the poem, the rigid pattern is violated: line 7 of stanza 6 does not exist. The explanation seems obvious: the poet's "failure" to fully satisfy the complicated technical feat he has undertaken parallels the failure of the poem's protagonist to consummate his journey. The inter-

---

[2] See Ps. 25:2, 5, 17, 34:6, 9–10. The 11Qpsalms Scroll supplies the missing verse (likewise the Septuagint). This verse, however, is close to v. 17, except for the initial substitution of *ne'eman* for *tzaddik* and the replacement of the Tetragrammaton with *Elokim*. Hence this version is presumably a scribal solution to the problem of the absent verse, rather than an original alternative. See also Amos Hakham, *Da'at Mikra: Tehillim,* vol. 2 (Jerusalem, 1984) 578f. and note 23.

twining of form and content in the work of a twentieth-century master craftsman renders more persuasive the notion of a similar phenomenon in the psalm.

In this example, the Auden analogy is integral to the argument. Just as in the previous discussion, you cannot adopt the idea and dispense with the allusion. Yet the two deployments of "cultural literacy" operate in totally different ways. You cannot divorce your understanding of Jewish thought from your confrontation with the history of human culture, because the two are inextricably linked. The Auden reference, by contrast, has no direct connection to the psalm. It only provides an analogy that makes a certain way of reading more plausible. The skeptic may still demand more proof, preferably from an Ancient Near Eastern source. The more innocent reader may feel no sense of enlightenment – they trusted the rabbinic interpretation all along. And while the student of Jewish thought ought to train himself towards a grasp of general philosophical study, because he cannot otherwise be faithful to the work of understanding and insight, it is absurd to demand that the student of *Tanakh* who, rightly or wrongly, feels no impulse to read modern English poetry, ransack piles of literature, excellent or mediocre as they might be, in the hope of finding some stray nugget of serendipity.

Melville on Jonah

Before embarking on the whaling expedition, Ishmael attends an ex-mariner turned minister's sermon on Jonah (*Moby Dick*, chapter 9). The first part of Father Mapple's discourse brilliantly brings Jonah to life by imagining his furtive behavior, the suspicions he must have aroused among his companions and his own tormented conscience; the vivid depiction echoes several themes found in *Pirkei de-Rabbi Eliezer*'s midrashic reconstruction of the episode (ch. 10). The preacher goes on to analyze Jonah's prayer from the fish's belly. He has apparently noticed that the prayer (Jonah, chap. 2) lacks any expression of remorse for his sin or straightforward petition for his life. This might suggest that Jonah's repentance is incomplete, that he is not yet willing to confront the realities of his spiritual predicament. The sermon, however, reaches the radically different conclusion that remorseful behavior is not all that important: "For sinful as he is, Jonah does not weep and wail for direct deliverance… And here, shipmates, is true and faithful repentance; not clamorous for pardon, but grateful for punishment… Sin not; but if you do, take heed to repent of it like Jonah."

As an interpretation of Jonah, the sermon has limited value, because it examines only the first two chapters and does not integrate them with the rest of the book. At a more detailed level, as I have hinted, Melville's priest ignores, or apologizes for, the unusual features of Jonah's prayer. From our perspectives as Jewish students, and as individuals obligated to repent, the sermon raises significant questions: Is the sinner's "weeping and wailing" a good thing or a bad thing? *Halakhah* mandates both regret and self-reproach for the sin, bitter recognition that the sin wasn't worth it, and re-solve for the future. Why does Father Mapple seem to dismiss the expression of remorse?

These questions lead to a consideration of repentance and of the way we think about repentance. We may be reminded of the inconvenient fact that remorse is often not the first stage of repentance but a substitute for it. "Wailing and weeping" may dissolve the penitent in a warm bath of self-pity, after which he is too exhausted and comforted to repent genuinely. This is one lesson that the preacher seeks to inculcate, in the spirit of the Mishnah's statement (*Ta'anit* 2:1) that God did not look at the Ninevites' sackcloth and fasting, but at their actions.

At the same time, one wonders why the sermon sets "wailing and weep-ing" in such either/or opposition to genuine repentance. Is it possible that the minister wishes to impress his audience of sailors, who may be accus-tomed to think of religion and repentance as the feminine domain, by em-phasizing that God is not served by tears and weakness, but rather by manly resolve and obedience? If that is the case, then we may wish to con-sider the implications of this gender division for the role of religion in American life, down to our own self-consciousness. Do we too think of religious devotion as effeminate, or do we, in our desire to think of our commitment in masculine categories, tend to suppress elements in *halakhah* and Judaism that require a frank confession of frailty and vulnerability?

The project of comparing Melville on Jonah with the Bible, as read by traditional Jews, is not especially ingenious. It could be lifted from a survey article on Jonah, under the heading *In the Arts* (though the *Encyclopedia Ju-daica* article on Jonah ignores *Moby Dick*). Carrying it out, however, presup-poses attention to Jonah, to American literature and culture, and to the en-tire assortment of tensions engendered by the juxtaposition of the two. Needless to say, there are many fruitful possibilities of confrontation be-tween our culture and *devar Hashem* that are not as obvious as contrasting a biblical text with its modern adaptation. For this there is no substitute for sustained and lively curiosity on the part of the teacher.

Netziv at Babel[3]

In his *Ha'amek Davar*, the Netziv of Volozhin (d. 1892) proposed that the Tower of Babel (Genesis, chap. 11) was constructed in the hope that humanity, united around the tower, would co-exist in universal brotherhood and uniformity. In explaining why this is a bad thing, he argues that groups dedicated to the perfection of society are likely to be intolerant of all those who decline to be part of their universal ideal. Associations of such people are liable to descend to violence and murder to get their way. The similarity between the Netziv's idealists and the practice of militant secular social utopianism in the nineteenth and twentieth centuries is too pronounced to ignore. In Netziv's own time the activity of Russian social revolutionaries provided a foretaste of the terror and the pseudo-religious pretensions of fraternity that still haunt our world. Dostoevsky's *The Devils* is the first of many great depictions of this mentality.

This commentary of the Netziv is powerful stuff. A full appreciation would entail examining the Netziv's internal background within the history of biblical exegesis. R. Nissim, in his Commentary to Genesis and in the second of the *Derashot HaRan*, already connected the story of the tower with the moral dangers of centralization. Seforno, whose sixteenth-century Italian commentary the Netziv valued, viewed the project as part of an attempt to enthrone Nimrod as a universal despot, where the Netziv spoke of a social totalitarianism.[4] A full investigation of the political and cultural implications would require us to go beyond Dostoevsky and other writers on nineteenth century Eastern Europe. One would inquire to what degree the idealism deplored by the Netziv animates a variety of later movements, including the cosmopolitanism that deprecates Jewish separateness today and even offers ideological comfort to those who encompass our physical destruction.

As we have already noted, it is impossible for a teacher of *Tanakh* to master the huge amount of historical, literary, philosophical and social scientific understanding pertinent to this discussion. Where this example differs from our previous cases is the explosive relevance of the Netziv's insight. Educators must properly consider how to harness such material within an intellectually honest framework.

---

[3] R. Yitzchak Blau suggested the significance of this example.

[4] In the light of his commentary on Gen. 10:9, Netziv might have been disinclined to present Nimrod along Seforno's lines.

Halakhic Presuppositions

Often the study of Gemara is stymied by the enormous difference between the fundamental world outlook of the *halakhah* and the mentality brought to the table by most contemporary students. The idea that under certain circumstances it is desirable, even obligatory, to die rather than commit idolatry or transgress sexual prohibitions, or the principle that only the husband can initiate a divorce, are notorious examples. Sometimes these questions can be sidestepped for the moment, as they need not distract the student from addressing the *sugya* at hand. Yet a persistent avoidance of such questions ultimately does interfere with comprehension, as students infer that "the *halakhah* is not supposed to make sense," to say nothing of the crippling consequences for the student's development as a God-fearing individual.

Even areas ostensibly removed from the practical life of modern people, when properly understood, precipitate conflict. In certain cases the *halakhah* maintains that, absent a significant, irreversible change in the object, the robber may return the stolen object, even if it has depreciated in the meantime. When the object undergoes alteration, the thief acquires title to it; he discharges the obligation of restitution monetarily, and can thus realize a profit from his transgression.[5] Likewise, the halakhic concept of tort imposes liability only in cases of direct causality; even R. Meir's principle of *garmi*[6] presupposes a clear connection between the act and the resulting damage. From a modern perspective, such laws are paradoxical. The modern legislator thinks of law exclusively in terms of its consequences, and the *halakhah* seems to reward the enterprising criminal. The modern economist defines the value of a thing in monetary terms, while the *halakhah* seems to ascribe to the object some inherent value of ownership that evaporates when its identity is formally affected. Contemporary jurisprudence cannot exempt tortfeasors from liability simply because the causal nexus is not clearly visible. Likewise R. Kook points out that the laws according to which a lost object no longer belongs to the original owner after he "despairs" of his ownership (*ye'ush*) imply a conception of "communal owner-

---

[5] See *Bava Kamma* 96b, 65a and 66a for examples of these cases and Maimonides, *Mishneh Torah, Hilkhot Gezeilah* 3:4 and *Hilkhot Geneivah* 1:11–14.

[6] See *Bava Kamma* 100a for R. Meir's more expansive definition of causal liability. *Shi`urei ha-Rav Aharon Lichtenstein: Dinei de-Garmi* (Alon Shevut, 2000), pp. 198–200, touches on the potential gap between theoretical constructs and practical judgment in these areas. The preface (pp. 7–9) contains reflections on the significance of style in the presentation of *lomdut*.

ship" that sometimes outweighs, and sometimes is subjugated to, the private dimension of ownership.[7] These *halakhot* have little effect on the lives of most people in our community: when push comes to shove, secular law governs. But they cannot be consistently banished from the classroom.

One aspect of this confrontation can be handled comparatively. R. Aaron Levine's *Economics and Jewish Law*[8] and its successors, as well as the works of others less prolific, is invaluable for translating *halakhah* into the vocabulary of capitalist economics and spelling out the practical ramifications of the *halakhah* in modern society. The questions I have raised regarding *hilkhot geneivah*, like the difficulties encountered in studying *Gittin*, cannot be resolved merely by bringing economics to bear. It is necessary to contrast the entire modern system, which sees private property as a commodity, with a religious outlook that conceptualizes the value of property in radically different categories. Here an awareness of economic theory must be supplemented with an imaginative conception of other ways of thinking and living.

This set of examples is particularly intimidating, and the reason is not only the intensity of reading and thought called for. Unlike *Tanakh* and Jewish philosophy, the study of Talmud generally follows a well-established paradigm, the mastery of which has little to do with these more "philosophical" topics. The textual skills and analytic techniques that go into *lomdut* are time demanding as well. If teachers in the other areas are tempted to highlight forays into side points at the expense of the set curriculum, the dedicated Talmud instructor often feels impelled to stick rigidly to the tried and true.

Yet even this is not the whole story. The questions we have just glanced at often alarm us because they are not the ones chosen by the teacher. Those of us who teach Jewish thought have experienced the issues first-hand and therefore know more or less how to tackle them. With respect to the study of *Tanakh*, we discussed "elective" insights, so to speak: if we have nothing of value to say on these subjects, saying nothing is an option. You don't have to bring in Melville or Dostoevsky if you're not ready to. Talmud teachers, by contrast, except for those who have struggled with these questions on their own, or have some natural affinity for them, are forced to deal with them willy-nilly, because they cannot do their jobs otherwise.

---

[7] *Iggerot ha-Re'iyah*, vol. 1, #89 (p. 99).

[8] Aaron Levine, *Economics and Jewish Law* (Hoboken, NJ: Ktav, 1987).

The Gods of Egypt and the 1954 World Series

After the sin of the spies, Moses pleads that if God does not relent, the Egyptians and other nations will attribute His failure to bring Israel into the Land to His weakness (Num. 14:13–16). According to Rashi, they will infer that God was powerful enough to vanquish Egypt but not Canaan; according to Ramban, they will claim that He could crush the gods of Egypt but not the gods of the Canaanites. Against these explanations one may posit a "transitive" view of divine power. In other words, some students assume that if G can beat E, and C can beat G, then C is more potent than E. Applied to our case, this implies that the gentiles whose thoughts Moses claims to be discerning are liable to conclude, dubiously, that the Canaanites are stronger than the Egyptians.

Of course, this intuition about transitivity is not compelling. To begin with, it is Moses' argument about a hypothetical situation. If God destroys His people and the gentiles speculate about the reason, they are apt to think that God was unable to conquer the Canaanites. It is not at all clear that such a belief would be the best explanation of God's abandonment of Israel – in fact, it would be a false explanation, because the true reason would be their sin – or that those who buy into it would have worked out the implications regarding transitivity. Nevertheless, it is possible that such a consideration may have motivated Ramban's alternative to Rashi: it might be more plausible for the gentiles to ascribe extraordinary powers to the Canaanite gods than to the Canaanite military. Perhaps questions about the logic of transitivity led R. Bahya, in his discussion of Moses' earlier prayer after the incident of the Golden Calf (Deut. 9:24), to suggest that divine abandonment of Israel at that time would have engendered doubt among the gentiles with respect to the Exodus, rather than the hypothesis that God had performed the miracles related to the Exodus, but then reached the limits of His power when faced by Canaan.

A careful study of Moses' arguments is thus likely to raise the transitivity problem. How much weight it deserves depends on the reasoning of the last paragraph. There is, however, a certain kind of logic that would attribute artificial importance to the transitivity factor. Such thinking is based on a double premise: first, that the calculation of transitive relations is a reliable key to the comparative power of armies or deities; second, that the gentiles in Moses' hypothetical argument base their thinking on such calculations. Here I have found it useful to contrast the proposed transitivity logic with analogous applications in other fields. It is true that military second guessers and sports fans often intuitively reason transitively. They may assume that because the United States defeated the Axis Powers, it should certainly win against the North Vietnamese, or that the lowly New York Giants would be no match for the record-setting Cleveland Indians in the 1954 World Series. Examining these applications highlights the limitations of transitivity argumentation vis-à-vis the biblical situation.

This kind of classroom discussion usually doesn't count as an interaction between Torah and the humanities. Unlike the other examples we have looked at, it does not deploy recondite expertise; a little knowledge is enough. In addition, the results are negative: we arrive at a better understanding of the way our unexamined assumptions may lead us astray in our study. Analogies deriving from popular culture also lack the cultural gravity that would normally add grace to a scholarly presentation. For many readers the very idea appears frivolous and self-mocking. Nonetheless, such analogies ought to play a role in our education whenever there is a need to bring hidden patterns of thought to self-critical consciousness. Humor and a modicum of self-parody help our education, and benefit our students as well.

III

The previous discussion offers an artificial cross-section of the interface between the humanities and Torah study. Let us beware of contracting our horizons to such instances. Although many of our examples can potentially expand into full-blown courses, the classroom, by its nature, provides a Procrustean bed. The tyranny of clock and calendar affect the primary Torah curriculum too. Learning how to be educated must include learning how to rebel successfully, when the occasion warrants it, against time constraints. Genuine study of literature, philosophy or history, in any event, cannot be confined to fugitive snippets and sound bites introduced into *limmudei kodesh* hours, which can provide only glimpses of the sweep and scope of a broad education, and the expressive, analytic and imaginative dimensions that can be imported into the study of Torah. Thus, full integration can only be consummated outside the class. There is much to be said for the Hirschian ideal of the Torah educator who combines Torah and secular knowledge and serves as a role model for both.

The structure of class or sermon may also deter the introduction of literature that cannot be woven into the texture of the session. No reader of Jane Austen's *Emma*, for instance, can forget the party where Emma cracks a witticism about the inoffensive Miss Bates's dullness (chap. 43): "Miss Bates…did not immediately catch her meaning; but when it burst on her, it could not anger, though a slight blush showed that it could pain her." To experience or analyze this scene of frivolous, minor humiliation is more likely to instill interpersonal sensitivity in an overly clever student than the most strident *mussar schmuss.* So even if the incident cannot be mounted on stilts of *pshet'l* and walked through a *shalosh seudot,* even if it can't be plugged into a worksheet, any Torah education that cannot find a place for this kind of insight cannot gain anything from the study of the humanities.

IV

The title of this essay comes from T.S. Eliot's "Tradition and the Individual Talent." Eliot compares the relationship between the personality of the poet and the work of art to the role of the catalyst, the thread of platinum, in the manufacture of "sulphurous acid."[9] The poet, "the man who lives and suffers," is essential, like the catalyst, to the process of creation. Yet the personal dimension is invisible in the final product, like the platinum that disappears from the resulting acid. Similarly, the pursuit of wisdom, insight and imagination through the humanities may refresh and invigorate our study of Torah, although, in the final analysis, the greater its contribution, the less overt the role. This is one face of our subject.

Eliot's early twentieth century comparison of poetry to science, abetted by his chemistry analogy, accords to poetry the objective, impersonal qualities associated with science. His intention is to reject the Romantic cult of the poet. It is the poetry that matters, not as self-expression of the poet, but as part of the classic tradition. Stated this way, our understanding of religious education is in line with Eliot's conception of culture, and it is not surprising that Eliot's spiritual pilgrimage arrived at the harbor of revealed institutional religion. Like the classicist, our goal is to conform ourselves to a revealed body of objective truth. The criterion by which novelty in Torah is evaluated is truth, not self-expression.

At the same time, education has a different function than art and culture. It aims not only to delight and to instruct, but also to provide a personal model for the student to emulate. If what is transmitted in the classroom corresponds to the poem (or the acid) in Eliot's essay, and the teacher is the poet (or the platinum thread), then, because Torah education, in particular, is not successful unless it communicates a tangible sense of religious experience, intellectual adventure and passionate commitment, the student must not only produce the acid but become his or her own platinum filament. The next stage of our discussion shifts away from the subject matter to the question of personal intellectual character.

---

[9] Eliot probably means "sulfuric acid" (H_2SO_4), not "sulfurous acid" (H_2SO_3).

V

We have already acknowledged the impossibility of doing justice to all the challenges and opportunities with which we are blessed. No doubt some of you wonder if I have any idea how little discretionary time the average educator can call his or her own. The pressures are brutal, especially in the early formative years of teaching when one's repertoire is still inchoate. Would that all of us could feel confident of our basic Torah preparation, let alone afford the luxury of the *vita otiosa*! For the teacher who likes what I'm proposing, but despairs of doing it, I have only the obvious advice: Get started with your liberal arts education before you have to play catch up; ease into your teaching career to avoid being overwhelmed from the start; acquire friends and colleagues of like mind; read the *New York Review of Books* and similar publications; waste less time; learn to sleep more efficiently.

You will notice, perhaps with dismay, that I have not directed you to some magic manual that will supply you with pre-cooked chunks of humanistic insight and erudition. It is not that I begrudge you the assistance or doubt its utility; it is foolish to forgo whatever aid one can get; we are not intellectual Robinson Crusoes. But there are limits, and they are the same that pertain to other aspects of intensive Torah study: you can authentically borrow someone else's reconstituted wisdom only if you know what it is like to struggle for the insight yourself. (Here is where wisdom differs from information.)

Why is it important for the teacher to cherish, and to pass on, this experience of first-hand grappling with the material? Why not market a gutted version of humanistic insight, with the hard reading and thinking edited out? Here we must interrogate our educational goals. When we foster interaction between Torah study and the rest of life, what do we want for ourselves, and what do we intend for our students, beyond the transmission of information?

One answer is integrity, both in the sense of wholeness and in the sense of honesty. The Torah we study is connected to the rest of life, to the issues we confront when we read literature, philosophy or history and reflect on the world we inhabit. We want our students to be able to do this, and see us doing it too. This does not mean that we must exhibit effortless versatility in all areas: being an intelligent, educated person entails thinking resourcefully and judiciously about subjects in which one lacks thorough expertise and seeing them in relation to what we care about. Our students are learning from the way we handle these intellectual negotiations as surely as they learn from our official curricular instruction.

Just the other day I heard of a rabbi who taught that Shimon Peres's inclusion in Ariel Sharon's emergency government was as absurd as if Churchill had retained Neville Chamberlain in a parallel post. I am not sure precisely what place this argument had in his exposition of Torah, but it helps to be reminded that "outside studies," in this case history or political science, penetrate our educational discourse in unpredictable and sundry manners, so that the choice is not really between introducing liberal arts topics and avoiding them, but between doing so competently and doing so recklessly. Relevant or not, the argument is flawed: until his final illness, Chamberlain remained a member of the five-man War Cabinet; another member was the Foreign Secretary Lord Halifax, an even more inveterate appeaser than Chamberlain.[10] Knowledge of the facts might have led to a worthwhile analysis of the advantages and disadvantages of compromise for the sake of unity in crisis.

Assuming that this subject is indeed pertinent to the life or study of Torah, the historical error is regrettable: error is always inferior to truth. Among intellectually honest folk, as we like to regard ourselves, and as our students should strive to become, the sovereign remedy for error is correction. Now let me ask you: Which teacher is more likely to exhibit the virtue of intellectual honesty (*modeh al ha-emet*) – the one who is genuinely interested in historical understanding and accuracy (even if on occasion he purveys faulty information), or the one who customarily pulls tidbits off the Internet or casual conversations carried on before, during or after davening? Which is more likely to influence students of whom we can be proud? Which is more likely to produce honest, intelligent students who are proud of us and committed to what we claim to represent?

A sense of religious-intellectual balance is also imperative. How much time and how much emphasis should be devoted to "outside" material and insights? In study, as in life, much depends on finding the right relationship between what is primary and what is peripheral. If we want our students to develop a healthy sense of the benefit to be gained from referring to "outside" material, we must develop such a sense of proportion ourselves. When teachers who have not mastered the art of intellectual integration introduce outside material and alien perspectives, the problem is not only

---

[10] Churchill eventually dispatched Halifax to Washington as ambassador, where he aroused anti-British sentiment when he was taken to a baseball game and left an uneaten hot dog on his seat. For the incriminating photograph, see illustrations in Andrew Roberts, *The Holy Fox* (London: Weidenfield and Nicolson, 1991).

the time lost from conventional Torah study or the irresponsibility of provoking questions that one is ill-equipped to handle. If the teacher has not thought through, and internalized, the material, he or she is liable to invest marginal pursuits with a heightened significance and interest, thus communicating an implicitly flawed paradigm for integrated study. Thus, students have been known to come out of class convinced that exotic speculation about Near Eastern parallels or the versions preserved in the Dead Sea Scrolls (or half-baked wisdom about international politics) is more exciting and more important than engaging the biblical text and the traditional exegesis in the quest for *devar Hashem*. The teacher who strives actively to acquire his or her *derekh ha-limmud* is not immune to distortion or disproportion of values, but nevertheless has an infinitely better chance of striking the right balance, over the course of a year and a career, than one entirely dependent on prefab teaching materials.

Last but not least, the teacher of Torah must be passionate about learning and must convey the passion. Not all of us can be immersed in Torah day and night, but we should all taste the consuming passion for understanding. To read a text religiously is to read it strenuously (with *yegi'ah*), an edifying but labor-intensive engagement. There can be passion in the mere reading of sacred text – some people enthusiastically read sacred words that mean nothing to them. But for most of us, and for most of our students, there is no passion without the struggle to understand. There can be passion in rote learning too, where each repetition is identical with its predecessor and there are no new questions or surprising discoveries. But for most of us, and for most of our students, there is no abiding passion without the prospect of novelty and freshness.

For all of us some of the time, and for some of us all of the time, the freshness and the novelty emerge from the unadorned study of Torah, unaided by perspectives and preoccupations imported from other intellectual and existential regions of our lives. If, however, teacher and student are to share the ideal of strenuous Torah study as a regular feature of existence, one cannot simply assume that the freshness and the novelty will arise automatically. If, for most of us, bringing "outside" concerns and interests to bear is a means of lubricating our *yegi'ah*, then that interaction must be pursued with passion. Because we cannot take it for granted that our students will acquire the needed passion and joy without calling upon the creative contribution of the liberal arts, that interaction cannot be consigned to a mechanical, "connect the dots" mentality. The teacher must exhibit a personal stake in this aspect of the learning process. What is worth doing is worth doing well.

Do not consider our aspiration for *yegi'ah* a luxury, pertinent only to the elite, or merely a means to "make the class interesting." Reading religiously, with passion and intensity, lies at the heart of our education in Torah.[11] Opponents of intensive Torah study know full well how central this ideal is to Orthodox commitment. They complain that the need for thorough immersion and unqualified commitment to the study of Torah excludes people like them from positions of authority and celebrate the advent of the computer database, which promises to level the playing field, allowing individuals who lack time or religious conviction to compete on equal footing with *talmidei hakhamim* who have achieved their expertise the old-fashioned way.[12]

Whether ready access to information renders hard-earned erudition superfluous and anachronistic in purely academic terms is not our present concern. Our difference from the anti-Orthodox outlook runs deeper. It extends to the way that this approach reduces the experience of Torah study to the efficient production of an intellectual commodity the political-academic utility of which is independent of the personal engagement, the passion and the love, that the religious individual has invested in the subject matter. The politically minded pragmatist can only comprehend traditional Orthodox study as a crafty exercise in self-serving elitism. The individual who knows the personal face of Torah study firsthand does not eschew reference aids and databases as means to knowledge and insight, but rejects them as a substitute for personal engagement. Every component of the curriculum, including the ingredients discussed in this essay, can and should fortify the cause of religious reading. Is this likely to occur without the active intellectual participation of the teacher?

The qualities I have praised – religious and intellectual integrity, intellectual proportion, passion and a commitment to the strenuous life of *yegi'ah* – are currently under attack. Given the frailties of our community, the deficiencies of our educational institutions, and the relentless drift of our secular, bottom-line-oriented culture, we cannot take it for granted that others will exemplify the virtues we are too busy or indifferent to cultivate in our-

---

[11] See Paul J. Griffiths, *Religious Reading: The Place of Reading in the Practice of Religion* (New York: Oxford Univ. Press, 1999) for the crucial differences between religious reading and the utilitarian secular style of reading fostered by contemporary culture. The author, a Catholic scholar of Eastern religions, is concerned about the dangers to traditional religion posed by increasingly prevalent habits of information consumption.

[12] The view here criticized has been asserted both orally and in print. Specific citations have been omitted in order not to cause embarrassment.

selves. To the extent that these virtues are tied to the interaction of Torah study with humanistic insight, each one of us must become a catalyst in the pursuit of wisdom. There is fire in the catalyst. There is fire in the human personality.[13]

---

[13] My work on this paper coincided with the last illness of my revered mentor Rabbi Walter Wurzburger *z"l*; the last pages were written during his *shiv`ah*. Though R. Wurzburger's substantial intellectual contribution, which fortified the understanding of Torah with the methods and achievements of philosophical ethics and political theory, did not resort to the kind of wide-ranging investigations described in the early sections of my article, the ideals of honesty and whole-hearted engagement extolled in the concluding section are very much part of his enduring legacy.

AWE, LOVE AND ATTACHMENT: RELIGIOUS DEVELOPMENT AND THE MAHARAL OF PRAGUE

YAEL WIESELBERG

The *rishonim*, whose value in relation to us was like the highest celestial sphere compared to a mustard seed, pursued paths of righteousness to guide their students in paths of truth, until they reached that which is fitting. And now, in this deficient generation, "poverty breeds even deeper poverty,"[1] and they have turned away from the straight path. From the moment the child begins to strive in Torah until he becomes old, he acts as a foolish man who sees an architect building a wall [by] digging a deep foundation in order that the wall should continue to stand. The fool thinks that this is a needless act, for why should one dig beneath the earth if all that is needed is that the wall should stand on even ground? [The assumption is] that there is no need for a foundation for the wall, and this causes the wall to crumble even before it has been constructed. This is [the pedagogical mistake] in these lands.[2]

MAHARAL OF PRAGUE (Rabbi Yehudah Loew ben Bezalel), more than most Torah giants, reflects on the innermost values of Jewish education. Speaking of his own generation, he writes that teaching requires ground rules, a depth of understanding rooted in traditional educational techniques.

---

[1] A variation of an idiom from *Bava Kamma* 92a, implying that the intellectual poverty of teachers will also impoverish students.

[2] *Gur Aryeh* to Deut. 6:7, ed. Yehoshua Hartman, p. 123. Translations of Maharal are my own unless otherwise indicated. References to Maharal are to the Chaim Pardes editions of *Netivot Olam* (1988), *Tif'eret Yisra'el* (1985) and *Derekh ha-Hayyim* (1996), and to the Yehoshua Hartman edition of *Gur Aryeh* (1990–1994). Other references correspond to *Kol Sifrei Maharal mi-Prag* (London, 1961; reprints: New York, 1969, and Benei Berak, 1980).

Without these, the walls of Torah learning are liable to collapse through lack of solid support. With particular reference to *pilpul* (intellectual casuistry), Maharal chides against attempting overly sophisticated intellectual analysis before the basic elements of *Tanakh,* Mishnah and Talmud have been understood. His imagery is apt: the wall of learning crumbles when it loses immortal foundations: the awe, love, and attachment contingent upon primary texts and traditional modes of learning.

In *Netivot Olam,* an anthology of moral discourses, Maharal navigates amongst the multiplicity of doctrines and goals that define religiosity, providing guidelines for prioritizing and actualizing them in education. In general, his approach to religious development is colored by his mystical theology, which advocates a layered consciousness of God based upon the structure of the *sefirot* (divine emanations). Like other mystics before him, including Isaac the Blind, Nahmanides, Meir Gabbai, R. Azriel of Gerona, and R. Moshe Cordovero, Maharal identifies *deveikut* (attachment, or "clinging" to God) as the ultimate in religiosity, with other attributes tending toward this goal. By dovetailing Maharal's mystical theology with pedagogical theory, we discern a model for cultivating a relationship with God that begins with wisdom, progresses to awe, and culminates with humility. Having considered the role of these values in religious development, we will end with their methodological implications for education.

Maharal's paradigm provides a gauge for some of the major questions of contemporary Torah education. Among them, we might ask which kinds of teaching are most likely to water the springs of inner life? Is the sense of God's immanence more likely to be inculcated through learning for *beki'ut* (with a broader awareness of Jewish sources) or for *iyyun* (a deeper analysis)? More specifically, in the area of Talmud study, how might one decide between a more harmonized engagement with the talmudic system versus intellectual meticulousness? Without addressing such questions directly, this essay explores the values standing behind these decisions, clarifying the goals rather than the methods of education. Methods are of course suggested: Maharal rejects the over-intellectualization of learning, encourages respect for the rabbinic Sages and aggadic writing, and prioritizes the teacher-student relationship. In particular, he is committed to breadth in learning,[3] maintaining the talmudic dictum (*Avot* 5:21) "At the age of five [the student should begin learning] *mikra*; at the age of ten, Mishnah; ...and at the age of fifteen, Talmud." But while methodolgical suggestions of this kind are as helpful today as they were in the sixteenth century, perhaps his

---

[3] See, e.g., *Derekh ha-Hayyim* 5:22, p. 632.

greatest contribution is his analysis of the meta-goals of education – the value system forming the basis of all educational decisions.

The Paradigm

In *Netivot Olam*, Maharal writes of an approach to Torah-learning founded upon a hierarchy of values: *hokhmah* (wisdom), *yir'ah* (awe), and *anavah* (humility), which is integral to *ahavah* (love) and *deveikut* (attachment). *Hokhmah* (including both general wisdom and Torah study) is only the first rung in the value structure, which ascends toward *yir'ah* and peaks with the qualities of *anavah, ahavah* and *deveikut*, the humble recognition of one's place in relation to God that makes it possible to reach Him. On the one hand, the structure is holistic insofar as only those governed by *yir'at shamayim* (awe or fear of Heaven) can hope to be crowned with the higher faculties of *anavah, ahavah,* and *deveikut*. On the other, Maharal carefully describes these faculties as discrete educational goals. Of the three aspirations that emerge, the first – *hokhmah* – involves accumulating connective knowledge. The second stage, *yir'ah,* speaks of an awareness of distance between the individual and God, while the third, *anavah,* intimates the humility that makes relationship possible. By integrating this third attribute, one accesses the attendant qualities of *ahavah* and *deveikut,* which Maharal understands to be inter-related. The deepest form of relationship – *deveikut* – takes place not through an overpowering sense of God's greatness, but through an internal connection with Him.[4]

Maharal's paradigm provides a guide to religious development that recognizes different levels of consciousness of God. In contrast with some contemporary academic approaches to Torah study, Maharal contends that *hokhmah* is fruitful only where it leads to spirituality, but futile without the fear of Heaven. Well-known for his opposition to abstract *pilpul*, which he rejects as an inherently divisive form of thought, Maharal instead suggests the kind of learning based upon interaction, dynamism, and unity. Maharal argues that without the values of *yir'at shamayim* and *anavah* that build our relationship with God, intellectual wisdom remains barren, its Divine truth restricted to a this-worldly phenomenon.

Maharal places *deveikut* at the apex of his value system because morality cannot exist within a vacuum – it needs the vibrancy of relational understanding to give it form and content. Recognizing that we stand in eternal dialogue with God, other people, and rabbinic texts – indeed, merely being conscious of viewing the self in relation to an "other" – is vital to religious

---

[4]*Netiv ha-Anavah* in *Netivot Olam* (ed. Chaim Pardes), vol. 2, chap. 1, p. 4.

development. *Deveikut* emerges as the dynamic feature because it epitomizes the meaning of encounter, inviting us to engage directly with God and creation.

The Problem of Intellectualism

In *Netiv ha-Torah*, the first treatise in *Netivot Olam*, Maharal speaks of *hokhmah* in at least two modes. In some contexts, *hokhmah* (or *hokhmah kelalit*, general wisdom) refers to intellectual wisdom, denoting either Aristotelian rationalism or secular philosophy – those forms of thought Maharal connects to the physical, empirical world. In other instances, however, *hokhmah* denotes revealed Torah, and, in more specific contexts, *hokhmah penimit* (inner wisdom) or *sitrei hokhmah* (hidden wisdom), referring to the inner wisdom of Kabbalah. Of the three forms of *hokhmah*, value is accorded mainly to inner or hidden wisdom, and although Maharal include philosophical terms within his lexicon,[5] he repeatedly rejects rationalist positions, most notably in *Be'er ha-Golah* and *Derekh ha-Hayyim*.[6] In the following passage introducing *Gevurot Hashem*, Maharal dismisses rationalist philosophy on the grounds that it exists apart from the Divine truth of Torah:

> Granted, God has given man understanding and wisdom, but it is all relative to and connected with the material; all his rationality is subjective and related to matter. How can he grasp that which is abstract? A person would know nothing about the ways and actions of that which is far removed from his world had not God revealed this to Moses and the other prophets, who in turn passed this knowledge on to the Sages, who revealed these hidden things to us in the *midrashim* and other teachings. These philosophers who have come along to analyze the ways of God through human understanding, have come up with ideas so absurd that we would not deal with them, except to fulfill the wish of the Sages who have said, "Study the

---

[5] Maharal's interest in pedagogy has been noted by a number of scholars, yet the main academic discussion of Maharal's philosophy of education, that of Aharon Kleinberger, takes Maharal to an intellectual extreme. Kleinberger refers for example, to the "evidently intellectual conceptualization of the Maharal" in a way that emphasizes intellectual rather than mystical forms of understanding. See Aharon Kleinberger, *Ha-Mahashavah ha-Pedagogit shel ha-Maharal mi-Prague* (Jerusalem, 1962). Ovadiah Gottesdiener, on the other hand, displays greater sensitivity to the mystical aspects of Maharal's thought, including those underlying his pedagogical position. See Ovadiah Gottesdiener, *Ha-Maharal mi-Prague: Hayyav Tekufato ve-Torato* (Jerusalem, 1976).

[6] See for example *Derekh ha-Hayyim* 5:7, p. 549, for Maharal's remark that Maimonides' Aristotelian position is found "neither in the knowledge of the sages, nor in the Mishnah, nor in the words of the *midrash*."

Torah with zest so that you may know how to answer the heretic" (*Avot* 2:14).[7]

In the absence of revelation, philosophy originates with human thought rather than with God. Maharal suggests that rational understanding remains "connected with the material," limited to the physical world and, one might add, to the concrete objects forming the basis of abstract systems of thought. For this reason, he dismisses secular philosophy as "subjective, related to matter," because without revelation, even conceptual philosophy is built upon empirical links. Where conclusions are drawn from material evidence, they remain physically based, reflecting our limited comprehension of the world.

Maharal insists that since human understanding remains constrained by this-worldly assumptions, it will not necessarily lead to truth. True wisdom is revealed wisdom, specifically the kabbalistic wisdom transcending the leaps of the human intellect. Greater than other modes of cognition, revelation makes it possible to understand God and the "ways" associated with Him, illuminating "the ways and actions of that which is far removed from this world."[8]

Without the element of spiritual direction, *hokhmah* cannot succeed in bringing its bearers to the world-to-come:

> This (ability to reach one's ultimate purpose) cannot be said of any body of wisdom; it is through the Torah alone that one reaches the world-to-come. Therefore it is especially fitting for Torah to be termed "Torah," which is the term for teaching, for directing an individual to the ultimate purpose that is fitting to attain. It follows that the verse "And He guided me and said to me: Allow my words to uphold your heart..." [Prov. 4:4] is to teach us that God shows us our ultimate destiny, namely how to reach the world-to-come, through allowing God's words to uphold your heart. And thus an individual who clings to Torah will reach his ultimate destiny, which is the world-to-come.[9]

---

[7] "The Second Introduction" to *Gevurot Hashem*, trans. Shlomo Mallin, The Book of Divine Power: Introductions (New York, 1975), p. 12; *Netzah Yisra'el* (*The Book of Power*), trans. Shlomo Mallin (New York, 1975), p. 12.

[8] *Be'er ha-Golah*, Sixth Well, pp. 105–6.

[9] *Netivot Olam: Netiv ha-Torah*, vol. 1, chap. 1, p. 9.

Maharal distinguishes between this-worldly wisdom and the enterprise of Torah; only the latter is capable of guiding its adherents to their ultimate purpose in the world-to-come. Worldly wisdom remains self-centered, concerned with factual knowledge that leaves man bound in his enclosed, earthly existence. Although Maharal values the *hokhmah kelalit* that is able to provide insights into the nature and order of reality, secular wisdom cannot itself advance moral values.[10] Only Torah, with its unique teleology, constitutes the language of teaching (*leshon hora'ah*) able to demonstrate (*lehar'ot*) the possibilities of a higher mode of existence.

From Maharal's perspective, Torah study therefore should not be confused with what we would today term "academic study." Authentic *hokhmah* is not a collection of facts or figures. Its value is intrinsic: it depends upon whether it generates inner spiritual wisdom and whether it remains connected with its source: "*hokhmah* has no ongoing existence other than from God, who is the cause."[11] While inner *hokhmah* necessitates God-consciousness, secular or academic *hokhmah* may not necessarily lead to fearing or serving God. In a similar vein, on the rabbinic statement (*Avot* 4:1) "Who is wise? One who learns from every person," Maharal explains that the true *hakham* cannot be defined by external forms of knowledge, but by the inner thirst for understanding:

The saying "Who is wise? One who learns from every person," implies that the name *hakham* as a description of a person can only be truly descriptive when it is an essential attribute. In the case of a person who owns a house, because the house is not an essential description (since he merely lives there), it cannot describe the man himself. Even if this were to provide some description of the homeowner even though the attribute does not stem from himself, in all events it does not constitute a complete attribute because it does not arise from his inner being. Therefore, it is not fitting for

---

[10] Maharal writes that those forms of wisdom capable of imparting knowledge about the nature and order of the world represent a "ladder leading to the wisdom of Torah." His position seems to conflict with the tradition forbidding the study of *hokhmah yevanit* (Greek wisdom), on the grounds that there is no time for study that is not outweighed by the obligation to learn Torah (a time that is "neither day nor night"). Maharal's solution to the prohibition is to radically reinterpret *hokhmah yevanit* as a generic term for illusory wisdom. Those elements of Greek literature that do impart knowledge about the nature of reality are permissible, while sophistry remains forbidden. See *Netivot Olam: Netiv ha-Torah*, vol. 1, chap. 14, p. 143.

[11] *Derekh ha-Hayyim* 3:11, p. 323.

an individual to be described by wisdom that is other than him, where there is no essential connection to the wisdom.[12]

Maharal uses the term "in and of himself" to define the wise man because this definition denotes something independent of ability or circumstance. The true *hakham* cannot be defined by the mere accumulation of wisdom, for information, like other quantitative attributes, such as physical strength or wealth, does not necessarily reflect the inner depth of personality. Maharal assumes that true knowledge cannot be accumulated passively – it needs the dynamism born of an internal spiritual aspiration. Choosing to learn from every individual reflects a thirst for learning that is objectively valuable, for it personifies an inner spiritual quest.[13] Pedagogically, the message is that knowledge must originate in desire, in the innate search that deepens the Divine aspect of personality.

Raising our Awareness of Awe

Hokhmah becomes meaningful where it generates greater awareness of awe and humility.

The awe of heaven is above wisdom, for from wisdom one attains the level higher than wisdom, namely the awe of God, which is primary and the beginning of wisdom. Awe is "the consequence of [lit. a heel to] humility" (Prov. 22:4), meaning that one who has the quality of humility must necessarily be a God-fearing person. This is not the case for wisdom, for it is possible to be wise without being God-fearing, such as those who have wisdom without an awe of Heaven...

Although wisdom is certainly a preparation, through which one attains the awe of Heaven, as Scripture says, "the awe of God is the beginning of wisdom" (Ps. 111:10), there is no absolute certainty in the matter. Wisdom is a preparation and a ladder through which one attains awe of Heaven, but it is possible to remain standing on the ladder without reaching the level of awe. However, when a person has the quality of humility and lowers himself, he will certainly manifest lowliness before the creator, recognizing his

---

[12] *Derekh ha-Hayyim* 4:1, p. 387.

[13] Michael Rosenak makes the same point in relation to awe: "The fear of Heaven and the acceptance of the yoke of Heaven was the fundamental end in itself of Jewish education, that which required no extrinsic justification. It pointed towards who the educated person was rather than what he/she did or knew." Michael Rosenak, *Roads to the Palace: Jewish Texts and Teaching* (Oxford: Berghahn Books, 1995), p. 95.

deficiency. This is the essence of awe, when one recognizes the essence of one's lowliness.[14]

Wisdom exists as a preparatory device, a steppingstone leading to the awe of Heaven. While the humble individual will necessarily display awe, conscious of the relation between himself and the Divine, those versed in self-contained *hokhmah* might still remain on the bottom rungs of religiosity. *Yir'at shamayim* advances moral development by leading us beyond the self, causing us to admit our lowliness to God in a move that also brings us to Him.

On the statement in *Avot* (3:11) discussing the dialectical interdependence of awe and wisdom, Maharal describes the essence of *yir'at shamayim*:

> Wisdom has no ongoing existence unless it stems from God, Who is the cause. Due to the greatness of the level of Divine wisdom, it has no ongoing existence in relation to corporeal man other than when it derives from God, Who is the cause. When a person is God-fearing, he is dependent on God entirely; and when one is dependent upon God, Who is the cause, one has ongoing existence in relation to the cause that stems from God's exalted being. Therefore when a person is God-fearing and may be considered a dependent in relation to the cause, then his wisdom has ongoing existence that is derived from the cause, who is God, sustainer of everything.[15]

Maharal presents the relationship between the cause and effect as a metaphor for what it means to be a God-fearing individual. Viewing God as the primary cause of our being enables us to admit our contingent and limited humanity. It reminds us that we have no ongoing existence unless guided towards a greater source, the cause and relation endowing us with some kind of permanence. Paradoxically, admitting our dependence upon God brings vitality to our humanity.

Living in awe of Heaven involves at least two components. Primarily, it involves a sense of dependence upon God and the words of the Sages, which validates tradition while motivating inner virtue. But it also means living in continual suffusion by the Divine presence.[16] While the first aspect

---

[14] *Netivot Olam: Netiv ha-Anavah*, vol. 2, chap. 1, pp. 2–3.

[15] *Derekh ha-Hayyim* 3:11, p. 323.

[16] Rosenak has noted: "[*Yirat shamayim*] was a complex aim. For while it had to do with one's duties ("keep his commandments") it was also, and perhaps first of all, a com-

of awe involves moral responsibility, the second speaks of a relationship with God predicated on continuing dialogue and an ongoing sense of His direction. By realizing ourselves to be the "effects" of Divine grace, and recognizing our dependence upon God's nourishment, we deepen our affiliation with the infinite. Pedagogically, this is Maharal's message: by linking cause with effect, and the awe of God with the material world, we bring meaning to personal experience.

The Immanence in Humility

More than any other character trait, the next stage of moral development, humility, generates an ongoing consciousness of the other, a mode God exemplifies by creating a place for humanity in the universe:

> Because the attribute accompanying God is humility, and this is the attribute more essential to Him than any other, as will be explained, the humble person participates in the attribute of his creator. This is certainly the greatest thing, for the attribute of reverence that is the awe of God involves manifesting lowliness before Him, and in this there is no resemblance to God at all, except for the recognition that He is the cause. About this it is said "that which wisdom has made a crown to its head, humility has made a shoe for its foot" (*Shir ha-Shirim Rabbah* 1:9), because the awe of heaven is greater than wisdom and less than humility. Because the humble person has some of the knowledge of his creator, he attains a higher level. This level is greater than the awe of God, because the God-fearing person, who is dependent upon God, who is the cause, [merely] clings to the cause. Humility is greater than awe of Heaven because the humble person has a [greater] resemblance to the attribute of his creator.[17]

The proof-text, "Awe is a consequence of [lit. a heel to] humility," meaning that awe develops from humility, renders awe secondary to humility just as the heel trails the body, always a lingering step behind. While the haughty individual, viewing himself as sovereign, cannot recognize his subservience before God, the humble person understands the meaning of dynamic encounter. More valuable than the pursuit of knowledge, and above awe, is the humility that enables union with God.

---

prehensive image of character, virtue and goodness. In the Jewish context therefore, while it did mean observance of commandments, and study of the Torah, it also preceded them, and it meant carrying them out with a certain pious intention." *Roads to the Palace*, p. 96.

[17] *Netivot Olam: Netiv ha-Anavah*, vol. 2, chap. 1, p. 4.

From within the mystical tradition, Maharal identifies humility as the quality most essential to God. In the hierarchy of God's inner being, it represents the dynamic decision to abandon transcendence in favor of creation. Choosing in his magnitude to embrace humanity, God expresses both humility and love, revealing his compassion through the intimate warmth of the revealed presence of God. For this reason, the attribute of humility likens us to God at a level that is "essential to Him more than any [other attribute]."[18] Maharal's value-structure accords a higher place to *anavah* than to *yir'ah*, for while awe enables us to meet God, a relationship based upon fear also implies inequality and distance, emphasizing the gap between God's greatness and ourselves. In contrast, humility enables *imitatio Dei*, the likeness to God that creates proximity to Him. Maharal suggests that we attain *anavah* by emulating God's most essential quality within the self, a result of our developing consciousness of God's greatness:[19] "wherever you find the greatness of the Holy One, there you find his humility" (*Megillah* 31a).

Maharal's apotheosis of *anavah* is reflected in his reverence for the rabbinic Sages and in the humility he finds in hermeneutics. He quotes: "Is it possible to cling to the *Shekhinah?* Only cling to the Sages, and Scripture will consider him as if he has clung to the Divine."[20] In place of intellectual solipsism, Maharal's interpretation finds respect for the rabbinic tradition. Conveying the notion that rabbinic teachings hold meaning – regardless of whether or not a student may discern it – is a central pedagogical message.

Humility is particularly important in a society that is sometimes affected by extreme forms of post-modernism. Rather than encouraging students to impose their reading upon the text (in line with the more politicized post-modernist position, which emphasizes only one's own presence in the learning process), Maharal's approach validates the existence of the "other," a textual presence that the student must respect as well as engage. Standing in a relationship of modesty to the text involves the element of deference: a belief in its inspirational possibilities that exist independently of the student's faculties of comprehension. The joining with another, exemplified by God Himself, involves both closeness and distance. From one

---

[18] Kleinberger, noting the centrality of humility in the learning process, comments upon Maharal's association of *anavah* with the search for truth. The student's consciousness of a lack of knowledge is itself likely to inspire greater success in learning, for "one who assumes that he is already a *hakham*...will not seek or strive to investigate further." Kleinberger, p. 159.

[19] *Netivot Olam: Netiv ha-Anavah*, vol. 2, chap. 1, pp. 5, 7.

[20] *Derekh ha-Hayyim* 3:11, p. 323, paraphrasing *Ketubbot* 111b.

perspective we approach God and the Torah on intimate terms, while from the other we experience the magnitude of His being as separate from ourselves. Our relation to the text of Torah needs to reflect our approach to God: while creative interpretation is invited, the text, in its greatness, exists as an independent entity.

The Durability of *Deveikut*

Maharal writes that *deveikut* is needed to bridge the gap between physical and spiritual wisdom. He explains: "A person must cleave to the Torah absolutely, until it cannot separate itself from him. Without this a person cannot merit the Torah, for this requires becoming one with the spiritual."[21] Torah, representing both spirituality and the spirit of unity, stimulates our yearning for God.

Literally translated as "clinging" to the Divine, *deveikut* speaks of a relationship based upon similarity, affinity, and the hope for completion. In addition, *deveikut* demands self-resignation, a purity of commitment that arises "when one turns over one's soul to God, because in this [act] one has clung to Him entirely, and this is the essence of love." Love and attachment are one:

> If one is drawn after God and desires attachment with God through the power of love, certainly one will also be afraid to transgress His will, which would annul both attachment and love. One who has love has a double reward, because included within this higher love is awe.[22]

First and foremost, *deveikut* stems from desire. With poetics echoing *Shir ha-Shirim*, Maharal speaks in his *Netiv ha-Ahavah* of the lover's need to be in the continual presence of his loved one. *Ahavat Hashem* includes attachment, in addition to awe, because love discounts those actions that might disappoint the other.

By embracing God through Torah study, we develop the aspiration for *deveikut* that furthers our relationship with Him: "Humanity has *deveikut* with God through wisdom, and that wisdom is specifically Torah, which is like a mediator between God and man."[23] In *Netiv ha-Torah*, Maharal suggests that Torah strengthens the heart and endows life, both cognitively, through learning its verses, and behaviorally, through the performance of

---

[21] *Netivot Olam: Netiv ha-Torah*, vol. 1, chap. 3, p. 32.

[22] *Netivot Olam: Netiv Ahavat Hashem*, vol. 2, chap. 1, p. 115 (see also pp. 105, 109, 119).

[23] *Derekh ha-Hayyim* 3:11, p. 323.

the commandments. *Deveikut* deepens when Torah becomes our channel for relationship with the Divine.

Developing Autonomy Through Dependence

The mode of study Maharal recommends is Torah *li-shemah*, learning that is undertaken for purely altruistic reasons, primarily out of love. The beauty of Torah *li-shemah* is its impact: by expressing our love of God through learning his Torah, we also revitalize ourselves:

> In the first chapter of *Ta'anit* (7a), "Rav Bana says: Whoever involves himself with Torah for its own sake, it becomes a life-giving balm for him, as is written, 'It is a tree of life for those who grasp it' (Prov. 3:18), and as is written, 'It shall be healing for your stomach' (Prov. 3:8), and as is written, 'Whoever finds me finds life' (Prov. 8:35). But whoever involves himself with Torah not for its own sake, it becomes a death-inducing balm for him, as is written, 'My lesson shall drop (*ya'arof*) like the rain' (Deut. 32:2) and the word *arifah* can only mean killing, as is written, 'And they shall there break the calf's neck' (Deut. 21:4)."
>
> The Torah is compared to a life-giving balm, for the balm is externally applied by the physician onto a person, so that it induces life. Likewise the Torah is apart from a person but is also attached, like the balm that remains external but connects with the person. And just as the Torah is a life-giving balm to a Torah scholar who engages in it for its own sake, so it is a death-inducing balm to a Torah scholar who does not engage in it for its own sake.[24]

The *aggadah* informing Maharal's discussion is based upon the promise in *Ha'azinu* (Deut. 32:3), in which Torah meets man in two ways, in response, respectively, to altruistic and narcissistic modes of Torah learning. Learning Torah *li-shemah* leads us to experience its life-inducing properties, whereas learning not *li-shemah* – not for the sake of God – leads to spiritual death. The aggadic proof-text brought by Maharal, "My lesson shall drop like the rain" is interpreted to mean that when God's words descend as rain, drenching the individual with its strength and weight, the message can be deadly, drowning the living entity beneath.[25] In contrast, when the

---

[24] *Netivot Olam: Netiv ha-Torah*, vol. 1, chap. 7, p. 69.
[25] The term *ya'arof* implies death because it evokes the *eglah arufah* ceremony in the wake of an anonymous murder (see Deut. 21:1–9).

words of Torah arise as a life-inducing balm, as the gentle touch of morning dew, they endow new life and growth.

In his reading of the *aggadah*, Maharal interprets the philosophic difference between rain and dew as the difference between the transcendent and the immanent, the first of which remains separate and abstract, while the second describes a closer, more intimate relation. What turns Torah into a prescription for life is the ability to become one with the transcendent and make it immanent. Experiencing the Torah as the nourishing benefit of dew means recognizing the transcendent otherness of Torah while at the same time experiencing its closeness and warmth.

Recognizing God's transcendent reality effects spiritual change. But in order for spiritual autonomy to advance, we must first recognize our dependence. And herein lies the paradox. Our autonomy depends upon the inspiration of spirituality. Just as our physical being depends upon air and food, our connection with God affirms inner life. Maharal's reading resolves the dichotomy between dependence and autonomy by suggesting that the first leads to the second. The quest for *yir'at shamayim* demands a focus upon Divine sustenance. Most evocatively, we notice "a near simultaneity of experiencing one's helplessness, even as one is 'raised' by the divine revitalization,"[26] suggesting that becoming aware of our contingency in relation to God's solidity makes it possible for us to gain strength from His presence. Deepening our conscious need for the transcendent also invites autonomy, because it generates a deeper, more harmonized sense of being.

The Teacher-Student Relationship: Balancing *Yir'ah* with *Ahavah*

The values Maharal places at the heart of religious development are equally foundational for his pedagogy. In fact, Maharal's perception of the teacher-student relationship parallels the relationship between God and man:

There are two ways in which the pupil relates to the teacher. From one perspective, the student joins with his teacher like a father and son, who also join together, while from another perspective, one is the teacher and one the pupil, and so they remain apart. By serving his teacher, like a servant who accepts the lordship of his master, he acquires awe of Heaven. The awe of Heaven is essentially God's transcendence, and therefore included in the student's service of the teacher are both a connection, which is loving-

---

[26] Bezalel Safran, *Hasidism: Continuity or Innovation?* (Cambridge: Harvard Univ. Press, 1988), p. 56.

kindness, and also a separation, which is the fear of his teacher and also the fear of Heaven. It is important to understand the reason for saying that [the teacher, were he not to allow the student to serve him, would] prevent the student from achieving loving-kindness, for this derives from the fact that the teacher is connecting with the student, and the connection between the teacher and student is loving-kindness. The reason for saying that the teacher would [in refusing service] take from [the student] the fear of Heaven, is that from the perspective of the student, fearing his teacher, namely serving him and yielding before him, leads him to merit a fear of Heaven. The awe of one's teacher is like the awe of Heaven – understand this because these matters are truly deep.[27]

The teacher mediates between the student and God, modeling a balance between authority and kindness reminiscent of God Himself. In the *yir'ah* mode, a space exists between teacher and student that enables awe for the teacher as well as for the body of information being conveyed. The relationship involves authority where the teacher represents the transcendent element of rabbinic tradition, bridging the gap between the student and the tradition by inspiring him or her with reverence. At the same time, however, Maharal refers to a more intimate mode of joining (*tzeiruf*) that characterizes the relationship between teacher and student. This bond, that of parent and child, intimates love, kindness and a ready identification of the student's needs and hopes. The "kindness" connection, namely the unconditional extension of loving-kindness, is at the heart of the teacher-student relationship – essential to the creation of *ahavat Hashem*.

With reference to the *yir'ah* aspect of the relationship, Maharal emphasizes the need for teachers to be as informed as possible of the insights and methods of our Sages of blessed memory:

And it says that he is given the means to learn [in addition to the means to teach], because in order to teach others one needs to know Torah as much as possible, in order to know how to answer students' questions. This is the reason for saying "one is given the means to study and to teach" (*Avot* 4:5), meaning that one is given the means to learn until it becomes possible to teach others. If on the other hand, one wishes to learn a certain amount of one tractate, one will not be given the means to learn the whole tractate, because [study] is termed the study of Torah even if it includes only one letter. Teaching others however, requires a significant amount of knowledge

---

[27] *Hiddushei Aggadot*, vol. 1, p. 160, commenting on *Ketubbot* 96a.

as we have said, and, in addition, people will not come to learn from an individual who has not attained a quantity of Torah. Therefore, one who
learns in order to teach others is given the means to study until the point
where he may teach others.[28]

Maharal focuses upon the teacher's own erudition, while also emphasizing that learning is most complete when geared toward teaching and, ultimately, action. Since deference to the text demands deeper understanding
of it before transmitting it, a talmudic tractate is better understood once it
has been taught. So long as one restricts oneself to private learning, it remains possible to rest with a lower level of knowledge, but learning in order
to teach demands bringing the words of Torah to their active completion.

While the *yir'ah* relationship between teacher and student is based upon
deference, the *ahavah* relationship is based upon acceptance, a manifestation
of the parent-child relationship, where each student is answered in accordance with his needs. Love involves both recognition and understanding:

> The Torah wrote [answers] to each one [of the four children in the Pass-
> over Haggadah] separately, because it is essential to respond to each one in
> accordance with his wisdom. One should answer the wise son according to
> the degree to which he is wise, and therefore one needs to tell him the laws
> of the Passover offering, namely all of the laws of the sacrifice. To the
> wicked son one must likewise respond in relation to his wickedness, and it
> is for this reason that [the Torah] mentions the answers to all four sons.[29]

A profound pedagogical message inheres in the answers given to the
four sons at the *seder* table. The Torah formulates different answers for the
different children, responding in kind to the goodness of the wise son and
the apathy of the wicked. By asking educators to "respond to each one in
accordance with his wisdom" Maharal implies that students should be answered in relation to their particular intellectual frame. The *ahavah* mode
anticipates that the educator will remain humble, capable of entering into
the personal experience of the student in order to consider the full implications of the questions addressed. Once familiar with individual personality
traits, the educator can more easily respond to the ideological underpinnings of the questions presented, so that both the wise and the simple sons,
for example, receive answers greater than the formulated questions.

---

[28] *Derekh ha-Hayyim* 4:5, p. 415.

[29] *Gevurot Hashem*, chap. 53, p. 233.

Articulating Learning in Partnership

The principle of *deveikut* also provides a model for learning in partnership. The *talmid hakham*, writes Maharal, should not remain excessively aloof, and should prefer to maintain his relationships with others: "Do not be completely separate from other beings, to the point where you cease to protect them, because the *talmid hakham* should have a connection with others."[30] The idea that the scholar needs a conscious connection with others is likewise the rationale behind shared learning. Although Maharal does not specifically refer to the *havurah* (group) or *hevruta* partnership, he speaks of the importance of learning together as expressed in the mishnaic statement "two who sit and share words of Torah, the *Shekhinah* rests among them" (*Avot* 3:3).[31] Torah, he explains, cannot ultimately be acquired by one as an individual. Although private learning may involve a level of engagement (*osek ba-Torah*), it cannot reach the level of genuine *limmud Torah* (learning of Torah) unless shared with a partner. Only shared learning will actively encourage students and scholars to listen to one another:

> "When two scholars pay attention to one another, the Holy One listens to their voices" (*Shabbat* 63a). When each one listens to the voice of his friend, so does God listen to their voices. This is not the same as the previous statement concerning two scholars who are amiable to one another. Here [the *aggadah*] says that when each person listens to the words of his fellow, and opens his heart to his words, the Holy One also listens to their voices.[32]

Maharal notes that when students of Torah listen to each other's words, God listens with them. More than simply being pleasant towards one another, this kind of Torah learning involves listening attentively, with an openness to understanding the other's position. Giving voice to the words of Torah thus invites God Himself to become the focus of shared experience. The unity emerging from the shared dialogue is so intense that God himself comes to hear, to partake in the harmony of the moment – "because those who listen to one another have a greater connection between them."[33]

---

[30] *Netivot Olam: Netiv ha-Torah*, vol. 2, chap. 4, p. 48.

[31] *Derekh ha-Hayyim* 3:3, p. 290, and *Tif'eret Yisra'el*, introduction.

[32] *Netivot Olam: Netiv ha-Torah*, vol. 1, chap. 6, p. 64.

[33] *Ibid.* See also Gilla Rosen's essay, in this volume.

Maharal further suggests that the faculty of speech, representing the vitality of transcendence, must be involved in Torah study:

R. Zeira said [one may infer] from the following: "A man has joy through the responses of his mouth" (Prov. 15:23). When does a man have joy? When he has responses in his mouth. R. Yitzhak said, "The thing is very near to you, in your mouth and in your heart, to do it" (Deut. 30:14). When is the thing very near to your heart? When it is in your mouth and in your heart to do it. Rava said [one may infer] from the following: "You have given him his heart's desire, and the utterances of his lips you have not withheld" (Ps. 21:3). When have you given him his heart's desire? When "the utterances of his lips you have not withheld." This means to inform us that the pleasantness of Torah is when Torah is present in actualized form, because when Torah is present in us we become spiritual, and there is no greater delight than this. [Torah exists in actualized form] when it endures in the memory.[34]

This suggests that the words of Torah are truly close to us when we articulate them and they become part of our most intimate experience. The moment of articulation is a moment of joy, for it means that Torah has become one with us. The element of activity in speech brings our potential to actuality, enabling us to actively engage in spirituality. Kabbalistically, this action (*asiyah*) translates a spiritual force into the physical world, and where the words of Torah create the sphere of dialogue and relationship, they transform creed into deed. As a helpful aside, articulation also strengthens the memory, impressing the words of Torah upon our minds and hearts and bringing us closer to our creator.

Maharal's Rejection of *Pilpul*

Given Maharal's emphasis upon uniting both individuals and ideas in learning, we may better appreciate his continued struggle against the study of *pilpul* (abstract intellectual casuistry) together with his staunch opposition to its didactic principles. Undertaken at the Prague academies of Maharal's day, *pilpul* often overextended the parameters of talmudic argument, attempting to reconcile different positions on the basis of obscure interpretations. Maharal's descriptions of *pilpul sheker* (intellectual sophistry) suggest

---

[34] *Netivot Olam: Netiv ha-Torah*, vol. 1, chap. 4, p. 49. The translation of *sikhli* as spiritual rather than intellectual is noted by Avraham Kariv in his introduction to *The Writings of the Maharal of Prague* (Jerusalem, 1960), p. 14.

that students of *pilpul* often ended by contorting the concepts they were trying to reconcile, creating division rather than unity, and forcing ideas into categories that contradicted their original depth and truth. While those in favor of *pilpul* were unconcerned by those flights of the imagination that left the realm of truth, Maharal was apprehensive that the Torah enterprise might lose its applications in reality.

While he admitted the value of *pilpul emet*, "true" insofar as it illuminates different aspects of existence, Maharal remained deeply suspicious of what he termed *pilpul sheker*, the philosophical abstraction that disconnects one from reality. Rather than being embedded in the world of the Sages, *pilpul* had developed into a form of learning based upon the abstract and the imaginary, upon sharpening one's arguments to impossible extremes just in order to outwit alternate opinions.

In *Netivot Olam*, Maharal refers again to the removal of the *Shekhinah* from the Jewish people when they cease to listen to one another, which he attributed to *pilpul* resulting in "a removal of good deeds and reverence from this generation."[35] In place of the intellectual hubris that sharpens conflict, Maharal advocates the kind of learning that builds bridges, promoting reverence and relationship rather than abstraction. Harmonized, holistic forms of learning (such as Maharal's study of *aggadah*), which unify the concepts of the Sages, are more likely to stimulate the values of *anavah*, *ahavah* and *deveikut*.

Revealing Integration in Interpretation

In *Netiv ha-Torah*, Maharal defines the essence of Torah as imparting one's knowledge to others; it develops from potential to actuality only once transmitted into action. From a more mystical perspective, the infinite source of goodness termed "*torat hesed*" (the Torah of lovingkindness) is brought to fruition only when its flow of goodness reaches a recipient.[36] Through his description of the meta-goals of education, Maharal gives us an idea of which values are most integral to *torat hesed*, along with their practical parameters in pedagogy. His paradigm presents a developmental guide for the Torah personality, beginning with intellectual wisdom (*hokhmah*), aspiring towards awe (*yir'ah*), humility (*anavah*), and love (*ahavah*), and ending with a dynamic focus upon attachment (*deveikut*). What motivates the

---

[35] Maharal continues, "In these generations and these lands, they walk in crooked paths," implying distorted paths of learning. *Gur Aryeh* on Deut. 6:7 (ed. Hartman, p. 123); cf. *Netivot Olam: Netiv ha-Torah*, vol. 1, chap. 5, p. 57. See also Dov Rappel, *Ha-Vikuah al ha-Pilpul* (Jerusalem, 1979).

[36] *Netivot Olam: Netiv ha-Torah*, vol. 1, chap. 8, p. 79 (cf. *Sukkah* 49b).

religious endeavor is finally the immanent relationship between God and humanity.

Methodologically, Maharal presupposes the existence of an aggadic discourse that may be covert but awaits discovery. By encouraging the attributes of *yir'ah* and *anavah*, he invites a respect for the words of the Sages that validates our relationship with God and with tradition. Rather than rejecting the text as irrelevant, the student governed by *yir'at shamayim* will place himself in a relationship with the Sages that enables their terminology to be redemptive. Appreciating the solidity of the text encourages us to engage it, revere it, and connect with it.

Maharal recognized that the presence of an "other" to whom we remain accountable is perhaps the most important contributor towards our humanity. While independent thinking is invited, an excessive focus upon autonomy leaves us bound within the parameters of the self, preventing the awareness of Divinity that stems from our interactions with others. If we are to develop a relationship with God, Maharal suggests, we must also relate to our collective Jewish consciousness, finding in the words of Torah, the Sages, and one another an informing and inspiring presence.[37]

---

[37] Few teachers manage to embody the spirit, dedication, and compassion of Maharal with unending resolution. Following years of energized teaching of Maharal, Professor Benjamin Gross continues to radiate warmth and devotion, and I am particularly grateful for the clarity of his vision, the rigor of his intellectual discipline, and the kindness of his soul.

AS GARDENERS IN THE GARDEN OF GOD: HASIDIC THOUGHT AND ITS IMPLICATIONS FOR TEACHER-STUDENT RELATIONSHIPS

Asher Friedman

> Fathers and teachers must know that their task is to educate and reveal children of the Lord and giants of Israel. They must see the children sitting in front of them as great souls still immature; their task is to get them to grow and flourish. A teacher is a gardener in the garden of God, assigned to cultivate it and guard it from harm.
>
> – Rav Klonymous Kalman of Piasezna[1]

Years ago, as I embarked on my first teaching experience, a friend recommended that I prepare by reading R. Klonymous Kalman of Piasezna's "A Discussion with Teachers and Parents."[2] The Rebbe's belief in every child's potential greatness inspired me, and his theories about the nature of adolescent spiritual growth resonated with my own experiences in working with teenagers. Over the past several years, my continued work with Modern Orthodox youth has served to intensify my conviction that the educational philosophy implicit in the Hasidic world view, and made explicit by R. Klonymous Kalman, can be profoundly useful in developing an educational vision for contemporary teachers.[3]

---

[1] "Author's Introduction: A Discussion with Teachers and Parents," in *Hovat ha-Talmidim*, in *A Student's Obligation*, trans. Micha Odenheimer (Northvale, NJ: Aronson, 1991).

[2] For biographical information on R. Klonymous Kalman Shapiro (1889–1944) see Aharon Sorasky's essay, included in both *Hovat ha-Talmidim* and *Aish Kodesh*, and Nehemia Polen's biographical chapter in his *The Holy Fire* (Northvale, NJ: Aronson, 1994).

[3] A theory of education constructed for one culture can never be directly applied to another. Instead, the theory must be "translated," maintaining the essential core of the theory but modifying its formulation so that it can be comprehensible and implementable in the new environment. Mordechai Rotenburg's multiple works on *hasidut* and

Why *Hasidut?*

Why turn to Hasidic thought for guidance in shaping our approach to education? Contemporary Orthodox educators often utilize innovative techniques, without inquiring as to whether the values these techniques carry as baggage are reconcilable to a Jewish world view:

> [T]he means and techniques that have been adopted by Jewish education are often imported indiscriminately from general education. Since the means of education are not neutral, it is quite possible that some of the means employed for Jewish education cancel out whatever there is in Jewish education that is related to "authentic" Judaism.[4]

If *how* we teach is as important as *what* we teach, if a teacher's attitude transmits subtle yet powerful lessons to the students about the nature of growth and learning, then this is an issue that must be grappled with.[5]

It is easy to underestimate the power of seemingly neutral educational decisions to transmit messages and values to our students. For example, the pervasive use of standardized testing seems a sensible, pragmatic approach – it is far easier to maintain consistent educational standards if disparate schools all subject their students to the same tests. But let us consider the impact that this approach has had on the way our students relate to the learning process. Accompanying the proliferation of standardized tests has come an abundance of test-preparation courses that teach those who can afford them the "tricks" necessary to achieve high scores. Teachers face intense pressure to focus on those subjects and types of questions that might appear on the tests. What message do the students receive from this? They learn to view the process of learning as a game, replete with tricks and strategies necessary to achieve correct answers. The pursuit of knowledge becomes the pursuit of the multiple-choice answer that is least likely to be

---

psychology (for example, his *Psikhologiah Yehudit va-Hasidut: Ha-Psikhologiah she-mi-aharei ha-Teologiah* [Tel-Aviv: Ha-Universitah ha-Meshuderet, 1997]) are good examples of "translation" from Hasidic texts to contemporary modes of thought and practice and have been models for my own work.

[4] Seymour Fox, "Toward a General Theory of Jewish Education," in David Sidorsky, ed., *The Future of the American Jewish Community* (New York: Basic Books, 1973), p. 263. See also Zalman F. Ury's, "Does Moral Education Have a Chance?" *Ten Da'at* (Winter 1989), pp. 3–5.

[5] For excellent illustrations of how teaching methodology itself powerfully shapes the attitudes of students to the process of learning and to their relationships with others, see Parker Palmer, *To Know As We Are Known: Education as a Spiritual Journey* (San Francisco: Harper & Row, 1993), pp. 33–46; and Elliot Aronson, *Nobody Left to Hate: Teaching Compassion After Columbine* (New York: W.H. Freeman, 2000).

incorrect. Thus, a seemingly value-neutral, pragmatic educational method transforms the way our students view the fundamentals of education. In fact, no educational decision is value-neutral, and educators therefore would do well to ensure that our teaching methods reflect a world-view compatible with the Judaism we intend to convey to our students. It is my hope that this essay will serve as a model of a consistent educational philosophy developed from a uniquely Jewish system of thought.[6]

In this essay, I will explain how certain basic assumptions about education flow from their roots in Hasidic thought and explore the way in which they play out in actual teacher-student relationships.[7] We will build an understanding of teacher-student relationships based on the theoretical teachings of *hasidut*, yet formulated in terms that can be implemented in the pragmatic realm of the contemporary classroom.

Each section of this essay can stand on its own but is best understood as a component of a dynamic system, affecting and affected by those facets preceding and succeeding it. In the first half I will examine the implications of Hasidism's optimistic view of the human soul for the teacher's image of the student. The second half explores the implications of approaching the student in terms of his or her actual locus along the spectrum of personal development.

I. *Hasidut*: Theory

Before commencing our exploration, I will briefly introduce some metaphysical assumptions underlying the Hasidic concepts that we will encounter:

---

[6] I don't intend to prove here that the educational philosophy implicit in the Hasidic world-view is the best approach to teaching in contemporary Orthodox schools. It is my hope that for those teachers whose educational intuitions resonate with the implications of *hasidut*, this essay will serve as a means of connecting their educational approach with a coherent Jewish world-view, and for those teachers who gravitate toward *hasidut* in their private *avodat Hashem*, this essay will elucidate the educational implications of their theology. For those teachers who are neither attracted to Hasidic theology nor to its educational implications, this essay is still useful – it can be viewed as a model of extrapolating educational philosophy from a particular theological/psychological world view. See Fox, p. 263: "There is…an urgent need for a serious discussion of what kind of Jewish education would reflect the various conceptions of Judaism. Such a discussion would result in the development of competing philosophies of Jewish education, but this, in turn, would make it possible for creative educators to develop means appropriate to the basic ideas in each of these philosophies."

[7] Hasidic thought is expressed in a vast number of works written over the past few hundred years and contains within it a wide spectrum of approaches. The system of Hasidic thought that I construct here is, to some degree, subjective – I chose texts that represent ideas that I personally have found useful and inspiring in my work as a teacher.

The secret of life is the Divine flow, and everyone must receive this flow, just as he is commanded to give of it to others. He who does not both receive and give is a barren tree.

                    – R. Tzvi Hirsh of Zidichov[8]

Complex Monism

The Hasidic world-view can best be described as one of "complex monism," an assumption that all of existence, as disparate and diverse as it seems on the surface, is ultimately connected back to one source. The statement of the *Zohar* that "there is no place empty of Him," became a central tenet of Hasidic thought – God pervades all of existence.[9] All things are essentially interrelated. According to *hasidut*, a single thought in the mind of a single human contains within it all of the worlds, all of the realms of existence. That is, a deep understanding of anything yields a comprehension of everything.[10]

For our purposes, the significance of this idea is that *hasidut* assumes that all things are ontologically connected. In the social realm, this means that human beings are not separate atoms that occasionally interact, but are, on a deep level, manifestations of a greater unity. In the psychological realm, this implies that to know some fact about the outside world entails a process of knowing oneself, and the process of knowing oneself entails a process of knowing the outside world.

For this reason, *hasidut* assumes that knowledge is *transformative* as opposed to merely *informative*. The latter approach to knowledge suggests that something is known when a person's thoughts correspond correctly to some objective reality. It assumes that knowledge is a phenomenon of the intellect and that that which is known is fundamentally separate from the knower. The former view, in contrast, assumes that something is not known to a person unless the knowledge has some existential meaning for her – if she remains the same person that she was before she was exposed to a given piece of information, she cannot be said to have learned it. Thus, knowledge cannot be solely cerebral; it is a phenomenon that relates to the knower as a whole – emotionally, behaviorally, and cognitively.

---

[8] In E. Steinmann, *Be'er ha-Hasidut – Galicia and Hungary* (Tel Aviv: Knesset Publishing), p. 196.

[9] *Tikkunei Zohar* 57.

[10] Cf. *Ba`al Shem Tov al ha-Torah, Naso* 4.

Theological Psychology

Since all of existence flows from one Source, and every fragment of existence is related to existence as a whole, every fragment yields insight into the nature of the whole of creation and the Creator. In particular, *hasidut* assumes that human psychology is reflective of the nature of God's interaction with His creation. *Hasidut* assumes that understanding the kabbalistic dynamics of God's unfolding emanations yields direct insight into the workings of the human psyche, and vice versa.[11]

> The *kabbalah* tended to describe the divine structures in human terms...
> [The *hasidim*], for whom the kabbalistic doctrines were a given, reverse[d]
> the order. [They] describe[d] man's personality in terms of divine *sefirot*.
> Thus, whereas the *kabbalah* elaborated an anthropological theology, [they]
> offer[ed] a theological anthropology, or kabbalistic psychology.[12]

Thus, many of the Hasidic texts that we will examine are written in kabbalistic terminology, yet will have direct implications for our understanding of psychological dynamics.

Transformative Relationships

Hasidut assumes that all relationships and events are transformative – our task in life is to gather insight, self-growth, and enlightenment from all of our interactions with the outside world. No encounter is by chance; every event demands a growth-oriented response. Since teaching involves the construction of a specific type of change-oriented relationship with students, Hasidic thought has much to contribute to our understanding of the educational process.

---

[11] The array of *sefirot* that describe the inner workings of God's emanations carry clearly anthropomorphic associations – for example, the second, third, and fourth *sefirot* are called *hokhmah* (wisdom), *binah* (understanding), and *da`at* (knowledge).

[12] Norman Lamm, *The Religious Thought of Hasidism: Text and Commentary*, (Hoboken, NJ: Ktav, 1999), p. 60, note 16. See also Arthur Green, quoted in Lawrence Kaplan and David Shatz, eds., *Rabbi Abraham Isaac Kook and Jewish Spirituality* (New York: NYU Press, 1995), pp. 29–30.

II. The Dynamic and the Static Self:
The Teacher's Image of the Student

And when a man wishes to walk on the path of *teshuvah*, he must become an expert in walking, and he must possess two realms of expertise, that is, expertise in surging forward (*ratzo*) and expertise in falling back (*shov*).
— R. Nahman of Breslov[13]

Are children like blocks of granite that must be sculpted, or are they like seedlings that contain within themselves the potential to sprout and blossom if properly nurtured?[14] In other words, do we shape and mold our successful students, or is a good education one that facilitates our students' own inner growth?[15] Of all questions that a teacher must pose to himself, perhaps this one has the most profound implications for his approach to education. We, who are entrusted with children and their growth, must face this question, for it asks, what is the source of growth? A teacher may side with one extreme or find some middle ground between the two approaches, but no teacher dare evade this basic attitudinal choice. As we shall see through the course of this paper, many of our basic educational strategies depend on this issue.

R. Klonymous Kalman seems to firmly adopt the position that children contain within themselves the seeds of their own growth. A teacher cannot shape a student into some pre-conceived mold, but rather engages in

> stimulating the growth and development of what each child is suited for by his very nature. This quality may be found in him only in very small measure, in total hiddeness; the task of the educator is to uncover it… Such an educator must adapt himself attentively to the student, must penetrate into the midst of his limited consciousness and small-mindedness, until he

---

[13] R. Nahman of Breslov (1772–1811), *Likkutei Moharan* #282. Cf. imagery in Ezek. 1:14.

[14] The classic proponents of these two extremes were John Locke, who saw a child as a *tabula rasa*, a blank slate to be filled with wisdom by his teachers, and Jean Jacques Rousseau, who assumed that children would blossom like wild flowers if only their parents and teachers would stay out of their way. See Neil Postman, *The Disappearance of Childhood* (New York: Random House, 1994), pp. 56–62, for further analysis.

[15] The psychologist John B. Watson, founder of behaviorism, remarked: "Give me a dozen healthy infants, well-formed, and my own specified world to bring them up in, and I'll guarantee to take any one at random and train him to become any type of specialist I might select – doctor, lawyer, artist, merchant-chief and, yes, even beggar-man and thief, regardless of his talents, penchants, tendencies, abilities, vocations, and race of his ancestors." John B. Watson, *Behaviorism* (New York: Norton, 1925), p. 82.

reaches the hidden soul-spark. Then he can help it emerge, blossom, and grow.[16]

This perspective, so powerfully expressed by the Rebbe, is rooted in Hasidic assumptions about human nature. In Hasidic thought, the soul is, in essence, an emanation of God, a *"nitzotz Eloki."* No amount of sin or corruption can completely eradicate this Divine spark, and therefore the potential for *teshuvah* and growth is never lost. A good educator will sensitize her students to their own inner greatness. Abraham Twerski relates that his father never punished him as a child. When little Avraham misbehaved, his father would shake his head gently and say, *"Es past nisht!* This does not become you!"* Instead of criticizing his son, the elder Twerski elevated Avraham's sense of self-worth by pointing out that he was too good for certain types of behavior.[17]

Ratzo (Surging Forward)

Rebbe Nahman of Breslov most profoundly expresses the relationship between awareness of one's potential greatness and spiritual growth. In a homiletical essay on the words "I will sing to the Lord as long as I exist (*be-odi*)" (Ps. 146:2), R. Nahman calls the true self the *"od,"* the source of infinite "moreness" – a fount of growth and potential that will yield greatness if only properly tapped. People despair when they lose sight of their *od,* when they feel trapped in their current mode of being, when their failures are taken to be definitions of their true selves.

It is easier to relate to others as static rather than dynamic beings, but this imprisons them in a pseudo-self that is incapable of change for the better. Through the process of searching out the small indications of potential beauty and goodness that can be found in any human, we realize that people are not static, they are not imprisoned in their perceived flaws, but contain the potential for unbounded growth.

The cost of viewing students statically, in terms of their perceived qualities instead of their dynamic potential for growth, was dramatically demonstrated in a school in England about a decade ago. A mistake was made in filing the results of an IQ test administered to the students. High-scoring students were listed as below average, and those who had scored below the average were listed as above average. A half-year later, when the mistake

---

[16] *A Student's Obligation*, pp. 4–5.

[17] Abraham Twerski, *From Generation to Generation* (Brooklyn: Traditional Press, 1985), pp. 14–16.

was finally discovered, the school readministered the test. Those students who had been mistakenly treated as above average in intelligence scored significantly higher than they had the first time, and those who had been reported to be below average scored far lower than they had the first time around. Teachers' assumptions about their students actually determined the students' growth.

When asked how they handled their "above average" students, the teachers responded, "For some reason our methods weren't working, so we had to change our methods." It was clear to the teachers that the students could grow; the only question was how to nurture that growth. They modified their teaching methods, and enabled these weaker students to flourish. If we relate to someone as if he is potentially great, he will perform accordingly.[18]

According to R. Nahman, it is not sufficient to passively accept the idea that every human being possesses potential greatness. Rather, one must actively search for signs of that greatness:

> Know, that you must judge everyone favorably. Even if he is completely wicked, you must seek out and find within him some small goodness, for within the realm of that goodness, he is not evil. By this means, by finding goodness within him and judging him favorably, you truly raise him up to favor, and it is possible to help him return in *teshuvah*.[19]

R. Klonymous Kalman saw the teacher as a guide who helps the student isolate and intensify his own strengths, both actual and potential. Students do not possess negative personality traits (*middot*); rather, they possess characteristics that have great potential for either positive or negative expression, and they need guidance in learning how to best develop their unique qualities. If they do not receive this guidance, then their *middot* may be expressed negatively.

In order to help a student, a teacher must be able to see him not just as he is now, but also as he *could be*. Thus, the teacher should see the student's

---

[18] This mishap is reported by Steven Covey, *7 Habits of Highly Effective People* (New York: Simon & Schuster, 1989), pp. 300–301. Of course, R. Nahman does not advocate a blindly optimistic perspective on humanity. He clearly indicates that we should view certain people as wicked, with the caveat that our view of them must simultaneously acknowledge their potential greatness. Obviously, a teacher cannot overlook a student's problems simply because the student has so much potential greatness. Rather, the teacher should view the student's problems in the context of his potential greatness.

[19] *Likkutei Moharan*, #282.

middot not only in terms of their current expression, but in terms of their potential, ideal expression. For example, when a teacher works with a volatile, angry student, he should visualize in his mind the potential passion this student will express in his *avodat Hashem*, once he learns to direct his energies productively.[20]

In order for a student to become aware of her own strengths and potential for greatness, an awareness that requires an ability to transcend her current situation and project far into the future, the teacher must develop this awareness herself. If a student is consistently treated as she is and not as she could be, her behaviors will be constantly reinforced and she will never reach a point where she can imagine other possibilities and certainly will never be able to take active steps toward growth.

In order to be able to focus on a student's potential even when most of his behaviors are negative, a teacher should take the time to think about each of his students individually and recall particular moments when the student did something that displayed his potential. Often, we teachers become entrenched, losing the ability to see our students as they truly are. In order to break free of this limited perspective, we would do well to turn to other teachers for insight into our students. It is also helpful to try to observe our students outside of the classroom. The student who in the classroom is silent and passive or wild and disruptive may behave very differently when he is in a more supportive environment, such as his home or the basketball court.

Mark,[21] a student of mine, was a problem case from the very beginning. He came to yeshivah with a long history of evading responsibility, behaving obnoxiously toward authority figures, and showing a generally rebellious attitude. Things didn't change when a *rebbe* told him to cut his long hair. He responded sarcastically, and the conversation ended in a shouting match. As the year went on, he teetered on the edge of being expelled. I deliberately avoided the role of disciplinarian and therefore was able to cultivate an amicable relationship with him. Mark and I had many conversations in which he brought his complaints about the yeshivah to me and I tried to encourage him to act in a more mature way in his dealings with authority figures. I found these conversations frustrating and wasn't sure if they really accomplished much. About halfway through the year, I realized that much of Mark's problem stemmed from his own miserable self-image and that

---

[20] *Student's Obligation*, pp. 7–8.

[21] I have altered the names and identifying details of the students described in these vignettes.

during our conversations I had bought into his feelings about himself instead of assessing his qualities on my own. I realized that Mark had a static perspective on himself, full of despair and lack of self-worth. Unless I developed my own dynamic image of him, enabling me to envision him as he might be, there would be no chance for growth. So I stepped back and wrote a list of his positive qualities and various glimpses of his potential greatness that I had seen in my dealings with him. Although the struggle continued for the rest of the year, this list helped me to focus on an awareness of his potential for growth during my frustrating dealings with him. It might be helpful to keep such a list for each of one's students, so that in case of crisis one will be ready to approach them from a dynamic perspective rather than their depressed, static self-images. When students cease to believe in their own potential, it is our duty to believe in it for them.

Shov (Falling Back)

Despite this emphasis on dynamism and potential growth, R. Nahman does not suggest that we lose sight of the actual state of the student. A certain awareness of one's locus in the realm of self-growth is necessary before willful movement is possible. R. Nahman describes a mode that he dubs "stillness before God" (*dom le-Hashem*), in which one fully acknowledges his low state of affairs.

There, in the depths of depravity, even to the depths of hell, even then he must not despair about himself forever, and he must constantly search out God, blessed is He, and strengthen himself wherever he may be, with whatever means he has available, for even in the depths of hell God is present, and even there he may attach himself to Him.[22]

The realization that God is present everywhere, even in the lowliest realms of existence, gives one the confidence to face one's actual state and prepare to move. We tend to deny to ourselves and to others our actual condition because we lack the conviction that it is possible to change. Thus I pretend to be someone that I am not, for to face the person that I actually am would mean to face the depths of despair. The first act that we gain the courage to perform when we attain a belief in our potential for growth is to accept the reality of our situation. Only then can we begin to grow.

Lack of faith in our potential for growth is not the only reason we fail to accept our current state. Another factor is the reality that growth is a slow, energy-intensive process. Instead of facing the gap between where we are

---

[22] *Likutei Moharan*, #6 (end).

and where we can be as a challenge, we relax, imagining ourselves to be far more advanced than we actually are. Few of us are truly ready for the hard work and long journey entailed in the process of growth.

R. Klonymous Kalman attributed the problems exhibited by the children of his generation to this weakness:

> The simplest and most important reason [for adolescent rejection of the Torah lifestyle] is that today's youth consider themselves grown-up before their time…an atmosphere of foolishness has surrounded the young people of our time, in which they have come to think of themselves as grown-up and independent – in their opinions and in their desires – though their mind is still upside down and their desires unripe and bitter.[23]

According to the Rebbe, the source of rebellion is the insistence of adolescents on viewing themselves as fully developed adults, instead of acknowledging that maturation is a developmental process and that they have much more growth ahead of them.

Educators have a responsibility to recognize our students' stage of development even if they are unwilling to do so themselves, and we must deal with them accordingly. I have seen an educator in a post-high school yeshivah become infuriated by his eighteen-year-old students who sleep late or show no enthusiasm for textual learning. Should it surprise us that a boy who has slept late, drunk in bars, and learned passively (if at all) throughout his adolescence continues his behaviors once he arrives in the Holy Land? We must not resent the state of our students; rather our job as educators is to work with them as they are, enabling them to become more.

Awareness of a student's place does not imprison him there, as long as it is coupled with awareness of where he can go. A teacher must juggle an awareness of the student's spiritual-developmental state, with a sense of the student's trajectory, his potential growth.

III. Constriction, Descent and Ascent:
The Teacher's Approach to the Student

We are accustomed to the idea that education entails change on the part of the student. In Western education, the student's knowledge base and skills are sharpened and broadened. In other educational systems, the student's world view and self-image grow more effective and more harmoni-

---

[23] *A Student's Obligation*, p. 11. See also Postman, pp. 4–5, for a similar analysis of contemporary adolescents.

ous with the surrounding world. But *hasidut* stresses that change on the part of the teacher is also an inherent element in the process of education. If both teacher and student remain static, a chasm lies between the two that permits no communication. The student's ability to traverse the gap is limited, and therefore it remains to the teacher to constrict himself, to move towards the student.

Tzimtzum

God, blessed is He, constricted (*tzimtzem*) His brilliance, just as a father constricts his intellect and speaks in baby talk with his infant child... This [Divine] constriction was for the sake of Israel. Love motivated this *tzimtzum*... When a father sees his son playing with nuts, his love motivates him to play with the son, even though from the father's perspective it is childish behavior. Nevertheless, out of his love for his son and his desire to derive pleasure from him, he constricts his mature intellect and immerses himself in childishness, so that the child can cope with it. But if the father dealt with him based on his own intellectual level, the son would not have been able to tolerate it, and the father would not have derived pleasure from him.
— The *Maggid* of Mezritch[24]

Lurianic *Kabbalah* sees deep paradox in the reality that God created the physical world. How can the many come from the One? If God is infinite, how can the finite world exist? If God pervades all of existence, how is it possible that each of us has independent consciousness, capable of desiring that which is contrary to the will of God? In response to these paradoxes, R. Yitzhak Luria (the Ari) proposed a new model for understanding creation. God did not create anything outside Himself. Rather, with an act of *tzimtzum*, of self-constriction, He made space for the finite within the infinite. In this ultimate act of love, God reduced Himself to make room for others, to make room for those who would receive His love.

Hasidut, with its emphasis on understanding kabbalistic concepts as psychological realities, gave a prominent place to the concept of *tzimtzum*. Thus understood, *tzimtzum* is the act of constricting one's own self in order to make room for the other, a holding-back that is in reality a great act of love. Some people give because they feel an inner drive to share their love with others. Repressing this drive hurts, and therefore they dedicate themselves to showering love upon others. This mode of love is insufficient. To

---

[24] R. Dov Ber of Mezritch (d. 1772) in *Or Torah*, #248.

truly love requires *tzimtzum,* an act that expresses a love sensitive to the needs of the beneficiary. The unique personality, strengths, and flaws of the recipient determine the shape and nature of the act of giving. In the realm of education, *tzimtzum* is the ability of the teacher to recognize and accept the more constricted cognitive, moral, and spiritual levels of his students in order to work with them on their own terms.

An excellent example of *tzimtzum* is found in R. Klonymous Kalman's own work. The Rebbe nostalgically described earlier generations, when youngsters were eager to absorb the values and knowledge of their elders and were therefore treated as *tabula rasa.* Only after a certain process of maturation were they given autonomy and responsibility for their own growth. However, he recognized the overly precocious mindset of his generation's children and adapted his educational strategy to it. He abandoned his own ideal conception of education because he realized that children were not equipped to handle it.[25]

Aside from its implications regarding broad educational policy, *tzimtzum* applies to the particular way in which we teach concepts to our students. Well-educated adults are accustomed to thinking in abstract terms, but youngsters encountering philosophy or Talmud for the first time often have difficulty dealing with conceptual thinking. A mentor of mine gave me the following guidance as I prepared to teach a course on Jewish philosophy: "If you wish to teach a concept for which you cannot think of an analogy or story to illustrate it, you have no right to teach it. Your inability to develop a *mashal* indicates that you don't fully understand the idea yourself." Rav Klonymous Kalman demonstrates this principle in all of his works — it is difficult to find a page in any of his books lacking some powerful image or parable that illustrates his conceptual points. *Tzimtzum* requires that we translate our ideas into the conceptual language of our students.[26] The *Maggid* of Mezritch compares this process of *tzimtzum* to pouring a liquid from a wide-mouthed jar into a narrow-mouthed bottle through a funnel.[27] The essential idea remains the same, but it is funneled so that it flows in a stream thin enough that the student is able to receive it.

The teacher must enter the world of her students to understand how they think and what type of formulation they most easily understand. We

---

[25] *A Student's* Obligation, pp. 12–15.

[26] For a discussion of "translation" in educational terminology as used here, see Michael Rosenak, *Roads to the Palace: Jewish Texts and Teaching* (Oxford: Berghahn Books, 1995), p. 99.

[27] Quoted in Rotenburg, p. 60.

expect students to invest themselves in our conceptual constructs and world views – is it not proper that we should do the same? We were once children; therefore we are capable of regressing to the thought patterns of youngsters. If one of us must build a bridge to cross the conceptual gap between teacher and student, the teacher ought to bear that responsibility.[28]

In addition to accounting for differing intellectual abilities and levels of conceptual thought, *tzimtzum* also entails the recognition of different motivations for study. While the teacher may be driven by sheer love of Torah study *li-shemah,* he may have students unready to respond to such a motivation. The teacher must discover what drives the students, not just because using appropriate motivations enhances class participation, but because students fully engage their intellects in a problem only if it promises some insight into an issue they are grappling with. The Ba'al Shem Tov used the following analogy to illustrate this point:

> A king wanted to teach his son numerous realms of wisdom. He hired many wise men to teach him, but the prince failed to grasp any of the lessons, to the point that they despaired of ever teaching him. Only one wise man stayed with him. One day, the prince saw a young woman and desired her for her beauty. The wise man complained to the king about this, and the king replied: "If so, since he has desire, even if it is for physical pleasure, this will be the key to his attaining all of the wisdoms." He commanded that the woman be brought into the courtyard of the king, and he commanded her that if the prince approached her, she should tell him that she would not speak with him until he had learned one realm of wisdom. She did so, and then added that he must learn another realm, and another, until finally he had attained all realms of wisdom. At this point, he no longer desired the woman.[29]

At different stages of development, different existential challenges prompt us to seek out understanding. A sensitive teacher will ask: "What are my students interested in? What subjects do they inquire after of their own volition, and how can I incorporate those subjects into my teaching?"

---

[28] I will argue below that when the student is ready, it is essential that the teacher retreat and allow the student to approach him. But this occurs only after the teacher has lovingly approached the student.

[29] *Ba`al Shem Tov al ha-Torah, Terumah* #4 (see #5 for theoretical underpinnings of this idea).

Yeridah le-Tzorekh Aliyyah – Descent for the Sake of Ascent

There once was a prince who became insane and imagined that he was a turkey. He sat naked beneath the table and refused to eat anything but grains of barley. The king summoned wise men and doctors, none of whom were able to help the prince. One day, a wise man came and said, "I will help him." He climbed under the table, undressed, and ate barley grains. Gradually, gradually, he said to the prince, "Could we perhaps eat other kinds of food here together? Could we perhaps put on pants?" Gradually, he raised him back to his former state.

> – R. Nahman of Breslov[30]

On one level, *tzimtzum* is a cognitive act – it is a teacher's willful constriction of her intellectual, emotional, and spiritual state in order to translate her wisdom into a language comprehensible to the students. It is an imaginative act, almost empathic in nature – the teacher must leave her own conceptual system and temporarily place herself in the conceptual "shoes" of the students.

But if *tzimtzum* is to be more than a mere pragmatic act of translation, another ingredient is required: love. When God created the world, His first act was *tzimtzum,* a constricting of His self. His second act was to return, filling the newly created void with His constricted presence. God descended to dwell in the physical world, and this second act was the *telos* of the first. So too, when we translate our ideas into terms that our students can relate to, we build a bridge between ourselves and our students. But the bridge does fill its purpose until we lovingly cross it.

This crossing of the bridge, this descending into lower worlds, is termed in Hasidic thought "descent for the sake of ascent" (*yeridah le-tzorekh aliyyah*). Connecting with a person on a lower spiritual level always entails a descent, a real lowering of one's self.[31] As the Ba'al Shem Tov states, "If a person wishes to help a friend who is stuck in the mud, he must get himself

---

[30] *Sippurim Nifla'im*, pp. 26–27. See also John Clay, *R.D. Laing: A Divided Self* (London, 1996), pp. 170–71, for a practically identical story about Laing.

[31] Some educators may feel uncomfortable viewing themselves as existing on a higher spiritual level than their students, and don't wish to see themselves as spiritual guides. But if they truly have progressed no further along the path of religious growth than their students, what are they doing in the classroom? To recognize one's current self as being more advanced in some ways than our students is not arrogance; rather, it's a prerequisite to our role as teachers. Nor does it preclude the likelihood that some of our students will eventually progress far beyond the furthest reaches of our own growth.

a little dirty, and thereby he will be able to come close to him and rescue him. But if he stays where he is, he has no way of rescuing him."[32] A teacher cannot help a student facing a spiritual difficulty, or even understand him, until he has found that same difficulty in himself. R. Yosef Yitzhak Schneerson of Lubavitch described in the following words the inner dynamics of a spiritual guide as he helps a *hasid* struggle with his flaws:

> For he too possesses this flaw within, as a trace, or a trace of a trace [of the *hasid*'s flaw], but regardless [of how minute the trace is], he possesses this same flaw within him. Awareness of this reality, and the fact that he finds a trace of a trace of this flaw within himself…gives the ability to the people of his generation to repair their sin.[33]

When an adolescent comes to us for help with his personal struggles, we have the ability to connect with those struggles because we, too, faced similar issues in our own adolescence.[34] We have confronted those challenges, and our personalities were shaped by that very process. No matter what spiritual level we have attained, we contain within ourselves a "trace," or a "trace of a trace," of our previous lower levels.

When a student comes to a teacher for help, he will often tremble in anticipation – will my *rebbe* think less of me when he hears about what's going on inside of me? Will he understand? As long as the student views the teacher as towering far above him, there is little chance that he can be helped. When the teacher descends, and faces the same inner difficulty that the student faces, the relationship is transformed momentarily. For that instant, the two share equal footing, each struggling with the same challenge. This moment of solidarity gives the student a new sense of his teacher. He is not merely a great person, but he is one who achieved greatness by growing past personal struggles. We may not view ourselves as great, but our students often do, and we must acknowledge that reality.

---

[32] *Ba`al Shem Tov al ha-Torah, Aharei Mot,* note 5.

[33] R. Yosef Yitzhak Shneerson, *Sefer ha-Ma'amarim u-Kuntresim* (Brooklyn: Kehot Publishing House, 1986), vol. 2, pp. 718–719.

[34] This is not to say that one must have undergone the exact same struggles to empathize with one's students. But the basic issues of adolescence are always the same, though they manifest themselves in varying forms: the struggle to establish an identity separate from that of one's parents, issues of sexuality, friendship and social pressure, the search for meaning. Thus, even a teacher who never faced the pitfalls and temptations that confront contemporary teens may be able to relate personally to their struggles.

This moment of identification with the teacher gives the student renewed confidence in his own ability to grow, to become like his teacher.

We despair when we recognize our flaws and assume that it's impossible to grow past them, that anyone who has made certain kinds of mistakes is beyond hope. Salvation occurs when we see someone else who shares this flaw, and yet is able to grow – it suddenly dawns on us that one can be under the table and yet wear clothes, one can be under the table and eat normal food. By realizing that others, who have not surrendered to their condition, share our flaws, we are freed from despair.

Such an experience with one of my own teachers had a profound impact on the course of my spiritual growth. In my first year at university, I was revisited by a host of spiritual crises that I had earlier dealt with during my years of study in Israel. I was wracked by doubt – doubt of the existence of God, doubt of the possibility of free will, and underlying it all, doubt of myself. In despair, I turned to a teacher who had helped me deal with issues of belief and faith the year before in Israel. When I mustered the courage to describe to him all of the terrifying uncertainties I suffered, he revealed that he too had undergone periods of struggle and doubt – including a stint during the time he helped me the year before. The sudden realization that I was not alone, and that my mentor actually identified with my own difficulties, transformed my perspective on the challenges confronting me. I still had to resolve my doubts, but the awareness that such a great man had faced similar problems and dealt with them healthily buoyed my faith in my ability to do the same.[35]

The feeling of solidarity accomplished by *yeridah le-tzorekh aliyyah* can be expressed in other ways, as in the following case: Ilan was a funny, good-natured boy, who, half way through the year, completely stopped coming to class. One day, I wandered down to his dorm room to see how he was doing. Heavy-metal music was blaring on the stereo, and he was lying in bed reading a novel. We had a very good talk about some self-growth issues that were worrying him. Not once did I mention my class. We agreed to talk more the following night. The next night I came by and he was in the

---

[35] See R. Aharon Lichtenstein, "The Source of Faith is Faith Itself," *Jewish Action* (Fall 1992), pp. 79–80, for his description of a similar experience in the development of his own religious commitment. It must be noted that some students are not ready to handle the reality that their teachers also struggle to attain greatness. These students need to retain the image of unattainable perfection for the sake of their own stability. A revelation such as the one my mentor made could be completely disillusioning and devastating. For me as well, I must admit that there was devastation and disillusionment mixed with the relief and elation I felt when I first saw the similarity between my teacher and myself.

shower, and I yelled into the bathroom that I had come by to say hello. The next day Ilan attended class for the first time in months, and actively participated. But this pattern did not continue. Once again, Ilan stopped attending class, and I assumed that his renewed interest represented a temporary phase and nothing more. I next saw him about a week later at a Shabbat meal. "Rabbi, what happened?" he exclaimed. "Why didn't you come back down to my room?" Shocked that our conversation had meant so much to him, I proposed that we meet in my apartment the following day. At that meeting, Ilan took some tremendously courageous steps in self-growth, all the while expressing fear that continued growth would mean that he would have to stop "having fun" and focus his energy on improving his own character. I sensed that his recognition that I was there to help him begin his journey gave him the confidence to plunge ahead.

In Ilan's case, *yeridah le-tzorekh aliyyah* transformed his attitude toward self-growth. The fact that I came to talk with him about issues that were on his mind indicated my concern for him. Furthermore, I was willing to descend to his environment – we spoke with *his* music playing in the background, in *his* room. It was very clear to both of us that I had entered his territory. *Yeridah le-tzorekh aliyyah* helps our students grow because it is a profound expression of our love, our willingness to move from our own places of comfort to be with them in theirs.

Ke-Mayim ha-Panim le-Panim

What happens when a student feels her teacher's love in the form of *yeridah le-tzorekh aliyyah*? From the perspective of Hasidic thought, the idea that "every action prompts an equal and opposite reaction" is as true in the realm of interpersonal relations as it is in the physical world. "As water reflects one's face, so too does the human heart reflect the heart of another person" (Prov. 27:19). This verse, central to many Hasidic discourses, refers to the reactive, reflective nature of human relationships. In the Ba'al Shem Tov's language:

When a man stands next to water, his reflection appears large upon the water. When he leans closer to the water, the reflection becomes smaller. As he comes closer and closer to the water, the reflection becomes smaller and smaller, until his face actually touches the water, at which point the face in the reflection meets the face of the man. So too, with regard to the heart of one man to another. When a man views himself as great, his fellow responds by bloating his own ego, and when a man humbles himself before his fellow, his fellow humbles himself as well, until he can constrict himself no further, at which point his fellow will follow suit [and through this process their friendship is strengthened so that nothing may break it]. Then equality is created between them, and they are made to be equal, and this is what Scripture says regarding Moshe (Ex. 33:11), "And God spoke to Moshe face to face, as a man speaks to his friend"...Since Moshe constricted himself before the Creator, blessed is He, the Creator, too, as it were, constricted Himself before Moshe and spoke to him face to face.[36]

This movement of "leaning forward" is associated with self-constriction. The student senses the love expressed by the teacher's risky, willful descent, and responds with love and a courageous willingness to take risks to continue the process of growth begun by the teacher.

The *Ba'al ha-Tanya*[37] points to God's descent to the depths of Egypt as the paradigmatic example of His infinite love for His people. When a Jew meditates on God's love for him, he automatically reflects that love with a welling up of his own love. Once Ilan (the boy in the story recounted above) felt that I cared for him, he opened up and began his journey of growth. To invest courage and energy in the process of growth demands enormous self-love, a commodity that many teenagers sorely lack. The realization that a teacher is willing to lovingly extend himself for his sake can be the spark that ignites self-love within a student.

Retreat and Pursuit

Despite the power of *tzimtzum* and *yeridah le-tzorekh aliyyah* to encourage self-love and growth, the teacher ultimately must pull away from the student in order to prevent the student from becoming passive and dependent. In the following teaching, the *Maggid* of Mezritch continues the metaphor of a father discovering his son playing childish games, but this time the father retreats from his son instead of descending toward him:

"Draw me, we will run after You" (Song 1:4). This is analogous to a father who sees his son playing childishly with small children. The father walks by him so that his son will see him. When the son sees his father, he drops his childish games and runs after his father, calling out, "Father!" When the father sees his son running after him, he turns and continues walking, which

---

[36] *Ba`al Shem Tov al ha-Torah, Ki Tissa* #15. See *Yevamot* 117a and Rashi for a similar understanding.

[37] R. Shneur Zalman of Lyady, introduction to *Sha`ar ha-Yihud ve-ha-Emunah* in *Likkutei Amarim (Tanya)*.

prompts the son to scream even more, "Father, Father!" and to swiftly run until he reaches him. In the beginning, when the father revealed himself to his son, he did so in order that his son would see him, abandon his childish games, and chase after him. This would give the father intense joy in the realization that his son is wise, and there is nothing more important in his eyes than coming close to him. When he sees his son abandoning all of his childish activities and chasing after him, the father hides his face and continues on his journey so that the child will despise his childish activities and yearn for his father even more… The great pleasure experienced by the father and son could not have occurred without…the father constricting his love and continuing on his path.[38]

Undoubtedly, the intense love shown by the teacher for his student when he descends to him is crucial for the possibility of growth. The student perceives a bridge built between his world and that of the teacher and feels the self-worth necessary to be able to begin to cross it. But as long as the teacher remains with his student in the depths, as long as the father plays childish games with his son, the son feels no incentive to move, to transcend his current level. At the proper moment, the *rebbe* takes a step back, and the gap between them reappears. Now it is the student's turn to traverse the chasm, to join the teacher on his level.

At first, our students may resent our withdrawal. Accustomed to passivity, they are bewildered by our invitation to cross the gap themselves. When a student once asked me an excellent question about a certain text, I acknowledged the brilliance of the question and asked him what he thought the answer was. "But Rabbi, I don't know anything – why don't you tell me? You're supposed to have all of the answers." I refused to share my own theory with him. Finally he came up with an answer that, although not my approach, solved the problem. This was one giant step across the chasm.

When a teacher descends to her student and then hides herself, she thrusts the student into an active role. The student, to maintain her connection with the teacher, must shake off her habitual passivity and chase after her. This newfound active mode of being can be exhilarating for students, and teachers can incorporate it into the structure of the curriculum. The learning environment can be structured in a way that allows both students and teachers to become receivers at times and to be givers at times.

---

[38] *Or Torah*, #188.

One of my most successful lessons utilized this approach. One day as I was about to teach I realized that my understanding of the *sugya* was faulty. I did not have the time to retrace my steps and discover my mistake before class time, so instead, I went before my class and admitted to them that I had made no headway in the *sugya* and that I needed their help. I split the class into two groups, and gave them one hour to learn the Gemara and *Rishonim* in groups. Then each group would be responsible to present their understanding of the *sugya* to the rest of the class. The boys spent the next two hours engaged in intense *talmud Torah*, relishing their new roles as teachers.[39]

IV. Double-Mindedness

After a long day of counseling his *hasidim*, the *Ba'al ha-Tanya* finally retired to his study and removed his long coat. His *gabbai* was astonished to see him completely drenched in sweat. "*Rebbe*, are you ill? Why are you so full of sweat?" he asked. "*Yehidut* (private consultation) with my *hasidim* is an exhausting task," the *rebbe* replied. "When a *hasid* comes in, I first have to take off my coat and put on his to understand his problems. Then I need to take off his and put on mine to deliberate on a solution. Then I need to take off mine and put on his in order to formulate a response, and then I need to take off his and put on mine in order to deliver the advice."[40]

Charisma is the ability to speak the language of one's students – to answer their unspoken questions and to respond to their suppressed fears.[41] This demands that one intimately know his students' basic needs and world views. But the danger is that during this "descent" to the constricted perspective of the students, the teacher may actually begin to identify with it

---

[39] In another case, a social worker friend of mine, who had recently made *aliyyah*, saw a client who suffered from low self-confidence. In order to reduce the boy's feelings of intimidation and of incompetence, he created a therapeutic alliance, with a twist. He asked the boy to help him. My friend was still struggling to acquire his Hebrew language skills, and asked the boy to teach him a new word each time they met, and to correct him whenever he made a mistake. In this way, he helped transform the boy's self image. The boy now saw himself as capable of helping others and was therefore one step closer to attaining the confidence he needed to help himself. For a fascinating description of a curricular implementation of this approach, see Aronson, *Nobody Left to Hate*.

[40] I have been unable to locate the original source of this story. Zalman Shalomi alludes to it in his discussion of the rebbe's investment in his *hasid*. *Spiritual Intimacy: A Study of Counseling in Hasidism* (Northvale, NJ: Aronson, 1991), pp. 180–82.

[41] My friend and mentor R. Alan Stadtmauer is the source of this formulation.

and lose the crucial ability to return to his more enlightened state. Less common, but even more destructive, is the case of the teacher who possesses tremendous charisma precisely because he is, in many ways, no more enlightened or sophisticated than his students. In both these cases, the teacher is unable to guide his students on their journey of spiritual and emotional growth, and likely will cause them to remain entrenched in their current state. The Ba'al Shem Tov and his students describe the solution to this danger:

> "I (*anokhi*) will descend with you to Egypt, and I will surely raise you back up" (Gen. 46:4). *Anokhi*, which refers to the *Shekhinah* (Divine presence), is a ladder with its base fixed in the ground, and its top reaching the heavens.[42] An analogy that explains this image can be found in the holy *Zohar*: If a person descends into a pit, he must take with him a ladder, so that he may return and ascend. The meaning of this is that the *Shekhinah* is a ladder… Ya'akov was probably terrified of the descent to Egypt,[43] the deep pit, lest he be lost there forever, God forbid, without ever being able to ascend. His fear clearly reflected his inner fear of being stuck in the depths. When he attached himself to this basic inner fear, which is itself the *Shekhinah*, he found himself connected to God, Who said to him, "Do not fear, for I, who am the *Shekhinah*, will descend with you." In other words, your fear lest you [permanently] descend from your [enlightened] level, which in itself is the *Shekhinah*, will descend with you.[44]

According to the Ba'al Shem Tov, if one is to "descend," he must first construct a "ladder," a cognitive device that will allow him to return to his previous level after accomplishing the goal of the descent.

In the case of my student Mark, I faced difficulties in helping him deal with his problems because I failed to prepare a "ladder" back up to my own perspective before descending to his perspective. Instead of independently assessing his strengths and weaknesses, I assumed that his poor self-image reflected reality, and I, too, became convinced that he had no way out of his situation. Only after pulling back and realizing how inaccurate and un-

---

[42] The imagery is from Gen. 28:12.

[43] In Hasidic homiletics, Egypt is identified with a state of spiritual narrowness and obstruction, based on the Hebrew name "*mitzrayim*," homiletically read *metzarim*, narrow straits.

[44] *Ba`al Shem Tov al ha-Torah, Vayyigash* 3 (and note 6).

healthy his self-image was, was I able to descend once more and begin to help him deal with his situation.

An effective "descent" involves a double-mindedness on the part of the teacher. While constricting his mind to the level of the student, the teacher maintains a subtle consciousness of his own, more enlightened, perspective. Thus, like the *rebbe* who exhausts himself exchanging his "clothing" with that of his *hasid* (walking in another's shoes, as it were), he moves back and forth between his mature understanding of the situation and the more constricted views of the student. He may quickly pull back and analyze his own empathic understanding of the student from a more expansive point of view, and then return once more to the student, counseling him in language and concepts that he can understand.

Failure to build a "ladder" before the descent not only impedes the growth of students; it also can be severely damaging to the teacher. A few years ago I was invited to attend an event sponsored by Jewish Alcoholics and Chemical Dependents and Significant Others (JACS) as a rabbinic observer. I spent the entire time sitting in recovery group sessions and listening to life stories full of pain. In order to connect with the recovering addicts, I had to descend within myself and find places within my own personality that were potentially addictive. But I did not know that I had to build a ladder, a constant voice in the back of my head reminding me of my own personal strength and stability. For a week afterward, I struggled with an image of myself as a potential addict. I had so fully identified with them that I was momentarily unable to find my way back up.

V. Influencing Students' Views of
Their Relationships With Their Teachers

I heard from the *Maggid* who said in the name of our master and teacher Reb Dov, that at the time that he desired to leave the Ba'al Shem Tov, he would not consent to this, and would delay him for some amount of time. The *Maggid* asked him why he delayed him, and the Ba'al Shem Tov responded that his mind is like a gushing spring, and as people draw more and more water from it, the spring gushes more and more.[45]

A teacher's creativity depends on his relationship with his students. Anyone who has taught a class knows that teaching forces one to attain a level of clarity and depth of understanding rarely achieved when learning

---

[45] Introduction to *Ba`al Shem Tov al ha-Torah*, #11.

on one's own. There is, however, a more subtle but equally important point. The Ba'al Shem Tov deliberately set up a situation in which he would have to express his dependence on his student, Reb Dov. He wanted Reb Dov to recognize his own important role in the relationship. When a student realizes that he contributes to his teacher's learning, it enhances his own self-image and begins to shape his own internal self-image as a productive thinker.[46]

Conclusion

In the course of this essay we have seen that, in the eyes of *hasidut*, teachers are "gardeners in the garden of God," entrusted to nurture our students with love, charged with the task of bringing forth their unique beauty. Ultimately, our students will learn to become gardeners of their own, but each must first discover that he possesses a garden to tend. It is this awareness that we teachers should cultivate in our students – that they are people of value, that they are full of potential greatness, that they are loveable and capable of loving. To transmit this belief to our students, we must tend to a duty that is so often overlooked in the hustle and bustle of teaching – we must believe it ourselves.

Every teacher and every educational context differs from the next, and therefore it is up to the reader to determine how these ideas may best be implemented in his or her classroom. Some teaching environments lend themselves more readily to the cultivation of the types of relationships described in this paper. Most of the examples in this paper were culled from my own experiences living on the same campus as my students. I had the ability to cultivate closer relationships than would have been possible had I lived further away. But a teacher need not live with his or her students to develop deep connections with them. And even a teacher with very limited opportunities to interact informally with students can adopt and communicate the attitudes described here. Students certainly sense, from classroom exposure alone, whether their teacher values them and their ideas, whether

---

[46] A teacher of mine, R. Mordechai Machlis, refers to all of his students as his teachers. Whenever he speaks to a student, he asks what "teaching" he has to offer today. When he sees a student learning something from a *sefer*, R. Machlis asks him to teach him something from it. At first this is somewhat humorous to the students, but, over time, this role reversal has a significant impact on their own confidence, feeling of competence, and desire to learn Torah.

she has faith in their potential greatness. Ultimately, these attitudes may have the greatest impact on the growth of our students.[47]

[47] This essay is dedicated to my parents, Dr. Myron and Sandy Friedman, whose *ahavat Yisrael* and *ahavat ha-Torah*, expressed in their dedication to Jewish education, inspired my own love for learning and teaching Torah. Many friendships have had a direct impact on the ideas presented here. My deepest thanks to: R. Jeffrey Saks, Menachem Kallus, Uri Etigson, Roberta Sternthal, R. Mordechai Scher, R. Shalom Carmy, R. Alan Stadtmauer, R. David Ebner, R. Tzvi Blobstein, Yoel Finkelman, Dodi Tobin, Yael Unterman, and Dr. Claire Ellen Weinstein, all of whom had a role in shaping the content or form of this paper, as mentors, teachers, and friends. Finally, I wish to thank all of my students. "From my students most of all" (*Makkot* 10a) does not merely refer to informational knowledge, but to transformational awareness. This writing was an excellent opportunity for me to reflect back on my first years of intense involvement in teaching, and realize how deeply I have learned from my students.

EDUCATING FOR MENSCHLICHKEIT:
A KOHLBERGIAN MODEL FOR JEWISH DAY SCHOOLS

STEVE BAILEY

PARENTS IN THE DIASPORA, who are concerned about their children's proficiency in college-preparatory curricula but also are serious about their religious development in young adulthood, are willing to spend thousands of dollars a year sending their children to private Jewish high schools. In Israel, parents are willing to pay extra costs and to transport their children over long distances to give them the best general and religious education.

After four years, these parents expect that their children will have received a high-quality Jewish and general education and that these young graduates will be knowledgeable in Jewish texts and Jewish practices while being prepared for the *bagrut* (post-high-school examination) in Israel or to compete for acceptance into prestigious universities in the Diaspora.

But parents also expect that each child will graduate as a "*mensch*." They expect that their children's attitudes and behavior will reflect Jewish values such as honesty, respect, caring, truthfulness, tolerance, compassion and social sensitivity. The fact is, most graduates may achieve academic success and competence in basic knowledge and skills, but many still remain seriously lacking in moral maturity, both in universal ethics and Jewish values.

Indeed, both formal and informal observations of Diaspora Jewish schools have revealed significant evidence of cheating, plagiarizing, and lying throughout the high school years.[1] Israeli schools fare no better. Dis-

---

[1] A number of authors have addressed these issues, among them: Karen Green, "Towards Teaching Menschlichkeit," *The Melton Journal* 19 (1985): 30–32; Louis Nulman, "The Launching of the Middos Curriculum," in Kaminetsky and Freidman, eds., *Building Jewish Ethical Character* (New York: Fryer Foundation, 1975); Michael N. Menitoff, "A Comparative Study of Moral Development in Jewish Religious School Settings," *Dissertation Abstracts International* 35 (1974): 897A.

respectful language and disruptive behavior towards teachers, administrators, and peers are commonplace. Overall, there are manifestations of social insensitivity, intolerance of differences, and immature moral judgment.

Certainly many of these schools graduate students who are strongly identified with observant Jewish life, but even these graduates often fail to absorb Judaism's non-ritually based ethics and morals. Worse, many graduates reject, ignore, or simply fall away from traditional Jewish life; in their rejection, they often replace Jewish values with the secular cultural values of their contemporaries.

Ethical reasoning and behavior, integral to Jewish education, come from the transmission of values that strengthen the young adult's Jewish identity in coping with the moral dilemmas of everyday life and from a firm basis in Jewish literacy and ethical traditions. If a Jewish adolescent enters young adulthood as a college-bound, morally stunted individual, we, as Jews, are in trouble. Where will we get the next generation of knowledgeable identified Jews who reflect Jewish ethics in their university, professional, and personal lives?

Who has the primary responsibility to transmit values and literacy – the home or the school? I believe that the school is a key player in addressing the critical issue of moral education for the following three reasons.

First, although the ultimate responsibility for character development is with the parents, schools are in a better position to influence the developing child's moral qualities, since children spend most of their waking hours in school. Hundreds of moral dilemmas are evident in school life, and educators can use these opportunities to sensitize students to ethical decision making.

Second, administrators and teachers are the child's models for ethical thought and behavior, intentionally or unintentionally. How educators relate to the child daily becomes the real teaching tool for the child's moral sense. It does not matter what traits and values are taught verbally; a student learns what a student sees.

Finally, a school-based moral education program is comprehensive and, therefore, more effective. Periodic moral exhortations or sporadic social-caring activities, at home or at school, do little to affect the internalization of values and ethical behavior. It is the day-to-day, real-life experiences that a child integrates. Therefore, schools that incorporate formal and informal techniques of moral education that are omnipresent have a strong influence on moral development.

Even if one argues that the home has the ultimate responsibility and the long-term impact on a child's moral education, the school is in a unique position to shape, apply, and reinforce these Jewish values and behaviors on a daily basis.

I will argue that a school-based comprehensive program that satisfies these three criteria, is a Just Community – a model for moral education, based on the pioneering work of Lawrence Kohlberg.

Kohlberg's Model of Moral Development

In order to discuss moral development, we need to clarify some terms. In the psychology of moral development, the term "moral" refers to that which is ethically correct – choosing what is "right" – in situations that present a person with a choice between "right" and "wrong" alternatives. "Moral reasoning" refers to the developing cognitive ability of the child to recognize, define, and analyze a moral situation. Therefore, the general term, "moral development" refers to the psychological processes involved in the continuing development of moral reasoning as the child grows from infancy to adulthood. Finally, "moral maturity" refers to the child's ability to *choose* the "right" – or ethically correct – alternative, when presented with a moral dilemma, according to age-related expectations.

Of course, the basic question is: What is considered morally "right" and what is considered morally "wrong"? For our particular purposes, we can characterize the domain of morality as follows: In secular pluralistic societies the "right" or "wrong" is reflected in *universal* values that are considered rights or virtues (such as the right to life, freedom, dignity, equality, property; and virtues of honesty, integrity and loyalty), and in religious communities, "right" or "wrong" is reflected in religious values that *include* universal values, but are more particular (such as belief in a God, a specific code of good deeds and virtues, prayer, etc.). Jewish tradition also teaches values through Jewish law, which has its basis in the written law and the oral tradition (for example, mishnaic, aggadic and responsa literature).

Moral development in Jewish education, then, comprises the psychological processes that are involved in a child's developing sense of what is right or wrong – which lead to moral action – based on both universal ethics and our specific Jewish value system.

Kohlberg[2] formulated a typology of the development of moral thinking. The typology contains three hierarchical levels of moral reasoning[3] and two

---

[2] Lawrence Kohlberg, "Continuities in Childhood and Adult Moral Development Revisited," in Baltes & Schaie, eds., *Life-span Developmental Psychology* (New York: Academic Press, 1973), pp. 179–204. Born in 1927, Kohlberg became the pioneering psychologist in the field of moral education at Harvard University, applying Piaget's developmental approach to changes in moral reasoning. Having a Jewish father, he identified as Jew-

related stages within each level. These levels and stages represent developing moral philosophies, that is, distinct ways of viewing moral issues, which change as the child grows. It is important to note that these moral judgments do not reflect external standards learned from parents or teachers, but rather the child's own morality, reflecting his or her particular stage of moral reasoning. Also, the child does not necessarily advance in moral reasoning with age or logical reasoning; age provides the *capacity* to reason at higher levels, it does not *cause* the child to reason at higher levels. Finally, the levels and stages are hierarchical, meaning that a child has to pass through lower stages before arriving at higher stages. According to Kohlberg, a child's moral maturity can be raised by specific techniques.

The Kohlberg model is a justice-based hierarchy – the more "just" or "fair" the response, the higher the level of moral maturity. This basic assumption, however, was challenged by Carol Gilligan,[4] who argued that Kohlberg's hierarchy of moral maturity based on a justice-centered approach to moral education was erroneous, since it valued caring and empathy lower than reasoning based on justice. Gilligan argued that Kohlberg's hierarchy inherently biased moral maturity in favor of males, who typified the justice approach, and against females, who expressed caring and empathy as the preferred reasoning. Gilligan argued that children speak with different voices: one reflecting the principles of justice and another the dynamics of caring. Neither is better than the other, but they are different.

---

ish and did much early research on *kibbutzim* in Israel. (As a young sailor, he had smuggled Jews through the British blockade after World War II.) A good summary of Kohlberg's work applied to education can be found in Lisa Kuhmerker, *The Kohlberg Legacy for the Helping Professions* (Birmingham: Doxa Books, 1994).

[3] Kohlberg called the first level the preconventional; the second he called conventional, and the third he named the postconventional or autonomous. The preconventional level takes an egocentric perspective, typical of young children, where the child considers only his own experience of good or bad consequences of his behavior. The conventional level, found most often in school-aged children, focuses more on conformity to the expectations of the group, whether family, friends, school, or nation. The widened perspective includes not only conformity with the social norms, rules, and laws but also maintaining or justifying this order. Finally, the postconventional level, typical of older adolescents and many (though not all) adults, expands the moral perspective to autonomous moral principles that have validity beyond the authority of the group or society norms. Within each of the three levels are two stages that further refine the level's perspective. Kohlberg based his ideas on Dewey's original three levels of moral thinking; see John Dewey, *On Education: Selected Writings,* ed. R.D. Archambault (New York: Modern Library, 1964).

[4] Carol Gilligan, *In a Different Voice: Psychology Theory and Women's Development* (Cambridge: Harvard Univ. Press, 1985).

Although Gilligan's research method and conclusions have been seriously challenged,[5] a Jewish approach to moral education supports the notion that although the "right thing" in Jewish law is based predominantly on justice (*din*), it is sometimes pre-empted by the principle of caring (*rahamim*, or perhaps *lifnim mi-shurat ha-din*), espoused by Gilligan.

Kohlberg's Model in Education

Kohlberg began applying his moral development model to education nearly forty years ago. In a short time, however, he expanded his program to address issues of justice and democratic values. This led to the development of the "Just Community" approach that was designed to create a "moral school" as the context for individual moral development.

Kohlberg taught that teachers should be advocates of values and represent the spirit and traditions of the community. But at the same time he warned against indoctrination, so that power and authority had to be grounded in participatory democracy, which would represent a system of checks and balances to guard against the abuse of authority. He compared his stance of teachers as advocates to the Israeli *kibbutz* leader, the *madrikh*, who advocates for collective responsibility by the entire community. This type of community-value advocacy, thought Kohlberg, provided a strong impetus for the moral growth of individuals within the group. Moreover, advocacy whose purpose is to create group norms that appeal to the moral reasoning of the group differs from indoctrination, which reflects the *personal* authority of the teacher or administrator.

A Modified Kohlberg Model: The Just Community

As the result of his experiences in these schools, Kohlberg came to emphasize new aspects of moral education and modify some previously held notions.[6] Having worked with adults and adolescents, Kohlberg viewed adolescents, typically at the "conventional level" of moral development, as the key population to target for moral education. He wished to create a Just Community to initiate adolescents into a conventional moral system reflecting fairness, equality and community. Kohlberg learned from his *kibbutz* visit that respect for rules is not allegiance to arbitrary regulations promul-

---

[5] See, e.g., Lawrence J. Walker, "Sex Differences in the Development of Moral Reasoning: A Critical Review," *Child Development* 55:3 (June 1984): 677–691.

[6] Some relevant aspects of our summary are discussed in Jack Reimer, "The Just Community Approach: Democracy in a Communitarian Mode," in *Lawrence Kohlberg's Approach to Moral Education*, ed. Powers, et. al. (New York: Columbia Univ. Press, 1989).

gated by an authority, but can be seen as a respect for agreements that the members of the group make among themselves and with their leader.

Another related area of movement from theoretical to practical was Kohlberg's acknowledgement that the *content* of moral education could not be separated from the *form* of moral reasoning. In other words, although moral development was focused on *styles* of reasoning – not whether a position was "pro" or "con" a certain action – it became clear to Kohlberg that there was no way to introduce conventional morality without specific content relating to a moral code of behavior. Kohlberg realized that when dealing with real-life moral dilemmas, *what* is decided is important, not only *how* it is decided. This practical and important limitation to the pure democratic value of equality is a crucial element of a realistic Just Community program for Jewish schools that emphasize a specific moral code and behavior over thinking.

A final point to discuss is Kohlberg's concern about indoctrination. He was always opposed to indoctrinating students and considered it a violation of democratic values. But given his acknowledgement that teachers should advocate conventional values and the community should transmit its values, how does one protect against indoctrination?

What Kohlberg eventually argued for was a Just Community approach, which would insure against indoctrination by a democratic governance approach to rules and policies. This meant that the rules would not be *monolithically pre-established* by the educators with no participation from the school community; instead, the responsibility for the formulation and maintenance of the rules would be shared by educators and students. To be sure, the educators retain the responsibility for educationally sound policies, but educators would have to base their policies on reasons that students can understand and accept, with genuine permission for dissent. This balance permitted the teaching of specific moral content and moral action, but within a context that allowed for critical thinking, discussion and responsible resolutions. Thus, educators were advocates of rules and policies, not indoctrinators.

What we need to do next, before detailing the structure and techniques of the Just Community and its application to Jewish education, is to address the issue of Kohlberg's secular moral education model vis-à-vis the goals and ideals of Jewish education. If we are applying a secular moral education program to a Jewish educational setting, we need to ask: Are the two moral educational goals compatible or are they directed towards different, antithetical ends?

Can We Adapt Kohlberg's Secular Model to Jewish Education?

There is no question that the Kohlberg model of moral education has to be modified for its application to Jewish education. The Kohlberg model was designed to address a universal hierarchy of values, based on justice, as the core for secular moral education in the public education system. Kohlberg did not design his program to reflect a particular religious orientation nor did he concern himself with transmitting particularistic values of sub-cultures within a society. He wished to teach democratic values, civic duties, and universal ethics so that children will be more likely to become responsible, ethically sensitive citizens and thus contribute to the overall good of society.

Those of us involved in Jewish education have an additional agenda. Not only do we want our students to become ethically sensitive citizens who contribute to the good of society, we also want them to be good Jews who express Jewish values in their everyday lives, who aspire to meaningful Jewish observance and identity, who strive for the refinement of the spirit called *kedushah*, and who contribute to the good of the Jewish people. For these goals, we need to go beyond the Kohlbergian system to issues of moral imperatives and religious values.

The question is whether we can accomplish the goals of Jewish education through the techniques and structure of the Kohlbergian Just Community. It may be that the underlying philosophical assumptions of Kohlberg's system are antithetical to the goals of Jewish education and to integrate their purposes would be a futile attempt at synthesis.

A number of Jewish researchers see Kohlberg's approach as compatible with Jewish educational goals. Some have cogently argued that the cognitive-developmental approach to moral education is highly compatible with the aims of Jewish moral education. Kohlberg and Judaism alike are concerned, they say, with a comprehensive morality that reflects the supreme value of human life and the central importance of social justice. The Kohlbergian utopia of universal peace, freedom, and brotherhood is reflected in the Jewish notion of the Messianic era. Therefore, these researchers argue, cognitive-developmental methods based on Kohlbergian moral developmental stages can strengthen the students' commitment to the basic moral standards of Judaism. [7]

Others have analyzed the similarities and differences between Kohlberg's notion of ethics and justice and that of Judaism. They point out that

---

[7] Leon Rosenzweig, "Towards Universal Justice: Some Implications of Lawrence Kohlberg's Research for Jewish Education," *Religious Education* 72 (1977): 606–615.

Jewish ethics goes beyond Kohlberg's notion of justice as equity. In Judaism, there is the imperative to "go beyond the law" with respect to kindness and caring for the welfare of one's neighbor. There is also an inherent difference between a universal system of ethics and a particularistic religious system. Having said that, these writers acknowledge that Kohlberg has developed a structured system to transmit ethics and values in contemporary times that can serve the needs of Jewish education. This view concludes that if Kohlberg's system could be expanded to include benevolence, not only justice, as a universal ethic, Kohlberg's model would achieve basic compatibility with Jewish educational goals. [8]

It is interesting to note that, contemporary with the study just noted, there was a major movement in moral education to modify the Kohlbergian model along just these lines. Carol Gilligan and her colleagues, in observing the difference between male and female reasoning, show the presence of a "care-oriented" reasoning that goes beyond the justice orientation – beyond the letter of the law. This stress on empathy and caring has been further developed into a "responsibility orientation" that is quite similar to the positive Jewish ethical obligation to be responsible for one's fellow human being, even when not obligated by the law. Gilligan's development of Kohlberg's model to include caring as a value often on par with justice further enhances the compatibility between Kohlberg's universal ethics and Jewish values.

Responses to Critiques

In contrast to those seeing Kohlberg's approach as compatible with Jewish education, others have presented arguments for the inherent *incompatibility* of the Kohlbergian and Jewish goals of moral education.

Some have emphasized the differences between the philosophical directions of Jewish law and those of Kohlberg's moral autonomy. This argument is focused on the inconsistency in Jewish education between autonomous reasoning using humanistic, universal values and the heteronomy of Jewish law.[9]

---

[8] Shirley Koolyk, "A Comparison of the Underlying Philosophical Assumptions Concerning the Concept of Justice in Kohlberg's Theory with those of Jewish Ethical Theory from a Halakhik Perspective," *Dissertation Abstracts International* 39 (1978): 2813A.

[9] Israel Wharman, "Jewish Morality vs. Kohlberg Morality," *Journal of Psychology and Judaism* 8:1 (1983): 30–41. Some of Wahrman's assumptions about the nature of Jewish law have been critiqued in Gilbert Shoham, "On Jewish Morality vs. Kohlberg Morality," *Jewish Education* 53:1 (1985): 33–35. Other critiques can be found in Abraham

Others have been concerned about the overall educational utility of the Kohlberg model for Jewish education. While acknowledging some areas of consonance, they deem the two approaches incompatible. Because these general concerns reflect those of most educators, I will review the main critiques (paraphrased in italics) and show how the proposed Kohlbergian moral education project addresses them. [10]

First, the critics say, *Kohlberg's system is primarily concerned with thinking styles and reasoning about moral dilemmas, while Judaism is primarily concerned with moral action, irrespective of reasoning.* While admitting that Kohlberg is also concerned with moral behavior, the argument states that Kohlberg starts with patterns of thinking, while Judaism starts with behavior. This is correct, but it does not present an incompatibility with the proposed model. The problem we are addressing in effective moral education is how to get the student to internalize Jewish values so that he or she will use these values to choose the morally correct action. Kohlberg believes that reasoning is a necessary but not sufficient condition to bring about this dynamic. Traditional Jewish education also values reasoning (e.g., talmudic logic, halakhic inference and *ta'amei ha-mitzvot*) but relies heavily on the power of the halakhic imperative or the power of modeling oneself after morally ideal personalities (such as the forebears up to the great sages of today) for behavioral compliance. The fact is that in our pluralistic society, the latter strategies are often not effective motivators to assure the behavioral end, while the Kohlbergian approach has been shown, by research, to be an effective method to bring one to moral action – though not sufficient in itself.[11] Acknowledging this insufficiency, the proposed model does not rely exclusively on moral reasoning, but rather uses a variety of means, including the halakhic imperative, to affect moral action. However, like Kohlberg, it holds that moral reasoning is a necessary component of internalizing values.

The second critique posits: *In the Kohlberg system, autonomous moral principles (stage 5/6) are ranked higher than heteronomous values (stage 4), while in Judaism, God is the moral source, and compliance with the imperatives of Jewish law – (stage 4), rather than the autonomy of level 5/6, becomes the level of morality for which to strive.* This sticky philosophical issue was the subject of research showing that

---

Feder, "Kohlberg's Theory and the Religious Jew," *Religious Education* 79 (1984): 163–182.

[10] The position I am attempting to counter is put forth by Barry Chazan, "Jewish Education and Moral Development," in Munsey, ed., *Moral Development, Moral Education and Kohlberg* (Birmingham: Religious Education Press, 1980), pp. 298–325.

[11] Augusto Blasi, "Bridging Moral Cognition and Moral Action: A Critical Review of the Literature," *Psychological Bulletin* 88 (1980): 1–45.

freely choosing to comply with Jewish law actually is an expression of autonomy (stage 5/6) that superficially appears like heteronomy (stage 4).[12] The argument is made that, even according to Kohlberg, an autonomous, freely chosen commitment to Jewish observance ranks no lower on the hierarchy of values than autonomous principles. The key issue is not the behavioral compliance with rules per se, but the motivation and reasoning for the compliance. Be that as it may, the proposed system for Jewish education maintains the dominance of Jewish law in moral reasoning for Jews and in their practice; Kohlberg's universal ethical core values are consistent with the halakhic view of justice and righteousness.[13] Therefore, the expected incompatibilities present no actual problem for Jewish education. In the proposed model, Jewish law is inherent in the school's policy and not subject to majority vote. On the other hand, understanding of the halakhic moral issues and the reasoning of the *posekim* (legal decisors) are taught as part of the moral dilemma discussion technique.

The third potential conflict states: *For Kohlberg, moral traditions and literature are suggestive and are to be considered a means to an end; while for Judaism tradition is a valid compendium of the right way to behave.* As mentioned previously, Kohlberg modified his approach relative to the transmission of traditional values, thus eliminating the force of this criticism. Kohlberg would agree that in a Jewish school, Jewish traditions as a source of values *should* be transmitted and advocated by teachers and the school, as long as they reflected the community tradition and did not represent merely the personal agenda of the teacher.

The fourth critique argues similarly: *For Kohlberg, the content of the moral dilemma is only a tool, but for Judaism, the moral dilemmas in Tanakh and Talmud are valuable as part of the Torah curriculum, not primarily as instrumental pedagogic techniques.* This is somewhat of a straw man. Kohlberg would have no problem using curricular material that has its own pedagogic value as the basis for discussions of moral dilemmas. In fact, he advocates the use of real historical dilemmas taken from existing curricula in social studies, civics, history,

---

[12] Janet Gottlieb and Stephen Bailey, "Transpersonal Moral Reasoning: A Proposed Measure of Motivation Underlying Religious Commitment," *The Journal of Pastoral Counselling* 16 (1981): 39–46.

[13] The rare exceptions reflect those biblical cases of primacy of nation over the individual. Kohlberg once told me that he did not agree that the biblical injunction to obliterate Amalek was consistent with universal moral reasoning. For Judaism, however, obedience to a Divine command and the survival of the Jewish nation take precedence.

and literature. In a Jewish school, he would advocate the use of existing Judaic curricula as the source material for dilemma discussions.

Finally: *Classical Jewish education does not have a clear hierarchy of moral development like Kohlberg, but rather a conception closer to a social-psychological dynamic of the complex relationships between cognition, emotion, social context, norms, etc.* Here, again, Kohlberg moved away from his narrower cognitive conception to the model of the Just Community, which takes into account all the factors (and more) listed above. The proposed Just Community for Jewish schools, moreover, integrates Gilligan's modification of Kohlberg's "pure justice" system along the dimensions of "caring orientation" and "responsibility" motivations.

In sum, the critics posit that any attempt to "Judaize" Kohlberg or to "Kohlbergize" classical Jewish education is artificial and will be unsuccessful. Similarly, they predict that no accommodation can be made between Jewish education and Kohlberg's approach to moral education. I believe that my counterarguments show these predictions to be unfounded, and that the Just Community for Jewish schools presented here represents a way to successfully implement Kohlberg's theories within Jewish education.

Practical Concerns About a Jewish Moral Education Program

Over the years, other Jewish educators have asked less theoretical questions about applying Kohlberg's approach to Jewish education. They have seen the need for a moral education program in their schools, but have had practical concerns. Here are a few of their pointed questions (and my answers) regarding apparent conflicts between Kohlberg's approach and contemporary educational practices:

Question: In traditional Jewish education, the teacher, by virtue of being a teacher, is the authority to be respected and heeded by students. Indeed, day school students are taught from elementary grades that the *kavod* (respect) due to one's parents must be extended to one's teachers. Thus, the parent is the authority in the home and the teacher is the authority at school. Teaching moral and ethical behavior in Judaism is based, primarily, on the authority of the parent and teacher, as representatives of Jewish values, who define for the child/student the differences between ethical and unethical values as well as right and wrong behavior. To propose democratic, rather than authoritarian, methodology in moral education seems somewhat self-contradictory in the context of these traditional pedagogic concepts of moral instruction.

Answer: It may come as a surprise to learn that in a democratically based Just Community, the educators are still the authorities, as well as the guides, for ethical behavior. The critical difference is that in an authoritatively based school (in contrast to an authoritarian school), authority is a position *earned* through mutual respect, trust, and acknowledgement rather than assumed automatically by virtue of role. The value of democratic techniques in Jewish education is in the nature of this relationship of mutual respect and trust, and in its development and expression. A teacher who listens to the student, respects the student, models fairness and sensitivity in the classroom, and cares about the student's success not only will be respected by the student but will be seen by the student as a model of ethical behavior. Furthermore, by being worthy of respect, the teacher is allowing the student to fulfill his or her obligation of "*kibbud morim.*" Conversely, if the teacher is authoritarian, arbitrary, intolerant, and defensive, the students will respect neither the teacher nor the subject being taught, nor will they see the teacher as a model to emulate.

Question: It seems from the structure of the Just Community that the authority of the administration and faculty is compromised and that the school is run on the democratic vote of the majority in all areas, including curricula, pedagogic goals, government requirements, and halakhic policies. That would be an irresponsible way to run a school. Students, administrators, and teachers are not all equal and should not have an equal vote in running the school.

Answer: To consider teachers and students as voting equals, of course, would be absurd. Administrators and teachers are trained professionals in education, and students cannot be expected to have equal authority on issues of curriculum, measurement techniques, assignments, or the overall educational plan of the school. It is equally absurd to invite democratic majority vote on issues of halakhic parameters and required observance in a traditional Jewish school. Similarly, compliance with governmental rules for health and safety are the responsibility of the administration and staff.

Therefore, the pedagogic, civil, and halakhic areas of the Just Community are not subject to the democratic voting options applied to the democratic classroom or "Town Meetings." This definitive limitation is explained to students each year and is accepted by them as reasonable, fair, and required in a modern, Jewish, college-preparatory educational institution. What is offered in these areas, however, is an explanation and rationale for all school policies and for halakhic parameters, even though they are not subject to vote. This maintains the level of mutual respect and trust necessary for the success of a Just Community.

Question: In allowing moral dilemma discussions in which students express their notions of justice and "rightness," we will be setting up conflicts with Jewish law. Two problems emerge. First, we are teaching the students that they have a right to their personal opinion about issues where there are, in fact, halakhic rulings to which the school (and each observant Jew) is committed. Second, correct behavior (the system of *mitzvot*) is not dependent on reasoning; we need to behave ethically regardless of our opinion about the behavior or our understanding of the reasoning. By associating the reasoning with the behavior, we are giving the students the wrong message about the unconditional obligation of moral action.

Answer: In a Jewish school's Just Community, Jewish law and Jewish values remain authoritative. As stated above, a school's policy determines the halakhic parameters of the school and is not subject to majority vote, although administrators and teachers need to be open to questions and need to be prepared to explain the assumptions of the *halakhah*. The technique of frequent moral dilemma discussions allows students to think about and analyze issues related to moral conflicts, which then gives them the skills and motivation to think about ethical issues in their everyday life. During the discussions, they are never told that a particular analysis is the "correct one," although the discussion leader guides the session towards mature, principled reasoning. What is significant is that a formal moral dilemma is always followed by an halakhic analysis of the moral conflict, thereby validating the inherent system of fairness/justice within halakhic reasoning and providing practical guidance for the students' ethical behavior. The halakhic analyses, based on talmudic and other sources, including contemporary responsa literature, rarely conflict with most students' reflective moral reasoning. In practical life dilemmas, we have not encountered a conflict between mature moral reasoning and halakhic imperatives. The positive result is that students see how their own thinking is reflected in Jewish legal analysis, and they are more likely to internalize the value and use it to guide their thinking in the future. In rare cases where a student's well-analyzed, sensible moral reasoning is not compatible with the practical halakhic outcome, the student's position is acknowledged as reasonable but the halakhic decision takes precedence in practical application.

Question: For centuries Jewish educators have transmitted Jewish values through direct teaching of text and stories using Sages and other holy personalities as models. Moral education has often been taught through techniques borrowed or adapted from the *musar* movement. Why do we need a radical new approach?

Answer: The main reason for a new approach is the fact that children are being raised in a pluralistic society of religious, secular, and non-Jewish subcultures and anti-Jewish values. Suffice it to say that children who are raised to value democracy, fairness, and reason need an approach to ethics that reflects these ways of thinking. If we could rely on social conformity, unconditional acceptance of authority, and unquestioning beliefs, we indeed would not need to try something different to influence students' ethical development.

The Just Community Model for Jewish Day Schools

Now that we have established a theoretical and practical compatibility between Kohlberg's model of moral education and the goals and purposes of Jewish education, we can look at how this model would appear in a Jewish school.

The Just Community model has two major characteristics: A school-wide government called an Authoritative Democracy and specific components that reflect the goals of moral education.

The traditional authoritarian educational process seeks to transmit the knowledge and values deemed worthwhile by the community to the next generation. Its goal, in school government, is conformity, and it is preoccupied with maintaining order and control. Inevitably, the authoritarian bureaucracy dominates the school community by coercion and subjugates the students to its own goals of ideological and behavioral conformity. Equally inevitable is the hostile "us versus them" relationship between students and administration and the consequent resentment by students of the values imposed.

At the other end of the continuum is the democratic education process. On the positive side, all members of the school have rights, privileges, and responsibilities in a democratic governing system. Students are empowered with the inalienable rights to be heard, for their reasoned judgment needs to be taken seriously, and to be treated fairly and respectfully by administrators and teachers. All are equal partners in seeking how to deal creatively with contemporary life.

But here, too, there are fundamental weaknesses. Adolescents cannot be expected to have the reasoned judgment of mature adults and, therefore, cannot be seen as equal partners in the education dynamic. Adolescents often are creative and energetic, but also impulsive and insensitive. Moreover, adolescents are not professional educators and cannot be expected to govern their formal education effectively. Accordingly, a "pure" democracy, where administrators, faculty, and students have equal rights in all areas, is a naive educational structure. Nonetheless, empowering adolescents to actively participate in their education and affording them rights of fairness and respect are critical to an effective educational strategy.

The two strategies appear incompatible in their extreme forms, but, in fact, both contain elements of an ideal model for contemporary Jewish education. In our moral education project, let us call this third strategy, which synthesizes goals and techniques of both authoritarian and democratic governance, an "Authoritative Democracy." Such a government is democratic in that it accords students the right to be heard, takes account of their reasoned needs to be taken seriously, and acknowledges their inalienable right to be treated fairly and respectfully by administrators and teachers. But the school also seeks to transmit traditional Jewish community values and achieve a significant degree of conformity to religious norms. In effect, it is a democratic bureaucracy, which is *limited* in three areas, where exclusive authority is retained by administration and faculty. These are:

1. Pedagogic authority – The school must retain sole authority over curricular and pedagogic goals by virtue of the school's contract with parents to provide an education that is approved by the civil authorities and congruent with parental aims. Thus, curriculum and graduation requirements are determined by the administration and faculty.

2. Religious authority – Jewish schools retain the authority to legislate policy on practices as required by Jewish tradition and ethics (i.e., halakhah).

3. Health and safety authority – The administration retains the authority to adopt and carry out policies that comply with health and safety measures as promulgated by Federal and State laws.

Components of a Jewish Just Community

Aside from an authoritative democratic government, a Just Community contains seven basic components that encourage moral maturity.[14] The fol-

---

[14] In September 1992, an innovation in Jewish education was initiated with the establishment of Shalhevet High School in Los Angeles. The school was created as an experiment in moral education to address the problems described in this paper. The approach used was Kohlberg's Just Community (supplemented by Gilligan's emphasis on relationship and caring), modified for a Modern Orthodox school committed to *halakhah* and a *"Torah im derekh eretz"* educational philosophy. The school's founders and parent body agreed that this modified Kohlberg approach and methodology should be central to the new Shalhevet High School education program and I was appointed Educational Director to create and shape this experimental project.

After the first five years I conducted a follow-up study, using a structured five-point scale questionnaire, and the results were striking. Students had been sensitized to moral issues relating to school life, such as cheating, dishonesty, and deception – as negative values – and respect for people and property – as positive values. Through democratic classrooms, dilemma discussions, a Fairness Committee, Town Meetings,

lowing is a summary of the basic rationale for each of these components, as it relates to the theory and practice of the Just Community reviewed in previous sections.

1. Democratic Classrooms

The Just Community is an Authoritative Democracy. As such, it presents students with the opportunity for their reasonable needs to be heard and taken seriously, and to be treated respectfully and fairly. In no other place is this more critical than in the classroom. Teachers need to establish classroom policies as models of ethical reasoning and democratic values to the students.

There is also a need for clearly defined and equitable discipline policies that are consistently applied. The combination of fair classroom and discipline policies creates a Democratic Classroom that reflects the Just Community goal of an ethical system representing democratic values of mutual rights and responsibilities.

From the students' side, students in a Democratic Classroom learn to take the perspective of the teacher, to balance her needs and theirs, to develop a sense of trust, to propose their own solutions, and to become sensitized to personal responsibility.

The policies cover as many areas of classroom procedures as possible, relevant to the particular course. Although it may appear overly detailed, greater detail makes misunderstanding and debate less likely in the future.

The policies cover both the responsibilities of the student and the responsibilities of the teacher. Just as students are to come prepared and on time, so are teachers. *Both* expectations are presented in the written policies. This written form is presented to the class for open and serious discussion. The teacher presents a rationale for each of the policies based on fairness and mutual rights and responsibilities, and students can comment, respectfully, on those policies they see as unfair, providing reasonable justification for their views. The teacher and students work on modifying policies that need modification and, by the end of the discussion, policies need to be accepted by all parties.

---

and community service, students had learned to articulate their opinions in a constructive manner, to respect the opinions of others, to be tolerant of differences, to show sensitivity and caring, to appreciate democratic values, and to develop critical thinking skills. Moreover, the methodology enhanced the excitement and involvement in classroom activity, as well as strong positive ties to the faculty and school community. We are awaiting a further five-year follow-up before publishing the longitudinal study. See Steve Bailey, "Democratic Techniques in an Orthodox High School," *Ten Da'at* 8:1 (1995): 35–37.

2. Moral Dilemma Discussions

The pioneering work of Moshe Blatt demonstrated that moral dilemma discussions in a classroom resulted in elevating the moral reasoning stage of the student. This technique has remained a cornerstone of programs aimed at raising the moral maturity of students.[15]

For example, students are presented with a story of "Sharon" and "Jill." Sharon shoplifts and leaves the store, while Jill is stopped by the manager and told to tell him Jill's name and address. The dilemma is: should Jill "give up" her best friend? Why or why not? The conflict of values for the high school student is "ratting" on your best friend versus responsibility to the law. Students participate in debating and challenging each other (which sensitizes them to moral issues) and no conclusion is offered. At the next meeting, the teacher presents Jewish sources that address this issue, and after the class is taught these values, a conclusion – from a Jewish perspective – is drawn. The process of dilemma discussions, presented according to researched techniques, serves to spur more mature moral reasoning and also serves to demonstrate the sources of halakhic reasoning. Students find reflected in Jewish law the mature reasoning they, themselves, generated.[16]

3. Town Meeting

We have noted that an effective moral education program requires an active, comprehensive approach to fairness, respect, and the democratic values of privileges and responsibilities in all aspects of school life. As an integral part of an Authoritative Democracy, students need to be given a chance to participate in their own educational experience by being given the opportunity to be heard and to participate in the development and maintenance of school policies.

Past experience has shown that since students are involved in rule making, there is an increased probability students will accept the responsibility

---

[15] Moshe Blatt and Lawrence Kohlberg, "The Effects of Classroom Moral Discussion on Children's Moral Judgment," *Journal of Moral Education* 4 (1975): 129–161. Aside from moral reasoning development, there are at least five other important goals of this technique, as noted by the staff of the Civic Education Project at Carnegie-Mellon University, in their workshop manual: Sam Gomberg, *Leading Dilemma Discussions: A Workshop* (Pittsburgh: Carnegie-Mellon Univ., 1980).

[16] Of course, there are students who disagree with the more mature reasoning or the halakhic reasoning, but the teacher has successfully demonstrated to the class that the *halakhah* is based on justice/caring and that the *halakhah* is the determinant of actual behavior. Eventually most dissenting students modify their immature reasoning in subsequent discussions. That is growth towards moral maturity.

to maintain the rules. Teachers and administrators have an equal right to have their views known and explained to the whole student body. Therefore, a bi-weekly Town Meeting is the setting in which students, administrators, and teachers discuss and work through school policies. Such open discussion teaches skills of listening, articulating, evaluating, tolerating, and respecting different views; analyzing conflicts of values; and balancing competing needs of justice and caring. Like moral dilemmas, these meetings are aimed at increasing moral maturity and social sensitivity as well as generating an appreciation of democratic values of a community.

An actual example of a challenging Town Meeting issue arose when some male students wanted to change the dress code policy to allow wearing baseball caps instead of *kippot* in school. Since this was not an halakhic issue, per se, it was allowable for democratic vote. The administration argued issues of the image of the school in the community and the secular "message" caps sent in an Orthodox Jewish school. The group of students who proposed it argued for freedom of expression and individuality. The administration's view persuaded the majority of students that the issue was the good of a few individuals versus the good of the school and the motion was defeated. However, had it been passed, the school would have adopted it. This is the risk that comes with democracy. But the values of respect and responsibility had been developed in the student body and they had acted responsibly; that is the ultimate payoff.

4. Fairness Committee

Typically, a student feels powerless when treated unfairly in school. Perhaps the student was excluded from a club unfairly or felt discriminated against by a teacher or administrator. There is no course of appeal, no action to be taken. This powerlessness often leads students to act out in nonconstructive ways like cutting class, acting disrespectfully to others, or damaging school property.

The purpose of the Fairness Committee, comprising student, teacher, and administrative representatives, is to deal with problems of fairness that arise among students, between teacher and student, and between administration and student. The teacher and student have equal rights to respect and fairness. In this context, fairness means that both parties have a right to have their needs balanced so that both sides can accept a resolution.

While the Fairness Committee should be viewed as a conflict negotiation agency – not a court – it has the power to recommend to the Principal a particular resolution by which the parties agree to be bound. One important by-product of the Committee is that students learn principles of the

Jewish system of justice through the participation of a rabbinical member of the Committee. Since the Committee is not a court, the rabbi does not decide the specific outcome, but he contributes to the discussion using Jewish law as guidance for evaluating the case.

An illustration of this committee's function involved a teacher who had made a student clean up the litter in an entire classroom after the student had not put his own litter in a trash can. The policy stated that a teacher can compel a student to clean up his or her own litter, but made no mention of additional punishment. The student appealed to the committee, stating that he had cleaned up his own litter but was not required clean up the room. The teacher argued that he had a right to teach the student a lesson. The committee found in favor of the student because of the written policy, which binds all members of the school community equally. This demonstration of fairness was quite impressive to the student body.[17]

5. Effective Discipline Policies

In a Just Community, a great deal of time and energy is spent on developing fair and equitable policies in the Democratic Classroom and formulating school-wide policies at Town Meetings. Also, the entire rationale for a Fairness Committee is to ensure that all members of the Just Community are treated fairly. Therefore, a lack of follow-through on agreed upon rules and regulations represents a violation of respect, fairness, and responsibility, the foundation of the entire moral education project.

In the adolescent's natural need for autonomy, it is predictable that some will try to ignore, disregard, blatantly violate, or subtlety circumvent rules. On the other hand, it is equally innate for an adolescent to seek structure from a consistent, predictable environment. Both these realities support the critical need for clear, descriptive behavioral expectations for all members of the Just Community and equally clear consequences for violations of these expectations. More importantly, the policies were made with the participation of students, and they accepted the responsibility to uphold the agreed-upon rules. Students quickly lose respect for a teacher or administrator who cannot enforce policies, and the entire message of the Just Community is undermined by allowing students, teachers, or administrators to abdicate their responsibility to maintain social order in the school as defined by school or classroom policies. While it is true that enforcing school

---

[17] It should be noted that there are few actual cases that make it to the Committee. Most are mediated between the parties informally. But the fact that there is a mechanism for student appeal has a positive effect on student morale.

rules takes a tremendous amount of time and energy, it is energy well spent in a school that teaches Just Community values.

6. Community Service

A key goal of the Just Community project is the integration of mature ethical reasoning, which will lead to morally mature, ethical behavior. Aside from the expectation of ethical behavior in school, there is an expectation of ethical behavior out of school as well – at home and in the community. This is consistent with the goal of generalizing students' moral maturity to new situations.

An excellent opportunity for behavior reflecting social sensitivity, caring, and ethical behavior is in volunteer work for community agencies serving the needy.

For example, students visited homes for the elderly on a weekly basis and each student developed a personal relationship with one resident. This went on through the school year and included singing programs for holidays, gifts, and cards. Students reported their experiences to the class at the end of the year. By devoting a reasonable amount of time consistently throughout the year, students experienced the satisfaction of actually serving others in concrete, practical ways. Such programs also instill responsibility, reliability, and trustworthiness, because the students' participation in the program is taken seriously by the school and the student has to keep time schedules and records and establish a responsible relationship with the agency being served.

7. Parent Training Workshops

Research in the Just Community has underscored the need for parents to be actively involved and personally invested in their children's education. In a Just Community, the responsibility is two-fold: to support and motivate the child's serious academic study and to promote the school's goals of democratic and Jewish values and ethical behavior.

Aside from supporting the goals of the school, an important rationale for parents to be trained in moral development techniques is that the dynamic of moral maturity evident in the school needs to be generalized to the home. We want students to behave respectfully towards their parents as they are expected to behave towards their teachers. We want parents to treat their adolescents with respect and fairness just as we ask of our teachers and administrators. We want to teach parents to communicate more effectively with their children, just as we want teachers to communicate effectively with their students. We want there to be fair discipline policies in the home just as there should be in school. A healthy environment that supports adolescents' psychological, academic and moral growth in school should be evident at home as well.

To those ends, typical topics for Parent Training Workshops were: "Helping Your Child Become a *Mensch*," which concentrated on what parents can do to develop their child's ability to make the "right" decisions when confronted with a moral dilemma, and "Dealing Effectively With Your Child," which focused on what parents can do to develop effective communication with their adolescents and carry out discipline policies that work. Parents learned how to listen, how to be assertive, how to be clear and unequivocal, and how to develop on ongoing trusting and respectful relationship with their children.

The Challenge

Part of the failure of contemporary schools to transmit Jewish values is related to the obsolete educational philosophies of administration and faculty. In the past, where community norms reinforced the absolute power of the teacher and respect was expected regardless of whether it was deserved, the school could obtain behavioral compliance from students out of respect for authority or threat of embarrassment to parents. In democratically conscious, pluralistic educational systems, however, respect and submission to authority is no longer absolute. We may prefer the educational norms of the past, but we need to acknowledge the realities of contemporary education.

Students are aware of their right to be treated fairly and respectfully, and they recognize that respect has to be earned by teachers and administrators, rather than demanded. This reality requires schools to rethink their administrative policies that attempt to control its students by power.

Ethical reasoning and behavior are integral to Jewish education. As Jewish educators, it is our responsibility to inculcate knowledge of Jewish values as the bases for students' behavioral choices and to develop the motivation and skill for integrating these values and acting on moral dilemmas in everyday life.

The challenge is to create a school community, within the confines of a pluralistic society, that is designed to influence the moral development and ethical behavior of its students such that they are more likely to integrate Judaism and Jewish moral values into their everyday lives, in and out of school. Such a program would have to incorporate those adolescent psychological processes and educational factors that are known to influence moral development and behavior while also initiating effective means of transmitting Jewish values as the content of the ethical structure. Research and personal experience suggest that Kohlberg's Just Community and its seven components, modified to reflect the Jewish values we aspire to pass on to our children, offers the most promising model for achieving those goals.

"IF YOU SEEK HIM WITH ALL YOUR HEART": NURTURING TOTAL INDIVIDUAL GROWTH IN YESHIVAH

Yael Unterman

"WHEN I WAS NINE, I was the king of the playground," he told me. "I ran, I played soccer. I wanted to be a prophet when I grew up. But now… I just *schlep* myself around. There's something empty inside." One would not know it to look at him; this was no dropout but, on the contrary, an exemplar of the best and brightest of Modern Orthodox Judaism. He spent years in an elite yeshivah and was now a Torah educator, inspiring students and enriching their lives. Yet his own life seemed so impoverished. I sadly asked myself what had caused the lively, deeply religious little boy to become this disheartened man.

If we are to believe his own analysis, part of the blame lay with his yeshivah experience. He had gained a great deal there, yet also lost so much when it damaged the very things it should have nurtured: his joy at being alive, his sense of wholeness and of a living spirituality at his core. To his amazement, I then told him of a few other acquaintances who harbored such an enduring resentment against their various yeshivahs that years later they set up "The Society for Casualties of the Yeshivah System." My acquaintance asked for their contact details and an ad hoc support group appeared to be in the making.

I must confess that I identify with this group. My years in yeshivah left much to be desired. To illustrate: my father, visiting me in yeshivah, was told by a certain teacher that I was an "undisciplined student"; agitated and aggrieved, with my self-image as an excellent student undermined, I debated what might have elicited this comment. Lacking the courage to simply ask the teacher, the best theory I could produce was that I had been asking too many philosophical questions in class that were off the topic. Admittedly, looking back now from an educator's perspective, I can see that for a teacher who is attempting to teach methodically it is bothersome to be sidetracked into discussing tangential truth/faith issues. Still, the fact is that following a *haredi* high school experience where I was reprimanded, "Those questions you're asking sow seeds of doubt in other people's minds," I had chosen to attend this particular yeshivah precisely so that I could finally discuss my questions with inspiring and mature mentors. Imagine my disappointment upon realizing that here, too, there was no time to ask the larger questions – they somehow appeared to be permanently tangential. Accordingly, loath to detain busy teachers in their free time, I awkwardly chose to bring up my unresolved issues in classes devoted to other topics, an "undisciplined" choice.

Alas, no teacher picked up on my confusion during my two years there. While I learned much excellent Torah in yeshivah, my overall experience was of overwhelming inner turbulence, isolated except for a few like-minded peers. My learning succeeded only in scratching the surface of what I needed, which was assistance in forming and bolstering my inner world. To pursue this need, and in an atmosphere of acceptance and nonjudgmentalism, I was later forced to turn to primarily nonreligious resources that lacked my religious outlook. The successful integration of the language of my inner world with that of Torah seemed to take place only in a very few fringe frameworks, many of them for *ba'alei teshuvah* – not a category I belonged to, for better or worse.

To readers of these words – rabbis, educators, parents and students – I wish humbly (and, I hope, without too much judgmentalism, although criticism is an inevitable precursor to change) to suggest that *something* was askew in the world of advanced Torah education as I experienced it. What my friend and I of diverse backgrounds – he an Israeli man, I a British woman, having attended different institutions – had in common was a yeshivah faculty who let us down in some way. They taught us much Torah and skills, but did not sufficiently help prepare us for our own lives; and thus several years down the line we found ourselves still in a state of confusion instead of maximizing our personal potential and thereby our contribution to the Jewish people and the world.

Although I have been told that changes have taken place in the institution I attended, I wonder if they are sufficiently far-reaching. I'm sure there have been many educational discussions on topics connected to mine, but I've never seen it explicitly addressed. What follows therefore is a formulation of the issues, together with some concrete suggestions – both fruit of many years of reflection and conversations with others who similarly attended large, well-known yeshivahs and were disappointed. The histories and personalities of these ex-students vary, but all are intelligent, spiritual and sensitive. Interestingly enough, several are now Jewish educators. Not surprisingly, they aim to be a different kind of teacher from the ones they encountered; and their students' gratitude and appreciation indicate that this choice was a wise one.

I am grateful for the opportunity to articulate my suggestions in this forum and hope that others will in turn propose improvements enabling the yeshivah to answer the deepest needs of its student population – a challenge I believe it can and should meet.[1]

The Root of the Problem

First, we must reexamine the goals of the yeshivah. The most observable objective of the Orthodox yeshivah – "learning Torah" – conceals a broad range of goals, one of which is socialization, i.e., molding the student in accordance with a desired social model.

In general, each yeshivah needs to be very aware of the model it promotes, whether subtly or explicitly. A female friend observed that several of her male acquaintances emerged from yeshivah with flat personalities and no emotional skills, having acquired chauvinistic opinions and a regrettable habit of arguing opinionatedly. In a different vein, others have contended that socialization to be "yeshivish" leaves students without sufficient learning skills.[2]

My suggestion, though, is that socialization of any kind may have detrimental results. A set of uniform societal values may harm a student's spiritual life (both at the time and later) because, being generalized, it overlooks individual needs. True, yeshivahs are not different in this from many other institutions, which, dedicated by nature to general goals, require the individual to deal independently with matters beyond their bounds. But this is simply not good enough. Even if the university, dedicated as it is to inculcation of knowledge, has become "a lonely, fragmented, and anxiety-ridden

---

[1] When I use the term "yeshivah" in this essay, I intend to refer to one-year and multi-year programs, men's and women's institutions alike; some of the suggestions are even applicable to yeshivah high schools. Obviously, the scores of institutions for higher Torah study (both in Israel and abroad) vary as greatly from one another as do the students they serve. Out of necessity, I have stated my argument with a certain degree of generalization, which may belie the realities of particular institutions. I feel it necessary to also declare that although I am putting forth a critique of the *yeshivot* (broadly defined), I would be remiss in not recognize the ongoing accomplishment of those *yeshivot*, and the educators teaching within them. On the contrary, it is out of conviction as to the ongoing potential of yeshivah study that I offer my observations.

[2] See, e.g., Yoel Finkelman's essay in this volume.

place for both faculty and students,"[3] the yeshivah is not the university, and its goals must reach beyond transmitting knowledge or shaping communities. It must be that rare environment devoted to finely tuned nurturing of the individual and the subtle processes of heart and soul; otherwise we will have students defecting to a place that *is* such an environment.

Therefore, I suggest we add a new set of goals for the yeshivah, including developing a personal relationship with God, finding one's own unique path in Torah, and nurturing spiritual completeness. Let us help students develop intrapersonal intelligence and self-awareness, so they can take steps towards balance and growth. While continuing to (carefully) inculcate our Jewish values and norms, let us simultaneously teach our students that norms are only the basis, only broad strokes of paint that do not exempt them from creating their own masterpiece on the canvas of life. Rabbi Tzadok ha-Kohen notes that each person is particularly connected to a letter of the Torah that is the root of his soul.[4] Let us teach our students to find their own letters, not ours; to be industrious in nurturing their unique selves; and to constantly strive to distinguish what "resonates" in them in whatever they learn from us, by asking them, "How is what we just learned relevant to *you?*" The resulting well-deliberated Jewish identity will serve them better in the future than would wholesale norms adopted through imitation.[5]

Rebellion and Seeking

In today's world of endless lifestyle options, people increasingly do not follow their community identity automatically; rather, they often undergo a drawn-out process of trial and error in identity formation before settling down. In the Orthodox world, as elsewhere, many teenagers and young adults find parents and religious educators unprepared for such turbulent processes. This leaves both sides feeling alienated, and some teenagers who

---

[3] Susan Handelman, "Dear Class," in S. Seldon & J. Greenberg, eds., *Essays on Quality Learning: Teachers' Reflections on Classroom Practice* (College Park, MD: Univ. of Maryland Press, 1998), p. 18. While this was said of the "large State University," and a smaller program may reduce loneliness, ultimately it is not the size but the *quality* of the attention that counts.

[4] See, e.g., *Tzidkat ha-Tzaddik*, p. 114.

[5] I am impressed by the mature identity of some "rebellious" students I have taught, who, having subjected their Jewish identities to constant criticism, understand them far better than many mainstream students do.

"act out"[6] through rebellious behaviors have therefore been labeled "at-risk." The destructive nature of these activities has finally attracted the Orthodox community's attention to this population within its bastions, and this is a positive step. Left unspoken of, however, is the existence of a second group at risk: those who also feel lost, but, because they are more refined, introverted or simply afraid, keep it bottled up deep inside. There it progressively eats away at them; and some are only vaguely aware of these feelings until they burst violently through into consciousness and wreak havoc.

In order to find solutions to the entire "at-risk" population – solutions that are not just reactive but preventative, attacking the root and not just the symptoms and, most importantly, attending to stresses below the surface too, we should closely examine what causes these feelings of alienation. I contend that when sensitive, reflective personalities begin a complicated journey of personal and religious *seeking* (a term I will use to cover the act of intensely questioning and searching, unwilling to put up with half-truths or with other people's choices) and in this vulnerable state encounter a restrictive and uncaring environment with insufficient space and support for such processes – the result is anguish, grief, and hatred of self and others.

This is the root of the alienation, an environment that is *emotionally* defective even if it is intellectually excellent. A Hasidic master warned long ago that an imbalance of the intellectual and emotional faculties in religious life will leave a vacuum that will force the soul to search for emotion anywhere, even in sinful behavior.[7] These young seekers do not want to be deliberately self-destructive; they simply wish to explore all facets of their identities, and their nonconformist behavior is possibly the healthiest response to a suppressive environment, indicating autonomy, authenticity and active control. I must stress how important this point is. A person who continues to be passively molded runs a risk of becoming depressed, paralyzed, or – God forbid – suicidal.

To any argument that these seekers are just a few overcomplicated students who are not worth our effort, I would first remind us that the Hazon Ish forbade yeshivahs to give up on any student, ordering the *Rosh Yeshivah*

---

[6] I doubt this explains all of this extreme behavior – some of it probably reflects an immature addiction to thrills. But in my experience, some of these rebels feel deeply misunderstood, confused and insecure.

[7] R. Klonymous Kalman Shapira, *Tzav ve-Ziruz*, chap. 9.

himself to learn with difficult students.[8] Having established this, I would further make a two-fold reply to such a contention. On the one hand, even if it is correct that they are fewer in number, such students have the potential for greatness. They are often the deepest, most original, sensitive and truth seeking, and if we can only keep them within the fold, they will provide sorely needed imaginative leadership for our communities. From Abraham, through Moses, David and R. Akiva, our greatest heroes have lived lives of change and truth seeking, rejecting norms presented by their respective environments; and given Judaism's emphasis on veracity, critical thought, self-awareness and growth, I view seeking as a very Jewish activity.[9] What is seeking if not acquiring knowledge as the Torah understands it: the Hebrew root *y-d-'* means not only to know, but also "to be in intimate relationship with" – the knowledge of experience, of the heart.

If the foregoing contention is, as I believe, incorrect, then adjusting somewhat our educational approaches may indeed benefit numerous students – including those who appear to be making reasonable progress, but in reality are not nourishing their inner worlds, just adapting well. Years later, some crisis or other event may trigger these students to reevaluate what they have been taught: middle-aged Orthodox Jews suddenly asking themselves who they really are, and discovering dreams or selves buried underneath piles of stale teachings. The danger is that they will look back at the yeshivah as the place where, their needs pushed aside, they were molded to fit someone else's agenda.

A few changes would thus make the yeshivah more effective for certain students in the long term and might alleviate some of the most destructive behaviors, as we grant the wildest rebels greater understanding. Understanding is not synonymous with condoning, and this is not a call to abandon discipline, but to help students re-channel energies.

Some *yeshivot* have already implemented these educational shifts, but they tend to be aimed at students on the periphery; I believe the methods need to be brought into the mainstream.[10] Having put forward my thesis,

---

[8] See, e.g., Zvi Yabron, "The Chazon Ish *zt"l* on the Educator's Responsibility to the Weak and Wayward Student," *Jewish Observer* 32:2 (November 1999).

[9] This may explain the disproportional number of Jews to be found trying out all sorts of odd cults and ideologies.

[10] I myself taught for four years on the faculty of one such institution and was privileged to personally witness the beneficial results. My constant thought there was "I wish I had had this kind of approach in my own yeshivah – I would have flourished." Less-religious teens and *ba`alei teshuvah* are also often treated to more open approaches, but there is also a growing movement of educators who challenge the assumption that only students of "irregular background" deserve such attention.

the following is a more detailed outline of possible improvements, any one of which would be a step in the right direction.

The Necessary Milieu

The ideal atmosphere for total individual growth in the yeshivah would begin with encouraging intellectual analysis and openness, while simultaneously providing quality emotional-spiritual content. To my regret, there seems to be a split between "intellectual" and "spiritual" yeshivahs, as if an intellectual person cannot have deep spiritual needs or spiritually must be simplistic. It is really only in studying selected spiritually sophisticated Hasidic texts that I have had both needs met simultaneously. Psychological counseling should also be available for students according to need. While a good start, even these realms must be refined in order for them to truly support seeking. For example, an atmosphere of intellectual openness, while highly commendable for the autonomy it grants in enabling the student to evaluate diverse Jewish philosophies and lifestyles, must be accompanied by active support for students confused by so many choices, so that they can work out what path is best for them personally. Similarly, while lessons of an unabashedly spiritual-emotional nature are crucial to a deeper spiritual life, there is a risk of teaching this material in a global fashion verging on indoctrination, as if all souls function in exactly the same way. Instead, individual differences need to be addressed, so that the student can gradually learn to recognize his or her own spiritual make-up and act accordingly. Lastly, the yeshivah cannot cast the burden of the student's inner spiritual turbulence onto the psychologist. Searching for truth is not a sign of mental illness but of mental health – and woe to us if we think otherwise. The therapist's role is only an initial one, to eliminate overwhelming emotional issues such as low self-esteem, depression, rage, and so forth, which deafen the student to the delicate inner notes that are his or her particular melody.

Who is Responsible for Addressing "Seeking"?

If the burden for individual spiritual growth cannot be passed on to psychologists, who then will assume it? In some yeshivahs there is a *mashgiah/mashgihah ruhani/t,* and if this figure is a sensitive, wise and comfortable address for "shocking" material, he or she may be very helpful to students (providing that his or her role is not merely a disciplinarian to enforce observance). A second figure, the youthful *rakkaz* or *rakkezet* (coordinator) or counselor, can also have a deep impact. One ex-student, today an educator herself, reports finding the yeshivah staff "frightening" but says of the intimate learning sessions with the *rakkezet* that "our weekly hour was the center of my development."

Now granted, even one figure who is accessible and who maximizes the use of emotional-spiritual intelligence can be a saving grace when the rest of the faculty is overly intellectual and distant, but this is certainly not optimal. First of all, some institutions have no *mashgiah* or *rakkezet*. Second, students need a choice, since the chemistry for a deep bond may simply be lacking with one person, however fine. Third, and most important, how does this leave the student feeling about the teachers and the Torah they represent? The Torah will become equated with lofty inaccessibility rather than with human warmth and communication. Certainly we would prefer the students to say, "At the center of my development was what I received from *the teachers*."

While many students do say such things, my impression is that many others do not. The head of a well-known Jewish learning institution in Jerusalem once asked me to name on the spot my two most influential Jewish teachers. When I replied that I could not name one, he informed me that this challenge, put by him to assorted Jewish educators, was met surprisingly often with this answer.[11]

Having myself had many dedicated, knowledgeable teachers (and even some brilliant and charismatic ones), it puzzles me how they and others could have failed to have a major impact on education-oriented students. I can only reiterate the above, and guess that the fault lies in neglecting the students' personal paths and deepest concerns.

Yeshivah students, having recently left home (itself not always such a supportive environment) are at a taxing stage of their lives, deciding what kind of people they want to be. Even if they do end up coming out of the yeshivah looking, talking, or even thinking like "good Jews" – and many do make drastic changes after being exposed to the yeshivah model – it would be irresponsible, not to mention naïve, for the faculty to pat themselves on the back and move on, without knowing each individual well.

Indeed, unless someone has accompanied the student throughout the year, discussing both current issues and future plans in depth, the seemingly strong religious identity may prove to be an illusion – resting on a rickety base of conformity to teachers or peers, which will collapse in a less religious environment (and sometimes even in a religious one). The key to a long-term effect on thinking students is what they internalized and were

---

[11] He noted that this was especially true of women. Perhaps men are more satisfied and impressed with intellectual brilliance, even without a personal connection.

transformed by during the year. Charismatic lecturing, constant repetition of the same messages, and even teaching information, skills, and habits – although essential for Torah education – are insufficient when not supplemented by a nurturing approach to seeking. It is those teachings directly relevant to the students' deep questions (and also those that evoke new questioning) together with the teachers' caring, open, and insightful support of the student's growth at his or her own pace that will do most to further anyone who is at all a seeker.

Teachers thus need to set their criteria for success higher, aiming to leave a lasting impression on the students. The following three suggestions may facilitate this aim: (1) outside the classroom, engage in caring, personal dialogue with students; (2) in class, introduce topics relevant to their current concerns and create group dialogue; (3) in both settings, provide a role model of courageous and dynamic religious process.

Outside the Classroom: Personal Engagement

Yeshivah educators are generally hired on the basis of their Jewish knowledge, teaching ability, and suitability as role models. It is not as clear if the yeshivah adequately weighs how much a teacher cares about, understands, and identifies with students. I hope that teachers do so, and I hope that this is a priority for administrations, but this entire dimension needs to be made an explicit part of the educational agenda. Teachers should not just teach and leave; they should be available for the specific purpose of personal conversation during the week. This costs more, but the truth is that a genuinely personal atmosphere in yeshivah is not a question of budget but of attitude – quality, not quantity. It begins with the *Rosh Yeshivah*, who can set a personal example of warmth, attention, openheartedness, and humility towards the administration and teachers. They, in turn, should be encouraged to relate to one another and to students in this way, so that any time spent with students can become quality time, involving genuine listening, respect for the student's perspective, and caring. If, rather than only noticing students who waylay them, teachers devote even a small amount of weekly thought to every student, they will know better what words to say to him or her, both in personal encounters and in the class setting.

The Role of Crisis

The strongest internalization of all occurs when someone goes through rough patches emotionally. We educators pass up many golden opportunities to have a positive impact on the students; every problem is a potential

Torah breakthrough, if we can only make it so. To do this, we need initially to listen to the student and validate the problem and only then give our advice, sympathetically. I believe, however, that the greatest impact comes when we are willing to divulge to students similar struggles of our own, and tell them how being a Jew grounded in Torah enriched us in those dark places. Certainly this has to be done with delicacy and caution, without overstepping important boundaries, but it is worth the trouble; when we create a direct channel from our individuality to theirs, students will never forget it. They will peek behind the distancing mask of teacher to learn what a true Torah personality is. Let us recall Rabbi Soloveitchik's inspiring figure, the lonely man of faith, who creates community specifically through his existential crises:

> [I]n crisis and distress there was planted the seed of a new type of community – the faith community...one lonely soul finds another tormented by loneliness and solitude yet unqualifiedly committed. [12]

Let me further illustrate with a personal anecdote. Grappling in yeshivah with the question of whether I should make *aliyyah* then or not, I turned to one of the warmer teachers, who indeed gave me some useful advice – but without finding out my particular circumstances, and without following up later. Consequently, I did not feel terribly supported. This was a missed opportunity. I wanted my Torah teacher to show that he cared, to help me see the broader spiritual context of this decision and its appropriateness for my particular life, and perhaps to share with me his own *aliyyah* experience and difficulties. What is a person with no address for guidance to do – turn to a therapist? Will this really suffice? I am concerned that therapists have more access to our students' deepest spiritual concerns than we do. We must beware of crowning psychology the "queen" of the inner world, leaving the Torah as "handmaiden" to dole out information, skills, and norms. The Torah has a higher healing to offer, as we learn from those *ba'alei teshuvah* who come to it still thirsty after years in therapy. Our sources are bursting with spiritual insight and relevance; let us train our teachers to utilize them to the maximum.

---

[12] Rabbi Joseph B. Soloveitchik, *The Lonely Man of Faith* (New York: Doubleday, 1992), pp. 39, 42.

Making Room for Personal and Existential Questions

Within the classroom structure too there is much scope for nurturing processes. Each yeshivah can check if there is enough of a forum in its educational agenda for questions relating to personal identity – relationships, growth, self-awareness – and also for the deep and difficult questions about God, Torah, *halakhah*, the human soul, and truth. These questions, even the ostensibly philosophical and abstract, can fester inside students and prevent them from absorbing much else. Many students come to yeshivah searching for illumination of these kinds of questions, and some leave feeling they did not get adequate answers. I know of a student who was requested to leave her school because she asked too many faith questions and was not happy with the answers offered her.

We must talk more openly about issues of faith and truth in class. Susan Handelman tells us that after teaching Bible at university, "one very bright fellow said, 'It was an excellent course…but we all cleverly avoided really talking about God, didn't we?'"[13] Although we in the yeshivah do not fearfully exorcise God from our text, it nonetheless seems that we sometimes exorcise Him from our hearts, forgetting to apply our learning to our relationship with Him. Rather than reading "And God said to Moses" and blithely continuing on, let us once in a while pause and ask "But how can God speak?" (philosophical question) or "What does God say to *you*?" (personal question). While learning all about the "trees" – *Tanakh*, Talmud, *halakhah* – let us not lose sight of the Divine "forest": what in fact is *avodat Hashem,* and what is *my* particular *avodat Hashem*? Let us introduce these topics in class – or, better yet, create entire courses devoted to frequently troublesome issues; and if these questions are attacked head-on, teachers will feel more prepared to discuss them than when they crop up randomly.

Discussion-Based Lessons

Yet even introducing personal and existential topics is not enough – there is still the matter of how. Frontal lectures are always an option, but let me suggest an excellent technique, too little utilized in the yeshivah world,

---

[13] Susan Handelman, "We Cleverly Avoided Talking About God: Personal and Pedagogical Reflections on Academia and Spirituality," *Courtyard: A Journal of Research and Thought in Jewish Education* 1 (1999): 103.

which enhances self-awareness and internalization: the facilitated discussion.[14]

Since in yeshivah there are usually no exams, there is actually time to give important issues the space they deserve. Rather than having difficult questions be a nuisance to the teacher, we can set out deliberately to take them by the horns and build an entire powerful lesson around one or a few of them.

How would this be done? First, we begin with a good question – not the routine rhetorical question so beloved of the teacher, but preferably one that has been the subject of some considerable reflection on our part and perhaps is not even fully resolved. Then, *before* addressing it via source texts or quotes, we elicit the students' ideas and answers. Our role here is that of facilitator, entailing listening carefully, repeating the comments in our own words to make sure we understood, encouraging shyer students to speak, pointing out any flaws, and comparing the students' positions with one another. In this way, we permit students to able to think for themselves first before introducing answers introduced precipitously, as is too often done in the Orthodox world, where doors opened by good questions are regrettably closed immediately by the answers.[15] Here in contrast, the listeners' active role will boost their internalization and recall of the topic,[16] and they will also learn to embrace questions as exciting gateways rather than fearing them.

Texts, too, can be made more powerful if the issues they raise are discussed beforehand and also if students are invited to offer their interpretations of them. A text dealt with in two minutes is unlikely to be remembered, but if differing opinions are heard, the student will be challenged and interactive, and more likely to recall the lesson. Best of all is when a student brings to light dimensions that the teacher had not noticed – if the teacher is honest enough to admit the *hiddush*, the student will remember it for a long time to come.

---

[14] See Asher Friedman's essay in this volume, in which he utilizes the Hasidic model of *tzimtzum* to describe how the teacher must withdraw to create space for the students. See also Handelman, "Dear Class," p. 27.

[15] If only the typical *devar Torah* could move from the format "Why A? Because B" to "Why A?," lingering on the question and having some discussion, and then considering "B." Those assembled would become a learning community for that time, and reactions of boredom – now all too common – would decrease.

[16] The act of speaking requires commitment and forces abstract thought into concrete terms. Nehama Leibowitz contends that active learning is endorsed in classical Jewish texts. See her *Torah Insights* (Jerusalem, 1995), p. 143.

The discussion is also a vehicle for broad personal engagement; teachers who have little time for one-on-one can still listen carefully in class, become familiar with their students' thought patterns and concerns, and respond personally when appropriate.

In sum: from my experience, children and adults almost always become excited and involved in a discussion, providing it is well-run and stimulating. I have witnessed mature people who have known only frontal lectures their entire lives become elated by this new, transformative education.[17] Such a session creates for its duration a dialogical community of people enriching one another's understandings of Torah, and – crucially – this is a model students can take with them, to reproduce wherever they end up.

A Model of Courageous and Dynamic Religious Process

My third suggestion depends on how open the teacher is willing to be in revealing his or her human side, behind the educational persona. I have already mentioned that this must be done cautiously but may reap outstanding benefits and be a breath of fresh air that the student later remembers best. I mean now to challenge us to reveal not only personal facts but also our religious struggles, past and even present. I understand that this may be a red light for some, and I ask for patience while I make the case.

To begin, let us be frank: Torah teachers, being only human, have their flaws. They are not always honest with themselves or their students; and when the aforementioned student was expelled for her faith questions, her teachers, had had they been totally honest, would have admitted that the institution was failing her, not vice versa. And what about teachers who are almost suffocating students under floods of methods and information while avoiding their burning questions? Is this really a deliberate educational decision, or might it rather reflect a misunderstanding of the students' needs, an inexcusable laziness, or a fear of opening a Pandora's box? I cannot but accuse teachers of turning a blind eye to students who are suffering under their very noses. Now I'd like to turn the tables and include the teacher, too, among my proposed beneficiaries, for the truth is that while the teacher's limitations restrict the students, they hamper the teacher even more.

---

[17] In the literature on adult education in the secular world, the need for learning to be transformative has been discussed at length. See, e.g., Stephen Brookfield, *Understanding and Facilitating Adult Learning: A Comprehensive Analysis of Principles and Effective Practices* (Milton Keynes: Open Univ. Press, 1986) and Jack Mezirow's *Transformative Dimensions of Adult Learning* (San Francisco: Jossey-Bass, 1991).

Teachers: "At-Risk" Too

Teachers may also be casualties of the yeshivah. They, too, need to grow and change as individuals, and are also sometimes trapped – by themselves, in their role. Rabbi Nathan Lopes Cardozo, who became Orthodox after a profound process of evaluation, tells of his amazement when several religious teachers divulged to him that they had lost their belief in Judaism. They wished *him* to tell *them* why it was such a great tradition.[18] While we may be justly concerned about their students, these teachers deserve compassion too. My guess is that they have fallen victim to the narrowing of Torah into nothing but a set of abstract intellectual concepts, dogmas and behavioral norms, which naturally results in static religious life and a stagnant relationship with God and self. These educators need to throw out any outgrown ideas, and rebuild their inner lives. This is, of course, easier said than done.

I think what is preventing these and other distressed teachers from moving on is fear – of loss of status, of loss of faith, of the unknown – and so they prefer to hide their true thoughts and suppress their questions. This, of course, is not a good solution. First, some students will surpass the teacher – not only in religious excitement, but also in integrity and confrontation of inner challenges, and, sensing the teacher's hypocrisy, they will lose respect. Then, the teacher will feel threatened by these students' contempt and secretly envious of their freedom to explore. A topsy-turvy generational situation will thus be created, which must be remedied as soon as possible.

Fear appears also to be behind the widespread avoidance of the facilitated discussion. These fears are understandable; open discussion, with its freedom of expression and potential for chaos, is a forfeiture of the teachers' absolute control, which for some is synonymous with discipline. Yet I believe a firmly guided discussion can in fact retain as much discipline as a frontal lecture can. Moreover, it gives the teacher the option of a control born of confidence and mutual respect rather than authoritarian rule.

Were it just a question of confidence in teaching, it could be addressed through teacher training; but a much stronger obstacle arises when fear of Heaven is cited. This issue leads me back to my initial subject – teachers disclosing their inner life. I imagine that the very idea elicits a strong reflex of opposition in some readers. I am assuming that arguments will be made for a certain distance between teachers and students, and claims put forth

---

[18] Nathan Lopes Cardozo, *Judaism on Trial* (Jerusalem: Urim Publications, 2000), p. 38.

that seeing a teacher questioning weakens the student's faith, that allowing students' independent interpretations will undermine rabbinical authority, and that teaching students to think will lead to heresy. Doubtless these points bear some validity, but, in truth, disclosure does not automatically put the teacher on the level of the students. (Indeed, teachers who feel vulnerable at the idea of ever dropping their mask might want to re-examine the basis for their class discipline.) Further, some students' faith might be weakened by *not* seeing teachers questioning and by never being allowed to express their own ideas. It very much depends on which students are being dealt with – mature or immature, in searching mode or of simple faith; and there is a price to be paid for erring too far in either direction.

There is also a risk of mistaking personal fear and a lack of confidence in Judaism's potency and breadth for genuine fear of Heaven. Those who believe their rebuttal of the too-intimate language of exploration is due to religious reasons might be surprised to hear that secular academics share their concerns:

> The strength of the taboo can be gauged by the academician's inevitable recourse to name-calling when emotion, spirituality, and imagination are brought into the curricular conversation: touchy-feely, soft, unrigorous, mystical, therapeutic.[19]

Perhaps, like the academic, our real concern is that we will find ourselves adrift in a world unfamiliar to us – that of the personal, emotional, imaginative, and creative. I contend that it is because we have not sufficiently explored it within ourselves that we feel uncomfortable allowing it inside the yeshivah. Consequently we send our students off with a profound mistrust of themselves too, and they live in fear of exploring any realm that seems just a little bit "dangerous."[20] This, of all things, should not be our legacy. Let us be more cautious about caution, and allow teachers to be more authentic, individual, and seeking, rather than stiff role models for a generalized norm. The students will be exposed to an example of courage and integrity and a dynamic process of constant "becoming" in one's spiritual life, and they will learn that a Torah personality does not have to fear questions. At the same time, teachers will be redeemed from

---

[19] Jane Thompkins, *A Life in School: What the Teacher Learned* (Boston: Addison-Wesley, 1996), pp. 213–214.

[20] This is especially so in the realm of sexuality, where the many religious singles have been handed a hefty burden of fear and guilt, which is surely a great drain, especially on top of the celibacy it is aimed at maintaining.

having to come in pretending (or worse, believing) that they know all the answers and instead will feel freer to learn from the students and from the work. For example, running a facilitated discussion is not just a matter of a new technique; it is a vital spiritual exercise. For a teacher to step back and switch to a mode that is primarily listening serves as an exercise in humility; as such, no Torah teacher should be let off the hook. How unsightly is an arrogant Torah teacher who likes to talk but not to listen. In addition, and marvelously, facilitated discussion serves to refresh the tired teacher. Stepping into learning mode, the teacher will experience every lesson as a further opportunity to hear via the fresh questions and perspectives of sincere young minds a divine voice calling for a renewal of comprehension. Hopefully the resulting energy will save teachers from burnout and stagnant religiosity, and they will be privileged to repeat the words of R. Hanina:

> I have learnt much from my teachers, and from my colleagues more than from my teachers, but from my disciples most of all.[21]

Summary of Practical Suggestions[22]

I suggested, first, that a good *mashgiah/ah*, counselor, or psychologist should be attached to the yeshivah, and that the curriculum should exhibit intellectual openness and sophisticated spiritual teaching together with necessary support for each individual's reaction to these elements.

Second, staff should be trained in how to run discussions and in asking questions that induce self-reflection, such as "How do you feel with this?," "How is this relevant to you?" Students thus will become habituated to absorb what they hear reflectively, so as to gauge the information's relevance to them personally. On these points I would add that the school can provide official frameworks for self-reflection and introspection. For example in the context of *Elul zeman* and *teshuvah*, a class or two may be devoted solely to discussing the yeshivah's and the students' goals and expectations for the year. Students can write down the areas in which they wish to grow, and share what they can aloud. In the middle of the year, in a follow-up session, they will ask themselves, "What have I gained so far, and how can I

---

[21] *Ta`anit* 7a.

[22] Implementing all of the suggestions would cause quite a revolution. I suggest every reader take what is useful for the framework in which he or she teaches (or at the very least take simple and practical steps to begin with, such as placing a suggestion box through which students may express their ideas) and also carefully consider which elements are appropriate to which students – for example, older students may want to be left alone to study more.

(and the yeshivah) improve what I can gain?" In the final session, students will look backwards and also towards the ensuing year; teachers will facilitate discussion of students' fears and hopes and give practical advice on how to set up a supportive community for continued learning of Torah.

Teachers should be provided with tools, including source texts, with which to properly address "big questions" (personal and existential) when these questions crop up or, better, in pre-planned discussion sessions. Such issues might include relationships with peers, parents, and non-Jewish culture; the true meaning of humility; individual and society; seeking, rebellion and autonomy; identity changes, faith, and doubt; and even teacher-student relationships. They can be taught through the stories of the Jewish greats previously mentioned, as well as those of Resh Lakish, Elisha ben Abuya,[23] the rebellious son, Nadav and Avihu and many others. Staff can also be exposed to creative techniques, for the daring teacher's use.[24] Teachers should be encouraged to reveal to the students some of their own religious questions and to view discussions with students as a resource for their own growth – a mutually supportive learning community.

A forum to implement several of the above suggestions might be an "open session" – a weekly hour for students to process the week's events with a teacher. The atmosphere is open, informal, and stimulating, as students recount the most interesting ideas they heard and also questions that are troubling them. The existence of this session will catalyze students to be more aware and active in their learning and to own their questions. Teachers will bond with the students and know what is going on, and students will learn to listen to one another and to view one another as a wisdom resource, which they should continue to do after they have left the yeshivah and its teachers behind.

Conclusion

We need to make the yeshivah more holistic in order to utilize these few yet formative years well. We must demonstrate to students that we truly

---

[23] The inclusion in the Talmud of such a dissenting voice galvanized someone I know to return to Judaism.

[24] Such as letter writing (see Handelman, "Dear Class," for her positive experience with this technique), or bibliodrama, a good explanation of which can be found in Peter Pitzele, *Scripture Windows: Toward a Practice of Bibliodrama* (Los Angeles: Torah Aura, 1998). Creativity is in fact central to the journey of the self, and educators need to learn how to nurture creativity within religious life. Credit goes to a teacher of Talmud I know who, having become involved in acting, shared publicly what this had done for him personally.

care about them for who they are and not just to mold them into a one-size-fits-all model. Rather than running to put out the fires of rebellion, we should instead stoke warm flames of self-esteem, self-awareness and self-reliance, and transmit the message of Jewish commitment in a non-authoritarian fashion of openness, connection, personal attention, and room for courageous exploration and creativity in them and in us.

As a postscript let me add that I believe that this entire essay is a reflection of a new *zeitgeist* sweeping through the world in recent decades. After many collectivist ideologies ignored – or worse, brutalized – millions, the world is placing much of its hope in the individual; and increased leisure time, extended years of study, and a plethora of psychological and spiritual theories have opened up new vistas of the inner world that have changed how we absorb knowledge. Many educators may sigh in irritation at today's youth. They can indeed seem very wearisome, but they cannot be forcibly suppressed: we are locking the cage after the tiger has escaped, since the seeking self is on the loose in modern consciousness.

We, both educators and parents, must face the difficult truth that we are at fault if our youth leave the fold. Just as the elders are held responsible when a stranger is murdered outside their town because they did not provide nourishment and accompaniment,[25] so are we responsible for not providing a habitable place for expansive souls that will settle for nothing but truth. It is we who will drive young people to explore in psychological, creative, and New Age frameworks that will, unlike us, support them, but that lack a Jewish frame of reference and often create rampant narcissism. We, in contrast, have the power to bring them to an awareness of their uniqueness that is balanced by such values as self-sacrifice, contribution to the world, and humility before God. But we need to understand that true Jewish humility is not oppressive and does not aim to destroy the unique, powerful self, but only the pride, attachments, and neglect of God that come with such a self. Moses himself was the greatest prophet and yet supremely humble. This is a paradox and a challenge, and must be taught repeatedly and with depth.[26]

The greatest things contain within them the most potential for evil. *Matzah*, the bread of freedom, is also the bread of affliction; the Torah may be

---

[25] Deut. 21:7 and commentaries there; *Sotah* 46b.

[26] A contemporary example of someone with incredible strength and determination yet also impressive humility was Nehama Leibowitz. It is a very difficult balance to achieve.

a medicine of life or it may be a deadly poison.[27] Rav Kook, in his important and well-known article *"Ha-Dor"* portrayed the unbridgeable gap between the older religious generation and the younger rebellious pioneers of his day, who rejected their parents' moral system as stultified and lacking in integrity. With great spiritual insight and courage, Rav Kook defined aspects of this rebellion as noble and expressed his desire to harness this energy back into the religious camp.[28] I believe we need leaders to show a similar spiritually deep understanding today,[29] to look beyond the selfishness of the "Me" generation and purge its dross – self-involvement, arrogance, superficiality, and indifference to the fate of the collective – in order to embrace and utilize its great power.[30] Perhaps behind the rudeness and self-absorption there actually lies an exalted spiritual purpose – the desire for integrity in faith rather than *"mitzvat anashim melummadah"* (habitual observance), the search for the unique spirituality of the individual soul. Rabbi Soloveitchik remarked:

> God willed man to be free. Man is required, from time to time, to defy the world, to replace the old and obsolete with the new and relevant. Only lonely man is capable of casting off the harness of bondage to society. [31]

Rav Kook noted that even in his day leaders were becoming less great while the people as a whole possessed increasing integrity and sensitivity.[32] So perhaps today we are all "lonely man," called to constantly grow beyond what society mandates, freer to choose than ever before. Let us remember that the *"na'aseh ve-nishma"* at Mt. Sinai was, according to the Talmud,[33] an enforced acceptance of the Torah, requiring centuries later a national reacceptance. The lesson is that acceptance under pressure is not the same as freely given consent. God taught this lesson specifically via the Purim story by hiding Himself – and giving the Jews the space to choose Him more authentically than at Sinai.

---

[27] *Yoma* 72b.

[28] R. Abraham Isaac ha-Kohen Kook, *"Ha-Dor"* in *Eder ha-Yakar ve-Ikvei ha-Tzon* (Jerusalem: Mosad ha-Rav Kook, 1995), pp. 106–116.

[29] The writings of certain Hasidic masters contain insights of this sort, but those writers unfortunately are long dead and are no replacement for contemporary leadership.

[30] "This is the *derekh ha-yosher*, to exploit one's energies rather than trying to conquer them, the *derekh ha-kovesh*." See R. Kook, *"Ha-Dor,"* p. 112.

[31] R. Joseph B. Soloveitchik, "The Community," *Tradition* 17:2 (Spring 1978): 13.

[32] R. Kook, *"Ha-Dor,"* p. 111.

[33] *Shabbat* 88a.

Finally, let us heed Rashi's words: "A man shall say to his son, be like Abraham!"[34] We must instruct our children, and we must remind ourselves, to be spiritual seekers like Abraham, when he beat out his path to the truth and to God.

---

[34] Rashi to Gen. 12:3.

RELIGIOUS COUNSELING
AND PESAK HALAKHAH
IN A YESHIVAH SETTING

JOEL B. WOLOWELSKY

MANY YEARS AGO, a student who had previously expressed no interest in studying in Israel after high school approached me with a request to arrange an interview the next day with a visiting *Rosh Yeshivah*. I spoke with him about the changes that were occurring in his thinking, agreed to arrange the interview, and the next day quietly slipped into the back of the room during the admissions test. The boy was exceptionally bright and did quite well. As the interview drew to a close, the *Rosh Yeshivah*, appropriately known for his keen insight, startled us both with an unexpected question: "Are you fully *shomer Shabbat*," he queried.

The boy was too uneasy to respond, so I spoke up from the back of the room. "Not yet," I said. "He wanted to be, but I told him to move slowly until he got to the yeshivah."

The *Rosh Yeshivah* responded somewhat incredulously: "You advised him to not fully observe Shabbat? That is quite a responsibility you have undertaken!" I replied with a smile that it was quite a responsibility to tell someone to *start* to observe *Shabbat* in its full details. Later, I explained to him that the boy lived near no *shomer Shabbat* friends and near no Orthodox shul. To be sure, it was important to try to develop immediate strategies to avoid violating basic Torah prohibitions. But to fully observe Shabbat in that setting meant, in effect, locking himself in his room for twenty-five hours. He would do it for one week, have a miserable experience, and that would be the end of *Shabbat* for him. But if he started fully observing *Shabbat* in the yeshivah, I said, it would be such a pleasant experience that he would own it forever. The *Rosh Yeshivah* didn't respond to my argument, but because he was establishing his relationship with our school, he accepted the boy.

The next January I visited the yeshivah in Israel and had lunch with the *Rosh Yeshivah*. I must admit that I was apprehensive as to how things would work out, but I was soon put completely at ease. He welcomed me warmly, saying, "I must apologize to you for what I thought of you last year. This was the first time I was in your school and you had the chutzpah to tell me – a *Rosh Yeshivah* whom you were meeting for the first time – that you told a boy who wanted to fully observe Shabbat to hold off. Frankly, I thought you were crazy. But after seeing the boy blossom here, I realized you were right."[1]

Could one write a *pesak*, a formal halakhic decision, telling someone who wants to fully observe *Shabbat* to go slowly for a few months? Frankly, I am not so sure it would be an easy task. But the point I shall be making is that *pesak* and religious counsel are not the same thing, and the halakhic rules are different for each.

"Din Melekh" and Meta-Norms

Let me digress for a moment to take note of a question raised by many high school students who are first learning the halakhic rules of convicting a criminal. In order to be convicted, the defendant must first have been warned by two witnesses not to commit the offense and must have acknowledged that warning and discarded it. How can a society maintain law and order with such a criminal justice system? Surely any criminal with a little savvy could always escape punishment!

Of course, this reality was not lost on the halakhic system, which has a parallel system of *din malkhut* – the king has the right to impose extra-halakhic sanctions in order to maintain law and order.[2] These extra-halakhic punishments may not meet the theoretical prerequisites of the *halakhah*, but they are necessary for maintaining the halakhic system as a whole, something which itself is a meta-norm of the halakhic community. In a time when we have neither a king nor a *Sanhedrin* responsible for maintaining

---

[1] I have deliberately left out the name of the *Rosh Yeshivah* so as not to necessarily tie him to what I learned from that experience. When I last checked, the alumnus – now a young professional with a growing family – was *shomer mitzvot* and a *ben Torah*. But it is important to realize that the correctness of an approach is not necessarily demonstrated by its outcome. Many times, a well-reasoned decision does not yield the desired outcome, and a mistaken decision might yield positive consequences. To be sure, unanticipated results should make one reexamine his or her assumptions, but there is no way of guaranteeing success. Just as a doctor must make a decision based on experience, knowledge, and a thorough evaluation of the circumstances, so too must a counselor choose an approach responsibly and hope for heavenly help.

[2] Maimonides, *Mishneh Torah, Hilkhot Melakhim* 3:10. Note also *Hilkhot Sanhedrin* 18:5.

social order,[3] we most frequently encounter these meta-norms in the context of *pikuah nefesh*, saving a person who is in a life-threatening situation, but they are not limited to it. Or perhaps it would be better to say that the meta-norms of *pikuah nefesh* apply to saving the *nefesh* too, not only the body.

I think we have a good intuitive feel for how this all works in many areas of life – areas in which we are quite comfortable. May one go about committing assault and battery on people? Certainly not. But a surgeon does not bring a *posek* into the operating room to ask how long an incision he is allowed to make; he has license to cut because he has license to heal. We have no trouble understanding that when he slashes to harm – even if he is wearing his surgical garb – he does so without halakhic sanction; but when he makes an incision to heal a dangerously sick person, it is he who must decide when and how to cut.

We know the difference between imposing martial law in time of war and imposing a police state to suppress dissent in a civilian society – and our secular courts likewise recognize such distinctions when a particular act is challenged. The Constitution with its Bill of Rights is important, but, in Justice Jackson's words, it must not be converted into "a suicide pact."[4] The king may impose extra-halakhic sanctions because he does so to protect and maintain a halakhic society. Indeed, society itself is in danger if it denies him that right.

That, I would suggest, is the essence of the difference between *pesak* and religious counseling in a yeshivah setting. Counsel is not *pesak*, and it is subject to different rules of engagement. Unfortunately, this distinction is lost on many people. Our generation is witness to books of personal advice given by *posekim* as if they were legal rulings meant to be public policy.

Sacrificing Fingers to Save Arms

At our high school reunion held a few years ago, I met an alumna and her husband, who was a yeshivah *rebbe*. A colleague mentioned to me that he recalled that she had become a *ba'alat teshuvah* when she was a junior in

---

[3] R. Yehudah Gershuni points out that when Israel had both a *Sanhedrin* and a king, the former had to judge only according to the theoretical *halakhah* (the "*mishpat tzedek*"), the just judgment with which the Torah charges judges (Deut. 16:18). But when there is no king, the judge assumes both powers, the authority of the judge and that of the king. See "*Dinei Malkhut ve-Dinei Torah ve-Hora'at Sha`ah*" in his *Hokhmat Gershon* (Jerusalem, 1997), p. 427.

[4] *Terminiello v. Chicago*, 337 U.S. 1, 37 (1949).

high school.[5] She had carefully negotiated her religious growth while avoiding any conflict with her parents. But when she was a senior, her parents insisted that she drive in the car with them on *Shabbat* when they went to a family event. They would not hear of any protests on her part, and they would fight any philosophy that intruded on their world view. He took a deep breath at the time, he told me, and told her to ride in the car with them.

The summer after, worried that he had mislead her, he consulted with his *rebbe*, the late R. Shlomo Zalman Auerbach. Yes, he was told, he had acted properly – sometimes a surgeon must cut off a finger to save the arm. Of course, what Reb Shlomo Zalman did *not* say was that *kibbud av va-em* requires violating *Shabbat* if so instructed, or that telling someone to ride in a car on *Shabbat* is not necessarily a violation of *lifnei iver* (the prohibition against causing others to sin), or that he himself would have necessarily given the same advice if asked. Indeed, what he said was that just as a surgeon has to make such decisions during surgery, so, too, must a responsible person giving advice be prepared to cut off a finger to save an arm.

We recognize this language as evoking that of the Rambam in describing the powers of the *Beit Din ha-Gadol*:

> If they see that the situation requires the suspension of a positive commandment or the violation of a negative commandment in order to bring many back to proper observance, or to save many Jews from stumbling in other areas, they may enact whatever they feel the moment requires. Just as a doctor amputates an arm or leg so that the person as whole might live, so too the *Beit Din* may rule at a specific time to violate some commandments on a temporary basis in order that they might all be upheld. As the Sages said [*Shabbat* 151b]: Violate one Shabbat so that many can be observed.[6]

This is certainly the spirit of which we spoke, but we must realize that the Rambam speaks of the *Beit Din* acting for benefit of the Jewish community, not a particular *posek* ruling for an individual – and certainly not a counselor advising a student. A central communal halakhic authority has a prerogative unavailable to the local *posek*: he can *change* the *halakhah*, albeit temporarily. Neither the *posek* nor the religious counselor has this right in confronting a difficult situation.

---

[5] Once again, I omit the colleague's name so as not to hold him responsible for my interpretation of the incident.

[6] Maimonides, *Hilkhot Mamrim* 2:4.

A Halakhic Logic

In having presented this issue anecdotally rather than analytically, I do not mean to suggest that it does not have a halakhic basis.[7] Indeed, R. Yehuda Amital provides such an analysis, by asking if we are permitted to instruct sinners to violate minor infractions of the *halakhah* in order to prevent them from committing greater sins, or in order to bring them to observance and belief in general.[8] At times, he concludes, in order to assist individual Jews to return to observance and to spare individuals from stumbling, there is a need to rule permissively and even to abet the violator indirectly.

R. Amital notes that many people rely on formally offering a place to stay overnight when inviting a non-observant guest for a Friday night meal. He admits, however, that there are situations where such reasoning cannot be employed. For example, he cites the question of allowing a teenager who lives far from the central meeting place of the local Bnei Akiva to join the organization. Allowing membership encourages the youngster to spend *Shabbat* traveling to and from the meeting, often in violation of Torah as well as rabbinic prohibitions. Yet many have allowed this in the realistic hope that the teenager will be positively influenced by the membership opportunity. There is a halakhic logic behind this, says R. Amital, and it was articulated by R. Auerbach, who had suggested elsewhere that

> ...while we do not allow someone to commit even a minor violation in order to save others from a greater sin, nevertheless, it is permitted to "put a stumbling block before the blind" [e.g., offer food to someone who will not make a *berakhah* and thereby cause him to violate that particular detail of the law] in order to help him avoid stumbling over an even greater "obstacle" [i.e., insulting him may distance him entirely from Judaism]... It turns out that there is no sin here at all, for in this case there is no obstacle being

---

[7] There is, of course, an extensive literature on the limits of *lifnei iver* that I am not quoting here, even though it may lead us to identical practical conclusions. I am pursuing a parallel and, I believe, complementary approach.

[8] R. Yehuda Amital, "Rebuking a Fellow Jew: Theory and Practice," in Jacob J. Schacter, ed., *Jewish Tradition and the Nontraditional Jew* (Northvale, NJ: Aronson, 1992), pp. 119–138. R. Amital's article appears in an expanded Hebrew version as *"Be-Inyan Mitzvat Tokhahah,"* in *Sefer ha-Yovel le-Mordechai Breuer,* ed. Moshe Bar-Asher (Jerusalem: Hebrew Univ., 1992), vol. 2, pp. 509–33.

set. On the contrary, it is the removal of a very great obstacle, by actively exchanging it with a less serious one.[9]

Avoiding Inappropriate Analogies

Well, then, we might ask, is not the position of encouraging someone to attend a religious youth group analogous in principle to the Conservative movement's 1950 opinion permitting driving to synagogue on *Shabbat*? That decision had rested to a large degree on the assessment that attending public worship on Shabbat was "indispensable to the preservation of religious life in America" and that the negative consequence of riding to synagogue was outweighed by the damage that would follow from being cut off from the community synagogue worship.[10]

The inappropriateness of the analogy, I would suggest, is to be found not in technical arguments regarding violating Torah and rabbinic prohibitions – although, to be sure, that is a crucial consideration – but in the difference between *pesak* and counsel. It might be proper guidance to tell a specific teenager to attend Bnei Akiva meetings on *Shabbat* or even to ride to a temple with her parents on Yom Kippur. It might be good advice because it is temporary counsel that tells the person how to get past a difficult – perhaps intolerable – situation and move on to halakhic observance, even though the action, taken out of the particular context, is completely prohibited. The problem with the decision of the Conservative movement is not simply that it took what might be sound counsel for some individuals and glibly applied it to the entire community. Rather, the advice was phrased as *pesak*; as such it was indefensible.

The Prohibited Remains Prohibited

This distinction can be inferred from a directive in a letter from R. Auerbach allowing a yeshivah to run an outreach program on Friday night: the parking lot of the synagogue in which services are to be held must be

---

[9] R. Shlomo Zalman Auerbach, *Minhat Shlomo* (Jerusalem, 1986), vol. 1, no. 35:1, p. 190. R. Meir Schlesinger relates that R. Auerbach referred him to this responsum in responding to the question of how parents should act if demanding *mitzvah* observance from their child results in the latter being resentful and therefore further distanced from Torah and its values. R. Schlesinger noted that training children in *mitzvah* observance is a rabbinic obligation, but developing in them a love of Torah and *mitzvot* is a Torah obligation. If circumstances regretfully bring about a conflict, it is the latter that takes precedence. *Hinukh* demands assessing the total picture and the over-all desired outcome. See his "*Mitzvat Hinukh*," in *Sha`alei Da`at* (Yeshivat Sha`alavim, 5749), p. 10.

[10] Morris Adler, Jacob Agus, and Theodore Friedman, "A Responsum on the Sabbath," in Mordecai Waxman, ed., *Tradition and Change* (New York: Burning Bush Press, 1958), p. 370.

closed for the entire *Shabbat* or *Yom Tov*, he insisted. We take this for granted, but it should be obvious why R. Auerbach thought it important to stress. Opening the parking lot undermines any possibility of a widespread perception of driving being forbidden on *Shabbat*. On the other hand, parking on the street down the block – viewed by some as hypocritical – actually creates a healthy tension. It forces the individual to be aware that driving is not part of the authentic *Shabbat* experience but is rather at best something being momentarily tolerated in order to get past a situation hoped to be transient.

If the counselor finds it acceptable to temporarily encourage or allow a specific violation as part of an overall approach, care must be taken to minimize violations as well as to avoid presenting the forbidden as actually permitted. The Conservative decision did not maintain that riding to synagogue was a prohibited act that was being tolerated for the moment so that one's religious commitment might be strengthened to the point where it would no longer be necessary. Rather, it suggested that "when attendance at services is made unreasonably difficult without the use of an automobile, such use shall not be regarded as being a violation of the Sabbath."

This is not to say that the outreach workers must constantly stress that a particular activity is forbidden. On the contrary, R. Amital notes that

> one of the leading halakhic authorities in Israel instructed those who work in *kiruv* not to discuss the laws of family purity with those married individuals taking their first steps towards renewed observance. Furthermore, he suggested that even if the subject is broached by the penitent him/herself, the instructor should plead ignorance.[11]

This, of course, is explained by the fact that the subject comes up in a closed private situation where the teacher is working with an individual and intends to eventually bring up this and other subjects at the appropriate time. That is to say, we are dealing with a counseling situation.

Procedures Worth Noting

What, then, are the rules for such religious counseling, one might ask. The point is that there are no hard and fast rules, because that is the nature of counseling. One cannot give a detailed list of *dinei malkhut*, because they must emerge from the specific social situation; one cannot anticipate all the implications of martial law because it is contingent and meant to be en-

---

[11] R. Amital, "Rebuking a Fellow Jew," pp. 128–29.

forced only when society is breaking down. Counseling is meant to deal with people in distress; the details of what to do depend on the specific person and his or her circumstances. But while there are no rules, there are certainly some procedures worth noting.

One should be aware that most probably the student intuitively knows the difference between *pesak* and counsel. A counselor need not fear that telling a student to wait a while before adopting a completely *shomer Shabbat* way of life will be interpreted as endorsing *hillul Shabbat* as a legitimate alternative. One should answer the question being asked; there is a reason why *posekim* wait for a question to be posed before offering an opinion. In listening to a student's question, one must be aware of the difference between asking what the law requires of me and what I should do in this situation. Indeed, it is often the preexisting knowledge of the answer to the former question that leads one to seek counsel on the latter.

By way of analogy, consider an obese teenager who finally asks a counselor how he or she can either lose weight or stop smoking. To the unsophisticated nonprofessional, the answer requires no significant expertise: simply either go on a diet and begin exercising or stop lighting up. But we need not list here all the possible reasons – psychological and situational – that might make immediate adoption of that program impractical in order to understand that this might be the wrong (or at least impractical) advice. Adolescents need reassurance that they can succeed before starting out on a difficult course. Premature attempts to begin a difficult regimen might guarantee failure. The dietician might be able to offer an authoritative "*pesak*" on the right number of calories to which the diet should be restricted; it is the counselor who must decide on how to reach that goal.

A youngster might truly want to become completely *shomer Shabbat* but fear that it will be too difficult a process. Indeed, it might well be at that time. To encourage the student to set out on a challenging campaign without making sure that all the resources for success are in place is irresponsible and an invitation for failure. The *posek* has to set out the ideal that there is no excuse for violating *Shabbat*; the counselor has to help the student reach that ideal.

On the other hand, not all religious counseling demands permissive advice. Sometimes the opposite is true, and the proper counsel is to suggest more restrictive action than the *halakhah* requires. (There seems to be less reluctance to adopt such an attitude nowadays, but that, I fear, is more a matter of sociology than principle.)

Confidence Tempered with Hesitation

The question of which approach to take is a complicated one. Recently, a friend reminisced about his experiences decades ago as an advisor and faculty member for NCSY. On one occasion he was housed for *Shabbat* with a family who were not members of the host synagogue. The father volunteered to tell him why they belonged, instead, to the Reform temple in town. It seems that when the time came for their son to celebrate his bar mitzvah, the Orthodox rabbi told them that he could be "bar-mitzvahed" only if the entire family stayed over in proximity to the shul and did not come by car. Although they drove to shul on other *shabbatot*, as did most congregants, the rabbi's policy was not to celebrate the acceptance of *mitzvot* in that manner. In disgust, the family promptly transferred to the local Reform temple, where they were warmly welcomed, and had been there ever since. My friend had learned a lesson from this at the time, he said, and concluded that *yikov ha-din et ha-har* – sticking to principle and the letter of the law, come what may – was inappropriate and could easily boomerang.

The very next week, he continued, he was in a different town for a *shabbaton*. He went into the shul kitchen on Friday afternoon to check up on the *kashrut* and had a conversation with the elderly lady who worked there. She told him, "You know, I have no respect for the rabbi here. I myself don't keep *Shabbat*, but still, is it not hypocritical to have a rabbi who speaks about *Shabbat* and yet regularly celebrates bar mitzvahs for boys who drove to shul that very *Shabbat* morning? What kind of Torah can he represent?"

In all honesty, he confessed, he saw her point, and concluded that principle is a very important thing, not least because of its practical effects. (His next conclusion, he continued, was that being a community rabbi was a very difficult thing, and might not be for him!) Indeed, having to decide which approach to take in any given situation can be a make-or-break decision. If the student is looking for encouragement to find the strength to move forward, counseling patience can result in missed opportunities (or worse). On the other hand, pushing the student too hard might spell disaster. *Posekim* must bring self-assurance and confidence to their ruling; religious counselors must temper their confidence with doubt and hesitation.

It is true that in *pesak*, one often has to speak to the situation and not simply the law. As R. Aharon Lichtenstein has noted,

A sensitive *posek* recognizes both the gravity of the personal circumstances and the seriousness of the halakhic factors... He might stretch the halakhic limits of leniency where serious domestic tragedy looms, or hold firm to the strict interpretation of the law when, as he reads the situation, the pressure for leniency stems from frivolous attitudes and reflects a debased moral compass.[12]

But religious counseling is not *pesak*. The issue is not to find a *heter*, but an *approach*. It is an extra-halakhic action, a prelude to halakhic living.

Counselor Qualifications

Of course, in many ways the religious counselor is just like any other competent counselor; it is therefore necessary to note the following caveat. The very same compassionate, utilitarian advice can have a very negative effect if offered by counselors who are not themselves *shomerei mitzvot*. This is not simply because one's intuition has to be backed up with an informed understanding of both the competing values within the *halakhah* itself and the differences between, say, rabbinic and Torah violations. It is, rather, that the meta-issue with which we are concerned is not simply helping students to "grow into themselves" – although that is certainly part of the job of a general counselor in the healthiest of situations – but rather helping students to grow into *benei Torah*. The suggestion to temporarily hold off on going forward – or to go forward slowly, moving step-by-step to increased halakhic observance – might generally be a laudable position that helps people accommodate less-than-ideal situations and adapt to them. But here, the message that has to be conveyed is that this is the best way to grow in *mitzvot*. Only a knowledgeable *shomer mitzvot* can convey that idea with integrity. If a non-observant counselor comes to the conclusion that a student is pressing too much too soon, an observant counselor should be brought into the discussion.

It is important to ensure that expressing acceptance of a person with all of his or her deficiencies – an important and legitimate goal of the religious counselor – will not be interpreted as endorsing those shortcomings. Whatever the area of religious conflict, this is best done by focusing on the possibility of observing all the *mitzvot* that are in one's power to fulfill. Indeed, one of the hardest messages to get through to teenagers is that the Torah does not require us to be perfect, but to yearn and strive for perfection. This is especially true when one is dealing with a student struggling with

---

[12] R. Aharon Lichtenstein, "On Abortion," *Tradition*, 25:4 (Summer 1991): 11.

sexual impulses, be it homosexuality, masturbation, or heterosexual prom-
iscuity.[13] Often, students must be reassured that they can discuss a subject
calmly before they can address it practically.

Learning Religious Counseling

Religious counseling is an art learned through apprenticeship. Psychologists routinely consult supervisors to discuss hard cases; lawyers discuss
briefs with senior partners; doctors exchange views with colleagues. Yet I
have found many teachers – usually young, but not exclusively – who routinely (almost cavalierly) offer serious advice without ever sharing the fact
with colleagues, senior or otherwise. They often do so without any understanding of the student's home situation, and with little appreciation of the
possible negative consequences of their advice. What is the source of their
unfounded confidence?

One of the roots of this problem is to be found, I believe, in our synagogue youth groups (like NCSY or Bnai Akiva), summer camps and learning programs, and school seminars. High school upperclassmen and college
students act as advisors and counselors, and in general they do a superb
job. They are, for the most part, great role models, and their enthusiasm for
growth in Torah is contagious. But most of these programs offer little if
any training, and there is usually no opportunity for the counselors to provide feedback to and interact with experienced faculty. They are not getting
a constant message admonishing them against offering unsupervised guidance on family and religious issues. Indeed, they often are confused by a
view that, since the *halakhah* is clear, there is no need to consult someone
else to know what to do in a specific situation.

Another root of the problem is to be found in the training – or lack
thereof – new teachers receive before they enter the classroom. Many new
teachers begin their careers with no formal teacher education and even less
day-to-day supervision. In some schools no one asks teachers what is going
on in their classrooms (unless there is an obvious problem). It is no surprise then that no one discusses with them the type of discussions they are
having with their students. Given the authority to run their classes as they
see fit, it is a small reach to the conclusion that if they are ready to be independent teachers, they are ready to be independent counselors. Often their
advice calls for ill-advised stringencies. But it is important to remember that

---

[13] See Bernard L. Weinstein and Joel B. Wolowelsky, "Initial Religious Counseling for a
Male Orthodox Adolescent Homosexual," *Tradition* 29:2 (Winter 1995): 49–55, and our
subsequent letter-to-the-editor in *Tradition* 29:4 (Summer 1995): 93–94.

such mistakes can be as dangerous and destructive as inappropriate leniencies.

This is not the place to outline formal training programs in general or religious counseling. But we surely can say that one needs an atmosphere in which all counselors relate their significant conversations to more experienced colleagues and mentors. (One might also consider maintaining a journal of significant conversations and the subsequent feedback from more experienced mentors.) To be sure, there is an obligation to protect the student's privacy and confidentiality; but the case can usually be discussed anonymously with any number of colleagues without violating confidentiality.

There is another reason to insist on routine consultation. There is a "high" involved, especially among young charismatic teachers starting out in their profession, in having young students hang on one's every word. It can generate a hubris that is best tempered by shared discussion with colleagues. One must be sure that it is the needs of the student that are being addressed, not those of the counselor. Acting routinely without consultation is a telltale sign of hubris.

Halakhic Review

Even though religious counseling functions on a parallel track to *pesak*, in the end it is subject to halakhic review. Civil courts may be loath to review or second-guess military decisions or martial law determinations made in times of conflict, but they reserve the right to do so. The king himself is rebuked by the prophet. The *posek*, who concerns himself with the ideal universe of *halakhah*, remains the moral compass for the religious counselor. One does not ask a *posek* for confirmation of advice – because that would be *pesak* – but, rather, gives him the opportunity to express concern and reservation.

But, of course, this means that the *posek* being consulted must be a competent religious counselor. Not all *posekim* fit that category and, indeed, many would be the first to admit this. In fact, in many Hasidic communities, there is a clear division between the *rebbe* and the *dayyan*. To be sure, the *rebbe* must be learned and the *dayyan* compassionate. But they usually receive different types of questions, and each knows which types of questions he is qualified to answer. Much of the tension that exists between *Roshei Yeshivah* and congregational rabbis stems from a confusion of their respective roles, often from a denigration by the former of the proper and necessary role of the latter.

R. Amital noted:

At times, in order to assist individual Jews to return to observance, and to spare individuals from stumbling, there is a need to ignore certain violations of rabbinic or even Torah laws; at times, there is a need to rule permissively, and even to abet the violator indirectly... Every deliberate overlooking of a sin, and every dispensation given in a specific case, may result in a cumulative negative effect with regard to the public at large... [This process] is a dangerous route "on which the righteous travel safely but the frivolous stumble."[14]

We therefore conclude, as did R. Amital, with a note of caution by R. Ovadiah Yosef:

The principle of permitting a minor violation for the sake of [avoiding] a more serious one must be exercised most sparingly. Just like in the case of healing the body, a doctor sometimes decides to amputate the hand to prevent the spread of the disease to the rest of the body, and sometimes decides to leave things as they are, all decided upon with the counsel of other doctors, so too should this procedure be followed with the healing of the soul. One must consult many erudite and esteemed Torah scholars, so that the decision should not cause any damage, God forbid.[15]

---

[14] R. Amital, "Rebuking a Fellow Jew," p. 128. ("Righteous travel safely..." is a play on Hosea 14:10.)

[15] R. Ovadiah Yosef, *Yabi`a Omer*, vol. 6, *Yoreh De`ah*, no. 3.

LEARNING FAITH FROM THE TEXT, OR TEXT FROM FAITH: THE CHALLENGES OF TEACHING (AND LEARNING) THE AVRAHAM NARRATIVES AND COMMENTARY

HAYYIM ANGEL

AVRAHAM AVINU IS ONE of the exemplars of faith in human history. His unswerving devotion through a lifetime of trials and tribulations demonstrates an eagerness to follow God even in the most difficult of circumstances. From early elementary instruction and beyond, educators rightly turn to our Patriarch in any discussion of faith.

But the Avraham narratives also present many trials and tribulations for teachers and students. While Avraham is tested repeatedly in the narratives, readers confront a maze of interpretation in determining what Avraham's reactions should teach us religiously. And the stakes are very high: commentators – our educators *par excellence* – know that the way they explicate the Avraham narratives will define our religious conceptions of having faith. Ideally, commentators are absolutely bound to drawing religious lessons from the biblical text; but religious preconceptions also are likely to enter the exegetical picture, especially when the implications are so significant.[1] Therefore, it is imperative for educators to elucidate which argu-

---

[1] It is critical to note that traditional commentators enter the exegetical fray with two religious assumptions: (1) biblical heroes are outstanding figures, whose spiritual accomplishments far exceed anything we can envision; and (2) the biblical text was composed as an eternally relevant teaching (cf. *Megillah* 14a) and therefore must be understood as applicable to our own religious lives. For an analysis of the way traditional commentaries have balanced these two assumptions, see Yaakov Medan, *"Megillat Bat Sheva," Megadim* 18–19 (1993): 67–78. See also Mosheh Lichtenstein, *Tzir va-Tzon* (Alon

ments in fact emerge from an analysis of the biblical text, and which are faith-related opinions stemming primarily from exegetes' religious inclination, rather than from textual considerations.

In this essay, we will consider three general responses of the commentators:

1. Accept the plainest sense of the text, and assume that what Avraham did was correct. Throughout the Avraham narratives, this option *always* appears to be the smoothest reading of the text, since God responds to Avraham's queries with assurances and covenants – and never overtly criticizes him.[2]

Exegetes who do not believe that a text teaches good faith may employ one of two alternatives.

2. Accept the plainest sense of the text, but criticize Avraham for what he did – either by searching for hints in the text which might indicate negativity, or simply by stating that Avraham did something wrong.

3. Provide an alternate reading of the text. In effect, this method eliminates the questions of faith that Avraham's actions may have raised.

By considering the passages in Avraham's ongoing dialogue with God, and how commentators have combined textual and religious motivations in their analysis, we will gain greater insight into the teaching of faith through the Avraham narratives.

Of course, educators must adapt material to the level of their classes. Much depends on age, level, homogeneity of students, and a host of other variables. Additionally, teachers have their own styles, and points of emphasis: are they focused primarily on teaching the Book of Genesis, *parshanut* methodology, or the topic of faith in general? While there is much overlap between these areas, the class structure will depend substantially on the answers to that and related questions.

This essay is intended as a resource, so that educators, aware of their own student populations and individual teaching styles, will be able to adapt this material to the needs of their particular students. This will enable them to draw students, regardless of age and background, into an active learning process related to the all-encompassing religious issue of faith.

Shevut: Yeshivat Har Etzion, 2002), pp. 235–257, as well as Uriel Simon, "The Religious Significance of the *Peshat*," *Tradition* 23:2 (Winter 1988): 41–63.

[2] Educators should contrast God's favorable responses to Avraham throughout the narratives with God's explicit criticism of Sarah when she laughs at a divine promise of children (Gen. 18:12–15; see discussion below), and of Moshe when he expresses frustration at the nation's inappropriate request for meat (Num. 11:21–23). This contrast will enable students to see how God appears to accept Avraham's questions as religiously valid – an assumption generally, but not always, adopted by the commentators.

II. Text Analysis
A. Genesis Chapter 12

God's first recorded encounter with Avraham sets the tone for the Patriarch's illustrious career: God instructs Avraham to abandon his family and begin a new life in a foreign land. Accompanying this command are promises of great blessing. Without so much as a word, Avraham embarks for Canaan, and constructs altars in gratitude when he arrives. Thus, Avraham's faith receives immediate affirmation in the Torah.

But before Avraham can settle in the Promised Land, a famine afflicts Canaan. The reader confronts a quandary: God had led Avraham to Canaan with guarantees of blessing; but now Avraham and his family face starvation. At this critical juncture, God conspicuously does not provide Avraham with any further instructions, as if to test him.[3] Avraham opts to go to Egypt, forsaking the Promised Land out of physical necessity.

Avraham's descent to Egypt generates a frightful challenge: he fears that the Egyptians will murder him in order to take Sarah. Should Avraham expect divine intervention, or should he take personal responsibility to preserve his own life? Avraham chooses the latter, asking Sarah to pose as his sister. Only at the last minute does God afflict Pharaoh, saving Sarah. Avraham and his family return to Canaan with great wealth.

In this chapter, commentators agree on what happened; they differ only in their assessment of Avraham's actions. Ramban sharply censures what he deems a deficiency in the Patriarch's faith.[4] According to Ramban, Avraham should have trusted God's original promise of blessing, waiting patiently in Canaan for God to bring rain. Moreover, he should not have given Sarah away once they did go to Egypt. Ramban suggests that Avra-

---

[3] See *Tanhuma – Lekh Lekha* 5, Rashi, Radak (on 12:10). Nahum Sarna, in *The JPS Torah Commentary: Genesis* (Philadelphia: JPS, 1989), p. 93, notes that famines were unusual in biblical Israel (see II Sam. 20:26; I Kings 17:1; II Kings 6:25, 7:1; Ruth 1:1). The fact that all three Patriarchs encounter a famine (cf. Gen. 26:1; 42:1) is therefore significant, possibly suggesting that God's promises of blessing are not always followed by repose. Sarna concludes, "all this continually impinged upon the religious consciousness of Israel. It generated a heightened sense of dependence on God's protection and a more intense awareness of His mysterious workings."

[4] See R. Samson Raphael Hirsch's penetrating evaluation of Ramban's opinion regarding the criticism of biblical heroes (on 12:10). For a more elaborate discussion of Hirsch's position and its implications, see Joel B. Wolowelsky, "'*Kibbud Av*' and '*Kibbud Avot*': Moral Education and Patriarchal Critiques," *Tradition* 33:4 (Summer 1999): 35–44.

ham was punished severely for his lack of faith in these instances; his descendants were enslaved in Egypt as a result.[5]

But the overwhelming majority of exegetes maintain that Avraham's responses were fully warranted in both of the above instances. These commentators follow the lead of *midrashim*, which state that God tested Avraham ten times and that Avraham succeeded in each of them.[6] He had to acquire food and do what he could to protect himself and Sarah from the immoral Egyptians.[7] According to the majority opinion, the Torah teaches that in the absence of explicit prophetic instructions, one may not depend on supernatural intervention in times of crisis.[8]

Educators should emphasize that this is a meta-textual debate, and utilize the opportunity to explore the religious positions of the commentators

---

[5] Although the Torah never explicitly links the slavery to any sin, several *midrashim* and later commentators search for possible explanations. See *Nedarim* 32a, which offers three opinions blaming Avraham himself for the slavery of his descendants. Abarbanel suggests that Yosef's brothers' jealousy and sale of Yosef, as well as Yosef's own role in provoking his brothers, are to blame. Seforno (on Gen. 15:13) avers that the Israelites in Egypt assimilated (see Ezek. 20:8–9) and therefore were punished for their own sins. Similarly, R. Yehudah Kiel (*Da`at Mikra: Bereshit*, vol. 1 [Jerusalem: Mosad ha-Rav Kook, 1997]) submits that the Israelites should have left Egypt after the famine in Yosef's time had ended; because they remained, they were enslaved (for a fuller survey of traditional opinions, see Kiel, pp. 426–8).

Abarbanel (Gen. 15, question #15) quotes Ran and R. Hasdai Crescas, who both assert that the Israelite slavery was not a punishment for any sins, but rather an educational investment. Ran suggests that the slavery was intended to humble Israel, so that they would be able to accept the Torah later on. Similarly, R. Crescas maintains that God wanted to perform miracles for the Israelites, so that they would learn that God, and not magic, controls the universe. Although Abarbanel initially prefers to believe that all calamities occur as the result of some sin, he eventually concedes that the slavery may have served to refine and purify Israel (similar to Ran; cf. references to Egypt as a "refining pot" in Deut. 4:20; I Kings 8:51; Jer. 4:11). In the end, the theological causes of the slavery remain a mystery to the reader.

[6] See, for example, *Avot* 5:2; *Pirkei de-Rabbi Eliezer* 26. Rashi and Radak (on 12:10) consider Avraham's lack of protest the required response for passing this test. In *Tanhuma – Lekh Lekha* 5, on the other hand, Avraham did protest Sarah's being taken to Pharaoh. He prayed, "Is this the reward for my confidence in You?" In this *midrash*, Sarah also prayed at that time, using a similar tone (cf. *Gen. Rabbah* 41:2).

[7] Ran (quoted in Abarbanel), Abarbanel, Seforno, S. D. Luzzatto, Hirsch, Malbim, and Hoffmann suggest that if Avraham were viewed as Sarah's brother, Egyptians wishing to marry Sarah would have to negotiate with Avraham directly, and he could refuse. Avraham's delaying tactic fell apart when Pharaoh himself became interested in Sarah, however. For a discussion of a possible ancient Near Eastern parallel relating to the unique legal status of a brother, see Barry Eichler, "On Reading Genesis 12:10–20." In *Tehillah le-Moshe: Biblical and Judaic Studies in Honor of Moshe Greenberg*, Mordechai Cogan, Barry Eichler & Jeffrey Tigay, eds. (Indiana: Eisenbrauns, 1997), pp. 23–38.

[8] See, for example, *Pesahim* 8b; *Kiddushin* 39b; *Bava Kamma* 60b; *Hullin* 142a. Radak (on 12:12) emphatically adopts this position as well. For further sources, see *Entziklopediah Talmudit*, vol. 1, s.v. "*ein somekhin al ha-neis*," pp. 679–681.

themselves.[9] When students reach the text ambiguities in the ensuing narratives, they will understand that at least some of the debates among exegetes emerge from a context broader than the local *peshat*.

B. Genesis Chapter 15

Genesis 15 introduces complexities not previously encountered in the Avraham narratives. Until this point, Avraham responded to divine commands, and to situations as they arose. Now, Avraham questions God for the first time – twice in the same dialogue. In interpreting Avraham's challenges, commentators debate whether any questioning or doubting is acceptable in proper faith.

1. Avraham's First Question

In chapters 13–14, God appears to Avraham once, and again promises the Land of Canaan to Avraham's progeny (Gen. 13:13–18). Though silent in the text, Avraham must have wondered who those descendants would be. After all, Sarah was approximately seventy years old and still barren. Lot, Avraham's presumed heir at the outset of the narrative, had distanced himself from the family both physically and spiritually by settling in the depraved city of Sodom.

When God promises reward to Avraham yet again, Avraham finally verbalizes his concerns. In fact, these are his first recorded words to God in the Torah (Gen. 15:1–6):

After these things the word of the Lord came to Avram in a vision, saying, Fear not, Avram; I am your shield, and your reward will be great. Avram said, Lord God, what will You give me, seeing I go childless, and the steward of my house is this Eliezer of Damascus? And Avram said, Behold, to me You have given no seed; and, lo, one born in my house is my heir. And, behold, the word of the Lord came to him, saying, This shall not be your heir; but he who shall come forth from your own bowels shall be your heir. And He brought him outside, and said, Look now toward heaven, and

---

[9] For elaboration on Ramban's position, see David Berger, "Miracles and the Natural Order in Nahmanides," in *Rabbi Moshe Nahmanides (Ramban): Explorations in His Religious and Literary Virtuosity*, ed. Isadore Twersky (Cambridge, MA: Harvard Univ., Center for Jewish Studies, 1983), pp. 107–128. Of the traditional exegetes, Ralbag probably adopted the view most diametrically opposed to that of Ramban. See David Horwitz, "'Ha-Haritzut Emet': Ralbag's View of a Central Pragmatic/Ethical Characteristic of Abraham," in *Hazon Nahum: Studies in Jewish Law, Thought, and History Presented to Dr. Norman Lamm*, ed. Yaakov Elman and Jeffrey S. Gurock (Hoboken, NJ: Ktav, 1997), pp. 265–309.

count the stars, if you are able to count them; and He said to him, So shall your seed be. And he believed in the Lord; and he counted it to him for righteousness.[10]

It would appear that Avraham, despairing of having children of his own, already had taken steps to adopt his servant Eliezer. In response, God promises that Avraham himself will father children; Eliezer would not be Avraham's heir.

Was it appropriate for Avraham to question God? A few commentators, including Ralbag and R. David Zevi Hoffmann, maintain that it was. The Patriarch did not see any reasonable likelihood of fathering an heir. Hoffmann explains that Avraham essentially was saying, "Give me a child," but respectfully did so indirectly by pointing out that he had no heirs.

Netziv likewise understands Avraham's question as it stands in the text, but he criticizes the Patriarch for doubting God's explicit promises. He therefore interprets Avraham's second statement (in v. 3) as a corrective – Avraham himself inferred from God's lack of response that he had doubted too much (in v. 2).[11]

Several other exegetes share Netziv's uneasiness with Avraham's questioning an explicit promise from God. But they appear to find God's favorable response proof that Avraham's statement was religiously justified. Consequently, they offer alternative readings of the text, which support their own conceptions of faith, and which also vindicate Avraham's behavior.

Rashi, Radak, and Ramban suggest that Avraham was worried that perhaps he had sinned, thereby forfeiting God's promises (see further discussion below). In this view, Avraham did not doubt God; he doubted himself.

Alternatively, Hizkuni, Abarbanel, Seforno, and Malbim maintain that Avraham fully trusted God's promise of progeny but was concerned that his son would yet be too young to inherit by the time the elderly Avraham expected to die. As a result, Eliezer still would emerge as the guardian of Avraham's estate. God responded that this son would be old enough to inherit by the time Avraham would die. This reading does not appear to be

---

[10] All translations of biblical and talmudic passages in this essay (with a few minor modifications) are taken from Soncino Press Judaica Classics CD-Rom.

[11] Several other commentators maintain that Avraham first thought his question in v. 2 and only verbalized it in v. 3. See, for example, Abarbanel; Kiel (p. 398).

the plain sense of the text; it emerges from these commentators' concerns about Avraham's faith.

To summarize, we have seen four interpretations of Avraham's first question:

1. Adopt the plain sense of the text: Avraham questioned God's promise, and God approved of this questioning (Ralbag, Hoffmann).

2. Find a textual hint at criticism of Avraham: Avraham questioned God's promise, but realized himself that he was mistaken in doing so (Netziv).

3a. Reinterpret the text: Avraham worried about the fulfillment of God's promise, but he did so out of self-doubt that perhaps he had sinned (Rashi, Radak, Ramban).

3b. Reinterpret the text: Avraham did not question God's promise at all; he simply worried that it would not be fulfilled soon enough (Hizkuni, Abarbanel, Seforno, Malbim).

In this instance, students should be shown that the text most likely supports the first view. But they should appreciate how attitudes toward faith motivated a large number of commentators to seek alternate explanations. With a heightened sensitivity to this balance of text and interpretation, and now aware of this broader debate, students may continue their own exploration of the nature of faith.

2. "He Counted it to Him for Righteousness"

Gen. 15:6 concludes the dialogue, relating that Avraham trusted in God, and *he* counted it to *him* for righteousness. The latter half of the sentence is ambiguous: did Avraham consider God's promises an undeserved kindness, or did God consider Avraham's faith in trusting God's promise of progeny a model for future generations?

Onkelos and Rashi aver that God regarded Avraham's faith as a model for future generations.[12] Ramban, true to his own religious outlook, asks: is it remarkable for a prophet to trust in God? Therefore, Ramban understands the second half of the verse as one of gratitude – Avraham considered it an undeserved righteousness of God to give him a child.[13] Of course, Onkelos, Rashi, and those who follow their interpretation would respond to Ramban's religious question: yes, it was admirable of Avraham

---

[12] See also *Targum Yerushalmi* to Gen. 15:6; *Mekhilta – Be-Shallah* 6; *Tanhuma – Be-Shallah* 10; *Song Rabbah* 4:8; Maimonides (*Guide of the Perplexed* III:53), Radak, Ibn Kaspi, Seforno, Hoffmann.

[13] See also Bekhor Shor, Hizkuni, Ralbag, Arama, Abarbanel, Netziv, S. D. Luzzatto, Kiel (p. 403).

to trust God's promises, given the lengthy delay in their fulfillment until that time.

In this instance, the text may be read either way. The context of Avraham's questioning and God's response in 15:1–5 supports Onkelos and Rashi.[14] But Avraham is the subject of the first half of 15:6, and the verse may be read according to Ramban's position, for there is no explicit transition of the verse's subject. As in chapter 12, much of the commentators' argument in this instance revolves around their own positions on the nature of perfect faith, rather than over the proper reading of the text.[15]

3. Avraham's Second Question

In the following vision (Gen. 15:7–8), God again promises the land to Avraham's descendants:

And He said to him, I am the Lord who brought you out of Ur of the Chaldeans, to give you this land to inherit it. And he said, Lord God, how shall I know that I shall inherit it?

Avraham's response appears astonishing. Moments ago, he trusted God; what would prompt him to doubt God now?

Shemuel (in *Nedarim* 32a), and several other *midrashim*, maintain that Avraham indeed was requesting further confirmation of God's promises. But he was wrong for doing so, and was punished severely: his descendants were enslaved in Egypt as a result.[16] It appears that Shemuel and the other

---

[14] Cf. the parallel usage in Psalms (106:28–31), cited by Ibn Kaspi and Hoffmann in support of the Onkelos-Rashi position:

They joined themselves to Baal-Peor, and ate the sacrifices of the dead. Thus they provoked Him to anger with their wrong doings; and the plague broke out upon them. Then stood up Pinhas, and executed judgment; and so the plague was stayed. And that was counted to him for righteousness to all generations for evermore.

[15] It is noteworthy that Ramban never appeals to the lack of subject transition in the verse; he simply rails passionately against the underlying religious assumptions of Onkelos and Rashi. Nehama Leibowitz, in *Peirush Rashi la-Torah* (Tel-Aviv: Open University, 1990), vol. 1, p. 159, conjectures that Ramban may have taken such a strong stance as part of his involvement in anti-Christian polemics. For further discussion of Ramban's views, see Ruth Ben-Meir, "Avraham in Ramban's Philosophy" (Hebrew) in *Avraham Avi ha-Ma'aminim*, ed. Moshe Halamish, et al. (Ramat-Gan: Bar-Ilan University Press, 2002), pp. 155–165.

[16] Cf. *Tanhuma – Kedoshim* 13; *Song Rabbah* 5:22; 30:16; *Eccles. Rabbah* 4:3; *Pirkei de-Rabbi Eliezer* 48; *Pesikta Rabbati* 47; Rashi to Isa. 43:27. See also discussion in n. 5.

Sages interpret the relationship between Avraham's question and the subsequent divine promise of slavery in v. 13 as one of cause and effect.

However, most later commentators do not perceive divine criticism towards Avraham; on the contrary, God makes a solemn covenant with Avraham in the wake of his second question. Although God accepted Avraham's question, these exegetes cannot believe that Avraham would express doubt at this point. Therefore, they suggest no fewer than five alternate readings of "how shall I know that I will inherit it":

1. Perhaps later generations will sin. How can I be assured that this covenant really will be fulfilled? (Radak, Ralbag, Ramban, Seforno, Malbim).

2. By what merit will I inherit? (*Gen. Rabbah* 44:14, Rashi [second opinion, 15:6], R. Bahya, S. D. Luzzatto).

3. In which generation will my descendants inherit? (Bekhor Shor, Abarbanel, Hirsch, Kiel).

4. How will my descendants know that the promise has been fulfilled? (Hoffmann).

5. The *berit bein ha-betarim* (Gen. 15) occurred some five years *before* the beginning of this chapter; therefore, Avraham did not doubt God immediately after trusting Him; he asked this question considerably earlier (Hizkuni).[17]

These commentators assume that Avraham fully trusted God's promise. But they still must provide a fair reading of the text. Those who adopt the first reading impose a theology of sin onto the text (see discussion below); therefore, other commentators seek different options. But the alternatives are difficult to fit into Avraham's words.

The common assumption of these interpretations is that the very possibility of Avraham's questioning in this instance is unacceptable. Shemuel and other *midrashim* accept the plain sense of Avraham's statement, and sharply criticize the Patriarch. The later exegetes reinterpret Avraham's words so that he does not doubt God's promise so soon after having accepted another one.

---

[17] Hizkuni bases his opinion on the chronology of *Seder Olam Rabbah*, ch. 1, which dates the 430 years of the Israelites "stay in Egypt" (see Ex. 12:40) back to the *berit bein ha-betarim*; and the 400 years of "living in a land not theirs" (see Gen. 15:13) back to the birth of Yitzhak. This reckoning, however, implies that the *berit bein ha-betarim* occurred when Avraham was seventy years old, five years before God commanded him to leave Haran to go to Canaan. Consequently, Ibn Ezra and Ramban already challenged this chronology. For a fuller survey of rabbinic opinions regarding the years of the servitude, see Amos Hakham, *Da`at Mikra: Shemot*, vol. 1 (Jerusalem: Mosad ha-Rav Kook, 1991), pp. 208–9, 233–4.

Nevertheless, the plain sense of the text appears to vindicate a questioning Avraham. One could argue that Avraham already trusted God's promise that he would have a child; now, he wanted an absolute sign of confirmation that his descendants would in fact inherit the land. God responds favorably to Avraham's request, having His fire "pass in between the halves." This is how Rashi (on 15:6, first opinion) and Ibn Ezra (on 15:7) view Avraham's question. Their reading upholds the plain sense of the text on both ends: Avraham questions (as maintained by Shemuel and the other *midrashim*), and God responds favorably (consistent with the majority of later exegetes).

Instead of viewing Avraham's question as a sign of little faith, it appears that Rashi and Ibn Ezra would find great religious heroism in Avraham's dialogue. He did not question from doubt; he questioned precisely because of his faith and his truthful relationship with God.[18]

To summarize, there are three predominant approaches to Avraham's second question:

1. Adopt the plain sense of the text: Avraham requested a sign of confirmation from God, and God approvingly provided one (Rashi, Ibn Ezra).

2. Find a textual hint at criticism of Avraham: Avraham requested a sign of confirmation from God, and God disapproved, punishing Avraham's descendants with slavery (Shemuel and other *midrashim*).

3. Reinterpret the text: Avraham was requesting something else, or was worried about future sins annulling this promise. God approved of this lesser question and solemnly swore that all will occur as promised (majority opinion).

4. Excursus: The Theology of Sin Annulling Promises

Several commentators ascribe one or both of Avraham's questions in Genesis 15 to a fear that perhaps he (or later descendants) would sin, thereby forfeiting divine promises. This line of interpretation emerges from a talmudic examination of a related question of faith: Yaakov repeatedly appears to doubt explicit divine promises. When fleeing to Haran, he states (Gen. 28:20–22):

If God will be with me, and will keep me in this way that I go, and will give me bread to eat, and garment to put on, So that I come back to my father's

---

[18] Kiel in *Da`at Mikra: Bereshit*, vol. 2 (Jerusalem: Mosad ha-Rav Kook, 1999), p. 23, quotes the midrashic principle that the righteous approach God audaciously, since they are confident that their God is true. See *Berakhot* 17b; *Yerushalmi Berakhot* 7:4 (11c).

house in peace; then shall the Lord be my God; And this stone, which I have set for a pillar, shall be God's house; and of all that You shall give me I will surely give the tenth to You.

But God had just promised protection in Yaakov's heavenly dream! (Gen. 28:15):

Behold, I am with you, and will keep you in all places where you go, and will bring you back to this land; for I will not leave you, until I have done that about which I have spoken to you.

Moreover, Yaakov continued to fear his brother Eisav years later, despite God's reassurances of protection:

The Lord said to Yaakov, Return to the land of your fathers, and to your family; and I will be with you (Gen. 31:3).

The messengers returned to Yaakov, saying, We came to your brother Eisav, and also he comes to meet you, and four hundred men with him. Then Yaakov was greatly afraid and distressed... Yaakov said, O God of my father Avraham, and God of my father Yitzhak, the Lord who said to me, Return to your country, and to your family, and I will deal well with you; I am not worthy of the least of all the mercies, and of all the truth, which You have shown to Your servant; for with my staff I passed over this Jordan; and now I have become two bands. Save me, I beseech You, from the hand of my brother, from the hand of Eisav; for I fear him, lest he will come and strike me, and the mother with the children. And You said, I will surely do you good, and make your seed as the sand of the sea, which cannot be counted for multitude (Gen. 32:7–13).

Why would Yaakov doubt God's explicit assurances, and even remind God of earlier promises? The Talmud (*Berakhot* 4a), perplexed by these stark incongruities, suggests that Yaakov worried that perhaps he had sinned, thereby forfeiting God's promises:

And, behold, I am with you, and will keep you in all places where you go, and the other verse reads: Then Yaakov was greatly afraid! [The answer is that] he thought that some sin might cause [God's promise not to be fulfilled].[19]

But this interpretation depends on preconceived religious assumptions. As in the case of the Avraham narratives, this interpretation is not universally accepted. Some exegetes criticize Yaakov for showing insufficient faith in God's promises.[20] Others reinterpret aspects of the narrative, thus mitigating Yaakov's apparent distress.[21]

But perhaps Yaakov simply was concerned about the ultimate fulfillment of such long-term promises, and God deemed his questions to be reasonable. A related *midrash* (*Gen. Rabbah* 76:2) states that "the righteous have no assurance in this world." Indeed, Yaakov suffered considerably throughout his life, despite God's repeated assurances of protection. He was threatened and cheated by Eisav and Lavan; his daughter Dinah was raped; his wife Rahel died in childbirth; his son Re'uven acted inappropriately towards Bilhah; and his sons sold Yosef to Egypt.

In any event, the fear of sin annulling divine promises appears nowhere explicitly in the Avraham or Yaakov narratives; therefore, this explication

---

[19] See, for example, Ramban (on 28:20–22), Rashi (on 32:11), and Kiel (on 32:8), who explain away Yaakov's fears with this talmudic reasoning. Several commentators propose possible sins of Yaakov: The *Zohar* (*Bereshit* 168a) faults Yaakov for not honoring his parents sufficiently, for not studying enough Torah, and for marrying two sisters. Ramban and *Keli Yakar* blame Yaakov for striking a covenant with the wicked Lavan. Hatam Sofer, following the midrashic lead of *Gen. Rabbah* 75:2, considers the very act of sending messengers to Eisav sinful. Kiel further suggests that Yaakov may have been fearful of his original sin – the deception of Yitzhak that had triggered Eisav's anger. For analysis of rabbinic perceptions of negativity in the deception, see Nehama Leibowitz, *Studies in Bereshit*, 7th ed. (1985), pp. 264–274; David Berger, "On the Morality of the Patriarchs in Jewish Polemic and Exegesis," in *Modern Scholarship in the Study of Torah: Contributions and Limitations*, ed. Shalom Carmy (Northvale, NJ: Aronson, 1996), pp. 131–146.

[20] Netziv (on 32:8) accuses Yaakov of being overly fearful of Eisav, and attributes his suffering in this episode to that lack of faith. Rashbam believes that Yaakov's sending gifts to Eisav was a ruse to enable him to flee. God sent an angel to wrestle with Yaakov to detain him so that there would be a confrontation with Eisav; God wanted Yaakov to see that He would protect him. Similarly, Radak and Hizkuni (on 32:26) view Yaakov's wrestling injury as a punishment for his lack of faith in God's protection. (Radak: because he wavered [*poseho*] over God's promises, he was condemned to limp [*posei'ah*].)

[21] On 28:20, Kiel quotes *Tosafot*, who argue that the condition imposed by Yaakov ("*if* God will be with me") should be translated as a declaration of confidence ("*surely*, God will be with me"). Alternatively, the *Zohar* (*Toledot* 150b) suggests that Yaakov made a conditional statement, because he remained unsure if his majestic dream was prophetic. *Gen. Rabbah* 70:3 suggests a third possibility: the chapter is out of chronological sequence. Yaakov in fact vowed *before* his dream, and God responded favorably in the dream.

of their questions remains possible, but not compelling in *peshat*. It is more likely that both Patriarchs genuinely had cause for concern, and God approved of their worries – they were reasonable indeed.[22]

To conclude, the brief dialogue in Gen. 15:1–8 gives rise to three significant exegetical debates regarding the nature of faith. Students should be shown which arguments are text-based, and which arise primarily from religious concerns. Avraham's first question appears straightforward, but some commentators remain uncomfortable with any degree of confrontation, and therefore either criticize Avraham or reinterpret his question. In 15:6 ("and *he* counted it to *him* for righteousness"), commentators rely partially on their own positions on having faith to interpret an otherwise ambiguous phrase in the text. Finally, most commentators reject the smoothest reading of Avraham's second question in 15:8, or criticize him for it, because it appears illogical or inappropriate to them that the Patriarch would express such clear doubt about a divine promise. The Torah appears to praise Avraham's tenacity in confronting God, and God responds by striking renewed covenants, considering Avraham's continued faith to him as righteousness – a model to all future generations. In short, Genesis 15 affords a singular educational opportunity to bring together textual and religious considerations, as interpreted by traditional exegetes.

C. Genesis Chapters 17–18

Following God's renewed covenant that Avraham will produce an heir, Sarah offers her maidservant Hagar to Avraham. Hagar gives birth to Yishmael. But after thirteen years of Avraham's raising Yishmael as his heir, God shatters Avraham's assumptions (Gen. 17:15–21):

God said to Avraham: As for Sarai your wife, you shall not call her name Sarai, but Sarah shall her name be. And I will bless her, and give you a son also of her; and I will bless her, and she shall be a mother of nations; kings of people shall be of her. Then Avraham fell upon his face, and laughed, and said in his heart, Shall a child be born to him who is a hundred years old? And shall Sarah, who is ninety years old, bear? And Avraham said to God, O that Yishmael might live in Your presence! And God said, Sarah your wife shall bear you a son indeed; and you shall call his name Yitzhak;

---

[22] Yehudah Elitzur suggests that *all* divine promises in fact are a call to action – to inspire a person to behave religiously, and to hope that God will bless his actions. See Y.M. Immanueli, ed., *Sefer Bereshit Hesberim ve-He`arot* (Tel-Aviv: Ha-Hevrah le-Heker ha-Mikra, 1977), p. 427 (and cf. *Tosafot* on *Yevamot* 50a, s.v. *teda*). It appears that this approach most suitably fits both the Avraham and Yaakov narratives.

and I will establish My covenant with him for an everlasting covenant, and with his seed after him. And as for Yishmael, I have heard you; Behold, I have blessed him, and will make him fruitful, and will multiply him exceedingly; twelve princes shall he father, and I will make him a great nation. But My covenant will I establish with Yitzhak, whom Sarah shall bear to you at this set time in the next year.

Commentators note that Avraham's laughter could represent two principal emotions: (1) exultation and joy, deriving from a wholehearted belief in this new promise; or (2) some degree of doubt and shock. Onkelos assumes that Avraham's laughter was exclusively one of confident joy. On the other hand, *Targum Yerushalmi* perceives some degree of doubt in the Patriarch's laughter. Later commentators are divided on this issue.[23]

There are two issues motivating the commentators. Once again, there is a broader debate on the nature of faith. Some allow the exemplar of faith some degree of doubt, while others do not. But on a purely textual level, everyone must account for the discrepancy between God's reassuring response to Avraham and His critical stance towards Sarah when she laughs at the same promise (Gen. 18:12–15):

Therefore Sarah laughed within herself, saying, After I am grown old shall I have pleasure, my lord being old also? The Lord said to Avraham, Why did Sarah laugh, saying, Shall I indeed bear a child, now that I am old? Is any thing too hard for the Lord? At the time appointed I will return to you, at this season, and Sarah shall have a son. Then Sarah denied, saying, I laughed not; for she was afraid. And he said, No; you did laugh.

Based on this discrepancy, one may conclude that Avraham's laughter must have been out of joy, while Sarah's expressed doubt. Otherwise, Avraham should have been criticized as well. However, the unmistakable similarity in language between Avraham's response and Sarah's renders this position inconclusive. The aforementioned *targumim* already capture this debate: Onkelos renders Avraham's laughter "was happy," but translates Sarah's laughter as "laughed." On the other hand, *Targum Yerushalmi* offers the same translation for both ("with some degree of doubt").

---

[23] Rashi, Radak, Bekhor Shor, Ramban, R. Bahya, and Ralbag adopt Onkelos' reading, while Ibn Ezra, Ibn Kaspi, Abarbanel, S. D. Luzzatto, Hirsch, Malbim, and Hoffmann prefer that of *Targum Yerushalmi*. Mitigating Avraham's doubt, Abarbanel, S. D. Luzzatto, Hirsch, and Malbim maintain that Avraham did not doubt God's promise but was astonished on a rational level.

Consistent with the reading of *Targum Yerushalmi*, *Midrash ha-Gadol* proposes a different resolution: God's reproach in Gen. 18:13–14 was directed against Avraham as well as against Sarah. God mentioned only Sarah's incredulity, leaving Avraham to become conscious of his own lack of faith himself. According to this view, God *does* rebuke Avraham for his doubting laughter in chapter 17 – albeit in a subtle, indirect manner. R. Sa'adyah, Hizkuni, and Kiel (on 18:13) adopt this reading as well.[24]

We have seen four approaches to Avraham's laughter:

1a. Adopt the plain sense of the text locally: Avraham doubted the divine promise, and God approved (*Targum Yerushalmi*, Ibn Ezra, Ibn Kaspi, Hoffmann).

1b. Adopt the plain sense of the text locally: Avraham was shocked on a rational level, but did not doubt God's promise (Abarbanel, Hirsch, S. D. Luzzatto, Malbim).

2. Find a textual hint at criticism of Avraham: Avraham doubted the divine promise, and God disapproved, albeit subtly (*Midrash ha-Gadol*, R. Sa'adyah, Hizkuni, Kiel).

3. Reinterpret the text, based on the parallel account with Sarah: Avraham laughed entirely out of joy, whereas Sarah laughed from doubt (Onkelos, Rashi, Radak, Bekhor Shor, Ramban, R. Bahya, Ralbag).

In this case, the textual difficulties do not lend themselves to clear resolution.[25] Students should be shown the different interpretations of the divine responses to Avraham and Sarah and apply what they know from previous narratives to this debate among the commentators regarding the nature of perfect faith.

D. Genesis Chapters 18–22

After God's promise that Sarah will have a son is reiterated, divine emissaries set out for Sodom in order to destroy it. God informs Avraham of this decision, and Avraham responds (Gen. 18:23–25):

Will You also destroy the righteous with the wicked? Perhaps there are only fifty righteous inside the city; will You also destroy and not spare the place

---

[24] *Midrash ha-Gadol* (ed. Margolit), p. 302. Cf. *Gen. Rabbah* 47:3 – "Twice Avraham fell on his face, and his offspring were twice denied circumcision, once in Egypt and the other in the desert." This *midrash* appears to support the more critical reading of Avraham's laughter.

[25] For two recent articles on the subject of Avraham's and Sarah's laughter, see Esther M. Shkop, "And Sarah Laughed," *Tradition* 31:3 (Spring 1997): 42–51; Aaron Lichtenstein, "Isaac and Laughter," *Jewish Bible Quarterly* 18 (1989): 13–18.

for the fifty righteous who are in it? Be it far from You to do after this manner, to slay the righteous with the wicked; and that the righteous should be as the wicked, be it far from You; Shall not the Judge of all the earth do right?

Viewed in isolation from the other Avraham narratives, the Patriarch's response seems shocking, since he boldly challenges the fairness of God's actions.[26] But after considering the previous texts, we have come to expect Avraham's willingness to confront and question God.[27] Several *midrashim* contrast Avraham's campaign on behalf of Sodom with Noah's silence prior to the flood. Avraham's pleading represents the proper religious response, whereas Noah's ostensibly faithful silence is erroneous.[28]

In fact, precisely because the reader is accustomed to Avraham's active responses, he or she should be amazed at Avraham's *silence* when God commands the banishment of Yishmael (Gen. 21:12–14) and the sacrifice of Yitzhak (Gen. 22:1–3). How could Avraham stand idly by, and not challenge God?[29]

E. Commands vs. Promises:
An Explanation of the Apparent Discrepancies

By considering the Avraham narratives as a whole, we may resolve this dilemma. Avraham's actions may be divided into three general categories: (1) responses to direct commands from God; (2) responses to promises or other information from God; and (3) responses to situations during which God does not communicate directly with Avraham.

1. Responses to Direct Commands From God

Whenever God commands an action, Avraham obeys without so much as a word of protest or questioning:

---

[26] See R. Aharon Lichtenstein, "Does Jewish Tradition Recognize an Ethic Independent of Halakha?" in *Modern Jewish Ethics: Theory and Practice*, ed. Marvin Fox (Columbus: Ohio State Univ., 1975), pp. 62–88.

[27] Those who consistently reinterpret the earlier narratives would find Avraham's confrontation of God anomalous in this instance.

[28] See *Gen. Rabbah* 39:6; 49:9; *Tanhuma – Noah* 9; *Aggadat Bereshit* 7:18; *Pirkei de-Rabbi Eliezer* 23. See further discussion and sources in Nehama Leibowitz, *Studies in Bereshit* (1985, 7th ed.), pp. 59–66.

[29] Kiel (vol. 2, p. 100) suggests that Avraham did not pray on behalf of Yitzhak because Avraham had a vested interest in that case. But Avraham had a vested interest in the earlier instances discussed above, yet he still engaged God in dialogue. Therefore, Kiel's answer is unconvincing.

1. Avraham goes to Canaan (Gen. 12:1–4).

2. Avraham circumcises himself and his household when Avraham is ninety-nine years old (Gen. 17:23–27).

3. Avraham names and circumcises Yitzhak (Gen. 21:1–4).

4. Avraham banishes Yishmael (Gen. 21:12–14).

5. Avraham is willing to sacrifice Yitzhak (Gen. 22:1–3). Here, Avraham says *hinneni* before hearing God's instructions, signifying his perpetual readiness to follow God's commandments.

2. Responses to Promises or Other Information From God

In these instances, Avraham praises God when gratitude is in order, and he questions or challenges God when he deems it appropriate:

1. Initially, when God makes promises, Avraham responds by bringing offerings in gratitude (Gen. 12:6–9; 13:18).

2. Avraham questions God when it appears unlikely to him that His promises will be fulfilled (Gen. 15:1–8).

3. Avraham laughs when God informs him that Sarah will have a son (Gen. 17:15–18).

4. Avraham challenges God's justice prior to the destruction of Sodom (Gen. 18:23–33).

5. After the angel blesses him at the *Akeidah*, Avraham remains silent (Gen. 22:15–18).

3. Responses to Situations During Which God Does Not Communicate Directly to Avraham

On all of these occasions, Avraham must use his own best judgment and respond spontaneously, without direct guidance from God.

1. Avraham goes to Egypt during a famine and offers Sarah to the Egyptians in order to save his life (Gen. 12:10–20).

2. Avraham resolves a conflict with Lot and his shepherds by offering his nephew first choice of lands (Gen. 13:7–13).

3. Avraham rescues Lot from four enemy kings (Gen. 14:12–16). He then offers one tenth of the spoils to Malkitzedek, and refuses to accept plunder from the king of Sodom (Gen. 14:17–24).

4. Avraham marries Hagar at Sarah's request and then allows Sarah to persecute Hagar when the latter aggravates her (Gen. 16:1–6).

5. Avraham offers hospitality to his three guests (Gen. 18:1–8).

6. Avraham travels to Philistia, and again says that Sarah is his sister (Gen. 20).

7. Avraham celebrates the birth of Yitzhak with a party (Gen. 21:1–8).

8. Avraham refuses to banish Yishmael, until God intervenes (Gen. 21:9–11).

9. Avraham strikes a treaty with Avimelekh and the Philistines (Gen. 21:22–34).

10. After the angel stops the *Akeidah*, Avraham sacrifices a ram he finds, and then names the mountain "*Adonai yir'eh*" (Gen. 22:14).

11. Avraham mourns Sarah and purchases the Cave at Makhpelah in Hevron (Gen. 23).

12. Avraham enjoins his servant to find a suitable wife for Yitzhak (Gen. 24:1–9).

13. Avraham marries Keturah and fathers more children. He then sends them away, establishing Yitzhak as his sole heir (Gen. 25:1–6). He dies at age 175.

To summarize: Avraham always followed God's commandments without questioning, but he reserved the right to challenge any information or promises. Therefore, Avraham's silence when following God's commandments to banish Yishmael and to sacrifice Yitzhak is to be expected. And so are Avraham's concerns about God's promises of progeny or information about the destruction of Sodom.

Avraham's last words in the Torah support the foregoing distinction. When his servant expresses concern that he may not be able to find a suitable wife for Yitzhak, Avraham responds (Gen. 24:7):

> The Lord God of heaven, who took me from my father's house, and from the land of my family, and who spoke to me, and who swore to me, saying, To your seed will I give this land; He shall send His angel before you, and you shall take a wife for my son from there.

Initially, Avraham voices resolute faith, proclaiming that God surely will assist the servant. But in the next verse (Gen. 24:8), Avraham makes provisions in the event that the servant is *unsuccessful*:

> But if the woman will not be willing to follow you, then you shall be free from my oath; only bring not my son there again.

Thus, Avraham's parting words capture the tensions in his faith. Since Avraham was acting on his own, he hoped and prayed for divine assistance.

But without a prophetic revelation, he knew that he could not be sure that his servant's mission would be successful.[30]

And after Avraham's death, God emphasizes the Patriarch's perfect record of observing God's commandments (Gen. 26:2–5):

> The Lord appeared to him, and said, Do not go down to Egypt; live in the land of which I shall tell you; Sojourn in this land, and I will be with you, and will bless you; for to you, and to your seed, I will give all these countries, and I will perform the oath which I swore to Avraham your father; And I will make your seed multiply as the stars of heaven, and will give to your seed all these countries; and in your seed shall all the nations of the earth be blessed; Because Avraham obeyed My voice, and kept My charge, My commandments, My statutes, and My laws.

It also is significant that in the decisive majority of cases, God leaves Avraham to act on his own.

III. Educational Challenges and Implications

Traditional exegetes battle passionately over nearly every point in the Avraham narratives, precisely because he is the paradigm of faith. They must balance good *peshat* in the text with broader issues of belief. Many of these issues remain unresolved by our greatest thinkers; and this uncertainty is precisely what can open serious discussion with students, beginning a learning process that should encompass a lifetime.

Of course, early elementary school educators cannot present the Avraham narratives in all their complexity. But as with any other topic, they must not distort the material or present the issues in a manner that later will need to be unlearned. Rather, educators of younger children should provide an uncomplicated picture that can be enhanced and deepened in later years. For example, they might build a portrait of Avraham as one who observed God's commandments, who resolved family conflicts amicably, who heroically rescued his nephew, who offered hospitality to unfamiliar guests, and who prayed on behalf of Sodom and Avimelekh.

But once students reach an age when they can understand complexity, educators must teach the Avraham narratives in their entirety. Based on our foregoing discussion, the biblical evidence leads to an approach like this:

---

[30] Ibn Ezra, Abarbanel, and Seforno (on 24:7) already note that v. 7 must be a prayer of Avraham (and not a prophecy), or else why express concern that his servant may not succeed? In contrast, Hoffmann suggests that Avraham personally believed that his servant would be successful; he concluded with v. 8 solely to placate his servant.

"Avraham always observed God's commandments, and trusted in God's ultimate goodness and fairness. He thanked God when he experienced blessing. Sometimes, he faced difficulties and did not always comprehend the world in which he lived. On those occasions, Avraham used his concerns as impetus to pray to God. Most of the time, God did not give instructions to Avraham, so he followed his own religious principles to react in those situations."

This composite message offers a parallel religious worldview for students: They are expected to observe *halakhah* unquestioningly – as did Avraham. When their lives are going well, they must thank God – as did Avraham. But they also may express puzzlement and confusion with expectations that do not always appear to be fulfilled. Rather than being trained to shy away from their questions, students should learn to exploit their religious dilemmas as impetus to prayer and introspection – as did Avraham. Finally, students should be shown that even Avraham – a great prophetic figure – functioned most of the time without explicit divine guidance. He had to use his religious judgment to determine many of his most difficult decisions. How much more applicable is this message in an age lacking the supreme gift of prophecy.

Additionally, much can be learned from the ongoing debate among our commentators regarding the acceptability of Avraham's questions. If our greatest sages disagree over such basic understandings of what good faith is, then we must realize that we do not have a perfect understanding ourselves. Rather, the two thousand year old dialogue with our commentators encourages a life-long search for new levels of understanding and religiosity.

As religious educators, we all are caught in the same paradox of trying to remain faithful to the biblical text, while also being driven by our own religious values and preferences. It is hoped that this essay can serve as a resource for Jewish educators in terms of material, with an emphasis on how the diversity of opinions can be a wonderful educational tool to explore a fundamental religious matter. Ultimately, a strong text focus, and a subsequent consideration of the commentators once we appreciate the underlying text issues, can be invaluable for our students, and for ourselves.

It is the challenge of contemporary educators to utilize the tensions within the text and among the commentators to open all available dimensions of complexity. In this manner, Avraham serves as an ever-deepening model of faith to those who study his life through the eternal word of the Living God.[31]

[31] This essay is based on a lecture given on August 20, 2000, at Cong. Shearith Israel of New York, commemorating the first anniversary of the untimely passing of Talia Nagar, ז״ל, a delightful eight-year-old girl in our Congregation whose life was cut short by a brain tumor. May her memory always inspire those she knew, as well as all those who pursue a religious relationship with God in times of crisis. I would like to thank my students Jonathan Duker, Ezra Fass, Daniel Frankel, Natan Kapustin, Yehuda Kraut, Joshua Weisberg, and Chananya Weissman for reading earlier drafts of this essay and for their helpful comments.

RELIGIOUS LANGUAGE
AND MODERN SENSIBILITIES:
TEACHING THE AKEIDAH TO ADULTS

ERICA BROWN

THE THIRD CLASS of twenty in a survey of the *Tanakh* has just ended. The doors of this synagogue in a rural New England town, crowded with adult students new to text study and unfamiliar with its demands, are about to close on a heated debate. The topic for the evening's adult education class was the binding of Isaac, the *Akeidah*. It is difficult to privilege some texts above others in order to squeeze in Genesis 22, but religious concepts of submission are an important key to unlocking tests of faith for biblical protagonists. We read the text and used it as a platform to discuss the function of *midrash*, medieval commentary, and exegetical debate. Then we simply read the text without embellishment and noted the silence of Abraham, the compliance of Isaac, the urgency of the divine emissary.

The students were angry. With a confidence they had not demonstrated in the first two classes, many questioned Abraham's willingness. Abraham did not pass a test of faith; he failed one by not disobeying God. Sarah must have died as a result of the binding since she no longer appears in our story, they claimed, and, after Genesis 22, God no longer addressed Abraham intimately. As open as their minds would be on nineteen other occasions to seeing new texts and new interpretations of familiar ones, were they closed that evening to the possibility that Abraham was indeed Kierkegaard's "knight of faith"? God fared worse; the divine being was likened to a Greek god: scurrilous, manipulative, and uninterested in the welfare of his subjects. This group, so new to Bible study and unacquainted with its riches, had stripped the text of its religious depth within moments and without any doubt of the verity of their interpretation.

I was exhausted. I am a better teacher than a defense lawyer. I was frustrated by the inability of such intelligent people to leave their psychological commonplaces for a different ancient world where more was asked of the believer. And I was angry at myself that I had not anticipated just how difficult it would be from the comfort of their suburban lives and their often lukewarm religious commitments for them to digest Genesis 22 as it stands. If I could turn back time, I would have started from a more basic place and listed the stock words and phrases common to religious life and asked for definitions before approaching the text. With religious fundamentalism on the rise and a heightened sensitivity to its dangers, we could have explored how other faith communities understand martyrdom and self-sacrifice. Alternatively or in addition, I could have asked them to write down a personal moment of religious epiphany; we might have shared those moments and analyzed their key characteristics.

There are adult educators who make wide use of journal writing or letter writing techniques so that adult learners can better process what they are learning and personalize it.[1] This can be an effective way of approaching material that can give off a surface impression of inaccessibility. Writing exercises during a class session can give adults the feeling of being more active participants in the acquisition of knowledge and allows some freedom from the pure lecture or discussion style. The limited class time available often prevents teachers from creating quiet and contemplative moments in a classroom for individual study. Yet with subjects that are religiously dense, it is precisely this type of experience and exercise that may best communicate the profundity that the teacher is striving to draw out of the material. While the age-old argument in education about relevance versus authenticity is an interesting one, it should not dissuade anyone from trying to bring demanding religious notions within the conceptual reach of adult students. In my zeal to cover ground and complete the textual unit, I failed to provide the philosophical or spiritual casing that would have personalized the *Akeidah* and "protected" it from the usual approaches, which either distort it to extremes or ignore it altogether.

The reaction to the poor approach I had used seemed, instead, to be an attenuated version of Philip Roth's controversial short story, "Eli, the Fanatic," where the father of a Hebrew school student complains that his daughter is being fed ridiculous stories like Abraham sacrificing his son. The tone is both mocking and incredulous: "This Abraham in the Bible was going to kill his own *kid* for a sacrifice. She gets nightmares from it, for

---

[1] See Steven Brookfield, "Grounding Teaching in Learning," in *Facilitating Adult Learning: A Transactional Process*, ed. Michael W. Galbraith (Malabar, FL: Kreiger Publishing, 1991), pp. 33–56; Susan Handelman, "Dear Class," in *Essays On Quality Learning: Teachers' Reflections on Classroom Practice* (College Park: Univ. of Maryland, 1998), pp. 17–32.

God's sake! You call that religion?"[2] Irving Howe, in his critique of Roth, was astonished by this fictional conversation, calling Roth's character both "benighted" and "stupid." "To write as if this middle-class Jewish suburbanite were unfamiliar with 'this Abraham' or shocked by the near sacrifice of Isaac, is simply preposterous."[3] Howe could not fathom that any Jew, even an ignorant one, would be unfamiliar with one of the Bible's most dramatic narratives. More than forty years after the publication of Roth's story, it might not be hard to find those with only a vague awareness of the silent climb up Mount Moriah. More troubling, however, are a new breed of modern readers familiar with the story, who describe it in anachronistic or psychological terms, often reducing its theology to gross error and misunderstanding. The emerging dismissal of Abraham's heroism signals many educational dangers and raises other questions of modernity's clash with religion.

Teaching the *Akeidah* to adults, even committed adults, is not the same as teaching it to children. Religiously observant adults who revisit and study the text can become, like Abraham's ram, stuck in its thorns, unwilling to accept the pat theology they might have been fed as children. Its complexities open up a larger question in adult education. How can we use its kind of religious language and the assumptions underlying that language in our modern context, where we are not often confronted with issues of self-sacrifice or martyrdom? How can we present texts safely but challengingly when we don't always have answers and, in some cases, aren't even sure of the right questions? This essay explores some of these issues and. Through teaching vignettes, exegesis of Genesis 22, and a survey of thinkers on the text and religious concepts in general, it ponders how adult education teachers can help modern readers approach the demands of religious language.

Today, many words in the lexicon of religion have fallen into disuse: submission, surrender, repentance, abstinence, modesty, dogma. The list

---

[2] Philip Roth, "Eli, the Fanatic," in *Goodbye Columbus* (New York: Houghton Mifflin, 1959). The short story also appears in *Jewish-American Literature: An Anthology*, ed. Abraham Chapman (New York: New American Library, 1974).

[3] Irving Howe, "Philip Roth Reconsidered," in *Jewish-American Literature: An Anthology*, p. 715. Howe's point also shows up the difference between the treatment of the *Akeidah* in American Jewish fiction and its appearance in Israeli poetry and fiction. The notion of such a sacrifice may be alien enough to the American Jewish psyche to have prompted Roth's fictional musing. In Israel, where army service – and the life-and-death risks involved – shapes the social fabric, the backdrop of the *Akeidah* has been twisted and turned to revisit themes of sacrifice. This feeds into broader cultural differences, which make fiction forgettable in one geographic location and autobiographical in another.

goes on, and each addition reminds us of the distance of these words and the concepts they signify from the contemporary imagination. They are overshadowed by other words that directly or indirectly challenge religious language – individualism, pluralism, relativism, multiculturalism, postmodernism. Today's "isms" have contributed to the linguistic atrophy of religious concepts. They have stymied our ability, even within Jewish religious circles, to use religious language confidently and unapologetically. As teachers, we hedge and sometimes hide behind the casuistic study of commentaries to avoid using it. Without it, however, our teaching loses its spiritual heft. When we are busy contextualizing religious concepts within ancient history or thinning out the words so that they achieve neutrality, we fail to transmit the religious dignity that this language conveys.

Another vignette illustrates the point. One *Yom ha-Sho'ah*, the day of Holocaust remembrance, I addressed an audience on the interpretation of *Kiddush Hashem* – sanctifying God's name – in rabbinic literature, particularly during World War II. It was a weighty day and an even weightier theme. We began with Lev. 22:32 – the command to sanctify God's name – and its talmudic and medieval commentaries, and examined codifications of the law in times of oppression. We considered legal interpretations of this biblical verse by rabbis in the Warsaw ghetto. Studying the tenacity of faith is both fascinating and draining. An elderly man rose from his seat with a question that soon became an accusation. He was a Holocaust survivor from the Carpathian Mountains. All that I had said was nonsense. The rabbis made up the whole idea because they were weak and spineless and had no leadership capabilities. People muttered around him. Many nodded in agreement. Can one challenge experience with theoretical study? Again I was stunned. I understood their objections but failed to see why these reasonable adults could not see another side – the side of beauty in religious devotion and the strength of belief that can accompany humanity to the darkest of places.

Teaching sacred texts about sacrifice and submission within a largely secular culture presents an instructor with a much debated dilemma: how to be true to the contextual reality and the religious significance of the text while not alienating students for whom these texts are inaccessible and possibly offensive.[4] We cannot delude ourselves into thinking that those for

---

[4] For more on this subject generally, see Michael Rosenak, "Authenticity and Relevance," in his *Teaching Jewish Values: A Conceptual Guide* (Jerusalem: Nachala Press, 1986), pp. 35–45 and "Explicit and Implicit Religious Life and Teaching" in *Commandments and Concerns: Jewish Religious Education in Secular Society* (Philadelphia: JPS, 1987), pp. 108–126.

whom these texts carry religious meaning are free from this need for decoding and relevance. Even, and sometimes especially, people of commitment struggle inwardly to make sense of religious demands and the language that expresses them. Here, E.D. Hirsch's distinction between meaning and significance is particularly important.[5] Students of text who are not observant can struggle with the *meaning* of a biblical verse but ultimately can push it aside when it does not speak to them. Committed Jews (and anyone of faith who reads sacred texts) must also live with the theological and legal *significance* of the text. There are texts that laud self-sacrifice and submission, sanctification and simple faith. We need not stop teaching them for fear of offense. Indeed, the influence of secular culture can be so pervasive that we need gentle reminders that key words in most religious vocabularies still exist even if the concepts they represent are quite foreign to the modern temperament.

The sociologist Peter Berger has written extensively about the difficulty a secular society faces in trying to appreciate such religious concepts:

[There are] truths that may have been lost in the process of modernization. Our ancestors didn't know about particle physics, but they spoke with the angels. Let it be stipulated that through the knowledge of particle physics we have gained a new measure of *truth*. But could it be that we have *lost* a truth when our conversation with angels came to a stop?[6]

Our "conversation with angels" is an apt way to describe a religious grasp on reality that secularization diminishes. Words do offer us, even with their limitations, a way of defining a transcendent experience. By not creating a vocabulary of religious language in a classroom, we may be denying students a different grasp of reality, a new lens with which to view the world and define experience. Religious silence and submission are concepts that need to be gently introduced and unpacked even for the committed reader. To this end, we also need to create educational awareness that a new trend in psychological writing on sacred literature has vastly undercut our ability to appreciate religious language. Such tendencies in modern Bible interpretation augment the secular and, in reductive fashion, emasculate the sacred. Perhaps nothing is more harmful to the frailty of faith than

---

[5] E.D. Hirsch, *Validity in Interpretation* (New Haven: Yale, 1967). The distinction is made on pp. 8–14, but the entire book, and particularly chapter 2, will be useful in understanding this difference.

[6] Peter Berger, *A Far Glory: The Quest for Faith in an Age of Credulity* (New York: Free Press, 1992), p. 13.

readings of sacred literature that reduce it to little more than a transcript of divine error and a Freudian foray into heroic consciousness.

It is understandable that *midrash* – either modern or ancient – translates a text into a new cultural modality, "sometimes even to the point of turning it on its head."[7] But when this cultural translation is also a radical departure from exegesis, it should demand closer investigation. What is the writer of modern *midrash* trying to communicate that he or she needed to borrow the ancient text as a platform for? How much does the interpretation collude with the text's wording and claim to be truly exegetical? Does this modern *midrash* aim to eliminate the values presented in the ancient text? The taking and transforming of an ancient character into a modern prototype has been termed "figuration."[8] Modern *midrash* is often less interested in exegesis and more entrenched in figuration. This trend, in itself, need not be educationally unsound. The Sages, too, used figuration in polemical and homiletic *midrashim*. "Turning a text on its head" holds potential risks and dangers, however, when the message it purports undermines the very faith that the text itself proclaims. The *Akeidah* is a staple text to illustrate the point.

*   * **

The *Akeidah* text is short on dialogue. The lack of speech heightens the dramatic tension as Abraham's journey is recorded in detail. We know more about the placement of the twigs for the sacrificial fires than we know of Abraham's inner thoughts. He responds to God's call in one word and offers Isaac a few more. "The journey is like a silent progress through the indeterminate and the contingent, a holding of the breath, a process which has no present, which is inserted, like a blank duration, between what has passed and what lies ahead."[9]

No one, however, lets Abraham stay silent. The *midrash* has Abraham dismissing Satan, encouraging Isaac's submission, and bargaining with God for the future destiny of his people, and Sarah so shocked by the act that

---

[7] David Jacobson, "The Development of Modern Midrash in the Twentieth Century" in *Modern Midrash* (Albany: SUNY Press, 1987), p. 3.

[8] Alan Mintz, *Hurban: Responses to Catastrophe in Hebrew Literature* (New York: Columbia University Press, 1984), pp. 99–100.

[9] Erich Auerbach, "Odysseus' Scar," in *Mimesis: The Representation of Reality in Western Literature* (Princeton: Princeton Univ. Press, 1969), p. 10. Auerbach argues that silence is not only an aspect of this text but a general literary style throughout the Bible, in contrast to other ancient literature. Not surprisingly, he uses Genesis 22 as the example of a biblical text that illustrates this point.

she herself dies when she hears the answer to her question, "My son, what did your father do to you?"[10] Post-midrashic literature on Genesis 22 also cannot stop talking, but in this regard it is often those who compare themselves with Abraham who need to speak. In Shalom Spiegel's *The Last Trial* we are shown another imposition on the text.[11] Throughout history, people used this story to write their own trials into an existing biblical test. Some concluded that their test was harder; they really did have to give up a child to death, or many children, or perhaps an entire community. Their story was a variation on Abraham's story, but their understanding of the text's message was ultimately the same: the power or duty of submission fell upon them and they took strength in Abraham's example:

> The reteller of traditional Jewish narratives shares with the midrashic exegete, the mythopoetic writer and the poet engaged in intertextual struggle with a precursor and attempt to appropriate a text from the past and transform it in order to better understand the experiences of the present.[12]

Genesis 22 provided a spiritual anchor for medieval suffering and helped its readers intellectualize their experience through the patriarch's trial. Yet, these poems or stories add more noise, more clamor, and additional voices to the silent text.

To appreciate the text's quiet we must turn to its companion *haftarah*, II Kings, chapter 4. In it, Elisha promises a Shunamite woman a son. She does not ask for the child, and, like Sarah, asks that the prophet not ridicule her, leading her to believe that there is destiny beyond biology. The child is born, however, and, after some years, goes out to the field to his father, takes ill, and cries, "My head, my head." The father does not treat the illness but has the child brought to his mother. The mother places the child on her knees. She is silent. Only after the child dies and is placed on the prophet's bed does she speak, urging her servants to make haste, dismissing Elisha's servant, Gehazi, and pleading with the prophet. What explains her earlier silence and passivity when she suddenly becomes so energized upon the child's death? She did not ask for the child. His birth was supernatural and so, too, is the protagonist's perception of the child's death. In the face of divine gifts or their relinquishment, the expected response is silence.

Abraham likewise did not expect the birth of Isaac. It took him 86 years

---

[10] *Tanhuma – Va'era* 23; also in *Eccles. Rabbah* 9:7.

[11] Shalom Spiegel, *The Last Trial* (New York: Behrman House, 1979).

[12] David Jacobson, p. 6.

to have Ishmael. He certainly did not expect another son at his advanced age when his heir had essentially been determined, let alone with his barren wife, Sarah. When Isaac was born, it was a great gift to the patriarch, and the party occasioned by Isaac's weaning was a celebration of viability. Thus, Isaac was not taken back; when God asked for Isaac, Abraham gave back the child he never expected. But there is more than Abraham and the Shunamite woman's quiet observation of divine workings. Genesis 22 must be read through the prism of Genesis 21. There, Abraham does fight on behalf of a child, Ishmael, and is told by God to be silent and to listen to Sarah, his wife, who willed the boy and his mother away.[13] The expectation when losing a child through God's direction is silence and obedience in chapter 21; and so, too, is there silence in chapter 22. The silence in the text is quite intentional. Many verbs convey movement and action in this chapter but none actively convey speech. Whenever Abraham talks throughout the text of the *Akeidah*, it is to answer and not to question or to initiate. We see a literary parallel in the Shunamite text, and we see Abraham's silence in the shadow of the Ishmael story. What is to be learned from this silence?

Kierkegaard views the silence as a statement of theological stateliness, of Abraham's formidable strength:

> Abraham had faith and did not doubt. He believed the ridiculous. If Abraham had doubted – then he would have done something else, something great and glorious... He would have been admired in the world and his name forever forgotten; but it is one thing to be admired another to be a guiding star that saves the anguished.[14]

Kierkegaard depicted scenarios of doubt, hesitation, confrontation, negotiation and showed that each fell short of the text's ultimate message: submission. That is the word, next to silence, that is most resonant with the chapter. Abraham submits his will to the will of his Maker but does not lose himself as a result; rather, he defines himself:

---

[13] For this and many other linguistic parallels between Genesis 21 and Genesis 22, see Uriel Simon, *"Gerush Yishmael: Ha-Akeidah she-Kidmah le-Akeidat Yitzhak"* in *Bakesh Shalom ve-Rodfehu* (Tel-Aviv: Yedi`ot Ahronot, 2002), pp. 54–57. One could argue, as has Bryna Levy in private correspondence, that the silence of Genesis 21 is one imposed by God on Abraham (and his wife), and that Abraham's silence in Genesis 22 is his own. However, one could also counter-argue that the silence imposed on Abraham in chapter 21 inspires his silence at the *Akeidah* precisely because he has been silenced once and now understands unquestioning obedience as the appropriate response.

[14] Soren Kierkegaard, *Fear and Trembling,* trans. Alastair Hannay (Middlesex, England: Harmondsworth, 1985), p. 54.

The call of God, as Kierkegaard hears that call, is a call to infinite possibility, to standing before God in subjectively free individuality. Anything less than this belongs to the ethical, to the family, to the state, which measures one from the outside. God's voice is the voice of possibility, which tells the individual that the choice is infinite and not determined already. And this "command of God" stands in opposition to the ethical demand to *define* oneself within extant social institutions.[15]

Submission is a frightening concept for a modern reader because it implies a loss of personal autonomy.[16] Today it is a pejorative word. Classically, however, submission within a religious context is religiously edifying. Giving up part of oneself to God or one's fellow human beings can present spiritually potent moments. We may lose ourselves in prayer; we may apportion time for religious studies. We may even act in line with duty when it conflicts with our personal wants. Ironically, for many the act of forgoing oneself may lead to finding oneself, as Kierkegaard tried to demonstrate. Perhaps Abraham understood the full extent of his faith only when he descended the mount.

The philosopher Robert Nozick in *The Examined Life* writes this about faith:

Faith's particular route to belief is the following. There is an encounter with something very real – an actual person, a person in a story, a part of nature, a book or a work of art, a part of one's being – and this thing has extraordinary qualities that intimate the divine by being forms of qualities that the divine itself would have: these extraordinary qualities touch you deeply, opening your heart so that you feel in contact with a special manifestation of the divine.[17]

Religion must have as much silence as it does noise, as much limitation

---

[15] Jerome I. Gellman, *The Fear, the Trembling, and the Fire: Kierkegaard and Hasidic Masters on the Binding of Isaac* (Lanham, MD: Univ. Press, 1994), pp. 14–15.

[16] For an understanding of the tension between religious demand and personal autonomy, see Moshe Sokol, "Personal Autonomy and Religious Authority," in *Rabbinic Authority and Personal Autonomy*, ed. Moshe Sokol (Northvale, NJ: Aronson, 1992), pp. 169–216. Although rabbinic authority is obviously not divine authority, Sokol outlines different levels of personal autonomy that may be useful in understanding the scope of the problem.

[17] Robert Nozick, *The Examined Life* (New York: Touchstone, 1989), p. 51.

as it does freedom. Without a full complement of terms for religious experience, we may be denying ourselves moments of transcendence. Again Berger makes us sensitive to the need for meaningful religious terminology:

> Invariably, human beings not only experience the world but reflect on that experience. But when it comes to the experience that put man in touch with the transcendent, a distinctive difficulty arises: Reflection occurs by means of language, but language is rooted in ordinary reality; it is best geared to the practical concerns of everyday life. Consequently, it is very difficult to put into language any experience that radically transcends ordinary reality. Theology, in the broadest meaning of the term, is an attempt to place religious experience on the scale of reason, or at least to formulate it in the language of reason.[18]

There is no language of reason that can fully capture the drama of the *Akeidah*. Perhaps that is why much of Jewish theology is conveyed through narrative and not dogma. Stories *of* suffering affect us more powerfully than theologies *about* suffering. But, again, understanding the suffering may require a religious lexicon:

> The awareness that being involves suffering is a religious sensibility. This is not only because religious man, by nature, is claustrophobic in the confinement of the here and now and thus prone to a sense of suffering. It is also because the precariousness of his being in the world is in danger of collapsing when confronted with pain and evil that bewilder and threaten to tear him apart... [In relating the suffering of a religious being to the biblical text] the hearer of the biblical story is expected already to be well on the way in the exhausting journey of suffering and its confrontation. The story does not, for even a moment, raise the question of why man suffers or of what the essential meaning of suffering is. For Abraham, the call to give Isaac up causes no surprise, though it does inflict infinite pain. Abraham is wise enough in his old age to know that pain is reality and that the ability to forego is the mark of religious man; Abraham's strength is being tested, not his belief...it is the deaf listener to biblical tradition who hears that dissonant chord in the straightforward story. The listener already knows the sadness and weariness of religiosity and is straining to hear of the massive strength with which Abraham raised the knife in trembling hands.[19]

---

[18] Berger, *A Far Glory*, pp. 134–135.

[19] Aharon Agus, *The Binding of Isaac and Messiah: Law, Martyrdom, and Deliverance in Early*

Submission creates an opportunity to forge a bond with one's Creator, communicate commitment, define one's being or priorities, confront suffering, face adversity with strength, or lose oneself in a greater cause. We don't often take the time out to ask our students what Abraham learned from this experience and why it was valuable. Instead, we often cloud our teaching with a bevy of commentators and religious concepts that we sometimes fail to unpack. Submission usually does not speak the "language of reason," and its meaning is not self-evident. Like Abraham on his journey, we need to take time to hear the silence with our students.

It is difficult to teach or even to hear Abraham's silence because of the noise made by the psychology employed by some modern scholars in studying the *Akeidah*. Burton Visotzky's *The Genesis of Ethics* seems to be one such culprit:

> It was grotesque, even kafkaesque, this snatching away of the son of Sarah after all of the miracles that were wrought to have him. Had not Abraham given enough to God as yet? Raising the knife twice for circumcision of the boys and himself did not satisfy this God's desire for their blood... Abraham thought briefly of drowning his sorrows as Noah did. At least Abraham had the solace of knowing that after the sacrifice of Isaac, he, the survivor, would have no offspring to lure him to sexual misadventure.[20]

After calling God a mafia "don" who came to Abraham to "collect his dues" for divine protection with Pharaoh and Avimelekh, Visotzky talks about the act itself and its repercussions.[21] He writes:

> Modern theologians have suggested that God's jealous test of Abraham is in response to something far more iniquitous than parental love. The claim hinges on the way in which Abraham and Sarah relate to their long awaited child. Their behavior toward Isaac is obsessive...the efficacy of the idol must be destroyed. That God spared Isaac in the end is then a symbol of God's mercy.[22]

Rabbinic Religiosity (New York: SUNY Press, 1988), pp. 1–3.

[20] Burton S. Visotzky, *The Genesis of Ethics: How the Tormented Family of Genesis Leads Us to Moral Development* (New York: Crown Publishers, 1996), p. 103.

[21] Jack Miles in *God: A Biography* (New York: Knopf, 1995) claims that the *Akeidah* presents a period of self-discovery for God wherein he can gauge how realistic it is to test the faithful. Here, he concludes that, "...it is as much God who contends defeat as Abraham." See pp. 58–61.

[22] Visotzky, *Genesis of Ethics*, p. 105.

In this vein we find another modern-day reading:

The binding of Isaac is a warning about the destructive potential that lies beneath the loving surface of the child-parent relationship. Even acts that begin in love can veer into narcissism or selfishness.[23]

This problematic mode of interpretation contends that the binding was a punishment for Abraham and Sarah who were excessive in their dotage. Their son had become an idol and God was too jealous to stand for it. This reading imputes idolatry to the founder of monotheism. In the end, God spares little Isaac out of mercy, but the test was conceived by an "immature" God unwilling to share love, and by parents too preoccupied with a child to give God enough attention. The story has left the sacred pedestal it occupies in the Bible, in the Talmud, in *midrash*, in a thousand years of exegesis, and even in Kierkegaard's philosophy to become a quasi-psychological manual on bad parenting. There is no religion left in it. These writers not only read the text; they judged it and attached intention and detail that do not appear in the narrative. While *midrash* and commentary may function similarly, they do not try to excoriate or rid a text of its religious dimensions.[24] More commonly, *midrash* and exegesis elaborate on nuances in the text, developing and enhancing spiritual lessons. There are red lines in *midrash*, but perhaps not sufficient red lines in modern *midrash*.

Interpretation can be a very subjective endeavor; it is only natural that we use the language of our culture to interpret our world. When that language is psychological and no longer religious, submission becomes selfishness and silence becomes narcissism. We find ourselves a far cry from Otto's painstaking attempt to understand the rudiments of holiness.[25] Instead, much of modern Bible interpretation invites us to heap scorn upon

---

[23] Naomi Rosenblatt and Joshua Horwitz, *Wrestling with Angels: What the First Family of Genesis Teaches us about Spiritual Identity, Sexuality and Personal Relationships* (New York: Delacorte Press, 1995). p. 201.

[24] See Anson Laytner, *Arguing with God: A Jewish Tradition* (Northvale, New Jersey: Jason Aronson, 1990), pp. 48–49.

[25] Rudolph Otto's underlying assumption is that people experience holiness and need to articulate it in terms that can be comprehended instead of leaving it in the realm of the ineffable. Otto says of the sublime, "It humbles us and at the same time exalts us, circumscribes and extends us beyond ourselves, on the one hand releasing in us a feeling analogous to fear and on the other rejoicing us." See his *The Idea of the Holy* (London: Oxford Univ. Press, 1958), p. 42. His beautiful description of that which is sublime makes us ponder if a Visotzky-like reading would ruin this experience; we would either doubt our ability to have it or question its legitimacy.

transcendence. In the making of modern *midrash*, authors and students are encouraged to be playful and make associations but are not sufficiently advised to wed their interpretation to the words themselves, to use proof-texts, to realize the craft of careful word choice. Not only do readings such as these give far less educated Jews license to play with and manipulate the text (after all, the rabbis of the *midrash* were not free, in their textual playfulness, of criticism of Abraham); they create doubt in the minds of educated Jews. Would the Bible include narratives that would arouse such suspicion and scorn for a biblical hero? One can acknowledge the hero's errors while still being aware that their presence in the text is to promote what is extraordinary about them, not what is commonplace.

One contemporary scholar of the Hebrew Bible expressed his consternation at a spate of scholars who are ridiculing the patriarch, contending that this modern trend was probably fueled by Kant's reading of the story in *The Conflict of the Faculties* in the eighteenth century.[26] There, Kant writes that Abraham should have replied to this supposedly divine voice: "That I ought not to kill my good son is quite certain. But that you, this apparition, are God – of that I am not certain, and never can be, not even if this voice rings down to me from heaven."[27]

Not only should Abraham have questioned God about the act, suggests Kant, he should have questioned God about His very identity. God, being God, would never have asked this of man, let alone of this man Abraham, his faithful servant. Kant terms this narrative "the euthanasia of Judaism." The problematic interpretations I have cited demonstrate that Kant's reading is now flourishing in academic halls and adult education classes. Modern concepts of God, submission, and theology make this text readable only if it can be misread. Against this trend, it is argued, we must see in Abraham's deed "a paradigmatic disclosure of deeper truths" that many contemporary writers fail to grasp because of their "impoverished religious imaginations."[28] Included in this list of truths are religious notions that are foreign to modern sensibilities but are, at the same time, still central to a spiritual persona:

---

[26] Jon D. Levenson, "Abusing Abraham: Traditions, Religious Histories and Modern Misinterpretations," *Judaism* 47 (Summer 1998): 259–77.

[27] Immanuel Kant, *Conflict of the Faculties*, trans. Mary J. Gregor (New York: Abaris Books, 1979), p. 115.

[28] Levenson, p. 272.

The person of faith must be willing to sacrifice what is most precious; all we have, even our lives and those of our dearest, belong ultimately to God; His claim must be honored; God's promises are often painfully at odds with empirical reality; God's acceptance of us is partly dependent on the exemplary conduct of our forebears, and our system of worship is a continuing commemoration and reenactment of the radical obedience of the heroes of faith or yore... All this is lost when...ethics monopolizes our approach to the text and the presence of immoral acts therein necessarily disqualifies the entire narrative.[29]

Modern impositions on the text prevent the text from speaking for itself. The binding narrative is about the sound of silence; in its literal form, Abraham offers a theology where both debate and silence must have a place. It is both debate with God and silence before Him that frame Abraham's legacy. Abraham had been willing to enter into negotiations with family members (chapter 13), allies (chapter 14), local princes (chapter 20), and even God himself (chapter 18), but at the *Akeidah* he is stricken with complete silence. Submission and silence have their dangers, but also have their beauty.

During the middle of a Boston winter, a lunchtime class of a hundred or so professionals studied *Kiddush Hashem* together as one of the major themes of the book of Leviticus. A tall man with curly hair made his way towards me and shook his head vehemently. He argued frenetically with me for ten minutes, unable to hear anything I said in response. Jewish law is utterly mistaken. God would never ask for someone's death. This adult learner could not stand the concept, so he negated it. I did not create the idea. I was only asked to teach it. This was not an answer, only an excuse. It was not what I meant to say. What I really wanted to say was that it is not difficult to dismiss the tenacity of faith if you lack faith. A retired professor of religion, a Christian, passed by and thanked me. Submission is the bedrock of his faith, he said defiantly. He, too, sadly shook his head, "No one talks about it anymore."

If Jewish educators present a religious vocabulary that introduces and defines theological concepts instead of shying away from them, we can provide religiously committed individuals with another means of interpreting experience.[30] If we invite adults who may have seen a text dozens of

---

[29] Id., pp. 273–274.

[30] Those who may feel cautious about this approach may benefit from Israel Scheffler's

times to confront it and strip it bare until it speaks its theology plainly, we can safely approach the many niggling questions they have in their heads. Unlike uncommitted adult students of religion, these learners may have the same questions but not the same lack of reserve. Through playful and sometimes convoluted trysts with the texts, we may ironically be divesting religious texts of their sacred meanings; in domesticating them, we lose an opportunity for spiritual and intellectual growth. We miss the supernal possibilities presented in, for example, Rabbi Soloveitchik's description of the halakhic persona: "Great strength and presence of mind, the acceptance of the divine decree with love, the consciousness of the law and the judgment, the might and power of the Halakhah, and faith, strong like flint."[31]

A Jewish educator should try to "point toward a reality that lies beyond the ordinary"[32] and strive to be the compass of these experiences by using sacred literature as a pointer or signal for transcendence. If, instead, we dismiss a text's sanctity by encouraging any interpretation, avoiding theology, or reverting to childish readings when the words and concepts are impossibly difficult, we may find that instead of creating interest in Tanakh, we help students close the good book.[33]

*   *   *

There is a text of national sacrifice parallel to Abraham's individual sacrifice. In Exodus 14, the Egyptians are in vehement pursuit of the Israelites, who are stranded on the edge of the sea. The people cry out at God and Moses. Moses responds to the noise in a sermonic attempt at calm (Ex. 14:13–15):

Fear not, stand still, and see the salvation of the Lord, which he will show you today. For as you have seen Egypt this day, you shall not see them again ever. The Lord shall fight for you and you shall be quiet. And the Lord said to Moses, Why do you cry to me? Speak to the children of Israel that they may go forward.

---

insights in his "In Praise of the Cognitive Emotions," in *Inquiries: Philosophical Studies of Language, Science and Learning* (Indianapolis: Hackett Publishing, 1986), pp. 347–362.

[31] R. Joseph B. Soloveitchik, *Halakhic Man* (Philadelphia: JPS, 1983), p. 78.

[32] Berger, *A Far Glory*, p. 139.

This is a text of noise. The people cry out. When Moses speaks, he introduces static verbs: see, do not fear, stand still, be quiet. In contrast to the nation's noise, Moses recommends observation and silence. And in contrast to both of these approaches, God recommends movement. Go forward. Only in surrendering yourselves will you save yourselves. Only then, after that act, do we have the statement, "Then they believed in God and in Moses, his servant" (Ex. 14:31). The Israelites had multiple miracles on account of which to believe in God while in Egypt, yet only as a consequence of submission and their own leap of faith – both literal and metaphysical – did they come to authentic belief. It was then that the wailing faded into the sounds of the crashing waves. Crying turned to silence. Passivity became active faith and skepticism transformed itself into transcendence. The walk through the sea must have been totally hushed. It was probably as quiet as an early morning on Mount Moriah.

---

33 I would like to thank Howie Deitcher, Bryna Levy, and Daniel Marom for their careful reading and comments on this essay.

THE BRISKER DEREKH TODAY: ARE WE PURSUING THE "PATH" ENVISIONED BY REB HAYYIM?

DONIEL SCHREIBER

THE STUDY OF TALMUD is the lifeblood of the Jewish people. Throughout our history we have been occupying ourselves with it tenaciously even during the darkest oppressions. Whether we study Talmud alone or in company – with our family, students, colleagues, or teachers – there is a sense of mission, history, and divine connection that somehow pervades. It is not surprising, then, given the centrality of talmudic study, that different *darkhei ha-limmud* (methods) of talmudic analysis have developed over time.

For more than a century, the prevailing method of *iyyun* (analysis) in the yeshivah world has been, in one form or another, the Brisker *derekh* (method), developed by R. Hayyim Soloveitchik (1853–1918) of Brisk. Very broadly, the hallmarks of this approach are its insistence on rigorous analysis, critical independence, precise classification, and emphasis on Rambam's *Mishneh Torah* as a focal point of Torah study. The "Brisker *derekh*" along with other forms of conceptual analysis are colloquially known as *lomdus*. The Brisker *derekh*'s exciting and insightful approach re-energized talmudic study particularly, and Torah study generally, firmly establishing the ethic of Torah learning in the psyche of the modern-day committed Jew.[1]

---

[1] For a historical review and analysis of R. Hayyim's method, see R. Shlomo Yosef Zevin, *Ishim ve-Shitot* (Tel Aviv: Betan ha-Sefer, 1952), pp. 43–70; Norman Solomon, *The Analytic Movement: Hayyim Soloveitchik and his Circle* (Atlanta: Scholars Press, 1993); Shaul Stampfer, *Ha-Yeshivah ha-Lita'it be-Hithavutah* (Jerusalem: Shazar, 1995); Marc Shapiro, "The Brisker Method Reconsidered," *Tradition* 31:3 (Spring 1997): 78–102; R. Mosheh Lichtenstein, "'What' Hath Brisk Wrought: The *Brisker Derekh* Revisited," *The Torah u-Madda Journal* 9 (2000): 1–18; and R. Elyakim Krumbein, "From Reb Hayyim of Brisk and Rav Joseph B. Soloveitchik to *Shi`urim of Rav Aharon Lichtenstein*: The Growth of a Learning Tradition" (Hebrew), *Netu`im* 9 (2002): 51–94. For a more personal and intimate perspective of R. Hayyim's Method, see R. Joseph B. Soloveitchik's

While the impact of the Brisker *derekh* on contemporary Talmud study has recently begun to receive nascent but important reassessment, the influence of *lomdus* upon the character, philosophy, and constitution of present-day Talmud students still awaits any form of review. It is my intent to continue the examination of contemporary *lomdus*, as well as articulate an initial assessment of its effect upon, and implications for, today's student. Periodic review of the Brisker *derekh*'s methodological implementation and its impact on the student of Talmud will hopefully assist teachers, parents, and students in forming an appreciation of the current talmudic educational environment and of the need for improvements and adjustments.

This essay's attempt at generating an evaluation of contemporary *lomdus* and the concept of *derekh ha-limmud*, however, requires two qualifications. Firstly, writing an exposition on the methodology or system of any type of thought generally presupposes a complete and comprehensive mastery of the subject under discussion. Accordingly, it assumes a measure of arrogance, which is amplified when the subject is the study of Talmud – the embodiment of our tradition, the revealed Will of God. Inasmuch as one cannot have complete understanding of the infinite revealed Will, the very endeavor of writing an assessment of the method of its study is questionable and, perhaps, even presumptuous. Therefore, it should be understood that I do not offer my observations in the guise of a master talmudist; rather, I haltingly, but purposefully, submit them as a concerned student and teacher of Torah.

This brings us to the second qualification. In the course of my experience, I – like most people who learn Torah – have traveled on a spiritual and intellectual odyssey. In the course of this journey, whether entrenched in the "four cubits of *halakhah*" in *yeshivot* and *batei midrash*, or engaged in casual discussion in their corridors and cafeterias, I have encountered much discourse and discord on the advantages and hazards of the Brisker *derekh*. Interestingly, these discussions were not limited to mere students. Young scholars, rabbis, and *Roshei Yeshivah* were often drawn to, if not the center of, these debates.

Thus, as this is a familiar topic for students of Torah, I do not pretend to offer newly discovered ideas. I merely aim to organize and present some of the various comments and observations that I have heard from, or discussed with, my *rebbeim*, colleagues, and students. Collectively, these insights put the Brisker *derekh*, or the contemporary conceptual method of studying

---

"Mah Dodekh mi-Dod" in *Divrei Hagut ve-Ha`arakhah* (Jerusalem: WZO, 1982), esp. pp. 70–85.

Talmud, into perspective – from its definition, usefulness, and implementation, to its drawbacks and pitfalls.[2]

While the benefits of such a *derekh ha-limmud* certainly deserve recognition, its limitations ought not, and cannot, be ignored. Indeed, reviewing and critiquing elements of the Brisker *derekh* as it is implemented today, and heeding the ultimate realization that we must rethink and refine some of its contemporary aspects, will serve Torah study's very definition – to humbly engage, encounter, and ultimately surrender to the will of God.[3]

Furthermore – and let there be no mistake – this endeavor will contribute to preserving, and not detract from, the illustrious legacy of R. Hayyim. Indeed, the "Brisker Method" – the brilliant integration of Torah intuition with the idea of systemization and technique – flowed from and sprang out of R. Hayyim's Torah personality as a Halakhic Man, and all that it entails for a Torah way of life.[4] As a result, the underpinnings of the Brisker Method – asking the question of "what," rather than "why" – reflect Halakhic Man's emphatic attitude of total compliance with divine imperatives and absolute subordination to God.[5] It is *this* "path" (*derekh*) of Halakhic Man – Torah character and halakhic persona *par excellence* – that must prevail, then, in order for the Brisker *derekh* (method) to survive, let alone triumph.[6] Consequently, let us consider the contemporary state of the Brisker "*derekh*" (in both its senses) and ask: Are we following in the footsteps of R. Hayyim, or have we strayed from the "path"?

II. The Attraction of Studying Talmud[7]

To better understand the preoccupation with *derekh ha-limmud* and why the Brisker method is a crucial contribution that must be perpetuated, one

[2] As my experiences as both student and teacher reflect an all-male yeshivah environment, I hesitate to expound upon how the entrance of women into the realm of serious Talmud study would or would not correspond to my observations. This is especially true for the essay's latter sections, which conjecture on the pedagogic pitfalls of the Brisker method. No doubt much of what I write here is germane for female Talmud students, but clearly that more recent phenomenon would have its own unique characteristics, some of which are discussed in the final section of Gilla Rosen's essay, later in this volume.

[3] Cf. Rabbi Soloveitchik's comments in "The Study of Torah," cited in Aaron Rakeffet-Rothkoff, *The Rav: The World of Rabbi Joseph B. Soloveitchik* (Hoboken, NJ: Ktav, 1999), vol. 2, pp. 203–04.

[4] Cf. R. Soloveitchik, *Divrei Hagut*, pp. 82–85.

[5] See R. Lichtenstein, "'What' Hath Brisk Wrought," especially pp. 5–6.

[6] Hence the pun in the title of this essay.

[7] This section, and section IV, are based primarily upon discussions with R. Michael Rosensweig, at Yeshiva University in June 1986.

must first explore what it is about talmudic study that establishes it as the centerpiece, and perhaps obsession, of the Jewish people. The answer strikes to the core of what Torah study is all about. When one is involved in the analysis of Talmud, reaching great depths of understanding, one achieves a genuinely rich sense of satisfaction. While this is partially due to the fact that one is involved in the important and basic commandment to learn Torah, it is largely because one is engaged in something that is the most meaningful and penetrating experience humanly possible. It is the endeavor, in our never-ending pursuit to draw close to God, to understand divine intent.[8]

The only real way finite "man" has to reach God is to be involved in what God has revealed to us. This, to be sure, includes performance of *mitzvot*, but especially pertains to Torah study in general, and Talmud study in particular, because it is the embodiment of the will of God. While thrashing out questions involving torts may not be as obvious a method of bringing one closer to God as analyzing the laws of prayer and blessings, it is nonetheless equally efficacious.

If one does not relate to this experience and is not inspired by it, one may be serious about talmudic study and derive a certain pleasure from it but cannot be passionate in it. Those who are genuinely fervent in their study of Talmud, to the extent that they are animated by an almost consuming passion and an unbending resolve in its pursuit, have most certainly encountered the *Shekhinah*, the divine presence.

III. Definition of Talmudic Analysis or *Iyyun*

This passionate form of connecting with God has so captivated the Jewish people that understandably numerous modes of analysis or *iyyun* were developed to assist in this endeavor. While all agree that *iyyun* entails more than superficially studying the simple meaning of the text, there is a wide spectrum of approaches to defining *iyyun*, and we can outline three archetypes.[9]

---

[8] R. Aharon Lichtenstein, *Rosh Yeshivah* of Yeshivat Har Etzion, once remarked that even were the study of Talmud not a *mitzvah*, the Jewish people would still be passionate in their learning of Talmud – as it is our primary and clearest substantive connection with God. See also R. Lichtenstein's article "Study" in Arthur Cohen and Paul Mendes-Flohr, eds., *Contemporary Jewish Religious Thought* (New York: Scribner, 1987), pp. 931–937.

[9] See also, R. Yitzchak Adler, *Lomdus: A Substructural Analysis of Conceptual Talmudic Thought* (New York, 1989), pp. v–ix.

One end of the spectrum, reflective of classic *iyyun* found in the geonic period, would place the elucidation of texts as its main goal. All questions and analyses, in this approach, aim to arrive at a better understanding of the texts. On the other end of the spectrum, reflective of more contemporary *lomdus*, is the attempt to understand concepts by classifying, conceptualizing and defining halakhic matter. In its extreme form, where the concept reigns supreme, text is relegated to peripheral importance, significant mainly in its relationship vis-a-vis the concept. Focusing on key lines in the Talmud, without seriously attempting to understand the flow of the text, and identifying critical formulations in *rishonim* without significant regard for their context, are reflective of this approach. In the middle of the spectrum, one finds a more balanced system, embracing both the importance of text and the centrality of concept. The text generates analysis of concepts, while concepts shed light upon new ways of reading text.

While these archetypes do not necessarily exist in their pure forms, various *shi'urim* (lectures) and *yeshivot* certainly favor one model over another. These forms are also found in talmudic commentators. The *ge'onim*, Rashi, and Maharsha certainly lean toward the text-oriented approach, while the Tosafists, Ravad, Ramban, and R. Hayyim Soloveitchik of Brisk pull in the conceptual direction. Indeed, the transition from classic *iyyun* to Brisker *lomdus* at the end of the nineteenth century was reflected by the focus on, and the categorization of, concepts.

To be sure, the original Brisker method of analysis has, over time, undergone various transformations through different schools of learning. For instance, the school of thought of Rabbi Joseph B. Soloveitchik has more clearly defined and developed many of the technical terms and concepts, and has more broadly applied the ideas to new *sugyot* (topics).[10] Additionally, R. Aharon Lichtenstein, *Rosh Yeshivah* of Yeshivat Har Etzion, has, as methodologist of *derekh ha-limmud*, reduced conceptual analysis into a conscious technique more accessible and understandable to the average student of Talmud, paradoxically elevating *iyyun* to a new level of sophistication. This methodology incorporates a wide range of analytical tools and procedures, which define the perimeters, parameters, and process of a *sugya*, in order to illustrate the spectrum of possibilities.[11]

---

[10] R. Aharon Lichtenstein, "The Rav at Jubilee: an Appreciation," *Tradition* 30:4 (Summer 1996): 47–48.

[11] More recently, in my experience, R. Michael Rosensweig, *Rosh Yeshivah* at Yeshiva University, has advanced *iyyun* into new spheres of analysis. It entails, on the one hand, a microscopic approach requiring exhaustive, comprehensive, and often tedious sifting of the most subtle halakhic minutiae. On the other, it requires one to ascend to a mac-

In its most sublime form, *lomdus* achieves rigorous, microscopic scrutiny, and simultaneous broad, panoramic vision. When *lomdus* masters both polar extremes, it enables one to integrate and interpret all forms of nuances and detail into the landscape of the *sugya* in the broadest sense of the term – the meta-*sugya*.[12] For example, elements of *halakhah* associated with the process of *beit din* (courts) may shed light on how to understand the broader concept of *din* (Jewish civil law); details in the topic of *edim zomemim* (scheming witnesses) could reflect on the larger picture of witnesses and testimony; minutiae in the discussion of *gittin* (bills of divorce), might clarify the wider topic of *shetarot* (legal documents). The incessant and rigorous investigation of a detail's relationship to the meta-*sugya* is the hallmark of this system and may represent the pinnacle of *lomdus* and the Brisker *derekh*.[13]

Finally, at a different level, another form of *iyyun* is learning Talmud for the purpose of arriving at a halakhic or legal conclusion and implementation (*aliba de-hilkheta*). Rif, Rambam, Beit Yosef and Rema, to name a few, represent this approach. There are many *shi'urim* today, at various levels, which typify this system.[14]

Whether *lomdus* and *pesak* (legal decisions) may be combined in an integrated system to cooperate with and enhance one another is a question that still needs to be addressed. Classically, *lomdus* and *pesak* are considered, at best, reconcilable, and at worst, ill matched. It is difficult, indeed, to merge a conceptual system of study whose agenda is abstraction with a practical system of study whose goal is concretization. Obviously, this is not to say

---

roscopic perspective, taking into consideration a wealth of *sugyot* revolving around a broad issue, and then peering downward upon the sweeping, halakhic landscape. This method, in essence, expands Brisker analysis to the farthest reaches of both ends of the *sugya*.

[12] For an excellent illustration of this method, see R. Michael Rosensweig, "Family Structure: Halakhic and Anthropological Perspectives," in *Sefer Higayon: Studies in Rabbinic Logic*, ed. Moshe Koppel (Alon Shevut: Zomet, 1995), pp. 1–24. I use the term meta-*sugya* to refer to what I experienced as a student of R. Rosensweig – his emphasis on analyzing classic *sugyot* and then treating each of them as a detail within a broader enveloping *sugya*, which in turn may become a detail in an even broader *sugya*, and so on.

[13] The "meta-*sugya*" method also rectifies the Brisker *derekh*'s almost exclusive emphasis upon the question of "what" in the *sugya*, which shut down an entire area of fertile possibility latent in the "why" dimension of the *sugya*. The "why" may be utilized, for instance, to help clarify the underpinnings of the *halakhah* under discussion. See M. Lichtenstein, "'What' Has Brisk Wrought," pp. 6–12, for a more developed argument in favor of incorporating the "why" into the Brisker framework, and how it can be accomplished.

[14] Sefardic and Hasidic *yeshivot* generally emphasize this practical sort of learning, while amongst Ashkenazi or Lithuanian-styled *yeshivot*, Yeshivat Merkaz ha-Rav, for example, actively pursues such an approach to Torah study.

there are no individual institutions or Torah scholars employing *lomdus* to attain *halakhah* rulings.[15] Rather, the development of this endeavor into a system and method has yet to be realized and become a source of study. This field, therefore, as a system, is still a fertile, challenging, and relatively unexplored dimension of *iyyun*.

IV. Implementing *Lomdus*[16]

Before one can even begin conceptual analysis, or *lomdus*, one has to believe that within the halakhic system there exists an inner logic, an inner coherence. When one emerges from a *sugya*, one should expect to have uncovered a topic in terms of the basic fundamental issues. The degree of seriousness with which one takes nuances in formulations and logical inferences indicates the extent one believes in this inner logic.

For instance, in the pursuit of understanding the definition of a certain halakhic principle, one is not satisfied with merely compiling a list of laws. Rather, one is interested in defining the structure and inner logic of the halakhic principle; this requires one to perceive the central concepts of the *sugya* and explore their interplay. Success, inasmuch as there are always new facts, new definitions and new situations, lies in the ability to perceive new concepts in new facts, to penetrate to their meaning as much as possible, and apply them to new situations. This is the pursuit of divine intent and its inner logic.

How is this accomplished? Broadly speaking, certain tools and devices (some obvious and others subtle) contribute to one of the most important elements of *lomdus* – identifying the major topics and central issues in a *sugya* in terms of the "what," and not so much the "why."[17] For instance, central issues may be derived from a contradiction between sources, or from an inconsistency in logic. Obviously, in studying Talmud and *rishonim*, one has to know how to approach contradictions and their substantive resolu-

---

[15] R. Moshe Sternbuch's *Sefer Mo`adim u-Zemanim* is an excellent example of utilizing *lomdus* to arrive at a halakhic conclusion.

[16] It should be understood, as a qualification to this section, that these remarks are merely a reflection of my personal experience. There are a multitude of different *shi`urim* and *yeshivot*, rich in their own tradition of *derekh ha-limmud*, which can offer alternative approaches and angles to learning; they are unfortunately not represented here. While it is true that all *yeshivot* have some common ground in their conception of *iyyun*, there are a myriad of differences in the details of this conception, and even more so in its implementation.

[17] It is interesting that Briskers classically ask "what" almost solely in regard to the opinion of *rishonim*. However, the question may be equally put to *amora'im*, and perhaps even *tanna'im*. While there are some who in fact apply the "what" to even this level, there is much to be done in the development of this area.

tions. Similarly, one has to recognize the broader implication of strange *hava aminot* (initial assumptions), odd individual opinions, peculiar formulations, or citations of *pesukim* where logic ought to have sufficed. Often, novel ideas and concepts are hidden within these peculiarities.

Any variation or counter-intuition strikes one who is serious and sensitive about every word and logical inference. What often transpires is the development of a hermeneutic circle whereby texts serve as catalysts for new understanding of concepts, which, in turn, shed light on a fresh reading of the texts (e.g., in relation to their contexts or other texts), allowing one to reassess concepts, and so on. In such a dynamic environment, new insights and readings spring from previously murky and seemingly unintelligible *sugyot*.

Yet, how does one implement this? What is the methodology and technique of conceptual analysis? How does one uncover and expose[18] *lomdus* and novellae latent in various *sugyot*? Several works have been written on how to accomplish this, and I do not intend here to present a "How To" manual. However, in order to demonstrate the power, utility, and broad accessibility of conceptual talmudic analysis, we can touch upon some basic tools one can use to develop an issue conceptually.[19] A list of six specific techniques or characteristics, although not exhaustive, will prove instructive.

---

[18] The term "expose," rather than "generate," is used here because *lomdus* is an internal process from which conceptual categories naturally emerge. "Generate," on the other hand, implies the importing and imposing of pre-conceived categories – an artificial process foreign to the intuitive *lomdus* of R. Hayyim. See R. Mayer Twersky, "A Glimpse of the Rav," *Tradition* 30:4 (Summer 1996): 84–87. There seems to be a difference of emphasis in defining the process of exposing lomdus. While R. Soloveitchik describes it as a "process of pure postulation" (see *Divrei Hagut*, p. 78), R. Hershel Schachter appears to define *lomdus* as a "discovery of fundamental principles," aligning it with R. Hayyim Volozhiner's conception of *hiddush*, i.e., "clarification in the process of study." See his *Nefesh ha-Rav* (Jerusalem: Reishit, 1994), pp. 8–9, 12–14. Further on this difference, see Lawrence Kaplan, "The Multi-Faceted Legacy of the Rav," *B.D.D.* 7 (Summer 1998): 65–7.

[19] Examples of such manuals include: R. Adler, *Lomdus* and R. Moshe Wachtfogel, *The Brisker Derekh* (Jerusalem, 1993). Due to the constraints of space, it is beyond the purview of this essay to provide worthy analyses of *sugyot* or halakhic matter that could serve as concrete examples of the various devices and methods presented here. However, those who are interested in studying actual examples of these methodological tools may consult, in addition to *Lomdus*, Yeshivat Har Etzion's on-line "Virtual Beit Midrash" at www.vbm-torah.org, whose *shi`urim* on various *masekhtot* and on talmudic methodology are substantive models of many of this section's conceptual tools.

1. Reducing Concepts

One of the fundamentals of *lomdus* is learning to pinpoint basic questions, summarize topics, and reduce positions to their basic concepts. One must be able to read a line of Talmud or *rishonim* and understand whether it is extending or limiting the scope of a law. It is important to be able to read an opinion and recognize the novelty of its approach. This is accomplished by stopping and then putting the opinion into other terms and assessing the idea's *nafka minot* (ramifications). One must reduce it and conceptually translate it, then challenge oneself by asking: "Is this something new, is it different; are these assumptions unassailable or is it merely logical but not compelling?"

2. The Peculiar Opinion

Sometimes "reducing" an idea yields a surprising opinion. Even if we reject this opinion, whether it is an independent opinion in a dispute or a *hava amina*, one cannot deny that it reflects something conceptually significant. The usefulness of the peculiar opinion is that through its extreme application it can reflect a doctrine more effectively than a mainstream opinion. The flaw in a mainstream opinion is that it is too universal, whereas a peculiar or extreme position highlights possibilities and facets that one would not have considered before. When one sees ideas in a different context, the breath of fresh air that it brings with it sometimes gives one a new perspective, allowing one to deal with more central and significant issues. In this new context, one can reexamine and reassess the mainstream opinion in light of the peculiar one.

Typically, one of the basic devices in reassessing a mainstream or accepted position in light of the peculiar one is to set up a framework. This is done by first meticulously determining all the possible assumptions of the peculiar or rejected opinion. Then, one compares and contrasts these assumptions with the mainstream position. Which assumptions does the mainstream position accept and which does it reject? Does it accept the principle, but not the application or detail, or vice versa? For instance, the very thing that convinced *Tosafot* to take an extreme position could turn out to have been the same thing that motivated Rambam to say something moderate but to disagree with Ra'avad who also said something moderate but slightly different. Then one must ask why Rambam basically agreed with Ra'avad, but not with *Tosafot*; what motivated Rambam to adopt his position? When this is accomplished, one will have arrived at a new and deeper understanding of the mainstream opinion.[20]

Thus, one who is merely looking at things for their independent and local value stands to miss a lot. For instance, if one loses interest in the *hava amina* because it is not normative, or if one analyzes a *hava amina* but does not consider whether there are any echoes or remnants of it in a more mainstream *maskana* (conclusion), then one has neglected a significant opportunity to fully grasp and understand the *sugya*.

3. Determining the Struggle Within a Position

As part of determining the basic assumptions of a position, when analyzing a commentator, for instance, it is important to ask: "What is bothering him; what is the struggle within his position?" One can know all of R. Hayyim Brisker's insights, but if one simply perceives them as facts, as opposed to becoming immersed in the *process* R. Hayyim went through, then one has a considerably different, and somewhat superficial, experience. On the other hand, if one is struggling with R. Hayyim, looking for weaknesses in his arguments – with due respect of course – then one is doing service to R. Hayyim. One is then involved in the inner process and workings of Torah study.

4. Local and Universal Themes

Another effective device is contrasting parallel issues and maneuvering between local and universal themes. Whenever defining a particular halakhic mechanism, i.e. a device which according to *halakhah* can function to achieve some end, it is natural to wonder what that definition has to do with the broader understanding of that mechanism in the rest of the halakhic system. Their alignment would be far less significant than their non-alignment, which may be due to the mechanism in our case being unique.

A variation of this investigation is defining whether the mechanism under analysis is, in essence, a known and familiar mechanism (an "old *din*") or a novel one (a "new *din*"). For instance, when analyzing whether a par-

---

[20] A good example of this type of dynamic can be found in the debate as to the definition of *lo tahmod* (lit. do not covet – Ex. 20:14). If one assumes that *lo tahmod* is categorized as a prohibition of the heart and mind, one is confronted with an obvious problem: What are the criteria for determining when one has violated the prohibition in one's heart? This question motivated a host of differing responses – some extreme, some moderate – among the commentators. See esp. Maimonides, *Mishneh Torah, Hilkhot Gezeilah* 1:9 (and Ra'avad there), *Moshav Zekeinim* to Ex. 20:14, and *Birkhat ha-Netziv* on *Mekhilta* (*Yitro* 8). See also R. Michael Rosensweig, "*Be-Inyan Lo Tahmod,*" *Beit Yitzhak* 19 (1986–87): 214–27, esp. pp. 216–20.

ticular blessing is a *birkat ha-mitzvah* or a new cast of *berakhah*, it is necessary to run a "litmus test." First, one must identify the hallmarks of the known category. Second, one must compare the unidentified mechanism with this list of elements. If it shares these components, then it is similar in identity and definition with the known. If, however, it does not share these characteristics, then it is probably unrelated. Furthermore, if it has some traits but not all of them, then the investigation becomes even more challenging in terms of defining the precise inner tension within this *halakhah*. This is helpful, as well, in assessing the degree to which a rabbinic law, legislated with respect to a Torah law, is different from the original Torah law.[21]

5. Spectrums

A further tool is placing varying opinions into a conceptual spectrum. The opposite poles, representing the extreme positions in the *sugya*, generally reflect the *hakirah* (inquiry), the two dramatically different ways of perceiving the *sugya*. This is useful because it defines the boundaries of the *sugya*, and thus clarifies one's frame of reference. All other approaches must fall somewhere between the two extremes.

Moreover, by separating the various elements in the *sugya*, one can appreciate and analyze each element on its own. This is helpful because, generally, the *sugya* does not exist in its ideal type, but is rather an amalgam of the extremes.[22] Thus, in isolating the opposing components in the *sugya*, one achieves a better understanding of the tension between, and integration of, the composite extremes.

6. Deductive Reasoning

Additionally, it is often helpful to consider the a priori positions of a *sugya* in order to facilitate the identification of the actual opinions. By deducing the basic options in a *sugya*, one enters into its process and inner tension, and will find the opinions more readily in any given commentator. However, one must be careful to not force these preconceived possibilities into the opinion of commentators; it is critical to maintain an open mind and a natural reading at all times. Moreover, in the event a supposed possi-

---

[21] A number of good examples of this technique (with respect to both Torah and rabbinic laws) can be found in R. Adler, *Lomdus*, pp. 1–14 (Hebrew section).

[22] The separation and comparison of extremes can lead to several conclusions. For instance, such a situation can yield the realization of "*tzvei dinim*" (multi-faceted laws), in which the *sugya* operates on two distinct channels. Alternatively, this dynamic can lead to interpreting the *sugya* as a moderate expression of one theme. See also R. Twersky, "A Glimpse of the Rav," pp. 84–87.

bility does not in fact exist, one needs to determine which component within the *sugya* does not allow for such a possibility.

The six aforementioned examples of methodological tools offer different ways to sensitize one to what is transpiring between the lines. They are important illustrations of patterns of thought that, with consistent application, become intuitive. This intuition is invaluable to the Talmud student allowing him or her to respond naturally, and thus more accurately, to the variety of complex *sugyot* to be faced.[23]

Hence, the Brisker *derekh*, when successfully implemented, allows one to respond to the text with intuitive precision and penetrating insight, enabling the application of novel concepts and ideas to new situations. A skillful *lamdan*, thus, transforms the passive absorption of information into an active encounter, an engagement, with the will of God. As such, *lomdus*, by providing the opportunity for a genuine spiritual experience, enables one to form – but does not necessarily guarantee – a deeper relationship with God Himself.[24]

V. Caveats and Concerns
Regarding *Lomdus*'s Implementation and Impact

Considering all the advantages of mastering *lomdus*, the Brisker *derekh* proves to be an important, useful, and meaningful contribution towards engaging *devar Hashem* (the word of God). Yet, as attractive as the Brisker *derekh* is, quite a few caveats are in order:

A. Implementation of the Brisker Derekh
1. Flexibility and Creativity

While the techniques and tools of *lomdus* are extraordinarily helpful, they can also be a hindrance. Ritualistic fidelity to method can interfere with or

---

[23] See R. Soloveitchik, *Divrei Hagut*, pp. 70–85, which describes R. Hayyim's brilliant intuition as the source of his deep insight and analysis. See also R. Twersky, "A Glimpse of the Rav," pp. 84–87. In addition, see M. Lichtenstein, "'What' Hath Brisk Wrought," p. 16, note 9, on the relationship between intuition and methodology. While intuitive reasoning cannot be directly transmitted to others, I believe techniques and patterns of analysis and thought can, after being taught and implemented, become intuitive over time. Clearly, one who innately possesses brilliant intuition has the advantage, but those who are born without it, can, with proper training, make great headway in closing the gap.

[24] As this essay maintains, a relationship with God requires the use of halakhic intellect in conjunction with the halakhic personality. Such a relationship reminds us of R. Soloveitchik's metaphor of *"nisu'in"* (marriage), used to describe the level of intimacy R. Hayyim Brisker attained with the Torah. See R. Soloveitchik, *Divrei Hagut*, pp. 71–74.

interrupt creative reading skills or even understanding of the topic. Becoming bogged down with a particular series of questions or with a particular structure threatens one's ability to recognize what is unique about a particular *halakhah* and that it requires a different approach. Furthermore, one should not ignore a *sugya* or position that does not conform to one of these devices. One should not be blinded by the imperfect alignment of *sugyot*, or to their being seemingly unrelated and irrelevant.

It is important to keep in mind throughout that *lomdus* is not a formal method that merely requires a series of steps, nor is it an artificial process consisting of stale categories of thought. Rather, *lomdus* is a response to internal stimuli: one must always endeavor to be creative, open to nuances, formulations, and shifting winds in the sugya; flexibility is critical. Thus, while these tools are useful, one must not let them dull sensitivity and constrict creativity.

2. Breadth of Knowledge

To use the Brisker *derekh* effectively and accurately, one requires a basic knowledge of the breadth of Torah. In the excitement of using a methodological tool, many aspiring *lamdanim* skew the understanding of a concept due to their incomplete knowledge of Torah. This may be acceptable so long as the *talmidim* treat their interpretations as provisional. However, such an approach requires a great deal of maturity. Many have mistakenly accepted their own *hiddushim* (innovative insights) as truth, and have even applied this "truth" to related *sugyot*, horribly distorting the talmudic concepts. While it is true that lacking an extensive background in learning frees one to read a text or interpret a position without being encumbered by preconceived notions, it also prevents one from realizing when he has strayed into the absurd.

Acquiring a basic working knowledge of our system of Oral Law will provide a sensitivity and intuition that will preclude distortions of *sugyot* and enhance one's appreciation of the subtleties in them. In its entirety, this includes studying and reviewing Tanakh, Mishnah, *Midreshei Halakhah*, *Talmud Bavli* and *Talmud Yerushalmi*. There are no shortcuts. Even studying Rambam, which is enormously helpful for learning terms and concepts, falls short of integrating the inner workings of our system of Oral Law. To develop the critical intuition and instinct required to distinguish a good *sevara* (rationale) from a poor one, a valid concept or idea from an invalid one, what is likely from what is absurd, demands many years of hard and tireless, sometimes painful, study and review of much of Talmud. Accordingly, the sophistication of one's talmudic intuition will emanate from the degree to which one has studied the breadth and depth of the Oral Law.

3. Guidance

An important dimension of students' growth in Torah is their attentiveness to the gap that exists between their own perspective of a *sugya* and the seasoned approach of their teacher. Obviously, a *shi'ur*, presented often as a final product, does not necessarily reflect the actual order and process the *rebbe* went through in studying the *sugya*. Nonetheless, the very structure and content of a teacher's lecture serve as an optimal model, prodding *talmidim* to achieve new heights and levels in their daily learning. Thus, a student, after experiencing a finely crafted *shi'ur*, can locate and isolate his own weaknesses, and learn from his own mistakes, by asking such questions as, "Why did I not think of that question," or "How is it that I missed that inference." I do not take for granted that this critical self-reflection occurs automatically – especially for novice students. It is, however, an invitation for pedagogical intervention; we must encourage our students' "dissection" of their own initial understandings.

While it is difficult for *talmidim* to appreciate the skills being taught to them unless they have the opportunity to apply those skills themselves, accurate use of methodological and organizational techniques depends in great measure on the interaction between the students and their teacher. Students must have access to a teacher's guidance and input, to ensure successful integration and employment of concepts learned.

While it is basic that *talmidim* apply these tools in their research prior to attending the teacher's *shi'ur*, it is important that they also have some opportunity to present a topic that they have studied and investigated on their own. At what stage this should be done, in what form, whether written or oral, and how often, all depend on the level of the student. Clearly, the reinforcement of mistaken ideas and applications must be avoided. Students who are relatively new to the process of *iyyun* often create elaborate, but skewed, interpretations of *sugyot*. These mistaken notions must be corrected before they are repeatedly misapplied and aggravated.

4. Constancy

The ease with which one becomes inept and careless in the application of these analytical tools, due to infrequent use, is alarming. Therefore, it is necessary for anyone who wants to succeed in this form of investigative analysis to constantly work at and apply it.

B. Students' Response to the Brisker Derekh
1. Overconfidence

While *derekh ha-limmud* can transform frustrating hours in the *beit midrash* into a fruitful and satisfying experience, it can concomitantly inflate one's ego. Confidence in one's analytical abilities can easily lead to pride and arrogance. This is an occupational hazard for the *lamdan*, as it can result in a lack of intellectual honesty and professionalism. Moreover, for some, engagement in *lomdus* represents an opportunity to flex and display one's intellectual muscles. Were they outstanding at sports, they would readily fit the bill of swaggering athletes. As *lamdanim*, they act instead as swaggering talmudic competitors. Rather than such errant and pretentious behavior, *derekh ha-limmud* should engender an appreciation of a precious and humbling opportunity to engage in *devar Hashem*.

As repugnant as conceit is in bona-fide *talmidei hakhamim*, it becomes positively bizarre in amateur students of Torah. The pride that average *talmidim* sense upon discovering that they have asked "Reb Hayyim's question" is appropriate as long as they maintain perspective. Patience, hard work, and *siyata di-shemaya* (divine assistance), as opposed to arrogance, bring the student to the portals of true greatness. Instead of *talmidim* losing perspective with regard to their true abilities, and entertaining visions of grandeur, the educator's modest example and constructive criticism will lead students to a more accurate, and in the long run, constructive, assessment of themselves.

2. Character Development

Another issue that bears mention is character development. R. Aharon Lichtenstein once commented that if he were forced to choose between fostering learning or character development, he would opt that people know less Gemara but have greater sensitivity for one another.[25] On many occasions, R. Lichtenstein has vigorously emphasized that "Fear of God is His treasure" (Isa. 33:6), and as such it must not only be heavily guarded and protected, but nurtured as well.[26] Moreover, Torah scholars are expected to occupy a higher, and more refined, plane of existence. As spiritual aristocrats, in the finest sense of the term, they must, for example, display extra forbearance, honesty, and refinement of conduct and appearance,

---

[25] See R. Reuven Ziegler, *By His Light: Character and Values in the Service of God – Based on Addresses by Rabbi Aharon Lichtenstein* (Jersey City, NJ: Ktav, 2003), p. 249.

[26] See *Shabbat* 31a-b, which underscores the centrality and indispensability of *yir'at shamayim*. See also *Yoma* 72b and *Nefesh ha-Hayyim* 4:4.

as well as act with an awareness that they are representatives of God and His Torah.[27]

Often, in the eagerness to acquire a *derekh ha-limmud* and to become a *lamdan*, much of this is forgotten. Students can become so enthralled with the satisfaction of mastering *sugyot* that they neglect the development of their own character.[28] There is a danger that brilliant *lamdanim*, who may be severely lacking in simple *middot bein adam le-havero* (proper interpersonal traits) and, perhaps, even in *middot bein adam la-Makom* (proper relationship to God), can become the role models for other students.

Indeed, the fact that people have become *lamdanim* does not automatically mean they possess the basic virtues of *rahmanut* (compassion), *derekh eretz* (common courtesy and decency), *zehirut be-mitzvot* (meticulousness in performing halakhic obligations), and *yir'at shamayim*. It does not ensure that they will greet others *be-sever panim yafot* (with a pleasant countenance), treat others with basic dignity, or display all the other noble characteristics described in *Pirkei Avot*. Similarly, it does not indicate that they will refrain from slander and gossip, cease self-aggrandizement, or desist from the multitude of human vices. Although many masters and students of the Brisker method have indeed attained spiritual excellence and character distinction, it is unwise to forget that numerous *lamdanim* who are fundamentally flawed as people or who are simply not *tzaddikim* do, in fact, exist.

To offset this, it is critical for Jewish society and its institutions to exalt kindness, righteousness, and character perfection in conjunction with Torah scholarship. In fact, our society should place on a pedestal only people who are *tzaddikim* first and *lamdanim* second, or those who are at least equally committed to being both. However, those who place *lomdus* before

---

[27] Cf. Maimonides, *Hilkhot De`ot*, chap. 5.

[28] This phenomenon is not new to the history of Torah learning. Note, for instance, *Sefer Yirei'im* (vol. 1, introduction), in which R. Eliezer of Metz complains that despite the advanced level of Torah analysis in his time there was a lack of *yir'at shamayim* and halakhic compliance. Rabbeinu Bahya ibn Pekuda complained similarly in his introduction to *Hovot ha-Levavot*. Nonetheless, either due to its extreme emphasis upon abstraction or simply because it is the predominant analytical method today, the Brisker *derekh* plays a large role in these current educational challenges. For a fuller discussion of this historical problem, see Yisrael Ta-Shma, "*Mitzvat Talmud Torah* as a Socio-Religious Problem in *Sefer Hasidim*" (Hebrew) in Ivan Marcus, ed., *Dat ve-Hevrah be-Mishnatam shel Hasidei Ashkenaz* (Jerusalem: Merkaz Shazar, 1986), pp. 237–252; Immanuel Etkes, *R. Yisrael Salanter and the Beginning of the Mussar Movement* (Jerusalem: Magnes Press, 1984), especially parts 1–3; and Haym Soloveitchik, "Three Themes in the *Sefer Hasidim*," *AJS Review* 1 (1976), esp. pp. 332–333 and 342–347. I am indebted to R. Mosheh Lichtenstein for these sources.

piety have no right to our adoration – only, perhaps, our censure and pity.[29] Not taking this path will put our students and children in spiritual peril, for it is tragically possible that, in an environment where *lomdus* reigns supreme, piety may even, in the collective mind, become associated with intellectual mediocrity.[30] Is this the message we want our children and students to absorb? We must not, and dare not, sacrifice the souls of our successors upon the altar of intellectual attainment.

3. *Talmud Torah* Proper

A preoccupation with the methodology and technique of Brisker *lomdus* can also lead to inverting one's priorities. Actual learning of Torah is vastly more important an endeavor than the study of *how* it ought to be accomplished.[31] One who is obsessed with "how to learn" runs the risk of neglecting and even forgetting to actually learn. While developing a method has its place, one must never lose sight of the fact that it serves rather than replaces Torah study.

4. Experience of *Talmud Torah*

Similarly, one must not allow conceptual analysis of *talmud Torah* to degenerate into a mere intellectual exercise. Rabbi Soloveitchik once declared:

The study of the Torah has never been simply a formal religious duty that mandates an intellectual act or performance. The satisfaction that I derive from it is much more than the fulfillment of a mitzvah alone. It is true regardless of how important a role the intellect plays in the study of Torah. You know very well that I place…a great deal of emphasis upon the intellectual understanding and analysis of the halakhah… However, this study is more than simply an intellectual performance. It is a total, all-encompassing, and all-embracing involvement of the mind and heart, will, and feeling – the very center of the human personality. The emotional side of man, his logical bent, the voluntaristic impulses can all be usefully employed in plumbing the depth of Torah. *The study of Torah is basically, for me, an ecstatic experience in which one meets God.*[32]

---

[29] *Yoma* 72b: "Woe to scholars who engage in Torah but possess no fear of heaven." See also *Mo`ed Katan* 17a andMaimonides, *Hilkhot Talmud Torah* 4:1 ("If the rabbi is like an angel of the Lord, only then seek Torah from his mouth…").

[30] Note the introduction to *Mesillat Yesharim*, by R. Moshe Hayyim Luzzatto.

[31] Cf. R. Aharon Lichtenstein's approbation to the book *Lomdus*, where he emphasizes this point in the context of studying conceptual methodology.

[32] Cited in: Rakeffet-Rothkoff, *The Rav*, vol. 2, pp. 202–03 (italics added).

5. *La'asok be-Divrei Torah* – Intensity and Consistency

Furthermore, an unhealthy emphasis on *lomdus* could lead one to the conclusion that the basic value in studying Torah is to emerge with a *hiddush* (novel idea). While, for instance, R. Hayyim of Volozhin (1749–1821) felt novel insights were the joy and highest level of Torah study, he most certainly did not consider them the definition of Torah study.[33] Nonetheless, some feel that if they have not completely mastered the *sugya* or produced an innovative insight, then they have not actually learned Torah. Such a notion is both false and tragic. It is false because the *mitzvah* is, as expressed in the blessing over Torah study, "*la'asok be-divrei Torah*," to toil in Torah, not generate *lomdus*, per se; furthermore we are instructed "*vehagita bo yomam va-layelah*," (Josh. 1:8) to work in Torah day and night, not necessarily to emerge with a product. And it is tragic that many formerly aspiring *lamdanim cum balebatim* (laymen) believe that learning a few *mishnayot* or a *daf* a day is not "authentic" Torah study. Since they have little free time, they end up not learning at all, because, in their view, *daf yomi* is not considered "real" learning.

6. Exclusivity

Additionally, one must reject the tendency to believe that one who has not been taught talmudic methodology in general, or the Brisker *derekh* specifically, is not adept in learning and does not deserve respect as a Torah scholar. Such an inclination is obviously ludicrous. No mature person of sound mind would truly entertain the thought for a moment that the Vilna Gaon, R. Akiva Eiger, Hatam Sofer, Hazon Ish, R. Moshe Feinstein, or R. Shlomo Zalman Auerbach, to name but a few "non-Briskers," were not Torah scholars of the highest order. Talmudic methodology and the Brisker *derekh* give people a point of view in approaching Talmud, but it is only one point of view, and a relatively new one at that. Let us not be smug in our knowledge of *derekh ha-limmud* when we are ignoramuses compared with the Torah giants mentioned above.

A personal experience serves to reinforce this idea. As a young student I once inquired of R. Aharon Lichtenstein if the method taught in the *yeshivah* is the "ideal" mode of Torah study. His response made a lasting impression upon me. He forcefully told me that no one may claim to have the ideal method of *limmud Torah*. However, he continued, one may assert that the method one has found is the most suitable for oneself. He found both the

---

[33] *Nefesh ha-Hayyim* 4:12, and his *Ruah ha-Hayyim* to *Avot* 3:9.

inaccuracy and the arrogance of claiming supremacy disturbing, and advised distancing oneself from such thoughts.[34]

7. *Halakhah le-Ma'aseh*: The Study of Practical Jewish Law

A further concern associated with concentrating primarily on *lomdus* is the neglect of *halakhah le-ma'aseh*. There are aspiring *lamdanim* who do not have the satisfactory knowledge required to live their daily lives as complete halakhic Jews, during the week or on *Shabbat* and *Yom Tov*. This is the result of their being wholly satisfied by the stimulating experience of learning *lomdus*, and being completely uninterested in the tedious effort of studying and memorizing *halakhah*. If *lomdus* comes at the expense of *ma'aseh* (performance), there is a problem. What possible value is there in engaging God through *lomdus*, if one is not also committed to learning the laws necessary to live as a complete and loyal servant of God?[35]

VI. Educational Challenges

In sum, *lomdus*, particularly in the form of the Brisker *derekh*, is an effective and coherent system of talmudic study that has revitalized and re-energized *talmud Torah*, becoming the core study of most contemporary *yeshivot*. This method, to its credit, has not remained static. Proponents of the Brisker *derekh* have developed it into a systematic method and have broadened its applications and horizons. Yet, despite its vitality and success, it is important to admit that Brisker *lomdus* has also created many troubling educational issues and challenges for the Torah community in general, and those entrusted with Jewish education in particular.[36]

---

[34] My discussion with R. Lichtenstein was prompted by a talk he had given at the yeshivah in March 1987, which has been recently published as "The Centrality of Torah Study" in *By His Light: Character and Values in the Service of God*, pp. 61–74. On many other occasions since that meeting, I have heard R. Lichtenstein emphasize how it is improper for a person or institution to believe that he or it is, for example, "uniquely qualified" for a task, preferring, instead, the phrase "highly qualified."

[35] See, for instance, *Yevamot* 109b: "Whoever says that he has nothing but Torah does not even have Torah. Why? Rav Papa said, the Torah states 'Study them and observe them faithfully' (Deut. 5:1). Whosoever relates to observance, relates to study, whosoever does not relate to observance does not relate to study." Moreover, *Kiddushin* 40b states: "The study of Torah is preeminent as it brings one to the performance of *mitzvot*." A final and more radical example can be found in *Avodah Zarah* 17b: "He who engages solely in Torah study is as one who has no God."

[36] See R. Jeffrey Saks, "Rabbi Joseph B. Soloveitchik on the Brisker Method," *Tradition* 33:2 (Winter 1999): 52:

> Another crucial point of interest is the Rav's presentation [of the practitioner of the Brisker *derekh*] as an expression of his vision of the ideal educator... [W]e must bear in mind that the Rav is adjuring us that the method is not merely a technique

Apprehension should be felt, and vigilance ought be applied, at the individual, social, and institutional levels, with particular regard to the misconception and misapplication of, and preoccupation with, the Brisker method. These deficiencies have, for instance, fostered in numerous students, in *yeshivot* across the ideological spectrum, a tendency to distort *sugyot* inasmuch as they are unskilled in the Brisker method's conceptual techniques or because their general knowledge of the Talmud is profoundly lacking. Yet, ironically, *lomdus* also has nourished an excessive self-confidence, and thus a lack of intellectual professionalism and rigorousness, in many students. This occupational hazard, too, leads to the distortion of Torah.

On a different plane, many, due to their immersion in *lomdus*, have a predilection for arrogance, a cynicism towards studying Tanakh, Mishnah, *beki'ut* or *daf yomi*, and an indifference to the seemingly simple and tedious study of practical Jewish law. But perhaps most frightening are the *lamdanim* who, as a result of their weariness for character improvement and inattention to *yir'at shamayim*, bear little if any resemblance to *tzaddikim*.

Our community must strive to correct these deficiencies without in any way weakening the implementation and crucial contribution of Brisker *lomdus*. While the Brisker method's prestigious legacy remains, and must continue to remain, a central element of Torah life and learning, we ought to rethink and widen our emphases, and provide proper education and preparation for the student's ultimate involvement in, and relationship to, *lomdus*.

The educational direction *yeshivot* take in this century of Torah learning will have important repercussions for the Jewish people. At stake is whether or not we will become concomitantly more knowledgeable and more skilled in our study and mastery of the Oral Law, and at the same time more devoted to *halakhah*, character development, and our overall relationship with God. Neglecting our duty could tragically lead to the ultimate irony – the Brisker *derekh* undermining *talmud Torah* and eroding our commitment to, and connection with, Hashem. Certainly, R. Hayyim did not envision that!

---

or a jargon: *hillukim* and *hakirot*, *heftsa* and *gavra*, etc. – which are certainly components – but must be the educative outcome of a princely personality, the very extension of an halakhic man himself. I believe that this raises some serious questions for education (teacher training not least among them!) that all who engage in this method ought to be asking.

EMPATHY AND AGGRESSION IN TORAH STUDY:
ANALYSIS OF A TALMUDIC DESCRIPTION OF HAVRUTA LEARNING

GILLA RATZERSDORFER ROSEN

R. Hama ben Hanina said: Why are the words of Torah likened to fire? –
As it states (Jer. 23:29) "Is not my word like fire? says the Lord." – To
teach you that just as fire can not be ignited and keep burning by itself, so
too the words of Torah can not endure in a single individual.

— *Ta'anit* 7a

WHEN TWO PEOPLE sit down to learn Torah they set out on a journey together. What is their goal? What do they hope to achieve through their
learning? Are they trying to "get" somewhere or is it the journey-the proc-
ess-that they are after?

Different dynamics arise between two *havruta* partners.[1] They may engage in sharp argumentation, relentlessly attacking each other's positions.
They may listen quietly and patiently to each other, mulling over their different ideas. Or they may go off on a single track, excitedly encouraging
each other and overturning previous conceptions as they race along to-

---

[1] *Havruta*, an Aramaic word meaning friendship, companionship, or connection, is used
throughout this essay in its common meaning: Torah study partner. It is important to
note that I am not concerning myself with the historical question of the use of *havruta*
study throughout the ages; rather, I am interested in using the issues raised by a particular text to open educational deliberation on how we teach and study Torah today.
On the historical questions, the interested reader is directed to Shaul Stampfer, *Ha-
Yeshivah ha-Lita'it be-Hithavutah* (Jerusalem: Shazar, 1995), esp. pp. 50, 127, 146–49, and
281 (especially his disagreement with Yeshayhu Tishby on precisely how widespread
havruta-style learning was in *yeshivot*). Aliza Segal's monograph, *Havruta Study: History,
Benefits and Enhancements* (Jerusalem: ATID, 2003) raises a number of important pedagogical issues that I have not been able to address here.

gether. What factors affect this dynamic? Certainly they include their personalities, the relationships between them, their assumptions about the learning process, and, I believe, their goals. This essay is an attempt to engage the reader in studying a passage from the Talmud that grapples with the dynamics of the *havruta* learning process. It is a study in self-reflection on the part of the Rabbis about a process that was central to their experience.

Talmudic texts often engage the reader through the beauty of their open-endedness. Their ambiguity results not from any lack of clarity but from the opening of totally new perspectives. The power of the texts often lies in their theoretical distance from the reader, coupled with the immediacy of the deeper issues they raise. In addition, the thrust and parry, and the juxtaposition of different arguments, create in the learner a sense of uncovering and discovering treasures.

The text we will examine, from *Shabbat* 63a, encompasses all of these qualities. But therein lies the difficulty in teaching it, and even more so in writing about it. How much to reveal and how much to leave to the student's discovery? The very first and most basic methodological question poses a dilemma. In what order shall I present the passage and other texts pertinent to it? This particular talmudic discussion focuses on modes of *havruta* learning. A number of models of studying in partnership are presented in the Talmud, along with their consequences. The significance of these different modes is heightened by the context in which they are embedded, particularly the Mishnah from which they literally unfold. Teaching this text and parallel sources with *havruta* learning itself preceding the *shi'ur* gives the students the chance to engage and organize the texts themselves – and, of course, to reflect on what the texts mean to them. In different learning situations, I have presented the various texts cited in this essay in different sequences. I invite the reader to read my presentation in an open, flexible manner, reorganizing and rethinking the various passages quoted and thus making the material his or her own.[2]

Additionally, the primary text presented may be understood in a number of ways. The various modes of Torah study may be seen as complementary or mutually exclusive. In our analysis, the models are presented as alternatives juxtaposed to emphasize their differences. Another analysis may see them as complementary parts of the same process, brought together to show the necessary components of ideal study. Rather than offering a con-

---

[2] As my presentation below is an explication of selections from *Shabbat* 63a, the reader is invited to review that passage before proceeding.

clusive analysis of the talmudic text in *Shabbat* 63a, this essay is an attempt to show the way one particular mode of interpretation of the text may be used as an educational tool.

The Background

The talmudic text which we are about to engage describes different forms of learning, including one in which *havruta* partners sharpen each other's wits, and another in which they are exceptionally good listeners. Where would we expect to find such a discussion? I might have thought in Mishnah *Berakhot*, where the *Shema* is discussed, or in relation to the Mishnah in *Kiddushin* that analyzes the parental obligation to impart Torah to a child. Indeed, a probing discussion is found there dealing with the problematics of *talmud Torah* between father and son. But our discussion, surprisingly, appears in the tractate *Shabbat* following a Mishnah that discusses not Torah study, but the tools of war and the validity of warfare. The Mishnah is found in chapter 6 of *Shabbat*, which discusses what articles of clothing and ornamentation may be worn on the Sabbath and what may not, usually because of the prohibition against carrying in the public domain. In general, the chapter follows accepted norms of societal behavior and definitions of male and female attire according to social convention. Here, however, the Mishnah explicity raises the possibility that a moral value should override cultural norms:[3]

> A man may not go out into the public domain on Shabbat with a sword, a bow, a shield, a lance, or a spear; and if he does go out [with one of these implements of war] he is liable for a sin offering [i.e., he is considered to have carried the object in question]. R. Eliezer says: they are adornments for him [and thus part of his attire]. But the Sages maintain: they are nothing but a disgrace, for it is stated (Isa. 2:4): "They shall beat their swords into plowshares, and their spears into pruning hooks. Nation shall not lift up sword against nation, neither shall they learn war any more."

Our Gemara begins its analysis of this Mishnah with a question about the relationship between it and the *mahloket* (difference of opinion) between

---

[3] It is possible to interpret a number of *mishnayot* in this chapter in a similar manner. See, for instance, the *Yerushalmi* on the prohibition to wear spiked sandals, similar to those worn by the Roman legions, on *Shabbat*. The *Yerushalmi* argues that the Mishnah wishes to prevent a Jew from *ever* wearing them. Since people generally owned only one pair of sandals, prohibiting their use on *Shabbat* would achieve this goal all week long.

Shemuel and other sages as to whether the use of force (and thus the necessity of weapons) will persist during the Messianic age. This debate may reflect the extent to which warfare is considered acceptable.[4]

The Talmud then turns to examine Rabbi Eliezer's opinion. How could he maintain that weapons could be ornaments? (Cultural norms do not seem to suffice for the Gemara.) The Gemara cites a passage from Psalm 45 to justify Rabbi Eliezer's view. This psalm, which becomes the leitmotif for the Gemara's ensuing discussion, reads (Ps. 45:1–5):

> …A love song. My heart is astir with gracious words;
> I speak my poem to a king;
> my tongue is the pen of an expert scribe.
> You are fairer than all men;
> your speech is endowed with grace;
> rightly has God given you an eternal blessing.
> Gird your sword upon your thigh, O hero, in your splendor and glory;
> in your glory, win success;
> ride on in the cause of truth and humble righteousness;
> and your right hand will teach you awesome things.[5]

It is hard to know who the hero of Psalm 45 is; it may be the messianic king. Refuting Rabbi Eliezer's opinion that the psalm endorses the use of weapons as ornaments, the Gemara understands this psalm metaphorically. The "hero warrior" is the *talmid hakham*.[6]

Can one just ignore the *peshat* (literal meaning) in favor of an allegorical interpretation of a verse or an entire chapter? The Gemara now begins a short tantalizing discussion on the subject. But we may ask another question. What, especially in the context of this Mishnah, does the Gemara achieve through this allegorization? The hero of the psalm had been fight-

---

[4] Emanuel Levinas, presenting a totally different interpretation of this dispute, suggests that all the rabbis agree that there will be a total cessation of political violence in the Messianic age. They differ merely as to the level of human moral struggle that will still be necessary. See his *Difficult Freedom: Essays on Judaism* (Baltimore: Johns Hopkins Univ., 1990), pp. 60–68.

[5] Translation based on *Tanakh: The New JPS Translation* (Philadelphia: JPS, 1988). It is also suggested that the reader review this chapter in the original, as its verses will be expounded by the Gemera, and used throughout this essay.

[6] Such an interpretation is not unusual in the Talmud Bavli. See, for example, references to the *hakhamim* as *ba`alei trisin* ("shield bearers") (*Berakhot* 27b) and *Bekhorot* 36a (and Rashi to each), and the use of Ps. 127:4 ("As arrows in the hand of a mighty man…") in *Kiddushin* 30b and Rashi s.v. *"ke-hitzim"* and *"ken benei ha-ne`urim."*

ing for the sake of Torah values. Was that insufficient? Is not aggression or force a positive value as long as it is used in the figurative "war of Torah"? How shall we define that fight?

Furthermore, what is the source of this relationship between *talmud Torah* and combat? Is the Talmud choosing here sublimation of violent impulses? Or is the aggressive impulse seen as something more positive – a part of human nature that can find its true meaning and place in Torah study? Alternatively, is it the nature of Torah study itself which is being described? Does halakhic study demand a dialectical process of thought and argumentation that naturally leads to clash and resolution? Or is this possibly an image of a subtle process inherent in the *havruta* situation in which the "other" makes demands upon the self?

It is interesting that Rashi, in his commentary, tones down the militaristic tone, emphasizing not the aspect of actual combat but the readiness that is the normal state of a soldier: "Be careful to review your learning so that it will be ready in time of judgment to bring a proof like the sword on the hip [ready] to win at war, and that is your glory and majesty."[7]

Havruta Study as the Mutual Sharpening of Minds

This is the departure point for the Talmud to discuss an adversarial form of *havruta* learning. Having defined the hero of Psalm 45 as the *talmid hakham* and the Torah as his sword, the Gemara goes on to translate this metaphor into the learning process on the basis of subsequent verses:

> R. Jeremiah said in R. Eleazar's name: When two scholars sharpen each other in *halakhah*, the Holy One, blessed be He, gives them success, for it is said (Ps. 45:5), "in your glory (*ve-hadarkha*), win success." Read not *ve-hadarekha* but *ve-haddadkha* (your sharpening). Moreover, they ascend to greatness, as it is said, "ride on in success."

Two scholars who argue, challenging and even attacking each other's points of view, can achieve a great deal by clarifying distinctions in points of law and "sharpening" each other's minds.

A parallel passage in *Kiddushin* 30b may serve as an enlightening variant:

> Our Rabbis taught: [Scripture states, Deut. 6:7] *"Ve-shinnantam* – And you shall teach them diligently." This conveys that the words of Torah should be *mehuddadim* (sharp or clear-cut) in your mouth, such that if someone asks

---

[7] Rashi, *ad loc.*, s.v. *"Be-divrei Torah ketiv."*

you something, you will not stammer before answering him but rather you will (be able to) answer him immediately, for it says (Prov. 7:4): "Say to wisdom – you are my sister."

In this passage, sharpness is defined as speed and accuracy and the image of the sister suggests loving closeness.[8] (Rashi, as we have seen, follows this interpretation in his commentary to our passage in *Shabbat*.) However, the issue of aggression, and even the parallel to warfare, appears later in this section as well.

Another passage (*Ta'anit* 7a) portrays *havruta* learning as essential and describes the dangers of individual study.[9] It uses the imagery of mutual sharpening of minds in a number of ways, including a comparison to the use of iron to sharpen iron. Its most interesting addition to our study involves the role of the student or the *havruta* partner with less background or ability:

> R. Nahman b. Isaac said: Why are the words of the Torah likened to a tree, as it is said (Prov. 3:18), "It is a tree of life to them that grasp it"? This is to teach you that just as a small tree may ignite a larger tree so too it is with scholars, the younger sharpen [the minds of] the older.

Despite its advantages, this method of *havruta* study has potential pitfalls, for this is an odd clashing of swords. The goal of the fight should be at all times not to defeat the opponent, but rather to seek truth. What if the goal becomes to "win" – to be right? What if the partners become true adversaries?[10]

Our passage in *Shabbat* quotes the continuation of Psalm 45: "In your glory, win success; ride on in the cause of truth…" The *talmid hakham* must not lose sight of his or her true goal, the study of *Torah li-shemah* – for its

---

[8] See, however, parallel passages in *Shabbat* 145a and *Sanhedrin* 7b (and Rashi's comments), in which the image of the sister is understood differently.

[9] Some of the problems involved in independent study in the talmudic period may not be relevant today. Since at the time most material was orally transmitted, an individual cut off from the main stream of halakhic discussion might go off on some path of his own, based, for instance, on an interpretation of a biblical text. This also applies to the problem raised later in the text in *Shabbat* regarding two beginners who study on their own without a teacher.

[10] It is interesting to note that the passage in *Ta'anit* 7a which does not differentiate between ways of relating and learning together (describing *havruta* study only in these terms of fire and of mutual sharpening of minds) is framed by discussions regarding how to relate to the *talmid hakham* or the student who is not of good character.

own sake. This is the warning of our Gemara in *Shabbat*: "One might think [that success and greatness are bestowed] even if the study is not *li-shemah*; therefore Scripture states 'in the cause of truth.' (Ps. 45:5)" If the *havruta* partner challenges the other simply for the sake of the challenge, or to destroy the opponent's position without reflecting upon its truth, he or she has lost sight of the true goal.

Furthermore, "one might think [that these blessings come] even if the scholar becomes conceited or arrogant. Therefore Scripture states: 'and humble righteousness.'"[11] Too much ego prevents the individual from hearing or incorporating Torah.

The Talmud continues:

And if they do this [study in this manner] they will merit [the acquisition of] Torah, which was given with the right hand, as it is stated in the verse: "your right hand will teach you awesome things." Rabbi Nahman bar Isaac said: they will merit [receiving] things that are ascribed to the "right hand" of Torah: length of days as well as wealth and honor.[12]

The Talmud does not elucidate the psychological and metaphysical reasons for these relationships between forms of Torah study and consequences. This leaves the *havruta* partners opportunity for theoretical discussion.[13]

---

[11] That humility is a necessary condition for Torah learning and teaching is a recurrent theme in Rabbinic thought, epitomized by the description of Moses as "the humblest of all people" (Num. 12:3). See, e.g., *Ta`anit* 7a: "R. Hanina b. Ada said: Why are the words of Torah likened to water? To teach you that just as water forsakes an elevated location and flows to a lower place, so too the words of Torah are retained only in one of humble mind." See also "Torah and Humility," in *Shiurei HaRav: A Conspectus of the Public Lectures of Rabbi Joseph B. Soloveitchik* (Hoboken, NJ: Ktav, 1994), pp. 91–96.

[12] Rashi suggests two possible interpretations of this section. According to the first, the *right* way of learning is directly related to the thrust and parry of discussion, which helps to search out and clarify the precise reasons for the Torah's teachings. Alternatively, the preferred form of study alluded to here refers to the aspects of *li-shemah* and humility raised immediately above. These two interpretations reflect two radically different readings of the text. In the first, the importance of argumentation and sharpening the mind is further emphasized. Conversely, in the second interpretation, the Talmud is reinforcing its limitations on this form of learning. See also Maharsha, who prefers Rashi's second interpretation.

[13] Maharal understands that the correlations are both metaphysically and psychologically significant. For instance, he explains that the wisdom of the Torah as something intrinsically beyond the physical world is made attainable through the unique dynamic of the *havruta* relationship. It is also not fully accessible to someone who is involved in more worldly or selfish concerns. See Maharal's *Hiddushei Aggadot, ad loc.,* and his *Netivot ha-Torah*, chapters 2, 6, and 7.

Talmud Torah as Dialogue

There are, of course, other ways to envision the learning of Torah in *havruta*, just as there are other aspects to dialogue. True dialogue implies listening to each other with an "open mind" – open to the possibility of allowing the other to change one's own point of view. It requires listening with the aim of finding the inconsistencies not only in the other's argument but also in one's own. Furthermore, it suggests one partner drawing out another, listening for nuances in the other's words, and even helping the other shape ideas of which he himself was not fully conscious. It holds out the possibility of the partners coming together and deepening their bonds of friendship.

The issue of humility raised above leads into the continuation of the Gemara's discussion. The Talmud now introduces three quotations in the name of Resh Lakish on the subject, two of which may be variants of each other.[14] The first reads:

> R. Jeremiah said in the name of R. Simeon b. Lakish: When two scholars are pleasant toward each other when discussing *halakhah*, the Holy One, blessed be He, listens to them, for it is said, "Then they that feared the Lord spoke one with another, and the Lord hearkened, and heard" (Mal. 3:16); speech (*dibbur*) implies gentleness.

The second seems to go further:

> R. Abba said in the name of R. Simeon b. Lakish: When two scholars listen to each other in halakhic discussion, the Holy One, blessed be He, hears their voice, as it is stated (Song of Songs 8:13), "You who dwell in the gardens, the companions hearken to your voice: Let me hear it." But if they do not, they cause the *Shekhinah* to depart from Israel, as it is said, "Flee, my beloved…" (v. 14).

What is the relationship between these quotations and the discussion above? The difference I find most striking is that we actually do not know whether the two partners in Resh Lakish's model "succeed" in their learn-

---

[14] These two quotations are separating in the Gemara by a short passage regarding the performance of *mitzvot* and the importance of the individual's intentions. It may be seen as a digression based on the continuation of the verse quoted in the first passage, and I have not included it in my discussion. A different analysis, however, might regard it as an integral part of this section.

ing or whether they personally rise to great heights. The consequence, or possibly the reward, is of a totally different nature. We find ourselves in a completely different frame of reference. These two partners bring God into the *havruta* partnership, making space for the *Shekhinah* in the world. God listens to their learning.[15] This suggests that a different goal for Torah learning is involved: not personal success or even the enhancement of Torah itself, but rather a dynamic change in one's relationship to God and even in God's relationship to the world.

Furthermore, there is a definite sense of movement from the first quotation to the second. I would suggest an enhancement, if possible, of the closeness between the two partners learning Torah and God. A totally new paradigm is used to envision the *havruta* experience itself. We have most emphatically left the sphere of warfare and have entered the sphere of friendship, even of love – the world of the Song of Songs. God appears almost as a jealous lover who cannot be kept out of the *havruta* relationship – "The companions listen to your voice – let me hear it (too)."[16]

This selection parallels a passage in *Berakhot* (6a) that reads:

> Ravin bar Rav Adda said in the name of R. Isaac: …How do you know …if two are sitting and studying the Torah together the Divine Presence is with them? For it is said (Mal. 3:16): "Then they that feared the Lord spoke one with another, and the Lord hearkened and heard." And [how do we know] even if one man sits and studies the Torah the Divine Presence is with him? For it is said (Ex. 20:20): "In every place where I cause My name to be mentioned I will come unto thee and bless thee."

Why does this occur? This passage from *Berakhot* suggests the creation of a holy space. Our passage in *Shabbat*, however, suggests that it is the interpersonal relationship of love that invites the *Shekhinah*.[17] Maharal, in

---

[15] While it is possible that the phrase "God listens to them" or "God hears their voice" refers to listening to their prayers rather than to their learning (and this fits in well with other quotations brought between these two passages), the verses from Song of Songs seem to suggest God joining in the listening/learning relationship.

[16] In a similar vein, the *midrash* suggests that God asks the Jewish people to build the *mishkan* after giving them the Torah because he cannot be parted from their circle. See *Ex. Rabbah* 33:1.

[17] Indeed, the expounded text, Psalms 45, is titled *Shir Yedidot* ("Love Song," but also "Song of Friendship"). See Maharal, *Hiddushei Aggadot* to *Shabbat* 63a. Compare Rabbi Akiva's views on the *Shekhinah* in marriage: "when husband and wife are worthy, the *Shekhinah* is amongst them; when they are not worthy, fire consumes them" (*Sotah* 17a). See also *Kiddushin* 30b and 31a.

Netivot ha-Torah, suggests an explanation in which the Torah and the individuals learning are intertwined:

> Further, when they amiably discuss the Torah and pay attention to each other's views in Torah, they become an integral unity through the Torah – which (itself) is a unity. When they fail to unite because they do not attend one another's views, it is as if, God forbid, they cause a division in the Torah. The *Shekhinah* therefore departs from the Jewish people; its presence among the Jewish people is only because they were given the Torah, which is a unity – that is the reason the Holy One, blessed is He, Who is a Unity, resides with Israel.[18]

Of course these dicta originally had a life of their own, but within the context of the Gemara they may act as a critique of the first method of learning. *Sanhedrin* 24a quotes Sages in Israel who criticize the overly adversarial form of learning in Babylonia:

> R. Oshaia said: What is the meaning of the verse, "And I took for myself two staffs: the one I called "graciousness" and the other I called "attackers"? Graciousness refers to the scholars of *Eretz Yisrael*, who treat each other graciously when discussing *halakhah*; attackers, to the scholars of Babylonia, who injure each other's feelings in halakhic debate.

On the other hand, other passages suggest that there is a loss in analytical clarity when people do not attack each other's arguments.[19] The passage in *Kiddushin* (30b) quoted above seems to accept adversarial interaction as an integral and inescapable part of the process of intense and passionate study of *halakhah*. Indeed, that section continues: "Said R. Hiyya b. Abba: Even father and son, master and disciple, who study Torah together at the same gate become enemies of one another..." But the Gemara understands that the passionate argument brings about a deepening of the positive bond

---

[18] Translation based on *Nesivos Olam: Nesiv HaTorah – An Appreciation of Torah Study* (Brooklyn, NY: Mesorah Publications, 1994), p. 144.

[19] For example, see *Yevamot* 14a, where Beit Shammai is described as sharper (*mehaddedin tefai*) and, according to one view, this analytical precision could take precedence over the majority opinion in deciding *halakhah* (in the period before *halakhah* was set according to Beit Hillel).

between father and son, because, "...they do not stir from there until they come to love each other."[20]

Rabbi Akiva Eiger, in his commentary to *Pirkei Avot*, claims that the need for brazenness in the study of Torah is real but only temporary:

> In Torah study it is necessary for there to be brazenness, as Scripture says, "and the one who is ashamed [to ask] does not learn" (*Avot* 2:5), but in the future "the earth will be filled with knowledge" (Isa. 11:9) and even Torah study will not require brazenness.[21]

This interpretation suggests a more complex reading of our passage. It links the question in the first section of our text about whether warfare will persist in the messianic period with the second part, in which the "warfare" described takes place in the study of the Torah. Viewed in such a perspective, the different passages may be seen as reflecting a historical development: from Torah study that includes an element of aggression, competitiveness, or adversarial striving, to Torah study that is peaceful.

Do the *havruta* partners who learn in the Resh Lakish model succeed in their learning even though they do not sharpen each other's wits? The Gemara (*Eruvin* 13b) may have an answer to this question in another famous passage:

> R. Abba stated in the name of Samuel: For three years there was a dispute between Beit Shammai and Beit Hillel, the former asserting, "The *halakhah* is in agreement with our view" and the latter contending, "The *halakhah* is in agreement with our view." Then a heavenly voice went forth and declared: "Both are the words of the living God, but the *halakhah* is in agreement with the rulings of Beit Hillel." Since "both are the words of the living God," what was it that entitled Beit Hillel to have the *halakhah* fixed in

---

[20] I had always understood this passage as suggesting that even a father and son would experience some conflict in the study of Torah together. I prefer an interpretation I heard that *even* if a father and son experience enmity during study together they will reach love through their learning.

[21] Rabbi Akiva Eiger in his commentary to *Avot* 5:20, which reads: "Yehudah ben Tema said: Be bold [or brazen] as a leopard, light as an eagle, swift as a deer, and strong as a lion, to carry out the will of your Father in Heaven. He used to say: The brazen go to Gehinnom, but the shamefaced go to the Garden of Eden. May it be Your will our God and the God of our forefathers, that the Holy Temple be rebuilt, speedily in our days, and grant us our share in Your Torah." Rabbi Akiva Eiger is dealing here, as he explains, with the surprising contingency of this series of statements in the Mishnah and their varied approach to brazeneness. I am grateful to my son, Shlomo Dov, for bringing this source to my attention.

agreement with its rulings? Because they were kindly and modest, they studied their own rulings and those of Beit Shammai, and even mentioned the actions of Beit Shammai before theirs. This teaches you that he who humbles himself, the Holy One, blessed be He, raises up, and he who exalts himself, the Holy One, blessed be He, humbles: from one who seeks greatness, greatness flees, but if one flees from greatness, greatness follows.

Is the reason that the *halakhah* follows Beit Hillel intrinsic or extrinsic? Is it a reward, an attempt to encourage better character traits (*middot*) among the people? Is it that neither answer is the greater truth, but that Hillel is more likely to have the answer more appropriate for the people? Or is this an intrinsic consequence of Beit Hillel's behavior? Is the good listener, the humble partner, more likely to reach a deeper truth? Is someone who hears and understands people's needs and their potential more likely to reach a more desirable halakhic decision?

The Talmud cites one more quotation in the name of Resh Lakish in this series about *havruta* study:[22]

> R. Abba said in the name of R. Simeon b. Lakish: When two disciples gather together (*madgilim*) to study *halakhah*, the Holy One, blessed be He, loves them, as it is said (Song of Songs 2:4), "And his banner (*degel*) over me was love." [23]

---

[22] The continuation of this Gemara cites a quotation in the name of Resh Lekish that raised the problematic issue of a *talmid hakham* who lacks good *middot*. This dictum – "Even if a Torah scholar exacts revenge and bears a grudge like a serpent, gird him to your loins" – contrasts sharply with Resh Lekish's previous statements. In light of this and the many stories about the complex relationship between R. Yohanan and Resh Lekish, how is one to understand that it is *specifically* Resh Lekish who speaks of such peaceful, loving, Torah learning? See also *Sanhedrin* 24a. Was this what Resh Lekish actually experienced or what he aspired to? An analysis of whether or to what extent it is fruitful to speculate upon the relationship between the biographical details related about the Sages and the dicta attributed to them lies outside the scope of this article, but a teacher might be interested in raising these questions.

[23] The word used here, *madgilim*, is unusual and difficult to interpret. It may come from *degel* (i.e., flag; see Rashi's reading, which suggests the disciples gather together around the flag, or under the banner, to study). But see the very *different* interpretation cited by *Tosafot* in *Avodah Zarah* 22b (s.v. *Ragla*), in which the word seems to mean "to trip up" (perhaps from *daleg*, to skip): our *talmidei hakhamim* are causing each other to err, and thus apparently failing to understand the essence of their Torah study. Nevertheless, God loves them. This may have implications for the discussion of aggression, above.

How can we compare this *havruta* partnership to the others? What form of study is being described and what does the phrase that "God loves them" mean?

In this case, as in the first passage, the Talmud limits the scope of Resh Lakish's dictum. "Said Rava: Providing they know the features of a subject, providing also that there is no greater (scholar) in the town from whom to learn." Rava's comments suggest that Resh Lekish is describing beginners who really need a teacher. They are loved because they are doing the best they can. The motif of active love on the part of God ends this series. The passage in *Kiddushin* also ends with love. There the affection is between the *havruta* partners themselves.

We have thus at least three models of *havruta* study:[24] First, study through analytical argumentation (tempered by humility), leading to the acquisition of the Torah given by God and the consequent wordly rewards. Second, study through empathic listening, which leads to God's "listening in" and an intensified sense of the presence of the *Shekhinah*. Third, collective study which arouses God's love.

Is there a hierarchical relationship among these different models? Are they complementary aspects of *havruta* study? Could they reflect the same students' experiences in varying circumstances or at different moments? Could they reflect a historical process, as suggested above, leading to a messianic form of Torah study?

I would venture to suggest that it is precisely the lack of explicit editorial reflection on the part of the Gemara, as well as the context in which it is embedded, that make studying this selection so fruitful an experience. Each dictum stands on its own and also casts its shadow on the other passages, leaving both the individual quotations and the passage as a whole open to interpretation.

Educational Implications

What are some of the further pedagogical challenges presented by these passages? My goal when teaching is to give the students the chance to use these texts in order to understand themselves better: to evaluate the ways in which they learn best and the way they interact in relationships. Thus, these

---

[24] There are possibly four models, depending on two possible varients of Resh Lakish, as explained above.

passages can help students observe themselves as if from outside and notice the way they study in *havruta*.[25]

From an educational or experiential point of view, there is another angle of interest. These passages begin with the learning process and then deal with its effects. The Talmud suggests that certain types of study lead to particular consequences. One may be able, however, to reverse the process. I would suggest that the students' goals, the anticipated consequences – possibly explicit, possibly even subconscious – affect the dynamics of the learning process itself. *Havruta* partners striving for clarity may learn differently than those striving for beauty. A person seeking to acquire specific information may interact differently from one looking for a spiritual experience. Studying these passages may help people clarify what they are looking for when they study and fine-tune the methods they use.

The entire discussion is important from another point of view as well. One of the more riveting discussions about Jewish education today involves the question of the entry of women into the sphere of Talmud study and its dialectical, often highly analytical form, of thought. The questions asked range over the application of many issues raised by feminist thought. For example, according to the view that there are deep intellectual and attitudinal differences between men and women, if women seriously enter the forum of Talmud study, will it take a different form? For instance, would it be less rule-oriented and more aware of the individual needs of specific human interactions? Alternatively, would any possible impact be erased both by the particular character of the women who entered the field and the sheer force of established halakhic structure and precedent of thought?

Another question of interest involves not the content of Torah study but the process. Specifically, do women study in *havruta* partnerships differ-

---

[25] One method is to study the passages and then use role-play to act out the different *havruta* models, something I have experimented with in my own teaching. In one such experience, we broke up into four groups to study the topic of *mitzvah ha-ba'ah be-aveirah*, each group acting out one of the *havruta* models described (we differentiated between the first two models brought in the name of Resh Lakish). The students could treat their particular model in a positive or negative light, seriously or humorously. In addition, the participants were asked to reflect on the way they themselves interacted in *havruta* during the rest of the day. Surprising things occurred. Many participants felt that their initial assumptions were challenged. Students revealed unanticipated problems, such as insufficient analysis and rejection of ridiculous statements among the empathic listeners. Some participants who had thought that aggressiveness and competitiveness were out of place in Torah study recognized its advantages. Others perceived how much could be accomplished without aggressiveness.

ently than do men? Are they less aggressive or competitive and better listeners, as sometimes suggested?[26]

The talmudic texts involve different models without reference to gender, but they are remarkably similar to the ones being proposed today on the basis of gender. The Resh Lakish model of empathetic, respectful listening is generally described in the Gemara as the way Torah was studied in *Eretz Yisrael,* in contrast to the more adversarial, competitive, and analytical Babylonian model.[27] Alternatively, Beit Hillel's mode of study and interaction is contrasted with that of Beit Shammai. These texts thus provide an opportunity to explore important issues and differences without explicit reference to gender. It also suggests that with the entry of women into the *beit midrash,* we may be dealing with a greater emphasis on a particular model, or a slightly different combination of already existing elements, rather than a fundamental change in the *havruta* learning process.

These passages also create an awareness of the heterogeneity of experience possible within the world of Torah learning. They beckon the reader to explore the texts that underlie our conceptual worlds and daily halakhic lives and to creatively develop and enrich these texts.

Finally, from a sociological point of view, the *havruta* relationship forms a small, relatively stable unit within the larger framework of a Jewish community and intellectual dialogue. An intense, burning point of Torah study, it is an integral component of a vibrant society and helps to shape its character. The possibility of *havruta* study draws individuals out of their states of aloneness into a shared pursuit of truth and beauty. Although the *havruta* relationship generally begins with rigorous textual study, it also demands loyalty, perseverance, honesty, and humility between the partners and before God. It creates a unique space that figuratively fulfills the Torah's command (Ex. 25:8): "And let them make me a sanctuary that I may dwell among them."

---

[26] Since women do not have as many role models, they do not enter a traditional *beit midrash* that exists already, but create their own. As a result, any difference found may actually reflect not only a gender difference but an historical, contemporary trend that, in the case of women, is allowed to flower.

[27] Indeed, the Land of Israel is often characterized as feminine.

HERMENEUTICS AND VALUES:
ISSUES IN IMPROVING CONTEMPORARY TALMUD TEACHING

AVRAHAM WALFISH

IT IS SADLY PARADOXICAL that while the number of Talmud students in the Jewish community grows in unprecedented fashion, the difficulty with and alienation from talmudic study increases within major segments of the Orthodox community. In talmudic times, the study of Talmud was confined to an elite minority, as evidenced by the well-known midrashic statement:

> It usually happens that out of a thousand who enter upon the study of Scripture a hundred are successful... out of these ten who proceed to the study of Talmud one emerges [who is fit to render legal decisions].[1]

Today, study of Talmud encompasses all levels of Orthodox Jewish education, from the upper grades of elementary school through advanced yeshivah study, and all male students – and many female students – who have studied in Orthodox institutions of learning may be expected to have spent a considerable amount of time studying talmudic texts. The quantity – if not the quality – of competent talmudic scholars is far greater than at any previous time in Jewish history. But, the broad expansion of the scope of Talmud study has not had universally positive impact on Jewish education. The *haredi* world measures academic and social success (for male students) largely by the yardstick of talmudic proficiency, and the impact of this emphasis upon *haredi* society is beyond the scope of this essay. In the religious Zionist or centrist Orthodox camp, however, there is a growing sense of crisis in recent years regarding talmudic education and its discontents. A much-cited study of religious education in Israel revealed that, while Talmud was the subject to which the most hours were devoted, most

---

[1] *Lev. Rabbah* 2 (s.v. *"dabber el"*) (trans. J. Israelstam; London: Soncino Press, 1939).

students rated it as the subject they liked the least.[2] Conferences, committees, and newspaper articles have been devoted to describing, diagnosing, and proposing solutions for an increasingly acute and pressing problem.

An educational problem of these proportions will, almost axiomatically, have many dimensions, encompassing all of Joseph Schwab's well-known four "commonplaces" of education: the subject matter, the student, the teacher, and (for our purposes) the community. Undoubtedly a full solution to the problem will require a multilayered approach that addresses issues such as teacher training and the relation between the school and the community. In this essay I will address primarily the subject matter aspect of the problem, although this examination will touch on the other commonplaces as well. More specifically, I will discuss certain hermeneutical issues underlying the study of Talmud that, I believe, have a significant impact on the problems students face in grasping the subject and appreciating its value. Identifying and addressing these hermeneutic issues will help me to outline a program of Talmud study that, in my view, will make it more accessible and more attractive for Modern Orthodox students.

In order to clarify the centrality of these hermeneutical issues to Modern Orthodox Jewish education, we need to address a central question: why should Talmud continue to serve as a focal point of Jewish education? Our discussion of this question will lead us into an investigation of the nature of religious authority, an issue with profound impact on the way in which we should approach religious texts in general and the Talmud in particular. Our conclusions from these two discussions will guide us in our approach to the hermeneutical issues involved in studying and teaching Talmud.

Why Talmud? – The Dilemma

Many objective barriers make Talmud (and even Mishnah) inaccessible to the average modern student. Most people – including competent talmudists – have little fluency in Aramaic, and both Mishnah and Gemara are written in a terse style condensed almost to the point of obscurity. The material and social environment presumed by mishnaic and talmudic discussions differs vastly from that of the modern world. The Mishnah and the Talmud reflect styles of thinking and of presentation that the modern reader finds puzzling and alien. Perhaps most significantly, the legalistic formalisms and fine distinctions characteristic of Talmud do not seem to

---

[2] See S. Weiser and M. Bar Lev, "Teaching of Talmud in the Yeshiva High School: Difficulties and Dangers" (Hebrew), *Nir ha-Midrashiah* 8 (1990): 233–256. While this study focuses on Talmud instruction in Israeli religious high schools, I believe it is relevant for Diaspora education as well.

possess universal appeal – why should the average literate Jew find the legalisms of talmudic laws regarding torts or bailments more fascinating than the intricacies of their modern secular counterparts?

None of these problems is insuperable. They may be surmounted by instilling within the students – and the community at large – the conviction that the study of Talmud is of vital importance for one's religious life and spiritual development. The all-encompassing devotion to Talmud study that characterizes the *haredi* community has enabled them to confront these problems with a large measure of success. But other sectors of the Orthodox community do not display the same monolithic devotion to Talmud study. In an environment in which other pursuits and intellectual challenges, more congenial to the modern temperament, are accorded equal – oftentimes superior – status, the centrality of Talmud study to religious life cannot be assumed. Moreover, the greater openness of these communities to modernity exposes students to conflicts between the social mores and ethical assumptions of the Talmud and those that characterize a modern sensibility. In the liberal-pluralistic and scientific-critical environment in which modern consciousness is molded, neither the authority nor the superior wisdom of the Talmud can be taken as axiomatic.

Despite these formidable challenges, I believe it imperative that religious Jewish education retain a strong emphasis on Talmud. As Haym Soloveitchik has observed, contemporary Jewish observance has grown increasingly text-oriented.[3] Alongside the reasons that he and others have suggested for this development,[4] I would argue that in a contemporary culture that revolves around texts of various kinds, neither faith nor observance can flourish unless it is founded on a solid textual basis. Both Jewish practice and Jewish belief center on two foundational texts: the Bible and Talmud. A Jewish education must provide students with basic knowledge and familiarity with these two texts, as well as with basic textual skills.

A central issue involved in presenting Talmud to the students with whom we are concerned is the problem of authority. Traditionally, Talmud was studied by and taught to those for whom its authority was axiomatic, and this governed both the motivation for and the method of Talmud

---

[3] Haym Soloveitchik, "Rupture and Reconstruction: The Transformation of Contemporary Orthodoxy," *Tradition* 28:4 (1994): 64–130.

[4] Isaac Chavel, "On Haym Soloveitchik's 'Rupture and Reconstruction': A Response," *The Torah U-Madda Journal* 7 (1997): 122–136; Haym Soloveitchik, "Clarifications and Reply," id., pp. 137–149; Hillel Goldberg, "Responding to 'Rupture and Reconstruction'," *Tradition* 31:2 (1997): 31–40; Mark Steiner, "The Transformation of Contemporary Orthodoxy: Another View," id., pp. 41–49.

study. Study focused entirely on content, analysis, and skills, inasmuch as the relevance of the study was presumed, and students were largely assumed to be self-motivated. The basic methodological presumptions or techniques of the Talmud needed no justification, and the student's energies were channeled into following the intricacies and implications of the discussion in the Talmud and its traditional commentators. Teaching students for whom these presumptions cannot be taken for granted makes it vitally important to make Talmud study meaningful, relevant, intellectually challenging, and spiritually rewarding. But in order for Talmud to play a central role in religious consciousness, it needs to be taught as a text possessing commanding authority. For this reason, leading rabbis such as R. Aharon Lichtenstein have rejected in principle attempts to vitalize the teaching of Talmud by making the study relevant and spiritually rewarding.[5]

I contend that it is possible to teach Talmud in a manner that fosters a sense of relevance and spiritual meaning without sacrificing the sense of obedience to divinely sanctioned authority. My educational model for doing so will posit a form of religious authority for which I cannot argue here but that has been discussed both in Jewish and non-Jewish writings of recent years. Instead of taking a *dogmatic* approach to religious authority, which views all sacred texts as divinely inspired and demands of the religious personality a self-effacing surrender of all rational judgment in the face of the commanding word of God, I will follow the *inductive* model of religious authority, which roots obedience to divine texts in a rational process justified by induction from experienced events.[6]

---

[5] Aharon Lichtenstein, "Teaching Gemara in Yeshiva High Schools" (Hebrew), *Shanah be-Shanah* (5761): 315–327. "Making the study relevant" is used here to indicate gearing the learning toward issues and concepts that the student is likely to find interesting or rewarding, rather than toward the ideas that seem to be demanded by the text.

[6] The term *inductive* has been borrowed from Peter Berger, and indeed the two models of religious authority outlined here correspond to two of the religious postures described by him in *The Heretical Imperative* (New York: Anchor Press, 1979). Cf. Michael S. Berger's term "epistemic authority" in his "Rabbinic Authority: A Philosophical Analysis," *Tradition* 27:4 (1993): 62 ff. These approaches may be further compared to Kierkegaard's categories of "immediacy" and "immediacy after reflection," as well as to Moshe Sokol's categories of "hard" and "soft" autonomy, in "Personal Autonomy and Religious Authority," in M. Sokol, ed., *Rabbinic Authority and Personal Autonomy* (Northvale, NJ: Aronson, 1992), pp. 169–216. It should be stressed that most religious personalities combine elements of both positions: a "dogmatic" leap of faith is grounded in some experience that justifies such an act, and an "inductive" process of rational judgment leads to a commitment that limits one's range of autonomy. Nevertheless, there are different ways of balancing these two factors, leading to heavier emphasis on one or the other.

The *dogmatic* approach, which is successfully practiced in the *haredi* world and in certain sectors within the Zionist Orthodox and (so-called) centrist Orthodox communities, requires no "relevance" within the learning of Torah, and effectively obliterates tensions between one sacred text and another, as well as between the texts and current belief and practices. The student's awe before God and the extraordinary personalities who composed the sacred texts is described therein. This determines the student's understanding of these texts through traditional commentaries and teachings, and it ensures both the religious and experiential significance of Torah study and the lack of probing critical questioning capable of undermining the sense of the Torah's seamless unity. The inductive approach, on the other hand, regards the authority of the sacred text not as a presupposition, but as a quality that needs to be developed from the way in which the text is experienced. The student, educated within a framework of belief and observance, is trained to be attentive to all the nuances of the biblical text in order to hear the commanding divine voice that addresses us from the text.[7] Similarly, the student will accept the authority of the Sages not as a postulate, but as a natural consequence of learning to appreciate the profundity of their understanding of God, of man, and of Scripture.[8] Of course, Jewish tradition requires that ultimately the religious personality attain a faith in God and subservience to His authority that transcends his rational judgment and enables him to respond obediently to the divine command and declare (Ex. 24:7), "we will do (i.e., first, obey) and we will

---

[7] Several modern scholars have argued that attentive and spiritually open reading of the Tanakh can reopen modern secular man to the notion of a sacred text. See Michael Fishbane, *The Garments of Torah* (Bloomington and Indianapolis: Indiana Univ. Press, 1992), pp. 121–133, and compare his presentation in earlier chapters there on the views of Buber and Rosenzweig. See also Robert Alter, *The Art of Biblical Narrative* (New York: Basic Books, 1981), p. 46.

[8] See R. Soloveitchik's description in *Reflections of the Rav* (Jerusalem: WZO, 1979), pp. 135–136:

> The authority of a teacher is not imposed... A Torah teacher is freely accepted and joyfully embraced. His authority emerges from his personality; his learning and selflessness are acknowledged... At times he inspires emulation of his way of thinking and his general deportment, but this does not result in the enslavement of his disciples. The students are not crimped and circumscribed; their souls are not shriveled through fear and conformity. On the contrary, there is an enlargement and growth of the total personality... Teaching and learning are creative activity.

See further R. Soloveitchik's two models of "king-teacher" and "saint-teacher," pp. 161–163. These two approaches to the authority of the text may further be related to the "functional" and "hermeneutical" approaches to religious canonical texts outlined by Shlomo Biderman, *Scripture and Knowledge* (New York: Koeln, 1995), and see my "Religious Zionism in the World of Hermeneutics" (Hebrew), in S. Raz, ed., *Kovetz ha-Tzionut ha-Datit* (Jerusalem: Mizrahi, 1999) pp. 463 ff.

hear (only then, understand)." Nonetheless, the inductive approach may serve as the educational and phenomenological foundation for fostering the sense of authority that ultimately will enable such leaps of faith.[9]

The educational strategy suggested here rests on the premise that the inductive model, as described above, provides a foundation for an approach to canonical texts that can balance the simultaneous commitments within the Modern Orthodox community to faith and observance on the one hand, and to autonomy and critical judgment on the other hand.[10]

In the next section we will examine the hermeneutical and educational corollaries of this premise.

Experiencing the Text

Inasmuch as the educator in a Modern Orthodox framework cannot assume that students take the authority of the Talmud for granted, he or she must teach talmudic texts in a way that fosters the student's respect for and commitment to these texts. As noted above, the Talmud presents formidable obstacles to achieving this goal for most students. Some of the obstacles, such as barriers of language and of elliptical style, are technical in nature, and need to be addressed by finding appropriate tools and methods for teaching the students the "language skills" necessary for making sense of the text. The obstacles that concern me here are more fundamental, touching on the very nature and purpose of talmudic study. I will focus on two issues that, in my view, bear profoundly on the willingness and ability of many students to tackle the challenges and difficulties presented by the Talmud. First, the heavy focus in talmudic texts on the formalities and fine

---

[9] This does not mean, of course, that this sense of authority flows automatically from inductive premises. The Modern Orthodox community is plagued by ambivalent attitudes towards the notion of religious authority. See Daniel Tropper, "The Distress of Contemporary Religious Authority" (Hebrew), *Akdamot* 11 (2002): 79–96; Daniel Gutenmacher, "The Conservative Principles of Orthodoxy," *Akdamot* 10 (2001): 101–124; Tamar Ross, "On the Inner Role of the 'Outer'," *Akdamot* 11 (2002): 161–166; D. Gutenmacher, "An Unclear Boundary is Still a Boundary," *Akdamot* 11 (2002): 167–168; Yosef Ahituv, *Al Gevul ha-Temurah* (Jerusalem: Ministry of Education, 1995). The more nuanced and sophisticated thinking regarding religious authority that is required by centrist and Zionist Orthodoxies demands of educators heightened awareness of the issue, as well as greater clarity regarding spiritual goals and means of achieving them.

[10] Some recent thinkers, such as Shimon Gershon Rosenberg (R. Shagar), have been arguing that the "Modern Orthodox option" is outmoded, in light of the influential trend towards postmodern modes of thinking and behavior. I believe that this position has overestimated the influence of postmodernism both on the culture at large and on the religious world in particular, while underestimating the radical nature of the postmodern challenge to religion.

points of *halakhah* strikes many students as nitpicking and picayune at best, arcane and outmoded at worst. In addition, much of talmudic discourse is based on interpretations of earlier texts, such as Tanakh and Mishnah, that employ hermeneutical methods that the modern student finds difficult to understand and even more difficult to appreciate. The first of these issues affects the student's ability to identify with the goals of the talmudic discussion, and the second affects the student's ability to fathom the means by which the Talmud achieves these goals. A student who has problems on these two levels will thus appreciate neither the purpose nor the method of talmudic discussion.

To address these issues, I suggest three central goals that should underlie the teaching of Talmud: highlighting the values and spiritual concerns that underlie the formalities and subtleties of halakhic discourse; paying careful attention to the stylistic and literary qualities of talmudic texts; and confronting head-on the hermeneutical assumptions that govern talmudic interpretations and attempting to make sense of these assumptions. Attaining these goals will contribute to successfully addressing both of the foregoing concerns and enable the student to develop an "inductive" respect for the Talmud, with regard to both the goals and the methods that inform its discussions.

I will now outline how each of these three goals may be achieved in teaching Talmud and offer illustrative examples of Talmud texts presented in accordance with the method outlined here.

Values and Spiritual Concerns

It is both intellectually honest and educationally legitimate to ground the formalism of talmudic *halakhah* and its concern for minutiae in the Sages' devoted commitment to fulfilling the commanding divine will. Most talmudists would dismiss attempts to discern ethical and spiritual values within halakhic texts as *ta'amei ha-mitzvot* – a homiletic quest for understanding the unknown reasons underlying the inscrutable divine will, lacking any serious intellectual or theological basis.[11] Nevertheless, in order to foster an "inductive" acceptance of the authority of the Talmud, it is crucial for the teacher to afford the student insights into ethical and spiritual values that are given expression by talmudic discussions.[12]

---

[11] This presumption is rooted both in the all-consuming formalism that characterizes normal Talmud study, as well as in an implicit legal positivism – at least regarding divinely mandated law – that I believe characterizes the thinking of most talmudists.

[12] In addition to the educational advantages of doing so, I believe that a "natural law" point of view better fits the framework of an "inductive" approach. Among Jewish

The values underlying texts such as Mishnah, *Tosefta*, *midrashim*, and Talmud may be revealed in several ways. One way is simply to sensitize oneself to hidden issues that may not play a major role in the formal analysis or classic discussions of the halakhic issue at hand, but that are nonetheless clearly visible once one learns to look for them.

For example, the supreme importance that the Sages accord to the worker's responsibility to devote his working hours to his task and not to cheat his employer is reflected in *halakhot* that exempt the worker from standing in honor of a *talmid hakham* (*Kiddushin* 33a) and require him to recite *Shema* on top of the tree or building on which he is working (*Berakhot* 2:4). If we fully grasp the Sages' reluctance to allow even a brief work break outside the terms of employment, we will appreciate the dramatic importance they attach to a time-bound ceremonial *mitzvah* such as bringing first fruits, when they require workers to stand in honor of the first fruit procession (*Bikkurim* 3:4), as explained by R. Yose bar Avin (*Kiddushin* 33a): "Dear is a *mitzvah* at its appointed time."

The Mishnah's ruling in *Sanhedrin* 2:2 that a king cannot be judged would seem to place a king above the law, thereby seeming to contravene both the Torah's conception of a king as subject to divine law and the contemporary principle of the "rule of law." But the talmudic discussion in *Sanhedrin* 19a-b reinstates the "rule of law" by asserting that Judean kings are judged and that Israelite kings are not judged only because of a historical incident suggesting that the attempt to impose the rule of law upon recalcitrant kings can be highly dangerous to the court.

In these instances, the values underlying the text are apparent, but the use of value terminology in order to explain the text is not self-evident. The sensitive teacher will be alert to such "hidden" values within the text and exploit them by calling attention to them and spending significant time discussing them and their ramifications.[13]

A second way in which the teacher may reveal values underlying the text is by translating halakhic concepts from the formalistic language prevalent

---

thinkers who have debated whether Jewish law should be seen as positivistic or natural, I would cite Jose Faur, who has espoused a "positive law" position, and analyses favoring natural law theory by Rabbis Aharon Lichtenstein, Eliezer Berkovits, and J. David Bleich.

[13] Some interesting examples may be found in Yonah Fraenkel, "Educational Aims in Teaching Talmud" (Hebrew), *Mayim mi-Dalyav* (1991): 85–109.

in classic talmudic discourse into language of value that is both more accessible and more relevant to students.[14] For example:

In dealing with the *sugyot* on *Kiddushin* 9a-b, one may summarize the main conclusions of the talmudic discussion in classic halakhic terminology: unlike contracts of sale, which are written by the *makneh* (the one transferring ownership), a contract of *kiddushin* is written by the husband, i.e. the *koneh* (the one acquiring ownership), but there is an amoraic dispute whether the consent of the *makneh* (here, the woman) is also required; unlike most contracts, the contract of *kiddushin* must be written specifically for the sake of the particular woman to be betrothed (*li-shemah*), inasmuch as the Torah has significantly juxtaposed betrothal to divorce, which requires a bill of divorce written *li-shemah*. But examining these discussions with an eye trained upon the spiritual and ethical bases of the halakhic formalities suggests that underlying these differences between contracts of sale and contracts of *kiddushin* is a fundamental claim that the concept of *kinyan* ("acquisition") in the context of betrothal differs significantly from the parallel concept regarding transfer of mere property. The *halakhah* invests the *kinyan* of *kiddushin* with a personal and humanistic quality absent from the *kinyan* of property. *Kinyan* of *kiddushin* does not create, as in property transfer, a relationship of ownership between the *koneh* and the acquired object, but rather a mutual and personal relationship between a man and a woman. Consequently, the responsibility for writing the contract is not determined by the roles of *koneh* and *makneh*, but rather by the roles of man and woman, husband and wife. As in other contracts, there is an asymmetry between the two parties to the contract – the *halakhah* is not egalitarian – but the asymmetry between the roles differs. In property contracts, the writing of the contract is a completely unilateral act by the *makneh*. In a contract of *kiddushin*, however, the major active role is conferred upon the husband, but the wife is also recognized as a contracting agent of the *kiddushin* insofar as the contract must be written explicitly with her in mind and – according to one opinion – with her consent. Thus, the *halakhah* rec-

---

[14] Many instructive examples of this kind of thinking may be found in R. Soloveitchik's *Shiurim le-Zekher Abba Mari*. Rabbi Shimon G. Rosenberg (Shagar), "Method and Motivation in Teaching Gemara" (Hebrew), *Mayim mi-Dalyav* (1995): 363ff. terms this the "secularization" of the discourse of Talmud study. While I agree with the main points of his argument, I feel that the term "secularization" implies a more radical modification of halakhic thinking than is warranted. Emanuel Levinas's *Nine Talmudic Discourses* (Bloomington and Indianapolis: Indiana Univ. Press, 1994) aims to uncover the rabbis' concern with philosophical and ethical issues of contemporary relevance that lay beneath the formalities of talmudic discussion. While Levinas' method is highly midrashic and idiosyncratic, his sensitivity to the underlying values of halakhic and aggadic concepts is often instructive.

ognizes that "acquisition" of a woman in betrothal is designed to create not ownership, but rather a human bond of a different kind, marked by reciprocity (although not equality) in the relationship.

An additional example will prove useful. The concept of *ye'ush* (despair, or relinquishing hope of recovering a lost or stolen item), which entitles the finder of a lost item to take possession of it, may be presented as a formal halakhic concept, akin to *hefker* (voluntary relinquishment of ownership of an object in one's possession), and one may follow discussions of classic halakhic authorities regarding the similarities and differences between these two modes of relinquishing ownership.[15] If one is looking for values underlying the *halakhah*, however, one may follow the Mishnah *Bava Metzi'a* (2:5) in suggesting that the concept of *ye'ush* is rooted in an ethical perception, that the requirement of returning a lost item is dependent upon the owner's hope and expectation that he may recover the item. Perceiving the obligation of returning lost property as a matter of interpersonal morality rather than of formal consequences of laws of ownership and possession can help the student to understand that, subsequent to *ye'ush*, the owner has relinquished the moral demand he exerts upon the finder. Pursuing the matter further, one may see the laws regarding lost items as reflecting the moral and philosophical roots of the very concept of ownership. Ownership may be understood as a function of possession or control of the property and of recognition by society of one's right to the property, both of which involve intuitions rooted in morality and in an understanding of how society is organized. Losing one's property removes it from one's possession and subjects ownership entirely to the recognition by one's fellows that they are required to return it. Thus, study of the talmudic discussion of the laws of lost property can serve as a springboard for an in-depth investigation into fundamental moral concepts governing our attitude towards the foundations of society in general and of the concept of ownership in particular.[16]

---

[15] See *Tosafot* to *Bava Kamma* 66a s.v. *keivan*; *Entziklopediah Talmudit*, vol. 21, s.v. *ye'ush*, especially pp. 142ff.

[16] The analysis presented here is highly oversimplified, for purposes of brevity and clarity. Among the many sources bearing on this *sugya*, see especially *Birkat Shemuel*, Bava Metzia, #16–23, and *Entziklopediah Talmudit*, vol. 21, pp. 164 ff. An analysis of the concept of *ye'ush* that parallels many of the ethico-social concepts suggested here is offered by R. Yehiel Yaakov Weinberg, *Hiddushei Ba`al Seridei Eish* (Jerusalem, 1995), chap. 34 (pp. 248 ff.). Regarding the teaching of some of the *sugyot* mentioned here, see Yonah Fraenkel, "Educational Aims," pp. 90–93; Yosef Shimshi, "Returning Lost Property: Legal, Halakhic, and Methodological Aspects," (Hebrew), *Mayim mi-Dalyav* (1996):277–288; Shelomo Eitan, "Teaching the *Sugya* of Ye'ush she-Lo mi-Da`at on Level of *Peshat* and on Analytical Level" (Hebrew), *Mayim mi-Dalyav* (2002):23–38.

In this section we have presented several examples in which spiritual and ethical values may be perceived within talmudic discussions by means of conceptual analysis alone. In the next section we examine ways in which close textual analysis may signal the careful reader that there are ideas and values underlying the text, beyond those available to standard halakhic-conceptual analysis.

Style and Literary Qualities

Elsewhere, I have demonstrated the use by the Sages of stylistic and literary techniques, particularly in redacting the Mishnah, and have shown how they may be interpreted along the lines of spiritual and ethical values.[17] I believe that the very presence of such techniques in ostensibly formalistic-halakhic works is a powerful argument for the existence of a substratum of spiritual-conceptual values underlying the halakhic discourse of the Sages. Inasmuch as these points regarding Mishnah have been argued at length elsewhere, I will limit myself here to one illustration from the Talmud.

The laws of lighting Hanukkah candles are discussed in the Talmud in the second chapter of *Shabbat* (21a–23b). The simple explanation for this placement is that the Mishnah does not discuss Hanukkah anywhere and the redactors of the Talmud felt that the discussion of lighting *Shabbat* candles in this chapter was the most natural "peg" on which to hang another discussion candle lighting laws. Closer examination reveals that the Gemara redactor has created a "literary bridge" to ease the transition from the discussion of *Shabbat* candles to the discussion of Hanukkah candles. The reasons for forbidding the lighting of *Shabbat* candles with "wicks that the Sages said not to light for *Shabbat*" and "oils that the Sages said not to light for *Shabbat*" are offered by Rabbah (on 21a), followed by discussion, and the next two *sugyot* also open with "wicks and oils that the Sages said not to light for *Shabbat*" – Rami bar Hama asserts that these are not to be lit in the Temple and (following a brief discussion) three *amora'im* debate whether these may be lit for Hanukkah during the week and on the eve of Shabbat. Two points in common thus lead from the discussion of *Shabbat* candles to that of Hanukkah candles: the oils and wicks and the question as to what happens when the Hanukkah candles are lit for *Shabbat*.

The literary bridge between these two topics certainly enhances our respect for the redactor's literary concern and sensitivity. But if we turn to the end of the unit (on 23b), we discover that the redactor has created yet an-

---

[17] See my Hebrew articles in *Netu'im* 1 (1994), 2 (1995), and 3 (1996); and my English article in *Alei Etzion* 7 (1998).

other bridge between these two topics. At the conclusion of the unit, Rava argues that when one lacks the means to light both *Shabbat* candles and Hanukkah candles, *Shabbat* candles should be preferred because "the peace of the home" takes precedence over "publicizing the miracle." Thus we see that the Talmud's discussion of Hanukkah candles is framed by an envelope structure that underscores the connection between them and *Shabbat* candles. The two comparisons between *Shabbat* candles and Hanukkah candles at the two poles of the unit are related to one another, inasmuch as both of them highlight a fundamental difference between the two *mitzvot*: *Shabbat* candles, designed for benefit and "peace of the household" (23b), must be lit with materials ensuring that they will burn properly on *Shabbat* (21a); regarding Hanukkah candles, designed for "publicizing the miracle," it is less clear whether similar materials must be used, inasmuch as they are not lit in order to be used – indeed it is questionable whether one is permitted to derive any benefit from them (21a-b) – and it is not even clear whether their inadvertent extinguishing adversely affects one's fulfillment of the *mitzvah* (21a-b).

The literary framework of the discussion thus serves to highlight the meaning and purpose both of *Shabbat* candles and of Hanukkah candles. But it would appear that the redactor has further goals in mind. Between the discussion of wicks and oils for *Shabbat* candles and the discussion of wicks and oils for Hanukkah candles (on 21a), he has inserted another brief *sugya*, which discusses the use of these same wicks and oils in the Temple. Perusal of the talmudic discussion in its entirety will reveal that the presence of God in the Temple serves a model both for the lighting of Hanukkah candles (see the historical background on 21b and the testimony by Temple candles to the presence of God among the people of Israel on 22b) and for *Shabbat* candles (see the derivation of the time of lighting *Shabbat* candles from the "pillar of cloud" and "pillar of fire" on 23b). Thus, the interposition of Temple candles between *Shabbat* candles and Hanukkah candles on 21a is another signpost used by the redactor to indicate that *Shabbat* candles and Hanukkah candles, despite their differences, stem from a common source, as symbols of the Divine Presence. Hanukkah candles achieve this symbolism by publicizing the miracle, while *Shabbat* candles express the spirit of Shabbat peace, which creates an aura of sanctity within one's household.[18]

---

[18] The connection of *Shabbat* candles to the Divine Presence is intimated by Maimonides, *Mishneh Torah, Hilkhot Shabbat* 30:2, 5 (see discussion by R. Soloveitchik, *Shiurim le-Zekher Abba Mari*, vol. 1, pp. 62ff.). This may be further supported by midrashic and talmudic sources, such as *Gen. Rabbah* 67 (at end; cf. Mishnah *Shabbat* 2:6) and the

Finally, we may note a further point of contact between *Shabbat* candles and Hanukkah candles, reflected at several points throughout the unit. Both kinds of candles need to be lit in the framework of a house and a household. *Shabbat* candles, called "the candle of his house" (23b), are lit within the house for the benefit of the members of the household; Hanukkah candles are lit within the framework of a household ("a candle for a man and his household" – 21b) and at the entrance to the house (22a).[19] Thus, the language and structure of the talmudic discussion suggest that both *Shabbat* candles and Hanukkah candles serve, in different ways, to invest one's house with sanctity akin to the sanctity of the Temple.

The kind of literary features we have noted in these two sources may be found in many others. These features reinforce the argument that study of halakhic sources should include a quest for the spiritual underpinnings of the halakhic categories, while also providing the student a powerful tool for ferreting out these ideas and values. Not all these tools are suited for classroom teaching and discussion, but many of them are. In and of itself, the search by teacher and student for repetitions of language and interesting structures can be an important teaching tool, which helps foster close reading of the text and sensitizes the student to the text's language and nuances. The search for the ideas underlying the literary repetitions and structures can be carried out on many levels, and the teacher needs to find the level appropriate for his or her students. Since interpretation of literary patterns is an open-ended process, any level on which it is done may draw teacher and student together in a quest that has no packaged or predetermined result, and carries with it the thrill of discovery and creativity.

Hermeneutical Principles

One of the features of Talmud that makes it a particularly difficult text to understand is its multilayered character: the text is constructed as a series of commentaries, in which each new layer comments upon the previous. Thus, one may encounter a discussion that involves understanding how the *setama di-gemara* understands the way in which the interpretation of the Mishnah by an earlier *amora* was explained by a later *amora* in light of problems and solutions presented by *amora'im* of an intermediate period. Beyond the challenge of simply being able to follow the thread of the argument,

---

story of the two angels who accompany a man to his home on *Shabbat* evening (*Shabbat* 119b).

[19] More accurately, it should be lit at the entrance to the courtyard, so that it may be seen from the public domain. Nonetheless, it should be apparent to the public that it is connected to the house, as noted by Rashi (22a) s.v. *mitzvah le-hanihah*.

this feature of the Talmud presents a further, more fundamental problem – the tools and assumptions employed by the Sages of the Talmud in interpreting previous texts are often significantly different from the interpretative methodology employed in other areas of textual study. This problem, already noted by Rambam,[20] is magnified considerably for Modern Orthodox students of Talmud, for two reasons. First, it is more difficult for them to accept modes of thinking that are alien to their way of thinking, based on traditional authority alone. Also, they are exposed to the ways in which texts are interpreted in other disciplines, including literature and *Tanakh*, and the gap between the ways they are trained to understand texts and the mode of talmudic interpretation, creates a cognitive dissonance that impedes their ability or desire to understand the Talmud. Some students may raise questions regarding the validity of talmudic reasoning, which our educational frameworks are unequipped to handle. More troubling, the system often suppresses such questions from being addressed at all. The less capable student, although likely to be unaware of a cognitive dissonance, may find that his inability to comprehend the method behind the Gemara's textual interpretations fosters a feeling of inadequacy, in which talmudic reasoning seems mysterious and inscrutable. The inescapable conclusion, in my opinion, is that Talmud instruction for the Modern Orthodox student must include a thoroughgoing and honest confrontation with the question of talmudic hermeneutics: what are the assumptions underlying talmudic interpretation of earlier sources and how may these assumptions be justified?

Most students and teachers of Talmud, including many accomplished talmudists, have not been trained to confront these questions, which are more characteristic of academic Talmud study than of yeshivah learning. While there are aspects of academic methodology that I believe are neither necessary nor advisable for most elementary, middle school, or high school students,[21] it is essential that Talmud teachers begin to confront these is-

---

[20] *Introduction to Mishnah Commentary* (Kafih edition, p. 25; Shilat edition, p. 62).

[21] I refer here specifically to lower and higher textual criticism. Most analysis on these levels is, in my view, too abstruse for most students on these levels. Furthermore, too many questions about the textual integrity of a canonical work and too many conflicting and contradictory voices within an ostensibly unified text are not conducive to fostering the kind of faith and acceptance of authority at which we should aim. Compare my article, "*Beit Midrash* and the World of Academic Research – Part II" (Hebrew), *Shanah be-Shanah* (5757): 432–439. Hence, these methods should be introduced sparingly, if at all, until the student has developed both the ability and the commitment to handle them properly. For a different point of view on this issue, see Pinchas Hayman, "On the Teaching of Talmud: Toward a Methodological Basis for a Curriculum in Oral-Tradition Studies," *Religious Education* 92:1 (1997): 61–76, and his "Implications

sues honestly and consistently and develop sound educational methods to enable their students to confront them as well. I can only briefly sketch some of the basic guidelines that I would suggest for such an approach, and provide a few examples.

In order for the student to be able to understand talmudic hermeneutics, it has to be coordinated with hermeneutic assumptions to which the student is accustomed in other areas. Hence, the approach to a talmudic interpretation of a scriptural verse, a Mishnah, a *baraita*, or an amoraic statement must involve reading the original text on two levels. First, how do we understand the text, when we read it employing our normal tools of interpretation? And how, on the other hand, does the Talmud read the text? Reading the text on both levels highlights the novelty of the talmudic reading, as well as the central question we want to confront squarely: why did the Talmud depart from the simple reading and the plain meaning? Nehama Leibowitz and other teachers of *Tanakh* have already demonstrated both the intellectual and the educational soundness of such a dual approach to the text. Students taught by her method learn simultaneously close reading of the *Tanakh* and the breadth and beauty of traditional commentaries. They learn that while all interpretations, both *peshat* and *derash*, are part of our tradition and teach us important lessons, not all textual groundings are equal, and some readings have stronger claim than others to be regarded as valid *peshat* explanations.

A similar approach may be followed regarding the teaching of Talmud. Before actually learning the Gemara, the student should study the texts bearing on the talmudic discussion, starting with relevant scriptural passages and continuing through tannaitic sources. Each source should be studied carefully and thoroughly, utilizing the standard tools and methods of *peshat* interpretation: attention to language, syntax, and context; use of concordances, commentaries, and literary structure. The teacher should take care to direct the student to those questions and difficulties arising from the text that will serve as a basis in later stages of analysis for new interpretations and new ideas. These questions and difficulties should be addressed honestly and thoroughly, attempting to use the tools of *peshat* to resolve them when the abilities of teacher and student make this possible. In studying any text, the student should get the sense that there are tools accessible to him or her that can make the text comprehensible and meaningful, yet at the same time that the text possesses "fault lines" that open it

---

of Academic Approaches to the Study of the Babylonian Talmud for Student Beliefs and Religious Attitudes," in Yisrael Rich and Michael Rosenak, eds., *Abiding Challenges* (London: Freund Publishing, 1999), pp. 375–399.

up to deeper analysis and multiple creative interpretations. The first educational message is designed to give the student the confidence and the motivation to engage the text; and the second is designed to enhance his respect for the text's profundity and authority, as well as to open the text to the interpretations of talmudic sources. The talmudic discussion of scriptural and tannaitic sources can thus be experienced by the student as part of his ongoing dialogue with these earlier texts, rather than as a completed, closed, and largely inscrutable presentation of authoritative readings.

Due to space limitations I will present only one example. Prior to teaching the fourth chapter of *Berakhot* (*Tefillat ha-Shahar*), the teacher should discuss with the students the fact that the Tanakh includes many prayers and many prayer narratives, but, according to *peshat*, there is no source for a commandment to pray, certainly not on a daily basis. Biblical prayer is a voluntary, spontaneous performance, not a required and formalized recitation.[22] Turning to the *midrash* (*Sifre Devarim* 41, s.v. *u-le'avdo*), we find the Sages interpreting the commandment of "serving" God as including – among other understandings – "service of the heart," namely prayer. Close reading of this passage shows that this understanding of the term *avodah* (service) may be associated with the destruction of the Temple, as the *midrash* asks regarding a verse that describes Daniel serving God: "And is there indeed service in Babylonia?... Just as service of the altar is called service, so too prayer is called service." Discussion arising from these sources can focus on many central issues and values concerning prayer, including the advantages and disadvantages of fixing times and texts for prayer, the nature and meaning of service of God, and the reasons that the Sages felt that prayer was an appropriate substitute for the sacrificial service.

This prelude to the study of Mishnah *Berakhot* (chapter 4) can help the student to appreciate many of the emphases and motifs in the Mishnah. It is easy to demonstrate that the times for prayer in the first Mishnah correspond to the times of the daily sacrifices, with the exception of the evening prayer, which the Mishnah differentiates from the other prayers by declaring that it "has no *keva* (fixity)." The Mishnah alternates its discussion of the three daily prayers with more individualized prayers, such as R. Nehunia ben Hakanah's "short prayer" upon entering and exiting a *beit midrash* and the "short prayer" of a wayfarer in Mishnah 4. R. Eliezer's comment in Mishnah 4 that "whoever makes his prayer fixed – his prayer is not suppli-

---

[22] This is true regarding petitionary prayer. There is a greater degree of structure and formalization regarding praise and thanksgiving in the *Tanakh*, and we do find formal and mandated thanksgiving prayers, such as the recitation accompanying the bringing of first fruits in Deut. 26:5–10.

cation" can readily be seen as expressing the underlying tension between the inner individual and the formalized social aspects of prayer. One term the Mishnah employs to express this tension, *keva*, also raises interesting exegetical questions, which will illustrate how we may teach the Mishnah text both as an interpretable text in its own right and as a basis for talmudic interpretation.

The term *keva* appears both in the first Mishnah, describing the evening service as lacking *keva*, and in the fourth, expressing R. Eliezer's opposition to making one's prayer *keva*,[23] and the term is problematic in both contexts. In Mishnah 1, the context suggests that the meaning of the term is "fixed time," but this raises the question of why the Mishnah uses this term rather than simply stating: "the evening prayer [can be recited] all night" (see *Berakhot* 27b), just at it asserts that "*musaf* prayers – all day." In Mishnah 4, meanwhile, it seems unclear altogether what form of *keva* R. Eliezer opposes. Both of these questions may be addressed utilizing tools of peshat.

For simplicity's sake we will first consider Mishnah 4. Commentators such as R. Yehosef Ashkenazi (cited in *Melekhet Shelomo*) and R. Saul Lieberman (*Tosefta Kifshutah*, vol. 1, pp. 31–32) have noted that R. Eliezer's comment makes perfect sense when seen in the context of the dispute among the *tanna'im* recorded in the immediately preceding Mishnah, regarding the correct text to be recited for prayer: eighteen full-fledged benedictions or eighteen shortened benedictions. Assuming that the division between Mishnah units is faulty here, and that R. Eliezer is responding to the previous discussion, we understand his comment as follows: I object to both suggestions for a proper text for prayer, because in my view prayer should not have a fixed text at all.[24] Recalling that a fixed prayer text was first established during the period of Yavneh, under the direction or Rabban Gamaliel (*Berakhot* 28b), we can readily understand that the Patriarch and his colleagues R. Joshua and R. Akiva disagreed in Mishnah 3 about the nature of this fixed text, and that their colleague R. Eliezer voiced in Mish-

---

[23] I have dealt more fully with the use of this term, the Mishnah's wordplay, and the way in which these may be used for teaching in my article, "Teaching Mishnah as a Literary Text" (Hebrew), *Teaching Classical Rabbinic Texts – Studies in Jewish Education* 8 (2002): 41–45.

[24] I have followed the reading of R. Yehosef Ashkenazi; Lieberman suggests a modification of this reading, and also a justification for the assumption that the division between *mishnayot* is faulty here. Ezra Fleischer, "Regarding the Antiquity of Obligatory Prayers in Israel" (Hebrew), *Tarbiz* 59 (1990): 429, n. 75, follows R. Ashkenazi's understanding of R. Eliezer here, but see counterarguments of Joseph Heinemann, *Iyyunei Tefillah* (Jerusalem: Magnes Press, 1981), p. 77, and Jose Faur, "Towards Explanation of the Term 'Reading a Letter'" (Hebrew), *Alei Sefer* 15 (1989): 22 ff.

nah 4 a more fundamental objection. In his view, a fixed text for prayer undermines the very essence of prayer, which is to be "supplication," namely – a heartfelt expression of what the person feels individually, as opposed to recitation of a prepared text.

Regarding the use of the phrase "has no *keva*" in Mishnah 1, we may suggest two possible answers, using two different strategies of interpretation. One answer, following the Vilna Gaon's comment recorded in *Shenot Eliyahu*, is to differentiate between "has no *keva*" and "may be recited all day/night" in terms of its halakhic import. The Vilna Gaon explains that *musaf* is a prayer with a fixed time, whose time is defined as all day; the evening prayer, on the other hand has no fixed time at all – it is defined as a "filler" prayer, which may be recited any time between the fixed-time prayers of afternoon and morning. This, according to the Vilna Gaon, explains why *Berakhot* 27a-b assumes that R. Judah, who allows the afternoon prayer to be recited only until *pelag ha-minhah*, will automatically allow the evening prayer to be recited from that time. A second answer is based on the wordplay between fixed-time *keva* in the first Mishnah and the different usage of *keva* in the fourth: by using the same term for two different aspects of fixity, the Mishnah underscores that the issues and problems that attach to one (according to R. Eliezer) apply to the other as well. This answer may be supported by noting the *Tosefta*'s comment (3:1): "Just as the Torah established *keva* for *Shema*, so the Sages established *keva* for prayer." The *Tosefta* clearly is referring to the fixed times for reciting the *Shema* and for prayer, as is made clear by the continuation of the passage, and the need to compare prayer to *Shema* appears to be rooted in the *Tosefta*'s perception that fixing time for prayer is problematic. Hence the *Tosefta* asserts that were it not for the precedent rooted in Torah law that a *mitzvah* performed by speech and inner intent can be given a fixed time, the rabbis would not have been able to fix times for prayer. We thus see that the *tanna'im* did indeed see both forms of *keva* as problematic in the context of prayer.

Turning to the Gemara, we see that the *amora'im* have addressed both *keva* passages and have suggested interpretations that differ from the *peshat* understandings suggested above. Regarding Mishnah 1, *Berakhot* 27b explains that in addition to the primary meaning that the evening prayer may be recited all night, the statement that "it has no *keva*" further indicates that this prayer is not obligatory, but only *reshut* (recommended),[25] and it pro-

---

[25] *Reshut* in talmudic sources, as a contrast with *mitzvah* or *hovah*, does not mean "permission," but rather a recommended positive action or a low-grade prohibition. To the explanation of "has no *keva*" in the *Bavli*, compare the language of *Yerushalmi Berakhot* 4:1 (7b).

ceeds to elaborate upon this point by recording the dramatic confrontation between Rabban Gamaliel and R. Joshua regarding this issue. While it is difficult to accept this reading as the plain sense of the Mishnah, the teacher may help the student to understand the basis of the reading by noting the following points: (1) the Gemara is motivated by a genuine and troubling problem regarding the *peshat* reading of the Mishnah; (2) the Gemara solves the problem by reading the term *keva* in light of a known tradition regarding the status of the evening prayer, thus intensifying the denial expressed by the Mishnah – rather than stating merely that the evening prayer "has no fixed time," the Mishnah is understood to state that it "is not a fixed prayer" at all; (3) the centrality of the term *keva* throughout chapter 4 of the Mishnah as representing the concept of fixed prayer may provide greater plausibility to the Gemara's reading, which suggests that the Mishnah seeks here to deny to the evening prayer not only a specific time but the very notion of *keva*; and (4) the Gemara's reading of the Mishnah may be presented as a way of formulating the reading suggested by the Vilna Gaon, if we assume that a prayer not affixed to a time, which bridges the gap between two fixed prayer times, can be only a "recommended," but not an obligatory, prayer.

Depending on the level and nature of the students, the teacher will decide which and how many of these points are appropriate for their needs. Regardless of which strategy the teacher employs, the students will benefit from having independently addressed the exegetical issue raised by the Gemara, which enables them to scrutinize and appreciate the discussion of this issue in a deeper and more satisfactory fashion.

Regarding the use of *keva* in Mishnah 4, *Berakhot* 29b cites several amoraic explanations of the prayer of *keva* that R. Eliezer rejects as lacking the character of "supplication." It is suggested that one prays such a prayer of *keva* if his prayer seems to him burdensome; if he fails to use language of supplication; if he is unable to insert into his fixed prayer a "new" individual element; or if he does not pray at sunrise, a time when prayer possesses a special dimension of "fear of God." These ideas differ drastically from the reading suggested above, according to which R. Eliezer rejected the innovation in Yavneh of a fixed prayer text, discussed in Mishnah 3, immediately preceding the citation of R. Eliezer's objection. The Gemara assumes, rather, that R. Eliezer accepts the idea of a fixed prayer text, but seeks to inject into it an element of "supplication," in one of the ways suggested by the *amora'im*.

In order to explain the Gemara's way of reading R. Eliezer, the teacher may adopt one of two approaches: to find exegetical grounds for the Ge-

mara's reading or to seek halakhic or educational justification for the amoraic suggestions. On the exegetical level, the teacher may offer the following observations. First, the Gemara may have received the division of *mishnayot* as we have it before us, in which R. Eliezer is not participating in the
tannaitic dispute regarding the fixed prayer text; hence he must be understood to be objecting to an aspect of the fixed prayer and not to the very
practice itself. Further, the Gemara may have read R. Eliezer's statement in
light of a similar statement by R. Eliezer's colleague R. Simon (ben Netanel)
in *Avot* 2:13, whose context clearly indicates an "aggadic" rather than a halakhic understanding, namely that there is a fixed prayer text, but that it
needs to be recited in a manner that expresses "supplication." Neither of
these points will be found by all teachers and students to be decisive on
purely exegetical grounds, however, and so the teacher may adopt a different approach. Perhaps the purpose of the Gemara is to explain the position
of R. Eliezer not in accordance with its original import, but rather in a
manner that makes it relevant and meaningful even after the fixed text of
the *Amidah* prayer has become universally accepted halakhic practice.

Understanding Midrashic Interpretations of Mishnah by Gemara

The idea that the Gemara sometimes explains the Mishnah in order to
fit accepted halakhic practice or educational goals, rather than in accordance with purely exegetical considerations, may sound radical to the ears
of a traditionalist, but such an approach to understanding talmudic exegesis
has been suggested by such traditional scholars as the Vilna Gaon and R.
Yehiel Yaakov Weinberg.[26] Indeed there are passages in the Gemara itself
that indicate that, at least on occasion, traditions may even be altered consciously in order to achieve halakhic or other goals that may take precedence over precise historical and exegetical accuracy. Clearly "midrashic"
interpretation of this sort may not be emulated by our students, or even by
their teachers, but indeed this may be seen as the reason why many talmudic readings of *mishnayot* and *baraitot* do not fit the normal canons of interpretation. The premise behind understanding talmudic hermeneutics in this
way is that amoraic interpretation of tannaitic sources seeks to achieve two
goals, which do not always neatly correspond: to understand the text as
clearly and as thoroughly as possible, and to determine proper Jewish prac-

---

[26] Regarding the Vilna Gaon, see R. Yisrael of Shklov, *Pe'at ha-Shulhan*, introduction,
5c, regarding *hasorei mehasra*, and compare R. Menashe of Ilya, *Binnat Mikra*, introduction. Regarding R. Yehiel Yaakov Weinberg, see his *Seridei Eish*, part 4, pp. 237–241.
See also the first part of my "The Beit Midrash and the World of Academic Research:
A Survey" (Hebrew), *Shanah be-Shanah* (5756): 380–381, 389.

tice and belief. When the *amora'im* encountered tension behind the plain sense of the tannaitic text and what they considered – whether on the basis of tradition (Vilna Gaon) or their own understanding (R. Weinberg) – to be correct practice or belief, they sought to resolve the tension through creative interpretation. While these creative interpretations often reveal new and deeper dimensions of textual understanding, they may also go beyond what we can recognize as interpretation, reshaping the text in order to enlist its authority in the service of the ultimate goal of *halakhah* or of faith.

In the last example, I have suggested two strategies for dealing with amoraic interpretations of tannaitic texts that apparently differ from the *peshat* of these texts. The choice as to which strategy to adopt is a function of many factors, local as well as ideological. The attempt always to find deeper exegetical factors that render talmudic interpretation convincing on an exegetical basis certainly allows for a simpler, more palatable faith structure, in which there are few if any conflicts between exegetical truth and the truths of Jewish faith and practice, and the Sages of the Talmud are the keenest, most profound readers of canonical texts. In practice, however, it is not always possible to find exegetical points that will satisfy and convince us and our students. The teacher may argue that we cannot always fathom the profundity of the Sages' superior wisdom, but, given the nature of the modern Orthodox student, this strategy is unlikely to succeed unless it is utilized sparingly.

The second approach has the advantage of being simpler to apply convincingly in a broad variety of cases, but requires a faith structure that includes multiple sources of truth, with a measure of tension among them. Thus, the Sages of the Talmud would need to be presented as human beings, who don't have all the answers ready-made, and are not possessed of superhuman wisdom in mining profound meanings from texts.[27] Their greatness is measured by the honesty, wisdom, and depth with which they confronted the tensions that encountered them. By studying texts with the

---

[27] One who adopts an approach such as this needs to be aware that the postulates outlined here have been opposed, often fiercely, not only by the *haredi* community, but by many great rabbinical authorities (see, for example, discussion in my article [above, n. 21] and sources cited there). Opposition to this approach goes beyond fear of undermining halakhic authority (see, for example, *Mishneh la-Melekh* to *Hilkhot Nezirut* 2:8, end of first paragraph), and I believe it is rooted in concern that bifurcation between hermeneutic methodology and halakhic authority is liable to result in a split religious personality. In order to maintain a unified and stable religious personality, they believe that it is essential to root halakhic authority in the belief that the halakhic and aggadic tradition are grounded in truthful interpretation faithful to the divinely revealed word. As I have argued throughout this essay, this is a legitimate concern, which can and should be addressed by exponents of the approach argued for here.

Sages, and not only from them, we can better appreciate their wisdom and acumen, and we can ground their authority on inductive, rather than dogmatic grounds. The divinity of the *halakhah* they taught will be rooted in a theological model that includes human creativity, change, and development within the process by means of which the divine word given at Sinai is received and applied by Israel.[28]

I have sketched here some of the main principles on which I think the study of Talmud needs to be founded in order for it to be rendered both meaningful and authoritative for students in our community. The approach is founded on the premise that both the values and the nature of the talmudic text need to be addressed on a deeper level, and through a language different from those to which our teachers and most of our Talmud scholars are accustomed. I hope that the reader finds value in the presentation of the few examples that space allowed, and may be motivated to apply these ideas to other examples as well. The time is short and the work is abundant, but we desist from it at our peril.

---

[28] Many such theological models have been proposed by contemporary thinkers. See, for example, Shalom Rosenberg, *Lo ba-Shamayim Hi*, (Alon Shevut: Tevunot Publishing, 1997), esp. part 2; Aaron Kirschenbaum, "Subjectivity in Rabbinic Decision Making," in Moshe Z. Sokol, ed., *Rabbinic Authority and Personal Autonomy*, pp. 169–216 – and see the critique by Alan J. Yuter in his review essay in *Tradition* 27:4 (1993): 144, 149.

HISTORICAL PERSPECTIVES IN
TEACHING TALMUD

BEVERLY GRIBETZ

NOTHING IS AS SIMPLE as it seems in learning and teaching the Talmud. It is often thought that all one needs to study and teach a *sugya* from the Talmud is what the standard editions provide, plus a dictionary. Sophisticated advanced students know that various types of analysis, both traditional (such as comparing the *rishonim* and *aharonim*) and critical (such as comparing text versions and taking a source-critical approach to parallel *sugyot*), can enrich Talmud study immeasurably. Beginners, however, are typically regarded as unripe for such higher forms of analysis.[1] Advanced methods such as the text-critical, the dialectical (source-critical), the conceptual, and the historical are all to be "saved" for later, in this view. [2]

In the present essay I shall demonstrate the need for a teacher – and even a teacher of beginners – to delve into history in order to address a question that will inevitably arise in interpreting a certain *sugya*.[3] "History"

---

[1] See, e.g., Adin Steinsaltz, *The Talmud: A Reference Guide* (New York: Random House, 1989), pp. 79–80.

[2] As delineated by David Weiss Halivni, "Contemporary Methods of the Study of the Talmud," *Journal of Jewish Studies* 30 (1979): 192–201.

[3] The present essay is based on a chapter from my Ph.D. dissertation, "On the Translation of Scholarship to Pedagogy: The Case of Talmud" (Graduate School of the Jewish Theological Seminary of America, 1995). I am grateful to my friend Dr. Joel B. Wolowelsky, and my husband, Prof. Edward L. Greenstein, for their editorial counsel. The "beginner" I have in mind is the one I have had experience in teaching for over 25 years, a student aged 12 through adult. Developmental issues in teaching Talmud have not yet been systematically studied. Indeed, nearly all the research that exists is anecdotal, based on the experience of individual educators. The invaluable need for assembling and collating such anecdotal evidence from teachers is underscored by Lee Shulman; see, e.g., "Knowledge and Teaching: Foundations of the New Reform," *Harvard Educational Review* 57 (1987): 1–22. The many claims I make concerning the questions students will ask and the responses they give, as well as several matters of pedagogy that I raise, are part of my anecdotal record.

here refers not only to the history of Jewish practice that lies behind the textual material, but also to the history of the talmudic text and the later use of the Talmud in the Passover *Haggadah*. In the traditional study of classical Jewish sources, the history that is relevant is the narrative that those sources themselves relate. A historical perspective, in which both traditional and external sources are read critically, is sometimes, and in some circles, taken to be destructive of traditional foundations. History, purely applied, may indeed be a thoroughly secular discipline. But the application of a historical outlook in the context of traditional study may also complement, supplement, and enrich our understanding. Questions of an historical nature cannot but be raised in the study of certain texts and topics. Texts such as the *sugya* that will engage us here cry out for historical considerations.

Our *sugya* appears in *Pesahim* 116a; the reader is invited to review that text in advance of proceeding with this essay. In order to demonstrate the need for an historical approach, it will not be necessary to analyze and present a pedagogical method for teaching the entire *sugya*, brief as it is.[4] We shall content ourselves with treating that part of the *sugya* that requires the two previously noted types of historical criticism.

Preparing the *Sugya*: Questions and Guides to Answers

The typical Talmud teacher prepares the text from a printed edition of the entire Talmud, such as the standard Vilna *Shas*. This seemingly trivial observation takes on special significance in the present case. In the *sugya* beginning with the Mishnah on *Pesahim* 116a, the text of the Mishnah that is presented in the Talmud is different from the Mishnah text that appears in a standard edition of the Mishnah alone.[5] The Mishnah describes what takes place at the Passover *seder* when the second cup of wine is filled. A child who sufficiently understands what is going on, and who is sophisticated enough to formulate a question, is meant to ask the famous "Four Questions." The first two questions appear on the Talmud page as they do

---

[4] I see no reason that a teacher would not cover the entire *sugya*; but in order to deal with the latter part of the *sugya*, one would have to treat other matters, such as a critical comparison with the nearby passage on *Pesahim* 115b. In our passage, Rav Nahman asks a question of his servant, Daru, while in the nearby passage, Rava asks a question of Abaye. One would naturally wonder whether the situation in our *sugya*, in which a senior scholar asks a question of his servant, might be adapted from the nearby *sugya* in order to show how Rav Nahman exempted himself from reciting *mah nishtanah*.

[5] Another important question to consider is whether to teach the Mishnah separately from the Gemara, or to teach it as part of the running Talmud text; see my dissertation, pp. 30–32. For our present purposes, we shall assume that the teacher begins with the text of the Mishnah as it appears in the Talmud.

in the *Haggadah*, but everyone should immediately notice that the last two questions differ from their familiar formulations.

The third question in the Mishnah (as it appears in the Talmud) is: "On all other nights we eat meat that is roasted or stewed or boiled; tonight we eat only roasted [meat]." That question, of course, is no longer recited at the *seder* and is replaced by a question concerning how we recline. The fourth question in the Mishnah (as it appears in the Talmud) is: "On all other nights we are not obligated to dip even once; tonight we dip twice." This question appears in the *Haggadah*, but its wording is somewhat different. Most significantly, the formulation in the *Haggadah* does not include any terms of obligation, while the Mishnah's formulation (as presented in the Talmud) does. What is more, the *Haggadah* has this fourth question as the third of the Four Questions in the Ashkenazic version and the first in the Sephardic one.[6]

Teachers will already begin to think about some of the pedagogical issues that must be considered in teaching this *sugya*. Chief among the difficulties that students will have, or the questions that students will raise, is the dissonance between the version of the Four Questions found in the Talmud and the version in the *Haggadah*, which is familiar to virtually all students who have reached the point of studying Gemara. The teacher will begin to chart the various versions of the Four Questions.

A class will notice another curious fact about the way the Mishnah is presented in the Talmud. In the printed text, the fourth of the Mishnah's questions, the one concerning dipping, includes two sets of parentheses. Talmud-trained students know that such parentheses are a warning that there is something difficult or controversial about the wording of the text. At this stage, the class, made suspicious by the unexpected version of the Mishnah's formulation of its fourth question, may already compare it to the wording of the Mishnah as it appears in a stand-alone edition. They will discover there yet another version of the question.

We soon see that when the Gemara discusses the Mishnah, the language of the fourth question becomes a point of contention between Rava and Rav Safra. Surely we appreciate here the need to look closely into the nature of the differences among the various formulations of the question – in the Talmud, in the *Haggadah*, and, as we have now seen, in the Mishnah alone.

---

[6] Students should be made aware that the Ashkenazic and Sephardic versions differ in various respects, but we shall not explore that topic here.

Furthermore, alert students will notice another odd phenomenon with respect to the language of the fourth question as it is variously formulated in the Talmud. The discussion of this part of the Mishnah in the Gemara is introduced, as usual, by a *dibbur ha-mat'hil* (an introductory quotation from the passage that is being explained or discussed). Ordinarily, the *dibbur ha-mat'hil* reproduces the exact wording of the text being discussed. In this instance, however, the wording of the fourth question that is presented in the *dibbur ha-mat'hil* is not the wording of the Mishnah (as it appears in the Talmud).

History in the Text

All this highlights the fact that the texts of the Talmud, the *Haggadah*, as well as other classical Jewish texts, have a history. Both the peculiarities of the Talmud text at hand and the substance of the Gemara's discussion involve the history of the text. Dealing with textual history must, in a case like ours, be on our curricular agenda for the simple reason that some of the most fundamental questions that will inevitably arise in the study of our *sugya* can be answered only by recourse to historical perspectives.

A class may itself realize, or guess, that the explanation of the twin anomalies – one of the Mishnah's questions does not appear in the Haggadah and the Haggadah contains one question that does not appear in the Mishnah – must have an historical basis. It is reasonable to surmise that the dropping or adding of a question must have a cause, and that that cause has to do with some historical change.

Indeed, the traditional commentaries in this case alert us to an historical explanation. Any standard printed edition of the Talmud will be accompanied by the commentary of Rashbam (R. Samuel ben Meir), who completed his grandfather Rashi's commentary on the Talmud in the mid-twelfth century. The traditional student of Talmud, like any competent student of the text, will routinely seek the guidance of the commentaries of Rashi, and sometimes Rashbam, who tend to provide a *peshat* explanation of the text.[7] In explicating the third question of the Mishnah (as it is presented in the Talmud), Rashbam accounts for the fact that this question is present in the Mishnah's version of the Four Questions but absent from the *Haggadah*'s

---

[7] *Peshat*, in contrast to *derash*, refers to interpretation based on meaning in context; see Edward L. Greenstein, "Medieval Bible Commentaries," in Barry W. Holtz, ed., *Back to the Sources* (New York: Summit Books, 1984), esp. pp. 215–20. Contrast the more conventional definition of *peshat* as "the plain meaning of the text," e.g., Steinsaltz, *The Talmud: A Reference Guide*, p. 79, with Greenstein's explanation that a *peshat* understanding is often far from plain in any sense.

formulation by reference to a historical change. His comment on "Tonight we eat only roasted (meat)" is: "During the time when the Temple was standing, he (i.e., the son) would ask thus."

We understand that the restriction on eating the meat at the seder cooked any way other than roasted has to do with the Passover offering (*korban Pesah*). That is the way that offerings in the Temple were prepared. After the Temple was destroyed by the Romans, there was no longer any sacrifice, and any type of cooking might have been employed.

Nevertheless, a thoughtful class will still have some questions about the difference between the Mishnah and the *Haggadah*. Jewish liturgy generally tends to preserve ancient formulations and is not inclined to replace them with more up-to-date language. To take an example that is closely related to the case at hand, the *Musaf* service refers to the sacrifices that contemporary Jews will bring to the Temple, even when there is no Temple. Why, we may – and should – ask, was the reference to eating roasted meat dropped from the Mishnah's formulation of the Four Questions and replaced in the *Haggadah* by another question? And why was the question about leaning, which is in no way reflected in the Mishnah or Talmud, added?

To summarize, the class will have identified two sets of historical questions. One involves the history of the text, as it is manifested in the different printed editions (Mishnah, Talmud, *Haggadah*). Another involves the change in the content of the questions, mainly the historical change in which the Mishnah's third question was dropped from the *Haggadah* and was replaced by another question altogether.

These two kinds of questions – the textual and the historical – are somewhat different. The fact that the Mishnah contains a question about eating meat and the *Haggadah* a different question, about reclining, will properly be attached to the question about historical change, with which it is obviously bound up. The textual problem, concerning the Mishnah's fourth question, about dipping, demands a different approach.

With respect to the textual question, the teacher should examine all the available sources. These will include not only the printed editions of the Mishnah and the Talmud, as well as the *Haggadah*, but also the *Tosefta*, manuscript versions of the Mishnah, the Talmud (*Bavli* and *Yerushalmi*), and early documents concerning the *Haggadah*. The teacher should then begin to organize the data by making a chart of the different formulations of the question. A very basic chart will include at least the following:

    a. the version in stand-alone editions of the Mishnah;
    b. the version in the Mishnah as presented in editions of the Talmud;
    c. Rava's version in the Gemara;

    d. Rav Safra's version in the Gemara;

    e. The version in the *dibbur ha-mat'hil* in the Gemara;

    f. The version in the *Haggadah*.

The teacher should read through the primary sources – the Mishnah, Gemara, and *Haggadah* – as well as the standard commentaries on them. In the present case, the discussion in the Gemara provides a rationale for the differences. They turn out to revolve around certain thematic issues that are made explicit in the Gemara.

The Issue in the Gemara

The Mishnah (as presented in the Talmud) presupposes that people normally dip once in the course of a meal. Accordingly, what is special about the *seder* meal is that during it, one dips twice. In the Gemara, Rava (a Babylonian *amora*) challenges the Mishnah's assumption. In his experience, people do not dip at a meal at all. Rava, therefore, alters the formulation of the Mishnah's fourth question to read as follows: "On all other nights we are not obligated to dip even once; tonight [we dip] twice." In this reformulation, however, Rava introduces a new element into the fourth question, or at least makes this element explicit. This is the element, and language, of obligation (*hiyyuv*).

Rav Safra, another Babylonian sage, implicitly agrees with Rava that people do not customarily dip at a meal. But he objects to Rava's introduction of the idea of obligation concerning the Four Questions. In line with the overall context of the questions and their explicit function in the *seder*, the notion of obligation does not belong. It is clear from the Mishnah that the purpose of dipping is to arouse the curiosity of the child, who is meant to ask questions about the unusual behaviors that he[8] witnesses at the *seder*. This understanding of the Mishnah is presented by Rashbam in his comment on our passage in the Gemara: "This is on account of children's awareness, so that (the child) will ask." Accordingly, Rav Safra reformulates the question as follows: "(On all other nights) we do not dip even once; tonight [we dip] twice." In Rav Safra's view, the double dipping is a pedagogical tool for arousing the curiosity of the children present, but it need not carry the halakhic weight of a *hiyyuv*. The class will, of course, recognize that Rav Safra's formulation is the one that is adopted by the *Haggadah* and that it is this familiar formulation that was used by the editor of the Gemara

---

[8] The Mishnah and later literature specify "the son."

as the basis of the *dibbur ha-mat'hil* that immediately follows this part of the *sugya*.

And so we have an answer at hand to the question of why Rav Safra's formulation was preferred by our tradition to Rava's. The notion of obligation does not belong in the question about dipping. But how will we explain the change in the Gemara and the *Haggadah* from the Mishnah, where the assumption is that dipping once during the meal was the norm? The answer will have to be deduced from the fact that Rav Safra accepts Rava's assumption, holding that people do not dip at a meal.

This question can be answered in more than one way. On the one hand, we can apply a typical talmudic technique of interpretation: the apparent contradiction is not really a contradiction because the two propositions (in this case, formulations) at issue are dealing with two different situations. In this way of thinking, the Mishnah and the *amora'im* Rava and Rav Safra are speaking of two different things. The Mishnah is speaking about the dipping of vegetables during the course of a meal, and the *amora'im* are thinking of dipping not during the meal but prior to the meal proper, as we now do at the *seder*.[9]

The class, which has been sensitized to a historical approach, and which has already felt the need for historical analysis in dealing with the present *sugya* in light of the difference in the content of the Four Questions between the Mishnah and the Haggadah, may seek an historical solution to the question. The difference between the Mishnah's and the Gemara's formulations of the question about dipping boils down, in the end, to a matter of eating customs. The Mishnah assumes that people dip during a meal, while the Gemara assumes they do not. One could surmise that the Mishnah simply reflects a time and place different from those in the Gemara. The Mishnah was produced in the Land of Israel around 200 C.E. The Gemara was produced in Babylonia, beginning only in the century after the Mishnah was completed. One might therefore conclude that in Roman *Eretz Yisrael* Jews were accustomed to dipping during a meal but that in Babylonia Jews were not so accustomed. Thus, some have proposed that Romans dipped vegetables into sauce as the first course of every main meal and that Jews of Roman Palestine unsurprisingly did the same.[10]

---

[9] One will find an explanation of this type in the modern commentary on the Mishnah by R. Pinhas Kehati.

[10] Jacob N. Epstein, *Mevo'ot le-Sifrut ha-Tanna'im* (Jerusalem: Magnes Press, 1957), pp. 383–84.

The Substitution of a Question

Now that we have identified and solved the textual puzzles of the *sugya*, concerning the Mishnah's fourth question, we may turn to the historical question of why the Mishnah includes a question about eating roasted meat at the *seder* while the *Haggadah* presents an entirely different question. The reader will recall that the major question has to do with why the reference to eating roasted meat at the *seder* was not preserved after the Temple was destroyed.

To seek an historical solution, we are well advised to look into the historical scholarship of the so-called rabbinic period. One might consult an historical treatment of Passover as it developed from biblical to medieval times, concerned with the history of the ritual and dealing only tangentially with the history that lies behind the rituals.[11] Nevertheless, teachers will find references to the pertinent historical scholarship in his book or in one of the few extensive histories of the Jews in the rabbinic period, such as Gedaliahu Alon's.[12] There, one finds an in-depth discussion of the history of Passover observance among the Jews following the destruction of the Temple by the Romans.

Alon, too, begins from the obvious fact that the Mishnah's description of the Passover ritual contains a reference to the roasted meat of the Temple sacrifices even after the Temple no longer existed. This might be merely a commemoration of the historical past, but – as was said above – such a commemoration would be out of place in this part of the *seder*, in which the child's attention is drawn to the living ritual. Accordingly, Alon combs the available textual sources for some clarification of the rite that is described in Mishnah *Pesahim*. He discovers such a clarification in two *mishnayot* connected with Rabban Gamaliel, the same Rabban Gamaliel whose declaration, "Whoever has not said (i.e., explained) these three things on Passover has not fulfilled his obligation...," is incorporated from the Mishnah (*Pesahim* 10:5) into the *Haggadah*.

In one of these *mishnayot*, it is related that Rabban Gamaliel, who lived after the destruction of the Temple, nevertheless ordered his servant Tabi: "Go out and roast us the *pesah* (i.e., the roast lamb offering) on the grill."

---

[11] A good example is Baruch M. Bokser, *The Origins of the Seder* (Berkeley: Univ. of California Press, 1984).

[12] Gedaliahu Alon, *The Jews in Their Land in the Talmudic Age (70–640 C.E.)*, trans. Gershon Levi (Jerusalem: Magnes Press, 1980). See also Jacob Neusner, *A History of the Jews in Babylonia*, 6 vols. (Leiden: Brill, 1965–1970); Isaiah M. Gafni, *The Jews of Babylonia in the Talmudic Era* (Jerusalem: Zalman Shazar Center, 1990).

(*Pesaḥim* 7:2). In other words, it was the custom of Rabban Gamaliel, and anyone else who had the same practice, to roast a lamb on the evening of Passover, even following the destruction of the Temple. Alon is able to shed further light on this practice by adducing Mishnah *Betzah* 2:7, according to which Rabban Gamaliel permitted the preparation of a "helmeted kid" (*gedi mekullas*) on the eve of Passover, while the majority of the sages forbade this practice. The "helmeted kid" is defined in *Tosefta Betzah* 2:11 as a "kid roasted whole, with its head and shanks placed within its entrails."

From these and a few additional references, Alon makes a plausible reconstruction of the issue that lay between Rabban Gamaliel and the Sages. Once the Temple was destroyed, no proper sacrifice could be performed. Sacrifice was permitted only within the Temple. Rabban Gamaliel, however, whose name is associated with the special ancient rituals of Passover in the Mishnah and the *Haggadah*, sought to preserve something of the ancient rite by specially preparing a roasted kid in place of the Passover offering. The helmeted kid served this purpose. But the Sages feared that the practice of roasting a kid on the eve of Passover would smack of sacrifice and become misinterpreted as an allowance of animal sacrifice outside the precincts of the Temple. Accordingly, they forbade this practice. It is this practice of roasting a kid that is rejected in the post-talmudic age, in which the Mishnah's third question, concerning the roasted meat, is dropped, and another question is added (more on which below).

Alon is able to corroborate his hypothesis by adducing some fragments of the Passover eve liturgy discovered in the Cairo Genizah and published in 1898.[13] From these fragments, dating from the post-talmudic age, it is clear that the child asks three, not four, questions at the *seder*, including the question from the Mishnah concerning the roasted meat. As though to reiterate the importance of the roasted meat in this version of the seder, it includes a special blessing that is not part of the Mishnah ritual or the *Haggadah*. In it we bless God for commanding "our ancestors to eat unleavened bread, bitter herbs, and meat roasted on fire...." The Genizah material shows that there continued to be Jews like Rabban Gamaliel for whom roasted meat was an integral part of the seder. The fact that the traditional *Haggadah* eliminated the question concerning the meat, and includes no blessing stating that we are commanded to eat roasted meat at the seder, indicates that the position of the Sages prevailed.

The class, now in possession of a reason that the question about the roasted meat was dropped in the *Haggadah*, must consider the question of

---

[13] Ibid., p. 265 with n. 38.

why the *Haggadah* added a fourth question, and why that question deals with leaning at the *seder*. The teacher who has read Alon, or another history of the Passover rituals, will know that there was an option – taken by the rite preserved in the Cairo Genizah and long before that by the *Talmud Yerushalmi*'s version of our Mishnah – of having only three questions in the *seder* rite. What is the purpose, or function, of having four questions? There is probably no one answer to this question, but we may consider a few possible ones.

First, there is the motive of conservation: if one question is to be dropped, another is to be added. Second, aside from the biblically ordained triad of the paschal lamb offering (*pesah*), *matzah*, and bitter herbs (Ex. 12:8), it is not the number three that is used to organize the different parts of the seder; it is, rather, the number four that stands out in the rhetoric and rituals of the *Haggadah*. In addition to the Four Questions, there are four cups of wine, four expressions of redemption, and four sons. The pattern of fours may well follow from the way that the Mishnah structures the seder with respect to the four obligatory cups of wine.

On the other hand, there may be an ideological explanation of the *seder*'s tendency toward four or, more precisely, its aversion toward the number three. Early medieval Judaism was already sensitive to polemics with Christianity. The number three took on a Christian association, on account of the Christian trinity, so that Jewish tradition chose to highlight the number four at the seder. It will be recalled that, in Christian typology, the paschal lamb is a prefiguration of Jesus, the sacrificial offering of God in Christian theology, who was crucified on Passover. [14]

In any event, after considering the question of why another question needed to be added, the teacher may proceed to seek an answer to the riddle of why the question that was added deals with leaning while sitting at the seder. To answer this type of question, one involving the history of practice that is associated with the Talmud's content, well-trained Talmud teachers will turn to a resource that serves them well in this, as in many other matters – the edition and commentary of Rabbi Adin Steinsaltz. [15]

There, one will encounter the post-talmudic, geonic version of the *Haggadah* that is described in the ninth-century order (*seder*) of the liturgy by Rav Amram Gaon. The question of both the Mishnah and the Talmud

---

[14] I learned this explanation from the late Prof. Moshe Zucker.

[15] This is not to suggest that any but the most elementary Talmud class should use either the Steinsaltz or ArtScroll editions of the text in the classroom. A reference book or resource should not be confused with a *shi`ur* text.

about the roasted meat has already been dropped, and a new fourth question, asking why "we all lean" at the seder, has been added. Steinsaltz here adopts a historical approach, one that responds directly to the teacher's question of why, now, this question is properly made one of the Four. In Roman times – the period of the Mishnah – people routinely reclined during meals. This is taken for granted in the *Tosefta* (*Berakhot* 5:5), which mentions that, "Rabban Simeon ben Gamaliel, Rabbi Judah, and Rabbi Yosi were reclining (in Acco) on the eve of a certain Sabbath. The *Tosefta* goes on to mention a situation in which "guests were reclining in a certain householder's (house)." In the time and place of the Mishnah, therefore, when people typically reclined during meals, it would have made little sense to characterize leaning as a distinctive feature of the *seder*. The question concerning reclining at the *seder* would become relevant only at some time after the destruction of the Temple,[16] and perhaps even after the period of the Mishnah.

We are now equipped with an answer to the historical question of why the question of reclining at the *seder* arose relatively late in its evolution. But Steinsaltz raises a further question. According to him, the Four Questions follow a general chronological sequence that corresponds to the order in which things are introduced at the *seder*. Thus, the question concerning leaning should take first place among the Four Questions (as it does in the Sephardic version of the *Haggadah*) because it is the first of those things mentioned in the Four Questions to occur at the *seder*. This, however, is not exactly so. It is true that reclining is mentioned first in Mishnah *Pesahim* 10:1. But dipping, which in the Mishnah is the fourth and last question, is mentioned as a *seder* activity ahead of *matzah* in *Pesahim* 10:3. Steinsaltz's principle does not, therefore, seem to work.

The Teacher's Task of Curricularizing

This, then, may more or less complete our analysis of the *sugya* with respect to the two sets of historical questions that were delineated above – the question of the versions of the Mishnah's fourth question (concerning dipping) and the question of the change from the Mishnah's third question (concerning the roasted meat) to the *Haggadah*'s fourth question (concerning reclining at the meal). The teacher, whose task is to curricularize the material that has been gathered and considered, must plan how to organize the subject matter – with respect to the content and the methods by which

---

[16] This somewhat narrow interpretation is the one espoused by Steinsaltz.

the content, as it exists in the fields of philology and history, is organized – into lessons for the class.[17]

The *sugya* with which we are dealing is very rich from a number of perspectives. It discusses a key part of the *seder*, where the ritual is explicitly made into an educational experience by insisting on the asking of questions – even, as the Gemara says, when only scholars are present. It goes on to describe the nature of the narrative that is recited at the *seder*, beginning with the degraded state of our ancestors before they emerged from idolatry and proceeding to the grandeur of God's redemption of Israel from bondage. This alone contains a good deal of stimulating curricular material. Here, however, I shall restrict our treatment of curriculum to the types of historical issues presented above, in keeping with the focus of this essay on the need for historical perspectives in the teaching of Talmud.

It will be recalled that we organized the various historical issues delineated above into two sets. The first set, involving the dropping of the Mishnah's third question in the *Haggadah* and the addition of a different fourth question, is a matter of historical change. We referred to it, by way of shorthand, as the historical issue. The second set of issues involves the various wordings of the Mishnah's fourth question, concerning dipping. It is a matter of textual development, and we referred to it concisely as the textual, or text-historical, issue.

How and to what extent teachers will address the two sets of historical questions we have delineated will depend in part on what other aspects of the *sugya*, and the Passover ritual, they will want to highlight and on the importance to them, or to the ideology their institution represents, of history and historical change in general. As already mentioned, I see the use of history within a framework of traditional Jewish study as complementary, enriching, and sometimes even clarifying, and not at all corroding. And I have chosen this *sugya* as a case in point to illustrate the use of historical scholarship in the teaching of Talmud because I see no way in which a competent teacher can avoid the subject matter of history in dealing with it. On what

---

[17] It will be clear to those familiar with curriculum theory that I am drawing here on the seminal work of Joseph Schwab. Schwab, in accord with certain philosophers of science and education, such as Michael Polanyi and John Dewey, stresses that a subject matter comprises not only substantive content but also the way in which a discipline organizes and works with knowledge; curriculum writing therefore requires the input of a specialist who understands and can articulate the underlying principles, conceptual structures, and methods of a discipline. See, e.g., Joseph Schwab, *Science, Curriculum, and Liberal Education*, ed. Ian Westbury & Neil Wilkof (Chicago & London: Univ. of Chicago Press, 1978). See also Joseph S. Lukinsky, "'Structure' in Educational Theory," *Educational Philosophy and Theory* 2 (1970): 15–31.

we have called the historical issue, students will surely recognize the fact that the ritual we use today has changed from what is described in the Mishnah. Similarly, on what we have called the textual issue, students will easily discern the differences between the question about dipping as it is formulated in the Mishnah and as it is formulated in the *Haggadah*. These facts are noted and given historical interpretations in the classical as well as the modern commentaries.

The teacher, then, will need some way to curricularize the history in the *sugya*. A teacher will decide in what context and sequence to address the matter of history, depending on what else the teacher wants to achieve in teaching the *sugya* and according to the teacher's – and the students' – comfort with the topic of historical change. A teacher may, for example, choose to deal first with the less complicated textual issue, particularly because the explanation of the textual differences will be provided by the discussion in the Gemara. Then, having already exposed students to the history of the text, the teacher, in treating the child's question about dipping at the *seder*, can proceed to the issue of historical change in the Passover ritual. The alternative is to teach the issues according to the sequence in which they arise in the course of reading the *sugya*, beginning with the Mishnah.

Teaching the Text in Sequence

My own approach to teaching the *sugya* and the many and diverse topics that may be connected to it is to read the text in sequence and to raise issues and questions as they occur. I do this for three reasons.

First, I regard Judaism as a text-based tradition; accordingly, I am inclined to begin the discussion of any topic (in a Jewish educational setting) with a pertinent textual source.[18] Theoretically, one might begin with a topic of history, or current ritual practice, for example, and then seek the textual sources that might give background or depth to them. It cannot be overstated, however, that each curricular and pedagogical move we make conveys our ideological views about our subject matter and in general. Thus, in keeping with my conception of Judaism and the role of classical texts within it, I would begin not with history or even ritual but with texts.

Second, I would teach the Mishnah, at least at first, without revealing any of the questions or issues that will emerge in the Gemara's discussion, in order that students "discover" at least some of the Gemara's questions –

---

[18] Cf., e.g., Gerson D. Cohen, "Preface," in Seymour Fox & Geraldine Rosenfield, eds., *From the Scholar to the Classroom* (New York: Melton Research Center, 1977), pp. ix-x; Michael Rosenak, *Teaching Jewish Values: A Conceptual Guide* (Jerusalem: Melton Centre for Jewish Education in the Diaspora, 1986), p. 72.

and answers, too, perhaps – on their own. Apart from the pedagogical advantage of enlivening classes by allowing students to find and ask their own questions, and the psychological advantage of enabling students to second guess the talmudic masters, allowing students to anticipate the questions and issues of the Gemara by themselves can have the salutary effect of demystifying the Talmud for them, making it more approachable and sensible. This is a virtually universal concern in teaching Talmud, especially to beginners. The Talmud's accessibility and relevance to students is enhanced to the degree that they find the Talmud's questions and issues to be their own.

Third, the Mishnah at hand expresses an extraordinary appreciation of the value of asking questions. Participants in the *seder* must ask questions. The questions arise in the course of the *seder*'s activities, in sequence. The explicit purpose of much of the Passover ritual is to encourage inquisitiveness.[19] It would be a sad irony indeed if a teacher studying our Mishnah with a class would fail to elicit question after question as the text is read with students.

Questions are, in general, prompted by curiosity, which, in turn, is aroused by a sense that we are encountering something unfamiliar, something that, for some reason, appears to be new and different. We do not raise questions about the expected but about the unexpected. The Mishnah begins with an exemplary instance of questioning, and it is with this that I would begin teaching the *sugya*.

The Mishnah opens with what might at first blush seem like an ordinary fact: "They pour him a second cup (of wine)." Yet it is precisely at this moment that the Mishnah stipulates, "the son asks his father" the Four Questions. Why, the teacher may ask the students, does the son ask the questions at this point in the seder? The timing could be attributed to nothing more than coincidence or to the practical matter of having the child ask before he falls asleep. But the prepared teacher will have an answer at the ready, the one that is given by the standard commentaries (Rashi, Rashbam, Rabbi Joseph ibn Haviv (author of *Nimmukei Yosef*, a commentary on Alfasi's Talmud explication), Rabbi Isaiah of Trani (author of *Tosefot Rid*, et al.). The teacher should be able to elicit the "standard" answer to the question before turning the students toward the commentaries.

The question arises out of the dissonance between the ordinary function of a cup of wine at a ritual meal and the lack of an overt purpose for the second cup. The first cup served the distinct purpose of making *kiddush* at the outset of the *seder*. The one cup of wine is part of the ritual at the onset

---

[19] See further, Bokser, *Origins of the Seder*, pp. 67–71.

of every Sabbath and festival. A second cup might make sense in the context of a meal – if the meal were served at this point. But it is not. One must, therefore, wonder at the purpose of the second cup of wine.

Once the students have articulated the question and answer, one can turn for confirmation and refinement to the commentaries. Rashbam only hints at the answer.[20] One finds more explicit explanations in *Nimmukei Yosef* and *Tosefot Rid*. The latter, for example, comments: "Here the son asks: When he sees that they pour a second cup (of wine) before the food. Normally, they break bread after *kiddush* (the blessing over wine) and here dip a vegetable."

As the teacher and students proceed through the Mishnah, they will find that the first two of the Four Questions do not give rise to matters of history; they hold no surprises. The teacher may choose to dwell on the symbolism of the *matzah* and *maror* and their biblical bases. The teacher may also choose to train the students in close reading by making sure they ponder the fact that the second question does not say, "only bitter herbs," in the manner of the first question's "only *matzah*," but simply "bitter herbs."[21] It is only in examining the third and fourth questions, however, that students will be startled and intrigued.

As was said above, the teacher may choose to delve into the historical issues of the Mishnah's third question only after going into the textual issues of the fourth, which become a topic of discussion in the Gemara. In the approach I have adopted, one will deal with the questions in the sequence in which they are encountered. Accordingly, one will tackle the third question first.

The Question of the Third Question

The issues revolving around the third question (concerning the roasted meat) require the teacher to separate the two key historical issues – why was the Mishnah's question about the roasted meat dropped, and why was a new question about reclining added later – and organize the various pertinent textual sources in accordance with these two issues. In the present instance, the key texts are from the Mishnah and the *Tosefta*, on the one hand, and from the *siddur* of Rav Amram Gaon and the standard edition of

---

[20] Rashbam: "Here, at the pouring of the second cup (of wine) the son (if he is wise) asks his father: 'What is different...,' now that a second cup of wine is being poured before the meal."

[21] On this question, compare *Tosafot*'s comment on the words "On this night bitter herbs": "Note that it does not say, 'only bitter herbs,' because we do eat other vegetables at the first dipping."

the *Haggadah*, on the other (see above). The Gemara of our *sugya* does not deal with the historical question of the roasted meat. The entire historical issue can therefore be investigated in the course of studying the Mishnah alone.

Traditionalist[22] teachers may want to do no more than raise the simple historical question – why do we not say the Mishnah's third question anymore? – and content themselves and their students with the answer provided in the commentary of Rashbam.[23] But the teacher who has been informed by Gedaliahu Alon's analysis of the historical question may want to go into a deeper and more nuanced historical analysis. This teacher will, as was said, organize the textual sources according to the two key issues. The teacher may choose to retrace Alon's argument along with the students, sharing with them something of the scholar's method; or the teacher may choose to tease the historical questions out of the students by presenting them with some of the tannaitic sources that indicate that there were Jews who continued to eat roasted meat on the eve of Passover even after the destruction of the Temple. The students' interest will then be piqued by the apparent contradiction between the straightforward explanation of Rashbam and the type of tannaitic sources adduced by Alon. Contrast, for example, Rashbam's explanation with the Mishnah *Pesahim* 4:4: "In places where it was customary to eat roasted (meat) on Passover eve, it may be eaten; where it was not the custom, it should not be eaten."

The teacher may trigger students' questions and guide their search for answers by presenting the diverse pertinent texts, as well as by suggesting possible answers to be examined. Of course, only by means of the teacher providing information, or by being sent directly to Alon's treatment, will students discover the way that the practice of eating roasted meat on Passover eve continued into the geonic period.

Teasing out the Gemara's Issue

With the sources assembled by Alon in hand, the teacher and students will be able to discern the controversy between Rabban Gamaliel and the Sages. In the course of discussing their results, the teacher and students may want to talk about the general issue that lies at the heart of the custom of eating or not eating roasted meat at the *seder*, even after the Temple was

---

[22] By "traditionalist" I mean someone who regards Jewish learning as self-contained, who believes that all questions arising in one's study can be answered within the sphere of traditional sources and teachings.

[23] Rashbam: "Tonight we eat only roasted (meat): During the time when the Holy Temple was standing, he would ask thus."

destroyed: Is this ritual – and are rituals in general – an effort to re-enact an historical experience by simulating it (in the way that the roasted meat simulates the Paschal lamb offering in the Temple of old)? Or is this ritual – and are rituals in general – commemorations of the past that give rise to more symbolic and thematic types of meaning? The teacher will surely want to elicit from students various examples of rituals that can be interpreted either as re-enactment or as commemoration, or as both; and relate these rituals and their interpretations to tannaitic and post-tannaitic controversies over whether ancient rites should continue to be performed as much as possible (the position of Rabban Gamaliel) or not (the Sages). In this way it will be seen that the tension between Rabban Gamaliel and his colleagues remains an insoluble conflict of perspectives in trying to interpret the meaning of religious rituals.

In dealing with the second major historical issue – the question of why the *seder* question about reclining was added in the post-talmudic period – the teacher will not need to articulate the problem. Students will know that our *Haggadah* has a fourth question that does not appear in the Mishnah. Here the teacher will have two different tasks. First, the teacher will need to organize the tannaitic (toseftan) material that demonstrates the inappropriateness of our fourth question to the Mishnah and present it to the students so that they themselves can draw the obvious historical conclusion. On the question of why a fourth question needed to be added, again it will probably suffice for the teacher to act as a resource. Suggesting the importance of the number four in the *seder*, the teacher should manage to elicit several examples from the students. On the other hand, the students will probably not realize that having a set of only three questions was an option, both in talmudic and geonic times, without the teacher providing them with the pertinent sources.

For many teachers, the symbolism of reclining at the *seder*, as a token of our freedom, will be the more important lesson to convey. Nevertheless, the fact that Jews have sometimes asked only three questions instead of four (the *Yerushalmi* and Genizah source vs. the Babylonian Talmud and *Haggadah*), or used a somewhat different set of four questions (the Mishnah vs. the *Haggadah*), provokes a sense of curiosity that many teachers might well wish to exploit, and satisfy, in teaching our *sugya*. The teacher who has looked into the history of the Four Questions will simply have more interesting material to present than the teacher who goes little beyond explaining the *peshat* meaning of the text.

The Pedagogical Use of Surprise

In teaching the text-historical issue of the ways that the Mishnah's fourth question underwent reformulation, the teacher's main curricular task is bound up with the pedagogical one. The reasons for the changes in the formulation of the question are apparent, and they are addressed directly in the Gemara. The effective teacher must be careful to generate surprise by permitting the students to discover the different formulations and their rationales by themselves. The teacher need serve only as a guide to the sources and to the textual signals that are embedded in the Talmud. Teachers of this *sugya* must practice the art of reticence, holding back the discoveries they have made and the answers they know in order to cultivate their students' powers of discernment – and not to spoil the surprises on which the *sugya* is itself constructed (such as Rava's reformulation of the question).

The teacher will be able to achieve the goal of delineating the textual variants and allowing the students to discover their interrelations and rationales by taking the students through the text one step at a time and by tracking the variants only as they are encountered.[24] "Taking the students through the text one step at a time" means, in this context, pausing to take note of every formulation of the question and, as was said, charting it on the board; noting every printer's indication of a cross-reference or aid (such as the parentheses mentioned above); and making sure that the students keep the version in the *Haggadah* correctly in mind throughout the investigation.

The teacher may find it necessary to ask the students to think about the reasons behind the changes in formulation; but the teacher should not need to reveal the reasons put forward explicitly in the Gemara until they are encountered there. The one place where the teacher may need to intervene in the students' process of discovery is in the event that the students are "too reverent" toward the talmudic masters, or too shy, to ask the critical question: How could Rava, an *amora*, challenge the assumption of the Mishnah, that people dip their vegetables during a meal?

It is this question that, once raised – by the students, or if necessary by the teacher – leads inevitably to the historical observation that the two *amora'im*, Rava and Rav Safra, share the assumption that people do not or-

---

[24] A simple yet effective technique for highlighting the differences within the formulations of the *seder* question is to write each on the board in a different color. Writing on the board and using colors to highlight differences as a visual memory aid would seem to be so obvious a strategy that it should need no mention. However, it is rare to find this technique employed in a Talmud class.

dinarily dip during a meal, while the Mishnah assumes that they do. One need only propose that the difference has to do with the fact that different Jews living in different times and places have different customs. The teacher, however, should be in a position to anticipate this historical solution. Students who have dealt with the historical issue involving the Mishnah's third question, concerning roasted meat, will be disposed toward the relatively uncomplicated type of historical explanation that is called for in the case of the textual issue.

History in the Lesson

The teacher may choose to make the fact of textual change, and the ways such change can be tracked, the heart of the lesson. Alternatively, the teacher can, as in the instance described above in teaching what we have for convenience called the historical issue, relate the example of textual change and the reasons for it that we find here to other instances of textual change in the liturgy or in some other area of Jewish life. It ought to become clear to the student, if it is clear to the teacher, that the kinds of textual and historical change that we can "discover" through the study of our *sugya* are the same kinds of textual and historical change that have occurred throughout the growth of the Jewish tradition.

I believe the example I have presented demonstrates that the use of historical material and methods in a Talmud lesson can greatly add to our understanding. However, our meta-goals obviously include fostering a love of learning and commitment to the religious values of the tradition. In cases where historical study might work counter to those goals I rely on the intelligent teacher or curriculum specialist to act responsibly. This being said, Talmud students should know and use history in order to deepen and broaden their understanding of texts. Teachers should also lead students to appreciate the fact that history is not only then – it is also now. The study of Jewish texts can erect bridges between the historical background of the traditional sources and the contemporary lives of the people who study them.[25]

---

[25] For exemplary illustrations, see Barry W. Holtz, *Finding Our Way* (New York: Schocken, 1990); Michael Rosenak, *Tree of Life, Tree of Knowledge: Conversations with the Torah* (Boulder: Westview, 2001).

REDEEMING THE AGGADAH IN YESHIVAH EDUCATION

YITZCHAK BLAU

LET US OBSERVE a Gemara teacher in a yeshivah high school planning the curriculum for the coming semester. Noticing an aggadic passage, the teacher decides to skip it, as the halakhic sections are both much easier and more conducive to teaching reading skills. Indeed, high schools that do not insist on learning each page in a *perek* consecutively tend to leave out aggadic passages when they select the sections to study. Among other factors, this choice reflects the fact that we have a much more developed *derekh ha-limmud* (study method) with regard to *halakhah* than we do with regard to *aggadah*.

Now, the same teacher thinks about a good text to energize a *shmooz*, an informal discussion about Jewish values. Many experienced teachers take out a large file of articles by Dennis Prager, Eliezer Berkovits, Abraham Twersky, and others to look for the appropriate text. These authors deal with the problems of our generation in the language of our generation. It often may not occur to the teacher that a rabbinic text of older vintage may provide greater insight in dealing with the same issues.

While both of the foregoing educational decisions can be justified, the result is that a significant portion of the Talmud as well as the aggadic *midrashim* get shunted aside. This in itself should be cause for concern for a Jewish educator. If we want to introduce our students to the totality of Torah (within reasonable limitations), ignoring *aggadah* seems problematic. Furthermore, we may be sending a subtle, problematic message to our students: that in the realm of values, *Hazal* had nothing to say. We expose them to *tanna'im* and *amora'im* only in the context of their debates over points of law and fail to reveal to them that those same individuals taught moral and psychological wisdom, thought about philosophical issues and even exhibited a sense of humor.[1] This provides further reason to motivate a change in the status quo.

Perhaps we should begin to outline an approach by restating the problem in other terms. I take it for granted that aggadic texts do contain a good deal of insight and that most of that insight remains as relevant now as when it was written. If so, why is it that teachers shy away from aggadic material? Contrasting aggadic texts with halakhic texts will facilitate our understanding of the situation.

For one thing, the terminology of halakhic texts is easier and more repetitive than that of aggadic texts. While aggadic texts will often feature words that appear only a handful of times in the Talmud, halakhic texts tend to employ the same essential words over and over. Thus, once the student achieves some familiarity with technical terms such as *ka mashma lan*, *peshita* and *matkif lah*, the Gemara becomes a little less daunting (not that it becomes easy). On the other hand, even advanced students frequently find deciphering a new aggadic passage to be arduous work. We naturally refrain from presenting the more difficult aggadic texts to high school students who find the halakhic material intimidating enough.

The ability to focus on key words makes halakhic sections not only easier to learn but easier to teach. A teacher who explains to a student the differences between three different phrases employed by the Talmud to refer to three different questions can feel that he or she is unlocking pages of Talmud for that student. *Meitevei*, *matkif lah* and *u-reminhu* await the aspiring learner on almost every talmudic page. With regard to aggadic texts, the teacher does not have the sense that teaching the students the Aramaic words for a given trade or item of food will necessarily enable the student to navigate through the sea of Talmud.

The availability of medieval and modern commentators is an additional advantage given to the halakhic texts. A wealth of *mefarshim* grapple with the ideas in most of the *massekhtot* in the *sedarim* of Mo'ed, Nashim and Nezikin. Therefore, a teacher can feel fairly confident that a student's good question has already been asked and a written discussion of that question can be located. Furthermore, the teacher has a good deal of material to choose from in looking for a text of commentary that a student will find both accessible and interesting.

In the world of *aggadah*, the situation is completely different. The classic medieval commentaries frequently ignore aggadic sections. When they do

---

[1] For an example of the humor, see the concluding lines of *Sotah* 49b. For commentary on that text with educational implications, see Netziv, *Ha`amek Davar*, Num. 12:3.

comment, the issues at hand are often halakhic in nature or peripheral to the central themes of the *aggadah*. The modern commentaries reveal a similar bias. Some of the rabbinic giants who did write on *aggadah* did so in a more mystical style and used a terminology that is difficult for us to grasp (see, for example, the commentaries of Maharal and Ben Yehoyada).[2]

In truth, later rabbinic literature includes a great deal of valuable commentary on *aggadah* in texts of philosophy, *derashot*, *hasidut*, *musar*, and *parshanut*. But because these texts do not appear as commentaries on individual tractates, it becomes very difficult to uncover their hidden treasures. This situation is diametrically opposed to the halakhic sections, in which most of the important commentaries appear either as page-by-page comments on a given tractate or as commentary on Rambam's *Mishneh Torah*, where the relevant sections are easily located. It is not that difficult to find out what *mefarshim* thought about *bari ve-shema*, *miggo le-hotzi*, or most other halakhic topics.

Finally, it must be confessed that we are often unsure what to make of many *aggadot*. It becomes a struggle to extract the religious and moral wisdom of a talmudic text that explains how the ashes of a certain cat enable us to see the spirits hovering about (*Berakhot* 6a). While there are occasionally baffling halakhic sections as well, the overwhelming majority of halakhic *gemarot* based on legal reasoning (as opposed to *midrash halakhah*) easily lend themselves to rational analysis. Thus, a myriad of factors bring about this educational distinction between *halakhah* and *aggadah*.

Despite the force of these factors, I believe we can incorporate *aggadah* into our curriculum. Sometimes, the force of an *aggadah* will speak for itself, whether or not an interesting commentary on the *aggadah* exists. On other occasions, the standard commentaries on *aggadah*, such as those of Maharsha, Maharal, Ben Yehoyada and those collected in the *Ein Ya'akov* provide help. When these works fail to assist, the broader range of rabbinic literature often includes meaningful explanations. Insightful commentaries do exist, if we have the drive and wherewithal to find them. As more and more *sefarim* are published with indices, it has become much easier to find relevant comments on a given talmudic passage. A joint effort of various educators will make the job much easier, and I hope that this current article represents only the beginnings of my contribution to this field.

---

[2] A useful tool for locating commentaries on assorted *aggadot* can be found in the first volume of Moshe Zuriel's *Otzrot ha-Aggadah Ein Ya`akov: Mafteah ha-Pe-rushim* (Benei Berak: Mishor, 1999), which indexes 170 classical and modern commentaries.

This project will have educational ramifications beyond those mentioned above. Teachers often question how to help those students who simply do not "have it" with regard to Gemara. Non-analytic thinkers struggle greatly in Gemara, and the gap between the talented and the less talented is sharper than in other areas of study. As I once formulated it, anyone can make a good comment in *Humash* but not everyone is capable of making a good comment in Gemara. Clearly, no magic solution exits for this dilemma but incorporating aggadic sections might give the student tormented by talmudic thought a chance to shine. Such a student might have the literary and psychological skills needed to interpret *aggadah*. This is different from the same student excelling in some other discipline, because now the student can succeed in the same class, with the same teacher, and with the same *Talmud Bavli* open in front of him.

As the previous sentence makes clear, the recommendation here calls for integrating aggadic sections into the regular Gemara class rather than inserting them into a Jewish philosophy class or creating a new class altogether. The goals of the project include showing the students another side of *Hazal*, and this is best accomplished when the halakhic and aggadic sections form a joint unit. The same class that addresses *gerama ba-nizakin* will also discuss *Hazal*'s approach to ethical issues.

For the same reason, I propose employing the standard Vilna Talmud and not a Steinsaltz Gemara or an English translation. One could easily argue that with regard to aggadic sections, the teacher should focus on content rather than on reading skills and that the punctuation and vocalization that facilitate the reading therefore justify using the Steinsaltz text. Nevertheless, the familiarity of the normal typeface will encourage students to connect the aggadic and halakhic sections.

The same concern can bear on the *aggadot* chosen. While the odds of finding the appropriate *aggadot* in the chapter being studied may be small, opening the field up to the entire *massekhet* will make things easier. Although teachers will no doubt want to select certain important *aggadot* from other tractates, as long as some of the chosen *aggadot* appear in that year's tractate, the class can turn to *aggadah* with their regular Gemara and not always depend on a separate source sheet. Schools that teach assorted *sugyot* rather than moving consecutively through a tractate should find the integration even easier. All of the above helps create a sense of continuity between the *halakhah* and *aggadah*.

Of course, the danger exists that the students might find the aggadic sections more enjoyable than the halakhic sections and constantly ask to spend the day on *aggadah*. If this happens, the teacher should feel proud that one part of the curriculum works very well and think about how to improve on other parts. In other words, the problems generated by successful educational programming are the right kind of problems to have. Such students would, after all, be asking to study Torah and not just watch and comment on a "Twilight Zone" video as they might in an informal educational setting. At the same time, the teacher must ensure that the lion's share of class time remains devoted to the halakhic portions of the Talmud.

One last problem relates to allocating time. It takes many hours to achieve proficiency at reading halakhic *gemarot* and teachers will understandably be loath to cede time to other pursuits, including those within the broader talmudic corpus. But despite the time pressures, I believe the gain outweighs the loss. In most *yeshivot*, the Gemara class meets more frequently than any other, and the Gemara instructor often becomes a *"rebbe"* in way that the teacher of other courses does not. In some schools, it is assumed that the Gemara *rebbe* will set aside some time to discuss issues of concern for our students from a religious perspective. The proposal here recommends that a portion of those discussions emerge out of textual learning; thus, the twin goals of formal learning and discussing pertinent topics can coincide.

For several reasons, this essay will not attempt to outline an overarching method for interpretation of *aggadot*. The thrust of the essay calls for finding the gems of interpretation already present in rabbinic writings more than it emphasizes the teacher standing alone with the talmudic text and producing a *hiddush*. Thus, the central question might be how to locate the material and not how to interpret the text.[3] Additionally, I cannot honestly claim to have worked out such a method. Perhaps most significantly, I am suspicious of an overemphasis on methodology that leaves the runner forever talking strategy about the race without ever leaving the starting gate. Teachers will learn more from watching a successful educator teach than from listening to that teacher lecture about what he or she does, and I hope

---

[3] A teacher may well ask about a method for locating significant *aggadot* and relevant interpretations. The classic work *Ein Ya`akov* affords easy access to all the *aggadot* of a given tractate. A helpful thematic listing of aggadic and midrashic material is C. G. Montefiore and H. Loewe's *A Rabbinic Anthology* (New York: Meridian Books, 1960). As far as finding the interpretations goes, I can only reiterate that one must widen the scope of the search beyond the commentaries on a given talmudic page. Read widely, consult with colleagues and do not despair if you can only find helpful interpretations for a minority of *aggadot*. That minority will suffice to achieve the educational goal outlined here.

that the examples discussed in this article will be judged successful by my peers in education.

Still, a few brief general points may be in order. Learning *aggadot* demands sensitivity to the details of a story. The location of a given story or the specific object that appears in a story may reflect symbolic significance and not just arbitrary choice. The discerning reader must show sensitivity to subtle changes in the narrative. Does the flow of conversation shift in mid-story or does a given character begin to exhibit a change in behavior? Attention should be paid to both the broader and more limited context of a given story. A perceptive reader may discover special meaning in a particular story appearing in this specific tractate or chapter. The immediately preceding and following sections of the Talmud can help illuminate a talmudic tale. The aggadic examples in this essay will illustrate all of these factors: attending to detail, looking for shifts in the narrative, and investigating juxtapositions and broader context.

The above methodological guidelines relate to the process of interpretation that begins while the teacher prepares at home. Of course, attention must also be paid to principles of pedagogy specific to the classroom. A teacher should be genuinely open to accepting and discussing a different interpretation suggested by a student without being distracted from the view that he or she wants to advance. Additionally, significant thought should go into selecting an example of the insight in question relevant to the world of the students. Some of the aggadic interpretations that follow include applications of the individual themes that the contemporary adolescent can appreciate.

In the remainder of this essay, I provide seven examples of *aggadot* relevant to the issues of contemporary youth. After citing each individual *aggadah*, I will employ an eclectic group of commentators to provide an analysis that should prove relevant to the issues faced by our adolescent and college-age students. The analysis will also refer to some of the educational questions particular to the *aggadah* in question. Of course, in the classroom, a teacher would first ask the class for suggested interpretations before outlining his or her own analysis.

Dependency and a Change of Color:

R. Johanan and R. Eliezer both interpret: As soon as a man needs the support of his fellow creatures, his face changes color like the *kerum*…. What is the *kerum*? When R. Dimi came [from *Eretz Yisrael*] he said: There is a bird in the coast towns whose name is *kerum*, and as soon as the sun shines upon it, it changes into several colors (*Berakhot* 6b).[4]

What were these sages getting at when they spoke of the dependent individual's face changing colors? Maharsha, one of the classic commentators on the *aggadah*, understands the color change as a reference to the red hue of embarrassment. The poor man whose hand reaches out in desperation for the money needed to support his family certainly burns with a sense of shame. If so, this *aggadah* might educate us to appreciate the loss of dignity suffered by the destitute.

R. Yehiel Yaakov Weinberg, author of the *Seridei Eish*, offers a different explanation. In his view, the *aggadah* refers not only to a pauper but also to anyone dependent on the opinions of others. In particular, it relates to those holding some public position. The change of colors describes much more than embarrassment; it refers to a lack of authenticity. Both the pauper and the politician who depend on the good will of others face the constant temptation to alter their beliefs and opinions to suit the feelings of their benefactors or their public. In this sense, they may frequently "change their colors." Following almost any recent political candidate around the campaign trail, seeing how their messages change from audience to audience, makes R. Weinberg's claim abundantly clear. As R. Weinberg points out, this trait is especially dangerous among community leaders who should be listening to their consciences more than their constituents when making decisions fateful for the entire community.[5]

This second interpretation strikes a significant chord for our youth. While they do not usually run for public office, they do face the challenges of remaining true to one's convictions – and indeed, formulating those convictions – in the face of social pressure. An adolescent's underconfidence and desire for popularity make this challenge a constant struggle. Entering into a discussion of this issue via the aggadic reading has certain advantages over an informal discussion not generated by a text. The students have probably discussed peer pressure *ad nauseum* and will instantly turn off if that topic is broached. Beginning with textual analysis and then discussing the politician can allow for a transition to the adolescent dilemma that will not raise immediate opposition.

---

[4] All translations of talmudic texts are taken from the Soncino edition with some minor modifications.

[5] R. Weinberg, *Li-Frakim* (Jerusalem, 1967), p. 179.

Tzitzit and a Woman of Ill Repute:

Once a man, who was very scrupulous about the principle of *tzitzit,* heard of a certain harlot in one of the towns by the sea who accepted four hundred gold coins for her hire. He sent her four hundred gold coins and appointed a day with her. When the day arrived he came and waited at her door, and her maid came and told her, "That man who sent you four hundred gold coins is here and waiting at the door"; to which she replied "Let him come in." When he came in, she prepared for him seven beds, six of silver and one of gold: and between one bed and the other there wee steps of silver, but the last were of gold. She then went up to the top bed and lay down upon it naked. He too went up after her in his desire to sit naked with her, when suddenly the four fringes [of his *tzitzit*] struck him across the face; whereupon he slipped off and sat upon the ground. She also slipped off and sat upon the ground and said, "By the Roman Capitol, I will not leave you alone until you tell me what blemish you saw in me." "By the Temple," he replied, "never have I seen a woman as beautiful as you are; but there is one precept which the Lord our God has commanded us, it is called *tzitzit,* and with regard to it the expression *I am the Lord your God* is twice written, signifying I am he who will exact punishment in the future, and I am He who will give reward in the future. Now [the *tzitzit*] appeared to me as four witnesses [testifying against me]." She said, "I will not leave you until you tell me your name, the name of your teacher and the name of your school in which you study the Torah." He wrote all this down and handed it to her. Thereupon she arose and divided her estate into three parts; one third for the government, one third to be distributed among the poor, and one third she took with her in her hand; the bedclothes, however, she retained. She then came to the *Beit Midrash* of R. Hiyya and said to him. "Master, give instructions about me that they make me a proselyte." "My daughter," he replied, "perhaps you have set your eyes on one of the disciples?" She thereupon took out the script and handed it to him. "Go" said he "and enjoy your acquisition." Those very bedclothes which she had spread out for him for an illicit purpose she now spread out for him lawfully (*Menahot* 44a).

On one level, we have a story about how the *mitzvah* of *tzitzit* prevents sin. One might suggest that the fringes strike at the man's conscience more than they physically smite his face. On another level, the story emphasizes both the heroic ability to desist at the height of temptation and how such heroism can inspire others to repair their ways. Rabbi Eliezer Berkovits finds another level of meaning that helps in the formulation of a Jewish sexual ethics. The key lies in noticing a shift in the interaction between the two protagonists after the man has chosen to desist. In the first part of the story, they never communicate directly. Each one speaks to the maid but no words pass between the customer and the harlot. As soon as the man leaves the bed, the woman speaks directly to him. Secondly, they do not inquire about the other's identity in the early section. Only after it becomes clear that they will not lie together does she inquire about his name, as well as the names of his teacher and school.

These two shifts convey the essence of Jewish sexual ethics. Prostitution represents the height of impersonal lust. In such a relationship, each party views the other as a commodity. The harlot views the customer as a source of money and the customer sees the harlot as a source of pleasure. From such a vantage point, there is no point to communicating or to learning the other's identity. When the relationship shifts from I-It to I-Thou, and the two parties become interested in each other as people, then the union can become sanctified. Various halakhic restrictions on the interaction between the sexes can be understood from this perspective. *Halakhah* strives to prevent the dehumanizing impact of a relationship in which human beings become reduced to material goods.[6]

Rabbi Berkovits also explains the story's conclusion. When I first learned the story, I was troubled by the happy ending. I thought that the fact that they end up together destroys the heroism of the man's gesture and conveys the mistaken notion that the righteous individual will always later receive the very pleasure he or she renounces. As R. Berkovits points out, however, the conclusion adds a crucial element. Declaring the importance of the I-Thou relationship should not obscure the fact that physical enjoyment remains part of a healthy marriage. Thus, our two protagonists finally succeed in forming a deeper relationship that also includes a physical component.[7]

The relevance of this theme to adolescents needs no elaboration. I have found that, with a little prodding, students will often come up with this very interpretation. Analyzing this *aggadah* provides a novel angle for a perennial point of significance and interest. As with any discussion of sexuality, it should optimally be done in single-sex settings. Those teachers with co-ed

---

[6] Cf. R. Joseph B. Soloveitchik, *Family Redeemed: Essays on Family Relationships*, ed. David Shatz and Joel B. Wolowelsky (New York: MeOtzar HoRav, 2001), pp. 86–95.

[7] Eliezer Berkovits, *Crisis and Faith* (New York: Sanhedrin Press, 1976), pp. 64–70.

Gemara classes will have to take this point into consideration before choosing to learn this Gemara.

Honi Demands Rain

The third *aggadah* combines two stories from the same talmudic page and is somewhat lengthy, so it will not be cited in its entirety.

Once it happened that the greater part of Adar had gone and yet no rain had fallen. The people sent a message to Honi the Circle Drawer, Pray that rain may fall. He prayed and no rain fell. He thereupon drew a circle and stood within it... He exclaimed [before God], Master of the Universe, Thy children have turned to me because [they believe] me to be a member of Thy house. I swear by Thy great name that I will not move from here until thou hast mercy upon Thy children! Rain began to drip and his disciples said to him, We look to you to save us from death, we believe that this rain came down merely to release you from your oath. Thereupon he exclaimed: It is not for this that I have prayed, but for rain [to fill] cisterns, ditches and caves. The rain then began to come down with great force, every drop being as big as the opening of a barrel and the Sages estimated that no drop was less than a *log*. His disciples then said to him: Master, we look to you to save us from death; we believe that the rain came down to destroy the world. Thereupon he exclaimed before [God], it is not for this that I have prayed, but for rain of benevolence, blessing and bounty. Then rain fell normally until the Israelites [in Jerusalem] were compelled to go up to the Temple Mount because of he rain... Thereupon Simeon ben Shetah sent this message to him, were it not that you are Honi I would have placed you under the ban; for were the years like the years [of famine in the times] of Elijah (in whose hands were the keys of Rain) would not the name of Heaven be profaned through you. But what shall I do unto you who actest petulantly before the Omnipresent and He grants you your desire....

R. Johanan said: This righteous man [Honi] was throughout the whole of his life troubled about the meaning of the verse (Ps. 126:1), *A song of ascents, When the lord brought back those that returned to Zion, we were like unto them that dream.* Is it possible for man to dream continuously for seventy years? One day he was journeying on the road and he saw a man planting a carob tree: he asked him, How long does it take [for this tree] to bear fruit? The man replied: seventy years. He then further asked him: Are you certain that you will live for another seventy years? The man replied: I found [ready grown] carob trees in the world; as my forefathers planted these for me so I too plant these for my children. Honi sat down to have a meal and sleep overcame him. As he slept a rocky formation enclosed upon him which hid him from sight and he continued to sleep for seventy years. When he awoke he saw a man gathering the fruit of the carob tree and he asked him, Are you the man who planted the tree? The man replied: I am his grandson (Ta'anit 22a).

How are we to evaluate the character of Honi? If we employ results as the criteria, the first story apparently indicates that his methods prove successful. At the same time, Simeon ben Shetah doubts the appropriateness of Honi's approach from the perspective of possible profanation of the Divine name. Simeon's concern focuses on the potential that God might not respond to Honi, who would then be forced to violate his oath. Perhaps Honi's method is problematic from another perspective and the second story follows to make this point. Aharon Agus, a contemporary professor of Jewish studies, develops an overarching theory about two personality types in the Talmud. There are those who look for immediate solutions in one great moment of heroism, such as martyrdom or the miraculous. Others endure difficulties and patiently await the unfolding of history as they direct their energies toward guarding the law. Honi, who demands of God that he solve the problem at once, represents the first approach. The obvious flaw in this approach is that solutions are not always immediate, and arriving at the solution sometimes depends on the ability to persist and endure.

From this perspective, the second story provides a critique of the first. Honi cannot understand the psalmist lauding the return from Babylon because seventy years of exile appears to him as much too long to wait for redemption. Similarly, he fails to appreciate the planting of the carob tree when the payoff remains so distant. Nonetheless, we need to eat carobs, and ancestors must plant with their grandchildren in mind. We also need to find solace even in the possibility of a slow return from exile. The lack of understanding shown by Honi in the latter tale reflects poorly on his approach in the former.[8]

In the classroom, it might be too distracting to summarize Agus' theories about the two types of talmudic personalities and I would skip directly to his interpretation of the Honi stories. All youth (and most adults as well) need reminding that the most important things in life require years of effort and much patience and that problems are best solved with long-range vi-

---

[8] Aharon Agus, *The Binding of Isaac and Messiah: Law, Martyrdom and Deliverance in Early Rabbinic Religiosity* (Albany: SUNY Press, 1988), pp. 69–87.

sion. Our students struggling with personal, social and intellectual problems need to hear such a message. A teacher might also want to discuss how contemporary culture has heightened our impatience. Without minimizing the benefits of modern technology, one can recognize that it also encourages the sense that problems depart with the press of a button. The drug culture often reflects another manifestation of choosing short-term bliss at the expense of long-term interest.[9]

Inadvertent Crimes

> Our Rabbis taught: Moses had set apart three cities [of refuge] on the other side of the Jordan and corresponding to them, Joshua set apart [others] in the land of Canaan…. Were three cities [necessary] in Trans-Jordan [the same as] three cities for the [whole] land of Israel (as there were many more tribes in Canaan, why would both areas require the same number of cities of refuge)? Said Abaye: By reason that murder was rife in Gilead (*Makkot* 9b).

Many commentaries object that Abaye's answer misses the mark. The cities of refuge serve as a home for those guilty of inadvertent murder so the mere fact that one city across the Jordan contained a more murderous society should not necessarily create a greater need for cities of refuge. As intentional murder is a capital crime, and its frequency should not influence the number of people migrating to the cities of refuge. Thus, Abaye's focus on intentional murder seems beside the point. Commentators offer various answers to this problem. Ritva suggests that intentional murderers pretended that their acts were accidental and fled to cities of refuge until the courts could sort out who belonged where. Thus, a more murderous society does require more cities of refuge.

Maharal suggests a more powerful answer. A society with many murderers clearly does not value human life nor recoil at the idea of causing a person's demise. Such a society will also have more inadvertent murder because it will not take the precautions that would limit such occurrences. Trans-Jordan needs more cities of refuge not because the intentional criminals will find their way there. Rather, crimes of both intentionality and neg-

---

[9] This criticism is certainly true regarding illegal drugs and may sometimes be relevant to prescribed medications as well. To the degree that mood-altering drugs are overly prescribed, that may also reflect the erroneous search for quick solutions. (Obviously, this last point should not be mentioned in the classroom out of sensitivity to those students taking such medications.)

ligence stem from the same root, and a society with more of one will also have more of the other.[10]

Although the sanctity of human life merits expression in the classroom, I would not focus the analysis on this point, for our students will usually appreciate the sanctity of life on their own. Instead, I would direct the discussion toward the relationship between negligence and willful misbehavior, a point of broad educational significance. Moral and religious success mandates internalizing the notion that "I didn't mean it" often fails to excuse. Among the many examples that come to mind, a high school teacher might mention the responsibilities inherent in receiving one's driver's license. Teenagers behind the wheel, tempted to show off for their friends, need to understand the sinful element of careless behavior. As with regard to the previous point, this message does not relate especially to adolescents but it certainly belongs in the classroom as an important rabbinic teaching.

A Remedy for Slander:

R. Hama b. Hanina said: What is the remedy for slanderers? If he be a scholar, let him engage in Torah…But if he be unlearned, let him humble himself (*Arakhin* 15b).

We can easily understand the second piece of advice. Some badmouthing stems from arrogance (although some stems from underconfidence too), and the humbled individual will not be so quick to point out the faults of others. But how does Torah study help curb one's tongue? Maharsha relates this *aggadah* to the general notion that Torah study protects us from sin. If so, R. Hama could just as easily have been talking about theft or eating non-kosher food. An alternative explanation might suggest a reason why Torah effectively aids against *lashon ha-ra* in particular.

R. Yisrael Meir ha-Kohen, the Hafetz Hayyim, offers such an explanation in his celebrated *Shemirat ha-Lashon*. He argues that human nature being what it is, people will invariably talk about *something*, and the central question is what the content of their conversation will be. Those with matters of substance to discuss will have quality conversations. Conversely, those lacking the wherewithal for meaningful dialogue will invariably lapse into talking about others. The Gemara's advice to study Torah truly means finding

---

[10] *Gur Aryeh* to Num. 35:14.

ideas worth discussing and thereby rendering the need for idle chatter irrelevant.[11]

When teaching this text, I have asked students to think about what goes on during the lunch break. At some tables, students sit and discus the latest gossip in their grade. At others, students talk about things of greater significance. While the more mature and sophisticated students will have an easier time understanding this point, all students need to hear it. Ideally, it may prod them to think about the quality of their various friendships as reflected in the nature of the conversations.

The Problem of Profanity:

Said R. Hana the son of Rab: All know for what purpose a bride is brought into a bridal chamber, but whoever disgraces his mouth and utters a word of folly – even if a [divine] decree of seventy years of happiness were sealed [and granted] unto him, it is turned for him into evil (*Ketubbot* 8b).

What does R. Hana wish to highlight when he emphasizes that though everyone already knows what a bride and groom do on the wedding night, a person still should not mention it? According to Maharal, R. Hana reveals the true problem with profanity and coarse chatter. If we try to explain the problem of profanity in the context of harming others, the argument breaks down. The problematic nature of a speaker's profanity stems not from the offense taken by the listener. Indeed, all already know what will occur behind closed doors, so those listening need not suffer any shock. Rather, the problem must be located elsewhere.

Maharal focuses on the term "disgrace of the mouth" (*nibbul peh*). The problem of profanity is not what it does to the listener but what it reflects about the speaker. The need to speak in a rude fashion about coarse topics reveals a lack of dignity and gentleness on the part of the person talking. The Gemara speaks about disgracing "his mouth" because it is an internal problem more than an interpersonal difficulty. Maharal broadens the point by developing the idea that in addition to the categories of *mitzvot* between a person and God and *mitzvot* between one person and another, there is a third category of *mitzvot* – between man and himself. Refraining from coarse talk belongs in this third grouping.[12]

---

[11] *Shemirat ha-Lashon: Sha`ar ha-Torah*, chap. 1.

[12] Maharal, *Hiddushei Aggadot* to *Ketubbot* 8b.

Of course, students may deny the assertion that such talk reflects poorly on the speaker. The best method for arguing otherwise may be to ask the students how they would react if their mother or someone they particularly respect (a rabbi or teacher) were to start telling dirty jokes. If they admit that this would make them uncomfortable, they may also come to acknowledge that such talk fails to coincide with a more dignified and exalted expression of humanity. Aggadic statements about *nibbul peh* represent a call for each individual to move from coarseness to refinement.

The Sabbath, Myrtle Branches, and the Common Man

Our final example begins in mid-story. R. Simeon bar Yohai is fleeing a Roman death sentence together with his son R. Eleazar.

> So they went and hid in a cave. A miracle occurred and a carob-tree and water well were created for them. They would strip their garments and sit up to their necks in sand. The whole day they studied; when it was time for prayers they robed, covered themselves, prayed, and then put off their garments again; so that they should not wear out. Thus they dwelt twelve years in the cave. Then Elijah came and stood at the entrance to the cave and exclaimed, Who will inform the son of Yohai that the emperor is dead and his decree annulled? So they emerged. Seeing a man ploughing and sowing, they exclaimed, They forsake life eternal and engage in life temporal! Whatever they cast their eyes upon was immediately burnt up. Thereupon a Heavenly echo came forth and cried out, Have you emerged to destroy My world: Return to your cave. So they returned and dwelt there twelve months, saying, the punishment of the wicked in Gehenna is [limited to] twelve months. A heavenly echo then came forth and said Go forth from your cave! Thus they issued: wherever R. Eleazar wounded, R. Simeon healed. Said he to him: My son! You and I are sufficient for the world. On the eve of the Sabbath before sunset they saw an old man holding two bundles of myrtle and running at twilight. What are these for? They asked him. They are in honor of the Sabbath. He replied. But one should suffice you? One is for *Zakhor* and one for *Shamor.* Said he to his son, See how precious are the commandments to Israel. Thereat their minds were set at ease (*Shabbat* 33b).

Analysis of this *aggadah* could head in many directions, but let us focus on the conclusion. After years dedicated to spiritual seclusion, R. Simeon and his son cannot initially reconcile themselves to the mundane quality of everyday society. They withdraw for an additional year in the cave and only achieve reconciliation upon seeing an old man preparing for the Sabbath. As with any story, one can ask whether particular details are of crucial symbolic import or just random. Would the ending remain the same if they had encountered a Jew running with a *mezuzah* or a *lulav*? Would the story change significantly if the Jew were holding food for the Sabbath rather than myrtle branches? The following reading argues for the centrality of the Sabbath detail and the potential significance of the myrtle branches.

Perhaps the same Jew running before the Sabbath had been busy all week working the fields. The two rabbis could not bear the thought of others directing their energies to pursuits with no direct spiritual import. But those justifiably involved in producing sustenance and supporting families need not be spiritually tone deaf. Give them a day free from work responsibilities, and their authentic spiritual yearnings may emerge. Thus, the Sabbath stands as the test case that reveals the truth about those with tool in hand all week. Seeing the old man convinced R. Simeon and son that Jews work in the field for religiously appropriate reasons and not merely to escape the study hall and synagogue.

If so, this story could lead to a discussion about *Shabbat* in particular and about leisure time in general. As a different Gemara already notes, how a person spends his or her free time may reveal more about the person than what the person does while at work.[13] The many hard-working Jews who utilize *Shabbat* as their real chance to attend a *shi'ur*, pray with patience, and devote significant time to family reveal where their priorities lie. Those who employ Shabbat to play ball, read vacuous novels, or sleep all day reveal a lack of spiritual striving. Although this theme may resonate more for working adults than adolescent students, its relevance extends to the latter group as well.

Additionally, the story addresses the conflict between scholars and the working class. A natural tendency exists for the former to denigrate the latter, and the story indicates that the scholars must learn to appreciate those laboring out in the field. This may explain the choice of the myrtle.[14] In the well-known *midrash* that compares the four species of Sukkot with four types of Jews, the myrtle represents those full of good deeds but lacking in Torah.[15] The old man with the myrtle branches symbolizes the genuine piety to be found even among unlearned Jews.

---

[13] According to *Eruvin* 65b, a person is known by his play.

[14] Jeffrey L. Rubenstein, *Talmudic Stories: Narrative Art, Composition and Culture* (Baltimore: Johns Hopkins Univ. Press, 1999), p. 337.

[15] *Lev. Rabbah* 30:12.

One contemporary example of this phenomenon may help generate a good discussion. Our students will have encountered zealous yeshivah students just back from learning in Israel who cannot easily acclimate to their old environment. Such returnees often feel the need to reject many aspects of their previous lives, and that sometimes includes criticizing those not engaged in full time learning.[16] We can teach our students to respect the youthful idealism of the young firebrands even as we emphasize the need to grow beyond the simplistic division between those in the yeshivah and those in the outside world.

Evaluation and Conclusion

The seven *aggadot* discussed above represent a taste of the proposed program. The topics they cover include authenticity, sexual ethics, patience, profanity, negligence, use of leisure time, and the content of one's conversation. I feel confident asserting that most high school teachers would find this list of topics quite appropriate for their students. Moreover, a number of factors suggest that these texts will often provide a better starting point for classroom discussion than alternative texts or eschewing the textual altogether. First, as mentioned, these texts will encourage our students to think of *Hazal* as wise people with relevant insights. Second, beginning with textual analysis may enable a teacher to get a point across without the students feeling that they are being preached to. The suggested dynamic allows a teacher to analyze the text more than lecture the students and to elicit the point from the students themselves. Finally, I believe the commentaries we have examined to be profound in their own right and worthy of study irrespective of other educational factors.

Three of the featured *aggadot* were stories. Stories have certain advantages in that they naturally tend to grab the audience, and the analysis of various details can lead in interesting directions. On the other hand, the stories are longer, and, if one follows the suggestion here of learning *aggadot* in the original Aramaic, some students may find the length intimidating. Conversely, the other *aggadot* we analyzed may lack narrative drama but their brevity allows for getting to the point without losing too many students in the process.

The commentaries employed in this essay reveal the wide array of texts needed to find good explanations of *aggadah*. They include contemporary academics, modern theologians (Berkovits), supercommentaries on Rashi on *Humash* (*Gur Aryeh*), eclectic works by twentieth-century rabbinic lumi-

---

[16] See Dodi Tobin's essay at the end of this volume.

naries (R. Weinberg and the *Hafetz Hayyim*) and commentaries on *aggadah* (Maharal). Locating this material or producing one's own exegesis is a burden beyond the abilities of the average individual teacher. But the pooling of talents that can go into planning, developing and implementing a curriculum can generate a successful team effort toward incorporating *aggadah* into the classroom.

A tannaitic source states, "If you want to recognize the One who spoke and the world came into being, learn *aggadah*."[17] Another source might state, "If you want to show students the breadth of talmudic creativity, teach them *aggadah*. If you want students to appreciate the accumulated wisdom of the Jewish tradition, teach them *aggadah*. If you want students to see the words of our sages as relevant to their lives, teach them *aggadah*." By all means, teach them the *aggadah*.

---

[17] *Sifrei*, Deut. 49.

WALKING BEFORE RUNNING: TOWARDS A MORE PRACTICAL JUDAIC STUDIES CURRICULUM

GIDON ROTHSTEIN

> It usually happens that out of a thousand who enter upon the study of scripture a hundred are successful... out of these ten who proceed to the study of Talmud one emerges successfully, as it says (Eccles. 7:28) "One man in a thousand have I found..."
> — *Lev. Rabbah* 2

CHANGE IS GOOD. But change is also upsetting, particularly to balances that have been painstakingly forged among competing priorities. Change often means success in many areas, but it also means that assumptions of the past can no longer be accepted, indeed are often obsolete. This essay discusses faulty assumptions underlying our Modern and Centrist Orthodox curricula,[1] assumptions that lead to our failing to offer our students

---

[1] This article consciously focuses almost exclusively on curriculum as opposed to methodology because I believe that is the more crucial question facing Jewish education. Many of our efforts are doomed to failure by virtue of *what* we choose to teach students, not *how* we go about teaching them. To the extent this article will succeed, it will be in convincing educators of the need to focus on different texts, regardless of pedagogic style. Were schools to focus on building skills in texts the students are ready to learn, and are going to use regularly as adult Jews, it would be a great stride in Jewish education. I also assume that day school students have a basic commitment to knowing what it means to be Jewish, but generally lack the skills or interest in covering the kind of ground in Talmud that would produce that kind of knowledge. They do have the skills to work in a sophisticated fashion with other texts; if reasonably skilled teachers offered them the chance to do so, the endeavor would be more productive all around. At this point, it is less important what a particular lesson looks like than that lesson deal with a text the students have the time and ability to meaningfully master. Given such texts, students would enjoy studying Torah the same way they enjoy other projects that challenge them within their capabilities, that show them avenues of growth in their personal lives, and that earn them the approbation of respected elders and peers when they succeed. Finally, my proposals emanate from my involvement in

either skills they can use or texts that they can engage with productively throughout their lives. Those changes have been brought about by remarkable successes in non-curricular areas of Jewish education, successes worth remembering before we move on to consider the next step.

Successes of Jewish Education

One success lies simply in our having converted an Orthodox education into a meaningful and feasible alternative for teenagers. Prof. David Berger once reminisced that in the early 1960's, religiosity was so foreign a concept that many of his bright contemporaries could not comprehend that he, an intellectually gifted young man, could believe in, and adhere to, an Orthodox world view.

Today, of course, that is no longer either the issue or the central challenge. Graduates of the day and high school system attend institutions of higher Torah learning in Israel in remarkable numbers; the social pressure to attend such a program means that at least a year of concentrated Torah study has become close to a given for many in our community.

We have also made great strides in the realm of Jewish pride and identification. Based on anecdotal evidence, Modern and Centrist Orthodox *yeshivot* seem to regularly succeed at providing a positive Jewish experience for their students, an experience that increases the likelihood that these students will maintain a strong connection to their religion throughout their lives. We no longer worry that vast numbers of the graduates of these schools will lose all attachment to observance during their adult lives; instead, high schools can feel reasonably confident that their graduates will have been provided a solid base upon which to build an active and committed Jewish existence.

In this case, quality comes *with* quantity instead of in lieu of it. Today's educators can easily teach more than one hundred students a year, meaning that each of them will meet more students in one year than many of the past's greatest rabbis encountered in their lives. Even many of the Torah giants particularly known for their educational activities often dealt exclusively with students who had already acquired significant Judaic and talmudic knowledge, a stage (in times gone by) achieved only by the most gifted and motivated young men.

A greater awareness of Torah, a positive attitude toward a Jewish way of life, and a large population touched by educators' efforts are a credit to the

American Jewish education, but I suspect they would benefit segments in Israel, as well as elsewhere in the Diaspora.

entire Jewish community, especially its professional educators. At the same time, these points of success contrast sharply with one area, textual study and proficiency, in which our accomplishments are more limited and should lead us to seek methods that are more productive. While the problem will need to be attacked from a few sides, this essay explores curricular changes that might help add one more area of achievement to those already mentioned.

Adapting to Our Success

Some of the problems we have with texts stem from one of our central successes, the range of students we have managed to bring into our schools. That range implies that those schools will need to cope with a similarly broad sweep of talents, interests, and degrees of motivation within its student body. Devising a curriculum that meets the needs of all its constituents is a continuing challenge, one that Orthodox schools have not yet dealt with effectively, at least not in Jewish studies. We seem, to a great extent, to remain committed to a model aimed at producing potential *talmidei hakhamim*, scholarly Jews, which leads us often to fail to help our students simply become Jewishly literate adults.

A central error, I believe, lies in our focus on exposing students to many different types of texts during their twelve years of primary and secondary education, with the most important of these being Talmud. With some variation, Modern and Centrist Orthodox schools introduce students to *siddur* and Hebrew in first grade, *Humash* in second grade, Rashi in third, *Navi* in fourth, Mishnah in fifth, and Talmud in sixth.

While we could argue with many elements of that picture – the number of different texts students see, leading them to master none, is one example – we will first focus on the centrality of Talmud, since rethinking that attachment will free us for a broader reconsideration of our curriculum.[2] From sixth grade on, approximately half of the time spent on Jewish studies is devoted to Talmud, an emphasis that would make sense for those

---

[2] My teacher, R. Aharon Lichtenstein, also suggests (in an Israeli context) that high schools might be better off directing their focus away from Talmud. See his "Teaching Gemara in Yeshivah High Schools" (Hebrew), *Shanah be-Shanah* (5761): 315–327. He raises some of the same issues I will discuss here (see esp. pp. 318–22), and recommends that Mishnah and Rambam might be more productive. Since he sees this problem in Israeli schools, mastery of Hebrew seems not to help with Talmud study; as I will note later on, though, it would still seem to be important for ease in understanding *Tanakh*, the *siddur*, and Mishnah.

who will be spending significant portions of the rest of their lives in its study.[3]

In the modern world, however, the students we are teaching are not, or at least not generally, those who will devote their lives to the study of the Talmud. In contrast to the assumptions that were reasonable in *yeshivot* of yore (and of nostalgia), most of our students will go on to lives spent in occupations that make onerous demands. They will need to devote significant amounts of time to the positive task of *yishuv ha-olam*, to developing society and thus to the habitation of God's world. Their Jewish education, then, should be preparing them for the lives they will lead, a desideratum our current curricula do not always succeed at achieving.

The Trouble with Talmud

The practicalities of teaching Talmud, aside from the question of our theoretical emphases, also point towards an overemphasis on it in our schools. An unsystematic poll of high schools in the New York area suggests that few graduates of yeshivah high schools have studied even a hundred folio pages of Talmud, less than four and one-half percent of the entire corpus. Some schools, trying to maximize students' exposure to substantive discussions (by avoiding the Talmud's sometimes lengthy digressions), spend the year studying several sections scattered throughout a tractate, rather than consecutive pages of Talmud. For those schools, the four-percent number probably overestimates the students' meaningful exposure, since they will more likely have seen bits and pieces of Talmud in many different places, rather than any sustained portions of text.

For a student, seeing such a small amount of Talmud (and many students only *see* this material, without properly learning it) can yield only rudimentary skills. Many such graduates, probably most, can decipher few pieces of Talmud on their own, and almost certainly cannot trace a topic from the Talmud to its codification in law. We must face the sad truth that, for all our effort, we are not generally able to give our students the skills necessary for true talmudic literacy.

Among the many reasons for the flaws in our teaching of Talmud, several result from our commitment to other elements of the educational experience. I review them here only to point out that our inability to produce

---

[3] This is generally true for men and for women in co-educational schools. Some women's schools, perhaps to insure that their students receive the same Talmud education as men, adopt similar schedules. This essay does not differentiate between men's and women's education, mostly because it would digress from the central issues raised here and is not necessary for my basic thesis.

talmidei hakhamim of the old model is a function of who we are (and want to be) today. Those limits, then, are inherent to the educational system we have chosen to create. Solutions will not depend on trying harder or better, but on accepting those limitations and rethinking our goals in ways that will be more productive for all involved.

A first reason for our lack of success in Talmud is lack of time. Talmud is an all-consuming endeavor, and beginners cannot meaningfully grow in its study by focusing on it for an hour or two at a time, a few days a week. In a curriculum that attempts to introduce students to a broad and complex world, with many different subjects clamoring for attention, we are unable to devote the time that Talmud needs.

This is not only a question of our commitment, for it may be impossible, as a purely practical matter, to keep typical children focused on the tedium of reading and translation for multiple hours a day, an activity that necessarily figures in the process of becoming talmudically literate. I would guess, based on my own and others' experiences with Talmud, that fluent reading, if achieved solely by studying Talmud itself, requires devoting multiple hours daily for several successive years. Only in that way can students develop comfort with the language, assumptions, and modes of logic that set the Talmud apart from other works.

The best of teachers, let alone the average teacher, will find it stunningly difficult to hold young students' attention to one text for so long. In post-high school *yeshivot*, students do not generally sit in a class for three hours at a time, since even they, with their greater commitment, simply cannot focus on a teacher's presentation at such length. They, however, are mature enough (or expected to be) to study on their own for long stretches and are allowed to take breaks when necessary, an expectation that is not reasonable for elementary and high school students. Without that extended focus, however, the class will not cover enough ground or absorb a rich enough pool of ideas to allow for meaningful growth in students' talmudic knowledge.

The "should" of such a choice also raises important questions. People who value knowing a range of subjects – *Tanakh*, *halakhah* (both actual practice and some textual familiarity with sources such as the *Shulhan Arukh*), Jewish philosophy and thought, and a range of subjects that are not specifically Jewish but might be a vital part of a well-lived life, Jewish or otherwise (math, science, literature, history, music, art, etc.) – must recognize the crucial importance of prioritizing choices. In that context, the extreme of devoting three hours a day to Talmud calls for extreme caution.

A second reason for our shortcomings in Talmud and other Judaic subjects stems from the diversity of our students. The source from *Leviticus Rabbah* that opened this essay remarks on the rarity of finding students both capable and attracted to deep study of complex Jewish texts. Granting the exaggeration in its estimate that only one in a thousand will succeed, it nonetheless valuably reminds us of the different educational goals necessary for our unprecedentedly large student bodies.

Previously, those who were educated beyond Bar Mitzvah (girls, with their range of talents and interests, were not part of the mix at all) were those who had demonstrated interest and ability far beyond the average. With the implementation of universal education in theory and in practice, we have ensured that fewer Jews will be foisted on the world bereft of any understanding of the religious system to which they adhere. At the same time, such a change in the student body of our institutions necessarily requires a change in the material we offer them.

Some of those students will never be capable of studying Talmud in a meaningful way. Some could, if absolutely forced, struggle with it for as long as they are so forced. Some certainly could study Talmud, but prefer other forms of knowledge acquisition, other topics than those covered in the talmudic tractates we can cover, or types of questions other than those presented by the Talmud. To spend so much time on an endeavor that tradition itself realized was highly specialized seems mistaken as well.

How Troublesome Is an Inability to Engage Talmud?

A word more is in place on the lack of unanimity regarding the importance of Talmud study. Most famously, the Mishnah in *Avot* (5:21) does not envision students beginning their study of Talmud (which, of course, in that context does not mean the text of Talmud, but some advanced thought about Torah) until the age of fifteen. Until that point, *Mikra* (Scripture) and Mishnah (epigrammatic law) were sufficient. The Talmud itself, obviously, was able to conceive of a fulfillment of the *mitzvah* of Torah study that did not involve the study of these texts (i.e., Talmud).

Rambam as well seems to have placed his emphases elsewhere than on Talmud study. His most famous commentary, and also his best preserved, was the one on the Mishnah; he never completed his Talmud commentary, nor has much of it survived.

True, when Rambam defines the *mitzvah* of Torah study, he bases himself on a talmudic statement that uses the word Talmud. He might have interpreted that as referring to some text, our Talmud or otherwise. Instead, he rephrases it in terms of a type of study, involving developing a deepened insight into the halakhic system and its relationship to Scripture.[4] His introduction to the *Mishneh Torah* suggests that he thought it would free people from the need to consult the Talmud itself in their attempts to understand Judaism. While others resisted that move, it does show his lack of concern with whether Jews would spend their time studying that text.[5]

Maharal also vigorously promoted emphasis on Mishnah rather than Talmud; he, in fact, favored following the age prescriptions of the Mishnah in *Avot*, mentioned above. Maharal's concerns focused on reviewing sufficiently before moving on to other material.[6] While those worries also deserve consideration – and argue for a more limited range of subjects than we currently attempt to teach – I am suggesting an alternative to Talmud for an even more fundamental reason: our inability to give the students adequately meaningful skills, comprehension, or exposure to talmudic ideas and modes of argument.

In suggesting that we step back from our focus on Talmud, I am to some extent simply joining a line of thinkers who recognized both the challenges involved in its study and the limited group that is interested, ready, and able to meet those challenges. The curricula of schools that focus on people outside that group must provide all those others with workable ways of studying Torah, ways we can reasonably expect they will continue to pursue throughout their lives.

A third barrier to success in our talmudic efforts is cultural. Facing reality squarely, we must admit that our students do not, outside of class, operate in a talmudic vein. That is, they, their families, and their friends do not think "talmudically," speak "talmudically," or in many cases even care about talmudic discussions and ideas. When an issue arises, they will not first wonder what the Talmud has to say about it and only then develop their own opinion. Their conversation is not peppered with the talmudic phrases and sayings that once regularly appeared in such talk. Talmud is, perhaps more than ever, foreign territory.[7]

Thrusting students from such backgrounds directly into the study of Talmud forces them to try to conquer a different culture, language, and logical structure all at the same time. Such cultural immersion might work if

---

[4] Maimonides, *Mishneh Torah, Hilkhot Talmud Torah* 1:11. See also Rashi to *Kiddushin* 30a, s.v. *Gemara*.

[5] On Rambam's critique of "excessive talmudism" see Isadore Twersky, *Introduction to the Code of Maimonides* (New Haven: Yale, 1980), pp. 200ff.

[6] Cf. discussion in Yael Wieselberg's essay in this volume.

[7] On the analysis of this point and its import for my proposal, see a dissenting interpretation (and counter-proposal) in Avraham Walfish's essay in this volume.

it were the students' only task for the whole day (although even then, the going would be pretty slow); in their overcrowded schedules, it simply cannot work.

Listing the problems with our current methods of study points the way towards real success, towards an ability to bestow on every student tools and knowledge that will help them be culturally literate adult Jews. The first step in moving towards such schools, however, is relinquishing our axiomatic commitment to Talmud study as the center of a Jewish studies curriculum.

I do not mean to take lightly the Talmud's role in Jewish thought and practice. In the best of worlds, graduates of Jewish high schools would be budding scholars already reasonably familiar with significant portions of such a central text. And even in our "non-utopian" schools, it is likely that the top echelons of each class could productively spend eleventh and twelfth grade focused on Talmud, assuming they had laid the proper foundation in their previous years of education.

But aside from needing to cope with a broader student population, I would argue that stepping away from Talmud study could help us more effectively ready our students to eventually master it. Rather than approaching the problem head-on, we could begin with texts for which the students are already prepared that, at the same time, bring them closer to the world of the Talmud.

From Talmud to Mishnah

Making Mishnah the central Jewish text for at least the first several years of students' acquaintance with Oral Law would seem to do exactly that. I do not mean simply reading and explaining many paragraphs of Mishnah, for that would be at least as "boring" as Talmud. But the study of Mishnah, viewed through the eyes of its various commentators – choosing particularly appropriate pieces of Talmud, Rashi, Rambam, and assorted other classical commentaries and halakhic codes – can lead to a productive intellectual and textual experience.

Study of Mishnah in this way is easily as sophisticated as it would be in a Talmud class, but it is centered on a text the students are linguistically better prepared to comprehend, and one that is structured more like the way they think in their own lives. Focusing on Mishnah does not even completely forgo introducing the student to the language and modes of thought of the Talmud, since the commentaries on the Mishnah introduce students to many phrases and types of questions they would meet in the Talmud itself. Mishnah opens the door to Talmud more easily than Talmud itself.

Mishnah provides the further advantage of allowing teachers to maintain a pace that exposes the students to a wider range of concepts than they otherwise could encounter. Allotting an average of twenty minutes for teaching a Mishnah,[8] students who learn four *mishnayot* a day for 150 days of the school year beginning in fifth grade would have covered a quarter of *Shas* before graduating elementary school, and half by the end of eleventh grade.

Such a student, sitting down to study a tractate of Talmud for the first time, is easily as prepared for the endeavor as the typical high school senior. Indeed, it seems likely that such students could, in the course of a year, study as much (or almost as much) Talmud as we currently achieve in all the years of Talmud education combined.[9]

Four *mishnayot* a day might take up the same amount of time as we currently spend on Talmud, with more productive results. Shifting our focus to Mishnah study also means, however, that we can make more reasoned choices about how we allocate precious Jewish studies hours. Were we willing to have students learn only a sixth of *Shas* by the time they graduate elementary school and another sixth by the end of eleventh grade, we would free up time for other areas of study. Some of these areas are somewhat neglected, though they are of demonstrably greater importance to our students' lives (and spiritual personae) than either Mishnah or Talmud.

Educating for Jewish Adulthood

In considering what subjects might be more or less important to students' adult Jewish lives, I accept the view of the goals of education articulated so well by Howard Gardner. Gardner points out that across time, place, and culture, education has consistently focused on readying children for the tasks of adulthood in their particular society.[10] Perhaps by thinking about how to give students a mastery of the texts they will regularly encounter as Jewish adults, temporarily forgoing more ideal pictures of what

---

[8] Arguing that it really takes longer than twenty minutes to teach a Mishnah only strengthens the claim that we have no business teaching these students Talmud. Any student who, presented with a carefully selected group of commentators on a Mishnah, still needs more than 20 minutes to comprehend it, is clearly not ready to study Talmud.

[9] This obviously depends on the level of depth for which we strive, but students whose study of Mishnah had provided them with a significant base of knowledge and of commitment should be able to at least triple the current yearly achievements of Talmud classes.

[10] H. Gardner, *The Disciplined Mind*, (New York: Penguin Books, 2000), p. 28.

their adult Torah study will look like, we can identify other areas to emphasize in our curricula.

We focus on textual literacy, because schools are meant to teach not just knowledge, but skills; as we are the People of the Book, some of those skills must be textual. To paraphrase a well-known saying, teach a student Torah and you've sustained her spiritually for a day; teach a student *how* to learn Torah, and you've sustained her for a lifetime.

The First Vital Text: Torah

Three relatively simple texts are encountered by observant adult Jews regularly and yet are only poorly understood by the vast majority of current yeshivah graduates. The first, perhaps the most important, is the text of the Torah itself, the entirety of which is read in synagogues the world over on a yearly cycle. Readiness for adulthood should surely include fluency in this text.

During their years in school, students probably see all, or almost all, of the Five Books of the Torah. Fluency, however, means more than just exposure; it means that students should be able to sight-read (read and understand without prior preparation) any portion of *Humash*. Several factors suggest that the importance of taking students to that level of fluency outweighs even the value of introducing students to Mishnah as a text of its own.[11]

The Talmud (*Kiddushin* 30a) defines the *mitzvah* of Torah study as minimally involving knowledge of the text of Scripture. Schools that regularly allow students to graduate who have not yet fulfilled even the minimal requirement of *talmud Torah* might want to reconsider their barometer of success.

Students themselves have a religious stake in setting such literacy as a goal. Regardless of synagogue attendance, *halakhah* clearly requires adult Jews to complete the Torah portion each week, *shenayim mikra ve-ehad targum*, twice in the text and once with either Onkelos or Rashi.[12] As schools ready students for the tasks of Jewish adulthood, they should be trying to help them reach the point where they can, in a reasonable period of time, fulfill this halakhic desideratum.

---

[11] In three different contexts (*Sanhedrin* 33b, *Shevu`ot* 14b, and *Horayot* 4a), the Talmud refused to categorize a mistaken quote about what Scripture says as a mere error. Since *"zil karei bei rav"* (even schoolchildren are expected to know the contents of Scripture), such missteps are more willful than errors.

[12] See *Shulhan Arukh, Orah Hayyim,* 285:1 and 146:2. Note that the latter source permits using the public Torah reading as fulfillment of one of the two mandatory readings.

Of course, achieving that level of understanding of the text of the Torah presents different educational challenges than those confronted in our current curricula. Reading the *Humash* sentence by sentence, and ensuring that students know what each word means individually and in context, is, as I mentioned in the case of Talmud, a tedious task that would probably destroy any classroom that engaged in it exclusively. Expanding time spent on *Humash* cannot simply mean reading more of the same text – spending two hours on *Humash* instead of one – since, with all good will, there is a limit to how much of one subject a student can learn in a day.

Expanding Time Studying the Text of Torah
Without Decreasing Interest

I offer here, therefore, several options that allow for spending more time on *Humash* while still respecting students' need for variety. Were variety our only concern, we could divide the time allotted to Torah among the separate books of the Humash, such as one class a day (or a week), studying *Bereshit,* one *Shemot,* and so on. A more sophisticated approach would be to divide the time by genres of writing (narrative, law, and poetry, for example) or broad themes (parents and children, the structure of a Torah society, the *mishkan* and the sacrifices, etc.). Dividing by genre and/or topic, in addition to making class time more interesting, opens the option of leaving the more advanced genres and topics for later in a child's education.

Whatever option chosen, it would be vital to keep in mind the goal of covering all of Torah, at least over the course of twelve years of education. Second, but no less important, we must remember that a stress on reading skills would have to be a constant presence in all of these classes. The overall goal would be that students leave school fully comfortable with the text of Torah, ready to spend a life deepening their appreciation of God's word.

Lest the reader assume that I envision students chained to their desks, mastering ever more *Humash* and Rashi year after year, let me spend a moment offering some ideas for how to teach *Humash* in a way that meets the foregoing goals. First, *Humash* and Rashi, handled correctly, provide plenty of material for hours of deep and productive thought and analysis. Teachers could address such questions as what it was about the text that provoked Rashi's amplification or explanation; what are the strengths and weaknesses of Rashi's reading; what conception of Judaism (or the particular element under discussion) is embedded in Rashi's idea, and so on.

As someone who returns to Rashi frequently, I rarely fail to find some new implication in many of his comments. Especially in light of students' weak textual proficiency, it is hard to imagine that they are already "beyond" Rashi. In this regard, the story is told of a man who came to the Hafetz Hayyim, seeking a letter of recommendation to be a schoolteacher. The Hafetz Hayyim asked the man what he knew, and was told that he knew *Humash* and Rashi. In response, the Hafetz Hayyim said, "If you *really* know *Humash* and Rashi, I should rise before you and ask you for a recommendation." We do not need to fully share that view to recognize that even Rashi incorporates a wealth of material that, properly taught, can provide plenty of stimulation for students' intellects.

Recognizing that we will probably not succeed at focusing only on *Humash* and Rashi throughout the years in school, we would widen the scope of commentaries that are introduced. Keeping in mind our earlier caveats about introducing students only to texts for which they are linguistically prepared, we might decide to discuss other commentators orally rather than textually. More ambitious students and classrooms might read selections of Ramban's commentary, a difficult and challenging text, but one that contains more than enough ideas and insights to enliven years of reading *Humash*.

Focusing on the commentaries printed in the *Mikra'ot Gedolot* edition of the Torah, while convenient, still might seem too narrow for the sustained study I am recommending. In narrative sections of the Torah, using the *Torah Temimah* productively allows students to confront the responses of the Talmud and *midrash* to the text, without falling into the trap of trying to study Talmud directly. Especially in contrast to a literal reading, as in Rashi and Ramban, seeing how the Sages used texts could be an essential part of students' education.

Engaging in an extended discussion of how to teach narrative is probably superfluous, since the legacies of various teachers of Torah, particularly Nehama Leibowitz, have enabled us all. We might, however, productively reconsider how we teach the legal sections of the Torah. Here, we will certainly want to use Rashi and the occasional Ramban, but Rambam's *Sefer ha-Mitzvot* and the thirteenth-century *Sefer ha-Hinukh* can become indispensable tools as well. Showing the students organized presentations of how the Oral Tradition interpreted the Bible helps them understand the text itself and continues their preparation for the eventual study of Talmud and Jewish law generally.

Aside from the practicality of studying texts for which the students feel ready and the value of Bible fluency, we should also properly appreciate the psychological value to students of mastering the text of Torah before going on to more difficult tasks. Giving students ownership of Torah, meaning that they know that they can pick up the *Humash*, review previous knowledge, and think of new angles with which to approach these texts, will increase the likelihood that they will see Torah, broadly speaking, as a continuing and compelling point of interest in their later adult lives.

Torah and Mishnah could easily fill twelve years of Jewish education, but the desire for variety and the importance of other contributions to Jewish literature force us to expand our horizons even further. Two other texts, also among those needed to prepare students for the tasks of adulthood, cry out for more attention and are much richer sources of Jewish knowledge than we tend to recognize.

The Siddur: A Neglected Text

Most adults today use the *siddur* (prayer book) more than any other Jewish book, and yet explanatory courses in prayer are usually accorded only a small portion of time and are boring besides. It seems clear that most adult Jews today, even observant ones, have little idea of the meaning of the words they say in prayer, a state of affairs that also serves to explain so much of their lack of engagement in the services. Striving to ready our graduates for prayer textually, emotionally, and spiritually would be a service to the students as well as to the broader Jewish community.

As in the case of Torah, teaching *siddur* must involve more than the reading and translation of texts; boredom almost never leads to productive learning. Rather, these texts must become the focus of stimulating study. That would involve, at least, coming to understand the words of the text, considering its structure (and the message that structure is meant to send), and developing a picture of the goal of the texts and the experience they are meant to convey.

As prayer is not only an intellectual experience, it is necessary for the *siddur* section of a curriculum to include more practical elements as well. Some useful examples include: practice runs at prayer (in non-prayer times) so students can watch and question what happens without needing to worry about the time pressures of a particular *minyan*; meditation/concentration exercises to help students learn to focus on prayer; and informal, free-flowing discussions of philosophical and experiential issues related to prayer, so students can develop a real picture of themselves as Jews standing before their God.[13]

---

[13] See *Notes from ATID: Educating Toward Meaningful Tefillah*, ed. Yoel Finkelman (Jerusalem: ATID, 2001), and R. Isaiah Wohlgemuth, *A Guide to Jewish Prayer* (Brookline, MA, n.d.).

A key component to success here would seem to be disciplining ourselves to wait to introduce the students to *more* texts only when they are comfortable with their understanding of the texts we already expect them to utter on a regular basis. The sky would not fall if pre-sixth grade students recited less than the full *shaharit* every morning. Beginning with *Shema* and the *Amidah*, moving from there to *birkhot keri'at Shema* and *birkhot ha-shahar*, and only then to *pesukei de-zimrah*, for example, might let us ascertain that our students are using these words as vehicles of expression rather than rote recitations.

Proper study of *siddur* would include not only the daily prayers, but also those for *Shabbat* and holidays. In all of that study, students would also be learning important texts that we would otherwise need to teach them anyway. Examples include: *Shema* and *shirat ha-yam* from Torah; parts of *Nakh*, such as the various verses (and chapters) found in *pesukei de-zimrah*, *hallel* and *tahanun*;[14] and even excerpts from Mishnah, such as *Avot* and *bameh madlikin*. Relevant background material could also be included, such as the sections of *Yoma* describing the service of Yom Kippur (crucial to understanding the repetition of *musaf* on that day) or the talmudic discussion of the reasoning that underlies the order of blessings of the *amidah* (*Megillah* 17b–18a).

Meeting the Prophets More Productively

Similar curricular changes in the area of *Navi*, study of the Prophets, would take a further giant step towards properly readying students for Jewish adulthood. *Navi* classes currently start with Joshua (around fourth grade) and work their way to the end of the Early Prophets by the end of elementary school, with sections of Later Prophets usually being undertaken in high school. While the urge to give students a full acquaintance with the range of the Prophets is admirable, it again does not match the capabilities or interests of the typical student. Sadly, many students will not confront *Navi* on a regular basis following their graduation from high school, and their having learned several chapters of numerous Prophets will not provide fundamental knowledge that can sustain them in later life.[15]

---

[14] An especially important lost art is the Jewish attachment to *Tehillim*; texts that used to be known even to the least educated members of society are now completely foreign to many of the most educated. Teaching *Tehillim* to students, not as pure text, but as a source to use (with understanding) in various kinds of life celebrations and crises could be another valuable part of a well-considered curriculum.

[15] Young women who attend an Israel program are more likely to see sustained study of *Nakh*, but the suggestion made here should in no way put them at a disadvantage.

Those same students will, in the course of a calendar year, meet many sections of *Nakh* not currently taught in schools. There are eighty *haftarot* to be read after various readings of the Torah, not to mention the five *megillot* read throughout the year. As with Torah and *siddur*, few high school graduates can currently read and understand the majority of these texts. Were elementary and high schools to devote their *Nakh* time to striving to ensure that students leave school with a clear textual mastery (not just content-awareness) of the *haftarot* and *megillot*, we would accrue the same benefits as mentioned earlier.

Teaching selections from various *Nevi'im*, of course, makes it necessary to properly introduce each section, its background, and major concerns in each work (the *Da'at Mikra* series on *Tanakh* provides introductions that serve as a good model[16]). Students would thus quite possibly develop a broader understanding of the times of the Prophets and the contributions they made to Jewish religious history than they currently do. Schools could also group the texts in such a way that students learn all of the narrative *haftarot* and *megillot* – Esther and Ruth – in elementary school, again adhering to the policy of introducing students only to those texts for which they are linguistically and cognitively prepared.

Hebrew Language: A Key to Jewish Knowledge

The issue of language, which has played a central role throughout this essay, suggests that we reconsider the time we spend on teaching Hebrew. Current class time spent on Hebrew, particularly in schools that do not speak Hebrew consistently in the rest of the Jewish studies curriculum, does not suffice for producing real fluency or literacy. I believe it is possible to help students become more comfortable, or literate, in Hebrew with much less formal class time – thus also freeing more time for the Jewish studies initiatives I have been proposing.

Hebrew fluency is not only an important Zionist value, though that cannot be stressed enough; it is also an important Jewish value. Virtually all of the central Jewish texts are written in Hebrew or have been translated into it. Ensuring the ability to fluently read a Hebrew text is part and parcel of our attempt to ready students for Jewish adulthood.[17]

---

[16] See Mark Smilowitz, "Review Essay: *Da`at Mikra*," *Ten Da'at* 13 (December 2001): 39–52 (on use of *Da`at Mikra* in preparing to teach *Tanakh* and its use in the classroom).

[17] See Rambam's commentary on *Avot* 2:1, in which he classifies learning and speaking Hebrew as a *mitzvah* – albeit a "light" one. I know of no earlier source for this contention – perhaps the issues I raise here were those that led Rambam to his conclusion.

Conversation and reading are vital to producing students truly comfortable with Hebrew, as they are in English. On the conversational side, teaching *Ivrit be-Ivrit*, conducting all Judaic studies classes in Hebrew, seems the only viable choice; there is simply no substitute for gently forcing students to operate in Hebrew for a significant portion of their day. *Ivrit be-Ivrit* might seem to present a barrier to comprehension, but that claim underestimates students' language abilities, particularly in the younger years.

When my daughter entered first grade, she was blessed with a teacher who absolutely insisted on speaking Hebrew. The first two months of school were difficult, but by the end of the year, she was able to read and comprehend simple Hebrew texts she had never seen before. As a high school student at the Yeshivah of Flatbush, I saw fellow students with poor Hebrew backgrounds learn to easily follow a classroom conversation within a year. Teaching *Ivrit be-Ivrit* sacrifices comprehension for a fairly brief period of time (and the earlier and more consistently it is done, the shorter the time) in the name of a lifelong mastery of the language of our texts and our people (not to mention our land).

A second element to focus on is reading. Just as in English, reading is fundamental to Hebrew literacy and fluency. Expanding our schools' libraries to include Hebrew books for students of varying interests and skill, and hiring librarians (or engaging current Hebrew teachers as librarians)[18] who could introduce students to the pleasures of reading in Hebrew, would open up extra class time, and give students better mastery of Hebrew at the same time.

Let me recall in this context the wonderful librarian from my elementary school, who knew every Hebrew book in her library, and would offer each student books that matched his or her skill level and interests. Motivated students were able to find Hebrew books that they could actually read and enjoy, and return for more when done.[19]

The extra class time created by replacing study of Hebrew language with *Ivrit be-Ivrit* and required reading on a consistent basis could be used for Mishnah or any of the other central texts discussed above. As always, the

---

[18] Many current Hebrew teachers could probably have a greater impact on students if they became library resource people, who would discuss with students the books they had read, and find them similar ones. Students could even, perhaps, be required to meet with a particular librarian for ten minutes a week, to review the book (or chapters) they had read, and get more to read.

[19] The librarian was Mrs. Aviva Lapid at the Yeshiva of Flatbush elementary school. I should mention that "Hebrew Library" was a grade on our report cards – students who read 500 pages a semester received an A+, 450 an A, and so on.

point is to make sure that we maximize our effectiveness in producing students truly ready for a meaningfully literate Jewish adulthood, as we do in English.

Recreating Sinai for Our Students

In thinking about the shift of our priorities involved in the kinds of changes suggested here, the role of grandparents in teaching Torah provides a useful model. The *mitzvah* of *talmud Torah* is one of the few related to children, if not the only one, that the Talmud sees as incumbent on grandparents as well as parents. The Talmud proves that grandparental obligation by citing the verse "and you shall make them known to your children and your children's children" (Deut. 4:9).[20]

The verse, however, does not refer to Torah as what the grandparents need to transmit, but to the Sinai experience. The relevant passage (Deut. 4:9–10) reads in full:

> Only take care for yourself, and guard your soul exceedingly, lest you forget the matters that your eyes saw, and lest they be removed from your heart., And you shall make them known to your sons and your grandsons; the day that you stood before the Lord your God in Horev, when God said to me: Gather me the people and I will make them hear My words, so that they will learn to fear Me all the days that they live on the earth, and their sons also they will teach.

While the Torah seems to have been concerned with the experience of Sinai, which might mean having the grandparent tell the story of Sinai in a manner similar to the Passover *Haggadah*, the Talmud (*Kiddushin* 30a) applies the verse to the text of Torah itself. Many reasons might be offered for this discrepancy,[21] but in our context I suggest that grandparents are uniquely suited to teach Torah exactly as it was taught at Sinai, where each listener heard as much as he or she was prepared productively to absorb.

Parents often allow their visions of what the child should be or become to cloud their vision of what their child is; they are the primary teachers of

---

[20] Note that Maimonides, *Hilkhot Talmud Torah* 1:2, and *Shulhan Arukh, Yoreh De`ah* 245:3 both codify this grandparental obligation as law. See also R. Soloveitchik, "The First Jewish Grandfather," in *Man of Faith in the Modern World* (Hoboken, NJ: Ktav, 1989), pp. 15–24.

[21] Another possible reason is that the Talmud envisioned the *mitzvah* of Torah study as actually serving to keep the Sinai experience alive in each generation; but that is a discussion for another place.

Torah, but their Torah comes with the emotional overtones that necessarily affect all parent-child relations. Grandparents, around less often, perhaps less influential in the child's life, but also less embroiled and invested in a specific vision of the child's future, can meet the child where she is, giving her the Torah knowledge she is able to absorb.

Rambam codifies the grandparental obligation and then seamlessly notes that any knowledgeable person is obligated to teach those who wish to learn. We as educators need to fulfill a grandparental role, to take our students where they are, accept their starting point as our starting point, and then work to advance them as productively as possible in the ways of Torah. The ideas suggested here are offered as an avenue that meets the challenges of our generation in a way that can increase our students' involvement with and capabilities in the study of Torah.

In times gone by, giants walked the earth, amassing greater breadth of textual proficiency at a younger age than we can currently imagine. In our schools, we may be "dwarves" by comparison, although we reach many more students than in the days of the giants. Accepting our relative limitations, and working within them, might allow us to stop trying to match their ideal standards, and instead develop ourselves more effectively to our potential. Properly prepared, we may find more of our students standing on the shoulders of their forebears, exceeding our fondest hopes for how far, Jewishly, they are enabled to see.

TEACHING RABBI SOLOVEITCHIK'S THOUGHT IN THE HIGH SCHOOL CLASSROOM

MOSHE SIMKOVICH

MANY SHARE THE OPINION that Rabbi Joseph B. Soloveitchik was the foremost Orthodox thinker in America in the twentieth century. As we enter the twenty-first century, we lack a visible leader who speaks with similar eloquence and insight about the meaningfulness of living an Orthodox life in the modern world. This lack reverberates throughout our community but is perhaps most painfully absent in the high school classroom. Under modern circumstances, we owe it to high school students, in their search for the way Torah informs and inspires us, to give them the keys necessary for developing a vital vision of the future. The teachings of the Rav (as R. Soloveitchik was universally known) reflect the relationship of the Jew with the modern world, and one would think those teachings would be a basic part of the high school curriculum in all schools that struggle with the encounter between Judaism and modernity.

And yet it is not commonly so. Many rationales are offered to justify the omission of a serious study of the Rav's thought in most high schools:

1. It is often too complex. To fully appreciate the Rav, one needs both the background of a genuine *talmid hakham* and a Ph.D. in philosophy.

2. The students are not yet ready for the Rav's thought. Cognitively speaking, the thought is too subtle for adolescents. For that matter, many adults are never ready to understand the Rav.

3. The Rav's thought must be studied in depth. There simply is not time to do it justice in the high school classroom.

4. Our teachers often are unfamiliar with the Rav's thought.

5. Students may get the wrong impression of the Rav, depending on the teacher. One teacher might focus on the Rav as *Rosh Yeshivah* in the Brisk

tradition; the next might stress the Rav's philosophical works; and a third might emphasize his communal impact. Which Rav should be presented?[1]

6. There are more important and basic things to teach in high school.

7. Many schools choose not to explore philosophical issues in depth altogether.

Indeed, it is difficult to teach about any great Torah leader, and certainly about one as distinctive as the Rav. And yet, can we afford not to do so? In the meantime, we prolong an environment where many students perceive their approach to Torah as a compromise between secular and Jewish worlds. Or they simplistically characterize their perspective on life as *Torah u-madda* or even *Torah u-parnasah*, without being able to analyze these slogans and determine whether they adequately describe the Rav's approach, an approach they claim guides their lives.

The frustration of trying to convey the Rav's approach is not unique to contemporary educators. He himself bewailed the teaching of Judaism as primarily intellectual and academic. To the Rav, such teaching lacks experiential depth and does not promote spiritual growth:

> Orthodox youth have discovered the Torah through scholastic forms of thought, intellectual contact, and cold logic. However, they have not merited to discover her [the Torah] through a living, heart-pounding, invigorating sense of perception. They know the Torah as an idea, but do not directly encounter her as a "reality," perceptible to taste, sight, and touch.[2]

The study of the Rav's works can be a response to the problem. But I believe that the argument for aggressively introducing the Rav's works into the high school educational setting should begin with the Rav's own understanding of the needs and goals of our youth, with his depiction of the

---

[1] High school teachers are not alone in confronting this challenge. Numerous articles have been written in the past several years on this subject. For an idea of their scope, see the array of positions portrayed in the memorial volume, *Tradition* 30:4 (Summer 1996), reprinted as *Rabbi Joseph B. Soloveitchik: Man of Halakha, Man of Faith*, ed. Menachem Genack (Hoboken, NJ: Ktav, 1998); and the primary and secondary bibliographical sources in Eli and Chaim Turkel, *Mekorot ha-Rav* (Jerusalem: Rubin Mass, 2001). After this essay was completed, a noteworthy collection of memorial essays and tributes was published as *Memories of a Giant: Eulogies in Memory of Rabbi Dr. Joseph B. Soloveitchik*, ed. Michael A. Bierman, series editor: Jacob J. Schacter (Jerusalem and New York: Urim Publications, 2003).

[2] In *Be-Sod ha-Yahid ve-ha-Yahad* (Jerusalem: Orot, 1976), pp. 407–408.

pedagogical challenges that await us and that should keep us up late at night.

The Challenge of Contemporary Education

In a talk on "The Future of Jewish Education in America," the Rav related an experience he had as a *heder* student in Khaslavichy during his childhood.[3] The *heder rebbe*, a Lubavitcher *hasid*, was teaching the story of Joseph's meeting with his brothers in Egypt. The students were inattentive, until suddenly the class took on a surprising intensity, as the teacher approached Joseph's question to his brothers from a new angle. Joseph asked the brothers, "Is your father still alive?" (Gen. 43:7) — as if Joseph didn't know the answer! What did he mean by this question? Was this information he could not get otherwise? Rather, the teacher exclaimed, Joseph was asking about the brothers' beliefs and commitments. Were they continuing on the path of their father, or was each for himself, no longer committed to the Jacob's beliefs? Could they see that even while their father conveyed an old tradition to them, he was telling them something new, exciting, and challenging? Or were they so arrogant as to think of themselves as independent, and of their father as outdated?

To the Rav, what was important about what he was taught that day was not an analysis of a difficult text, but rather how the teacher addressed himself to the young man's soul. He was attracted to the invitation to approach Judaism in an imaginative way, to become a visionary, to see how one could involve the heart in matters of tradition and religion. The Rav saw this classroom episode as a foundational experience in his own education, one conveyed to him by a teacher whom the Rav did not feel was outstanding as a Torah scholar, per se. But this *heder rebbe* was able to give him a key to experience Judaism as a powerful way of life, a key that the Rav incorporated into his relationship to Judaism.[4]

The Rav felt the transmission of this capacity to be missing from the education we give our children in America and in Israel. He saw that the substance of what was being taught in schools did not respond to the youth it had to involve. In his most highly personal essay, "*Al Ahavat ha-Torah u-*

---

[3] Cited in Aaron Rakeffet-Rothkoff, *The Rav: The World of Rabbi Joseph B. Soloveitchik* (Hoboken, NJ: Ktav, 1999), vol. 1, pp. 149–52. The talk was delivered in Lincoln Square Synagogue, New York City, on May 28, 1975.

[4] The Rav described the impact of this *melammed*, Reb Baruch Yaakov Reisberg, on his spiritual development, and his own affinity for the *Tanya*, on various occasions. See, e.g., *Yemai Zikkaron* (Jerusalem: WZO, 1986), pp. 149–50, and the stories related in Rakeffet-Rothkoff, *The Rav*, vol. 1, pp. 147–59, and, esp., vol. 2, pp. 212–13.

Ge'ulat Nefesh ha-Dor," the Rav described the new generation we are challenged to guide:[5]

> American youth tend to exaggerated extremism, amazing in its arrogance…[they] go in the way of easy resistance. In a word, they are confused about Judaism. And this confusion is the product of a world outlook incapable of leading to fulfillment.

The Rav hesitated to criticize others for this inability to respond to the youth, opting instead to criticize himself. Later, in the same text:

> I have not fulfilled my obligation as a guide and teacher in Israel. When I have succeeded…my students received much Torah from me, and their intellectual stature has been fortified and has grown over the years that they have been around me… But I have not seen a great blessing in my efforts in the experiential realm… My words, it appears, did not light the divine flame in sensitive hearts.[6]

The Rav could have been satisfied with the status quo. He was a leading *Rosh Yeshivah* and academic, a powerful community leader, and a successful, innovative educator. Perhaps it was his unique success in all these spheres that deepened the frustration he expressed about reaching the next generation. He, Joseph in the twentieth century, joined Joseph our ancestor in questioning and challenging those closest to him about what was so dear to him – the future of the Jewish people.

The Rav on What Must Be Taught

In that same talk on "The Future of Jewish Education," the Rav went on to discuss what the older generation had to convey to the younger generation. What is it that will prove attractive to that next generation? The Rav described two motifs, normative and romantic. Because these motifs are presented as essential goals of education, it is worth reviewing them with an eye toward pedagogical implementation.

The "normative motif" involves the student in developing a disciplined life. Resignation, resistance to the surrounding society's hedonistic, orgiastic pursuits, refinement of one's character and of one's thought – all are keys

---

[5] Appears in *Be-Sod ha-Yahid ve-ha-Yahad*, pp. 403–32 [reprinted in *Divrei Hashkafah* (Jerusalem: WZO, 1993), pp. 241–58]. The quoted passage appears at p. 408.

[6] *Ibid.*, p. 420.

to achieving *kedushah* (holiness). Involvement in Torah provides the ideal instrument for developing disciplined thought, as one of the benefits of the serious study of *halakhah* is that it guides the student to become an agile and methodical thinker. The focus on Gemara, on *lomdus*, on clear conceptualization, enables the student to master the structuring of coherent perspective. As the student grows, he or she begins to understand a system of world interpretation unique to the student of *halakhah*. Once this is mastered, the student has an entry point into understanding the world from other perspectives as well.

The "romantic motif" involves the student in the *experience* of Judaism. Beyond requiring analysis and understanding with one's intellect, Judaism demands to be experienced, to be lived, and to be enjoyed. The Rav elsewhere called this an exciting and cathartic preoccupation, capable of intensifying the experience of Judaism so that it is "able to make hearts tremble and shout." It is exactly here, if we take the Rav at his word, that he feared he failed. He confided in his audience that to convey this excitement is the most difficult job of all. Despite his ability to explain abstract concepts, break talmudic debates down to their component parts, and popularize the ideas involved in them, the Rav claimed that he could not convey the complex experience of inner serenity and restlessness, trepidation and certitude, that he silently observed and experienced in his youth on the Days of Awe, watching his family in prayer:

> Here, for example, I am sitting and explaining the Day of Atonement to my students... From an intellectual standpoint there is much I can transmit to my pupils from what I absorbed from my forefathers and from my mentors about the significance of the day, about the sanctity of the Days of Awe. What I cannot pass on are the experiences that I myself underwent on those days. I cannot give rise in them to that gamut of feelings that a Jew must experience... I cannot possibly transmit the emotion I felt when I heard my grandfather, Rabbi Haim, tremulously breathe the words which describe the service in the Temple on the Day of Atonement...One could well-nigh see that at that moment Rabbi Haim dwelt in another world, as if he were floating and journeying from Brisk to the Jerusalem of two thousand years ago... This is a feeling that a Jew must personally experience; it does not lend itself to transmission via theological tractates and essays, homilies and sermons. It is a feeling – and it must be experienced!... I may

not be such a bad schoolteacher, and I can give instruction on various subjects – but not on this.[7]

He believed these deeper insights and feelings defied explanation in words and that the medium of choice was silence in all its intensity. How can one transmit these feelings? To commune with another on this level is an art. Whether out of justification or modesty (after all, his many students would disagree, on the basis of their personal experiences), the Rav was frustrated with his lack of expertise in this art. But the art of conveying experience is at the heart of conveying Judaism to another soul, to another generation; and it cannot be ignored.

In outlining the goals of modern Jewish education, the Rav posited that the teacher must help students overcome and eradicate the pagan-hedonistic influences of our society (a theme he revisited time and again), encourage them to find meaning in the disciplining of their drives, and set them on the path to holiness. The teacher must also convey the art of experiencing awe and joy, not just insight. The teacher must make understood the content of what is taught, while also inspiring the student to incorporate the experience of life that goes beyond words and makes Judaism a way of life. The need to do all these tasks is urgent; the difficulty in accomplishing the experiential tasks, intimidating.

Why the Rav Must Be Taught

At first, one might think that the responsibility to educate students in these two modes rests solely upon individual educators. But in the essay mentioned above, the Rav makes clear that successful education is a responsibility shared by Jewish leadership:

The religious movements [in Israel] themselves must transfer the focal point of their public service from the Knesset to the school and the *yeshivah*, from gatherings of leaders to teachers and instruction, from the debates in the political arena to multi-dimensional spiritual impact. The Judaism of the *mesorah* must give content and meaning to the life of the individual and the community.[8]

Communal leaders need to refocus their energies to promote greater understanding and appreciation of how identification with Judaism gives

---

[7] *On Repentance*, ed. Pinchas Peli (Jerusalem: Orot Press, 1981), pp. 149–50.

[8] "*Al Ahavat ha-Torah*," in *Be-Sod ha-Yahid ve-ha-Yahad*, p. 432.

depth and meaning to the lives of each individual, and changes the nature of the community as a whole. That being said, it is clear that the focus is on the teachers. The best pedagogical approach is centered on the classrooms and *yeshivot*. Its success is in the hands of the educators who are directly in touch with the students.

This leads us to practical questions. In terms of the goals to which the Rav aspires, what is it that the teacher must transmit? What is unique about his philosophy that needs to reach the student, both in content and meaning?

First, they need to know that not everything that must be taught is unique to the Rav. That is, most of us would agree that Modern Orthodox thinkers (if indeed that is an appropriate term at all by which to describe Rabbi Soloveitchik or Rav Kook, for example) share with others a basis in *halakhah*, in the Judaism of the *mesorah*, which is not shared with non-Orthodox thinkers. It is significant to know that some of the *hiddushei Torah* developed by the Rav have similarities in both form and substance to insights of others who come from the same Brisker tradition.[9] This is no coincidence. There is more in common among the Rav, Rav Kook, and *Roshei Yeshivah* in Lakewood or Benei Berak than some of our students (and, perhaps, some of our colleagues) would be comfortable admitting. Indeed, no matter how modern we paint them to be, they can neither be identified with modern secular Jews or religious denominations, nor with "modernity" as popularly defined. But, then, what is the difference between the Rav and his cousins? Or among the Rav, Rav Kook, and R. Diskin?

What differentiates the Rav, R. Kook, and those who understand their approach from other Torah thinkers is their awareness of the need to conceptualize and elucidate Torah in the vocabulary and modes of thought that the modern world comprehends. This is not just a pragmatic response to modernity – it is a dynamic opportunity. To highlight this awareness, let us first examine R. Kook's motivations in writing a book on *teshuvah*, and then return to the Rav.

In the Introduction to his *Orot ha-Teshuvah*, R. Kook makes the point that modern people need insight into repentance that is new and that is un-

---

[9] Similarly, it is significant to note that Rav Kook (in *Orot ha-Teshuvah* 13:5) suggested that the ability to understand and be Torah-observant in civil law is the best test of a Torah Jew, much as the Hazon Ish suggested that the knowledge of and fulfillment of *Hoshen Mishpat* (halakhic civil law) is the most telling test of the Torah Jew. See his *Emunah u-Vittahon* (Benai Berak, 1954, and many reprints), 3:10–13 (see also 3:1–5). To be clear, the Hazon Ish is implying that halakhic civil law is the only legitimate way of mediating disputes, and that without *halakhah* a person might be tempted to use his own intuition to figure things out.

available via the classic traditional writers on the subject – whether in *Tanakh*, in Talmud, or in the *rishonim*. He wrote this knowing full well that the *Hovot ha-Levavot, Sha'arei Teshuvah,* and Maimonides' *Hilkhot Teshuvah* were compelling, remarkable works on the subject. Yet these classic works did not speak to the modern person's way of understanding the dynamics of personal change. As R. Kook explicitly pointed out, modern people envision their world through new frameworks:

> I feel compelled to speak about repentance, and particularly about its literary and applied aspects, to create an understanding of its impact upon our generation, and to its realization in life, in the life of the individual and in the life of the community.[10]

In other words, R. Kook was sensitive to the need to present repentance from the perspective of the individual and the society – through the humanities, through psychological, and socio-political glasses. The more philosophical and theological approaches of the earlier classics do not speak to the modern sensibility. To Rav Kook, the nation will not come to repentance and the world will not be redeemed until literature and poetry express the depth and vision of repentance, as Judaism understands it. This insight permeates passage after passage of his works.

Similarly, Rabbi Soloveitchik offers insights into Judaism that speak the language of the modern person. His awareness of these areas was not a means to "convince" people of the value of being an Orthodox Jew. It was the perspective that he himself had, one that highlighted the significance of aspects of Torah that had not been emphasized by others before him. And so, his goal of developing a Torah perspective that grew from *halakhah*[11] reflected the philosophical realization that things must be understood in their own terms. Thus, identifying with Zionism, which he did despite his uneasiness in breaking with his family's position, was not an adventure outside of *halakhah* for him. The decision to join Mizrahi came from an awareness of the direction in which Torah leads, a direction the Rav felt his halakhic roots compelled him to take:

---

[10] R. Abraham I. Kook, *Orot ha-Teshuvah* (Jerusalem: Galor Press, 1977), p. 5. On the Rav's conception of *teshuvah* in this light, see Yitzchak Blau, "Creative Repentance: On Rabbi Soloveitchik's Concept of Teshuva," *Tradition* 28:2 (Winter 1994): 11–18.

[11] Cf. *The Halakhic Mind* (New York: Seth Press, 1986), pp. 100–102.

Thus the Mizrachi must understand that Jews like me, and others, who joined the movement and who draw their nourishment from the ancient talmudic soil of Abaye and Rava, are in the category of Joseph. They are required to sacrifice on this altar their peace of mind as well as their social relationships and friendships. The Mizrachi must also understand that we do not use the phrase "Zionism plus religion" or "religious Zionism." For us, there is only one unique noun – Torah. Israel is holy and dear because the Torah sanctified it and because the Torah's future is tied to it.[12]

Had the Rav lived in another century, this might not have been an issue that he would have been aware of, nor would he have written about it as he did. But he had a modern awareness of the world, and this awareness led him in new directions that the framework of *halakhah* could suggest in response to modernity. The Rav's framework was always halakhic. His insight into the significance of the *halakhah* is where the Rav was unique in his thinking.

Nevertheless, a unique perspective is sometimes reflected in the decisions that the Rav made. Again, there is a similarity to Rav Kook, whose awareness and halakhic evaluation of national values and needs had an impact on his decisions in regard to *shemittah*, or in his willingness to participate in the opening of the Hebrew University. Likewise, the Rav's view of the world led him to emphasize the value of the pursuit of knowledge in all spheres at Yeshiva University or his Maimonides School, and to forcefully resist those who would want to be permissive in regard to the need for *mehitzot* during prayer.[13] The Rav's very awareness came from his understanding of *halakhah*. For him and for Rav Kook, it was not a foreign force that took them away from Torah; rather it was a dynamic force born in Torah upon which they could shed new light for a generation that needed that illumination.

The development of independent and original insights that highlight the significance of Torah concepts and law is hardly a new phenomenon. Maimonides infused his *Mishneh Torah* with illuminating new insights – creating a matrix of *halakhah* with ethics and philosophy.[14] Seeing Torah

---

[12] *The Rav Speaks: Five Addresses* (Jerusalem: Tal Orot, 1983), p. 36.

[13] See R. Soloveitchik's essays in Baruch Litvin, *The Sanctity of the Synagogue* (Hoboken, NJ: Ktav, 1987 [3rd rev. ed.]), pp. 109–18, 139–41.

[14] See the important analysis provided in R. Isadore Twersky, *Introduction to the Code of Maimonides* (New Haven: Yale, 1980), esp. chap. 6 ("Law & Philosophy"). See also R. Twersky's contribution to: *Visions of Jewish Education*, ed. S. Fox, I. Scheffler, and D.

with new eyes, informed by the new insights of one's time, is an opportunity that *gedolim* throughout history took advantage of and pursued. It was not merely a tactic. It was the very expression of their dynamic relationship to Torah. As our students are being raised in a society that struggles with the issues that the Rav grappled with, it behooves us to start teaching them more effectively about the approach that can make Torah understanding and observance into the sorts of experiences that provide desirable insights. We cannot allow them to identify with the perspective that anything less than "yeshivish" is a shallow Judaism that compromises our essential values both in learning and in praxis. Pedagogically speaking, to wait until a student will be mature enough to "understand" R. Soloveitchik is to ensure that many of them will never understand him – and never be touched by his insights that speak directly to them when taught appropriately. At the high school age, the content of what the teacher presents the student ought to convey a sense of the connection of the process of learning to the creative forces that must be applied to Torah, no matter what aspect of the Rav's thought is examined. Failing that, the teacher has not succeeded in teaching the student what the Rav understood as the goals of study – a disciplined mind that recognizes the depth and beauty of what it examines.

Can Experience Be Taught?

I have briefly mentioned *halakhah* and Zionism as areas in which the Rav confronted and incorporated aspects of modernity. Later, I will identify the areas that might be the best to focus on when initially studying the Rav's thought with high school students. But first, we should consider further the realms that the Rav found difficult to convey: those of religious experience. Was the Rav's frustration unavoidable, due to the nature of what he knew needed to be taught? And even if he did fail to convey the sensitivity to experience, did he nevertheless leave us with ways to improve and succeed in teaching?

There are ways to convey the experiential aspect, requiring different levels of sophistication. A fairly simple way is through providing the student with the Rav's own history. This indeed may be part of what the Rav intended in telling people stories of his youth (as he frequently did), but, whether it was or not, it inspires an approach for the classroom teacher. These stories can open students to the very sort of experience that the Rav saw as absent from the modern student's life. To talk of the *heder rebbe*, or

---

Marom (Cambridge and New York: Cambridge Univ. Press, 2003), esp. the supplement to chap. 4 ("What Must a Jew Study – And Why?").

to talk of his experiencing the Days of Awe with his grandfather, or to talk of his experience of learning with his father R. Moshe,[15] is to provide an inspiration and a model to students that reaches them in a subjective, non-academic avenue. In order to enhance the potential of such an approach, the instructor must give background. A brief history beginning with the Rav's youth, upbringing, and education in Europe, and continuing on into his challenges and successes as a leader in America, gives context and reality to the stories and anecdotes that bring Jewish experience to life. This history should emphasize the dedication he showed to learning from childhood as nurtured by each parent, and should show that in no way was his education in his first two decades comparable to the sort of education our students receive. It should also highlight the intellectual interests that motivated the Rav to attend universities, as well as the range of his interests in university. This will allow students to discover that though there may be remarkable differences between the Rav's background and their own, students can ultimately see the Rav's life and works as an admirable spiritual quest based on a solid religious foundation. For some, the Rav's framework for pursuing wisdom in academic settings can be a model for their experiences. Thus, it is important to carefully present the Rav's life in a manner that does not reverberate as a myth, that avoids the danger of setting the Rav so far apart from the reality of students that the history is neither true to the Rav nor distinguishable from other lives of Torah leaders. Only then can it become a model that students can hope to emulate in their own ways.

But there is a deeper challenge to us – one that frustrated the Rav. There are religious issues and sensitivities that the Rav investigated that speak to the insightful student. There are perspectives unique to the Rav that can help the student enter into a deeper Jewish life imbued with dynamic potential, with a greater sense of purpose. Whether it is by understanding the Jewish response to evil, evaluating the existence of the State of Israel, or grappling with the tensions between the lonely person and the social person, a student will grow by learning the Rav's insights about such issues. But the insights need to be deepened via experiences. If only we could help the student incorporate them within him or herself, make such experiences foundations of his or her self-awareness and identity, then the Rav's second level of education could be achieved for the modern student.

---

[15] For example, see *Shi`urim le-Zekher Abba Mari* (Jerusalem, 1985), vol. 2, p. 15. For more general biographical background and its impact on the Rav's thought, see essays by R. Lichtenstein and R. Twersky in *Tradition* memorial volume (note 1, above), and R. Lichtenstein, "Joseph Soloveitchik" in *Great Jewish Thinkers of the Twentieth Century*, ed. S. Noveck, (Washington, DC: Bnai Brith, 1963), pp. 281–297.

But to do so is challenging. In order to find a way to succeed, we must uncover what impedes the handing over of deep spiritual experience.

The Rav himself provides an answer that goes beyond what we have discussed thus far. Much of education as we know it – as it is provided in *yeshivot*, universities, and secondary and elementary schools – is tied into language. The educational mode in the classroom may vary, may be discussion, dialogue, or lecture, but is inevitably verbal. Homework assignments may vary, but generally speaking the teaching of beliefs and ethics, and particularly of Torah, uses the written word. In contrast, the Rav describes the experience we need to convey as a lonely experience, and the teaching of that experience requires a non-verbal process. The Rav expressed this insight in many places. Typical teaching will not succeed where words do not easily go. What follow are two examples of how the Rav's insights help us discover entry points into the world of inexpressible religious experience.

In "The Lonely Man of Faith" the Rav develops the theme of the loneliness of Adam II.[16] This is not the place to summarize the relevant themes in the Rav's essay. It is enough for us to recall that the Rav emphasizes the impossibility of sharing who one "really is" with others, and that this problem is inherent in one's very being:

> "To be" is a unique in-depth experience of which only Adam the second is aware, and it is unrelated to any function or performance. "To be" means to be the only one, singular and different, and consequently lonely. For what causes man to be lonely and feel insecure if not the awareness of his uniqueness and exclusiveness? The "I" is lonely, experiencing ontological incompleteness and casualness, because there is no one who exists like the "I" and because the *modus existentiae* of the "I" cannot be repeated, imitated, or experienced by others.[17]

If this is the case, how is the transmission of spiritual experience possible? Here we are not talking about emotions, nor are we talking about mere excitement. Here we are confronted with the problem of transmitting how the "I," the person on the level of deep experience, can teach another person something that can be incorporated into one's essential identity, something that will "make one tick." How can that be done? It is a daunting task, akin to Moses teaching the Israelites in Egypt that they could access

---

[16] I am grateful to Dr. Elie Holzer of Bar-Ilan University for bringing the pedagogical ramifications of this text to my attention.

[17] *The Lonely Man of Faith* (New York: Doubleday, 1992), pp. 40–41.

new levels of identity and existence.[18] And yet it also is different from Moses in Egypt. In Egypt, Israel had to learn to speak, to gain confidence as a society and a covenantal community, and to take on the modes of free people. Jews had to move beyond sighs to the point where they could recall and express their story. It was a move outside the self, a move in the realm of Adam the first. This move was accomplished by a combination of miracles, leadership, and the merit of ancestors. But here the challenge is to move as Adam II, to move deep into the self, beyond speech. What lesson can resound so deeply as to touch this inner level of lonely self?

In response to this challenge, one should bear in mind that teaching an unsophisticated adolescent can be an opportunity. For example, youngsters are often challenged and confused, delighted and depressed, by the seemingly coercive role of *halakhah* in their lives. They wonder how it relates to their inner loneliness. This search leaves students open to conversations and ideas that are discussed all too infrequently by Torah teachers but are illuminated by the thought of the Rav. Because they are beginning to make sense of their own relationships to society, high school students will relate to the sensitivity of the Rav's analysis of the relationship of the individual to the community, relationships that are bewildering and invigorating to them at this time in life, when they are defining their own identities. At the same time, students will relate to the loneliness of Adam II, will appreciate some of the ways in which the Rav gives structure and vocabulary to what they intuitively sense. In short, studying sensitively chosen parts of the Rav's works can:

1.   give credence to the inner/outer struggle by placing it in a dialectic form that makes it a desideratum to struggle with, to confront and balance;

2.   give adolescents a useful vocabulary that will enable them to express their self-discovery as they grow within and through the context of Judaism; and

3.   show how Western society, culture, and philosophy have struggled with questions of individual and society, provide a critique of its proposed resolutions, and highlight the sensitivity to these issues found within Judaism that prevents reducing and simplifying such struggles to one of the two poles. In other words, it can show how our tradition allows us to grapple with the complexity and subtlety of reality.

---

[18] On this topic, it is worth reviewing the Rav's article, "Redemption, Prayer, Talmud Torah," *Tradition* 17:2 (Spring 1978): 55–72.

In addition, the Rav describes ways that *mitzvot* move us beyond the limitations of sharing experience, ways that break the language barrier by using other modes of experience. In his discussion of the conceptual foundations of the laws and of the impact of non-verbal forms of divine service in the Temple,[19] the Rav demonstrates how one can praise God even if one can never do so appropriately because "to You, silence is praise" (Ps. 65:2). The Rav presented a number of examples of worship inside and outside the Temple that were non-verbal, including wordless song and bowing:

> In the Temple, the Torah permitted us another manner in which to fulfill the verse "to You, silence is praise" – through a unique action, the structuring of God's praise in a mute mode, without speaker or word, that through wordless melody via musical instruments...This inner passion [*hitlahavut*] is beyond all cognitive explanation or logical structuring... The fulfillment of silence [in praise] is actualized through the cessation of speech.[20]

In reference to bowing, the *halakhah* demands that when the s*hem ha-meforash* (Tetragrammaton) is pronounced in the Temple, the listeners silently bow. To the Rav, this was another application of the principle that silence is the ultimate praise, as the intensified contact between man and God available only in the Temple demanded a heightened sensitivity to the demands of appropriate praise.

But the form that we can best relate to in our day is that of the *shofar*. The Rav explained that *shofar* is itself a mode of prayer. On Rosh Hashanah, even in our day, without the opportunity to enter the Temple, we are before God. The *shofar* has been associated with the proximity of the divine presence throughout our history, such as at Sinai. On Rosh Hashanah it plays that role every year. And much as wordless song is praise in the Temple, the *halakhah* of s*hofar* is one of "song without words, in the simple voice of the s*hofar*. It imposes upon us the obligation of silence and stillness through the *shofar*, through a prayer that is wordless and speechless, the voice of the plain *teru'ah*."[21] It is in this manner that the *shofar* eloquently makes us aware of the limitations of speech in reaching the depth of spiritual experience, by removing words and substituting non-verbal experiences that inspire awe or allude to experiences such as Sinai, where the very

---

[19] "*Be-Inyan Tekiah ve-Shirah ba-Mikdash*," in *Shi`urim le-Zekher Abba Mari*, vol. 2, pp. 69–75.

[20] *Ibid.*, p. 72.

[21] *Ibid.*, p. 74. Cf. *Yemei Zikkaron*, pp. 137–52.

transcendent nature of the experience reverberated beyond words. At the same time, melody and bowing in the Temple and *shofar* on Rosh Hashanah all have the potential to trigger the depth of spiritual experience that words, even the highest praises, cannot reach.

The educator must remind students that they will not grow as Jews without such experiences. It is the instructor's challenge to highlight those aspects of Torah, *halakhah*, Talmud, and so forth that allude to this depth of spiritual experience. And, finally, we must search out those situations that bring forth that depth, and invite the students to participate in the great experiential aspect of Judaism. In this sense, the teacher must emulate the *heder rebbe* who succeeded that day in Khaslavichy. And in this sense, although the Rav protested that he had not done enough, he provided a model for doing more.

Why Not Wait Until Later?

A high school student is at a critical juncture in his or her life. Students survive high school, some gracefully and dynamically, others by the skin of their teeth. Many responsibilities they did not ask for are imposed upon them; many of their interests lack a place in school. For these reasons, it might seem too soon to approach a high school student with a challenging course of studies, and it might meet with cynicism and resistance.

But there is no better time. At this point, particularly toward the end of high school, one's cognitive abilities reach a mature level, and social interactions reach a new sophistication. One's vision of the future begins to take into account more than one's immediate needs. There is a new awareness of one's personal destiny as it is shared with one's family, one's people, and humanity. Students begin to lock into ideals and commitments. If we are to reach students on these levels, adolescence is the time. To deny them access to the philosophy that underlies their education is to deny them an opportunity to identify with that philosophy as idealists. To wait for them to gain a philosophy after high school risks their never encountering the core values and ideas we mean to promote. Finally, it also prevents some students from incorporating the self-awareness that would help their high school studies gain the significance that the Rav intended for students to experience.

Students in high school do not come by this knowledge without help. Sadly, many students spend their high school careers without encountering a serious presentation of the very ideas and ideals for which they were sent to a Jewish high school. In a talk to parents of the Maimonides School in 1968, the Rav described the ideas at the root of the high school in terms familiar from "The Lonely Man of Faith." He contrasted the predicament of the modern American Jew to the situation of the "old-fashioned" Jew. The old-fashioned Jew had a sense of security – he knew he was right in observing Judaism and in his confrontations with the non-Jew. The modern Jew does not have this sense of security. The modern Jew questions who he or she is and what he or she stands for, and is at a loss to fully explain the very claim to uniqueness in a society that is critical of his or her identity. The modern Jew is both lonely and alone.

Issues such as these are important – and are rarely presented in an intelligent, well-structured manner in the high school classroom. The Rav was an optimist when it came to the potential for students to become dynamic Jews and dynamic learners through the dual curriculum he inspired at Maimonides School in Boston. In talks to parents, he consistently reiterated that the goal of Jewish education was literacy as a Jew and as a human being, and that education ought to guide students to understanding their potential and destiny as Jews in the world:

> The philosophical reasoning responsible for this optimism concerning the compatibility of the sacred with the mundane, the religious with the secular, is rooted in the thought that Judaism has never distinguished between these allegedly two areas of being. Judaism believes there is no duality in nature... Either everything is profane or everything is sacred. It is up to man either to extend Kedushah to every niche and corner of the universe or to desecrate even the Holy of Holies, the last cubit in the Sanctuary.[22]

A student capable of taking up the challenge of a dual curriculum, in which he or she is expected to unify what much of the Orthodox world understands as an irresolvable dialectic between the holy and the mundane, ought to have every opportunity to examine the foundations of his or her educational philosophy. The best way to do so is by examining the life and thought of the Rav.

The High School Seminar
The vitality of Judaism in the mind of the high school student is a function of its capacity to make sense of and give meaning to life in the world and of its potential to give the student access to ideals, along with a vocabulary to express ideas. In this sense, the reluctance to teach R. So-

---

[22] "Legacy" (special edition of *Kol Rambam: Maimonides School Newsletter*, Brookline, MA, October 1993).

loveitchik's thought in an exciting, structured manner is a denial of vision to adolescents who are thirsting to discover and refine their vision. Indeed, it may be true that high school students are unfamiliar with Spengler or *Zohar*, Otto or Brisk. Yet, many students in the Rav's *shi'ur* were similarly unfamiliar with the world of sources that provided the background to his thought. They did not on that account deny themselves the benefit of the Rav's teachings to whatever extent they could understand them. Nor do we use a lack of Torah or academic background as excuses not to present the thought of Yehudah ha-Levi, Maimonides, or the Maharal in a classroom. Many high school instructors do not hesitate to present their students with intricate *pilpulim* or subtle *hakirot*. With R. Soloveitchik's thought available in both Hebrew and English, one must question whether his thought is not taught from his own words because it is inherently difficult or because teachers and schools are not adequately committed to making the learning approachable. To do so would involve the teacher in genuine pedagogical planning and curricularizing, in breaking the material down into steps, in giving sufficient background, and in reaching students with challenging issues to which we have no simplistic solutions.

I was involved in developing and evaluating a curriculum that introduces the Rav's thought to high school students. Variations of the curriculum are now being implemented in a number of schools throughout North America. In its original format the curriculum presented twelfth-grade students with the following:

1. A History of the Rav in the context of his times (without recourse to creating a "myth" of the Rav).
2. Introduction to the Rav's thought through the texts he himself wrote.
3. A diversity of texts – primarily from *Shi'urim le-Zekher Abba Mari*, articles from *Tradition*, and his books.
4. Coverage of four key areas: prayer, Zionism, Torah study, and response to modernity.

Important to the success of this curriculum is the attempt to encourage students to grapple with the text itself. The excitement of learning the Rav's thought demands discovering the Rav's method of analysis. Thus, it demands active and aggressive learning that recreates the struggle that creative and rigorous thinkers like the Rav experience when analyzing text. For example, when I taught a class about the Rav's perspective on learning Torah based on his *shi'ur* on *birkhot ha-Torah*,[23] I made sure that prior to seeing what the Rav wrote, students learned the passages from the *Mishneh Torah* that the Rav analyzed. I asked students to list the problems that Maimonides' statements and sources created, and to discover the contradictions and gaps in explanation that required examination. Once students had prepared the text, we shared thoughts about what needed resolution, and even hazarded a few theories in response to the questions that were raised. Only then did we examine what the Rav wrote. By doing so, I ensured that students would experience the triumph of being bothered by questions that bothered the Rav, while gaining an enhanced appreciation of the elegance of his resolution and the proofs offered for it (including his personal relationship to his father, mentioned above). Through this process most students (though, admittedly, not all) were able to grasp the intellectual excitement involved and sense the emotional vigor that was necessary to be thrilled with learning. They were neither too young nor too inexperienced to be engaged by Torah study. They got a taste of "service of the heart" through their learning about how *limmud Torah* itself is ideally "*avodah she-ba-lev.*" This text also prepared students for a number of themes that recur in the Rav's writings about the unique importance of learning.

Another key to the success of the curriculum is giving students the opportunity to research issues that concern them. The faculty made an effort to match willing students with issues the Rav discussed and helped those students prepare presentations on those issues. On the final day of the seminar, a group of students gave presentations to their peers, teachers, and parents at a *siyyum* based on the ideas of the Rav that they had learned from his writings and recordings. While experiencing the voice of the Rav and showing others what it said to them, they discovered that the Rav spoke to their situation in a manner that gave them insights, unavailable elsewhere, into their relationships with the Torah and the world.

In the years following the early implementation of the seminars, I asked a number of students about the impact the sessions had upon them. Typical responses included:

1. "Until the seminar, we had no clear idea throughout high school about the underlying themes of our own education. It made sense of it all."

2. "Even with the seminar, we did not appreciate what was being taught to us until we went to study in Israel or in college, and there had to explain,

---

[23] *Shi'urim le-Zekher Abba Mari*, vol. 2, pp. 1–16.

uphold, or defend the ideas represented in the Rav's thought. This in turn sensitized us to the uniqueness of his approach."

3. "We wish we had gained some perspective and self-awareness earlier."

The Rav was one of the few who trusted in the Torah and its ideals to "educate, not indoctrinate"[24] the next generation in preparation for the future. It is this approach that will lead to profound, rather than only social or cultural, commitment of our students to Judaism. It will help them partake of a Judaism of in-depth experience. The task of appropriately presenting the Rav's thought and life to high school students is still before us, and the need is still urgent. Ask the students; they will tell you so. It is up to us to respond by formulating better and increasingly sensitive ways to present Rabbi Soloveitchik's thoughts in his own words to our students, in the hope that with the right blend of substance, pedagogy, and inspiration, we will create visionaries committed to Torah. Many questions remain to be asked – such as the right age at which to present material and whether to work on halakhic analysis or philosophy. Perhaps there is no one answer – one size does not fit all. But as the Rav provided many with the perspective to grasp the future through Judaism, and was frustrated when he felt he could not do so, so too must we share that frustration until we have done something about it, something that helps others to redemption.[25]

---

[24] Cf. the Rav's comments in "Legacy."

[25] See the insightful remark of Shalom Carmy in "Of Eagle's Flight and Snail's Pace," *Tradition* 29:1 (Fall 1994): 29:

> The Rav wants more *for* us, and consequently asks more *of* us. Reluctant and disappointed, we summon the popularizers, the politicians, the polemicists, who, with their unfailing affinity for the superficial and the half true, bravely try to make him do, and purvey many anecdotes. Rather than blame the Rav for demanding too much of us, we would do well to rouse ourselves to take full advantage of what he offers us.

VIRTUAL VOLOZHIN:
SOCIALIZATION VS. LEARNING IN ISRAEL
YESHIVAH PROGRAMS

YOEL FINKELMAN

THERE ARE TWO PASTS. One is the sequence of occurred events, or actions which were performed... There is another past. This is the perceived past. This is a much more plastic thing, more capable of being retrospectively reformed by human beings living in the present.[1]

The Changing Context of Yeshivah Education

When R. Hayyim of Volozhin first founded his yeshivah in 1803, it allowed a few elite students to dedicate several years exclusively to Torah study. The yeshivah provided for all their needs so that the students would be free to study. Their studies had little or no pragmatic function, although many graduates used their knowledge to pursue careers in the rabbinate or in Jewish education. The majority of Eastern European Jewish men completed their formal education during their early teen years, and only the intellectual elite spent any time at all in institutions for advanced study. Yeshivahs were responsible for providing the ideal environment in which to maximize Torah study for this small group of elite students.

The yeshivah, in that context, was responsible neither for creating Jewish identity nor for ensuring that Jews would continue to observe *mitzvot*. The Jew identified as a Jew as a matter of course and took traditional halakhic observance for granted. For traditional Eastern European Jewish society, the yeshivah provided education for the next generation of rabbis, judges, and other religious functionaries. For the students, the yeshivah provided upward mobility, supplying the education that pushed them into

---

[1] Edward Shils, *Tradition* (Chicago: Univ. Chicago, 1981), p. 195.

the socio-intellectual elite and giving them the opportunity to marry into the economic elite.

As *haskalah* and emancipation swept the Jews of Eastern Europe in the second half of the nineteenth and beginning of the twentieth centuries, the majority of Jews ceased to be fully observant, and the social function of the yeshivah changed as well. Increasingly, identity as a halakhic Jew, or as a Jew at all, ceased to be a matter of course. "Orthodoxy," as a denominational alternative to non-halakhic streams of Judaism, developed over the nineteenth century, when the basic social structure became less encouraging of halakhic behavior. The yeshivah gradually came to play a more crucial function in the creation and maintenance of Orthodox identity. Over the course of the nineteenth and twentieth centuries, yeshivahs often became more isolated from the increasingly non-Orthodox environments, and they spent more time and energy inculcating Orthodox ideology and patterns of behavior.[2]

This trend continues, particularly in the Modern Orthodox one-year yeshivah[3] programs in Israel that cater to students from the Diaspora. Over the past several decades, a growing number of Modern Orthodox day school graduates from English-speaking countries, perhaps even a large majority of them, choose to spend a year or two of full-time Torah study in Israel following their graduation from high school. Tens of institutions – yeshivahs for men and seminaries for women – cater to the unique needs of this student body. Obviously, these yeshivahs are not meant to educate the next generation of Orthodox educational and rabbinic leadership, as the original Lithuanian yeshivahs were. Only a small percentage of contemporary yeshivah graduates will enter rabbinic fields professionally. The over-

---

[2] Shaul Stampfer follows some of these changes in his *Ha-Yeshivah ha-Lita'it be-Hithavutah* (Jerusalem: Zalman Shazar Center, 1995); see also his "*Ha-Penimiah ve-ha-Yeshivah be-Mizrah Eiropah*," in *Ha-Hinukh ha-Penimiati ha-Mamlakhti Dati be-Yisra'el*, ed. Matityahu Dagan (Jerusalem: Ministry of Education, 1997), pp. 20–31; his "Heder Study, Knowledge of Torah, and the Maintenance of Social Stratification in Eastern European Jewish Society," *Studies in Jewish Education* 3 (1998): 271–289; Charles Selengut, "By Torah Alone: Yeshiva Fundamentalism in Jewish Life," in *Accounting for Fundamentalism*, ed. Martin Marty and F. Scott Appleby (Chicago: Univ. of Chicago, 1994), pp. 236–263. On the transition from Europe to the United States, see my "Haredi Isolation in Changing Environments: A Case Study in Yeshiva Immigration," *Modern Judaism* 22:1 (2002): 61–82, as well as William Helmreich, *The World of the Yeshiva* (New York and London: Free Press, 1982).

[3] Unless otherwise stated, the term "yeshivah" in this essay will refer to those one-year yeshivah programs in Israel that cater to Modern Orthodox students from the Diaspora. Obviously, there are many other kinds of contemporary yeshivahs; they are not a focus of this essay, though my comments may bear some relevance to other contexts as well.

whelming majority will attend college and choose white-collar professions. The overarching goal of these yeshivahs is to educate the next generation of educated, active, and committed laymen. These programs help to resocialize students out of what yeshivahs often perceive as a problematic American Modern Orthodoxy,[4] and into a more ideal religious observance. Casual observation, and one scientific study, indicate that this year in Israel has a profound impact on the religious practice, ideological commitment, and social identification of students.[5] There is little doubt that the phenomenon of a year spent learning in Israel has a generally positive effect on the students, and, by extension, on the Diaspora Orthodox community as a whole. These very important successes make it all the more surprising to parents, educators, and students that many yeshivah alumni fail to gain the basic skills with which to study a *sugya* (topic in Talmud or *halakhah*) on their own.[6]

I would like to argue that part of the reason why many students fail to acquire these skills is that contemporary yeshivahs are not primarily designed to develop student independence in Torah study. Yeshivahs are caught between two goals, which seem to be compatible in theory but may be contradictory in practice. They are dedicated to the goal of teaching the students how to learn, but they often are more concerned with their function as molders of Orthodox identity and practice. At times, the furtherance of the socio-religious goals comes at the expense of academic goals. The manifest function of the Gemara *shi'ur* is to teach the text of the Talmud and its traditional commentaries and to further the students' ability to study Talmud independently. But there exists a significant latent function as well: to further the students' social and ideological identification with Orthodoxy in general, and, in many cases, with a "yeshivish" kind of Orthodoxy in particular. *Rebbeim* (Talmud teachers) frequently choose to sacrifice

---

[4] For the sake of this discussion, I prefer not to take a detailed position on whether the yeshivah's criticisms of American Modern Orthodoxy are accurate. I believe that there is much to improve in American Modern Orthodoxy, but that yeshivahs often exaggerate these weaknesses.

[5] See Shalom Berger, "A Year of Study in an Israeli Yeshiva Program: Before and After," (D.Ed. thesis, Yeshiva University, 1997). A much-abridged version of this thesis appeared as "The Impact of One-Year Israel Study on American Day School Graduates," *Ten Da'at* 12 (Summer 1999): 5–14.

[6] Some students emerge from yeshivah with independent skills in the basics of Talmud study; a great many others, probably the majority, do not. Unfortunately, we have no detailed evidence of the skill levels of yeshivah graduates, other than the informal observation of staff, students, and alumni, since yeshivahs do not administer any kind of standardized tests. Staff and alumni whom I interviewed agreed unanimously that many students emerge from yeshivah incapable of studying Talmud on their own.

the academic goals for the sake of advancing their socio-religious ones. I will argue that it may be possible to improve the skills-oriented achievements, at least for some students, without significantly damaging the socio-religious growth.

My comments are, to a great degree, anecdotal and may not be provable in any precise or scientific way. This analysis derives from my experience as a student, dorm counselor, and teacher in various yeshivahs, as well as from extended interviews I conducted with staff, students, and alumni. My comments focus primarily on mainstream men's institutions, particularly those that attract students of better-than-average academic record. These institutions are not monolithic, and my comments are deliberately at a level of generalization to be (I believe) accurate, though they do not correspond to every detail in every institution. Furthermore, these thoughts may or may not have any bearing on *haredi* (ultra-Orthodox) *yeshivot*, on Modern Orthodox women's programs,[7] or Modern Orthodox men's programs that specialize in weaker students, at-risk youth, or *ba'alei teshuvah* (newly Orthodox). Either these comments will resonate with the experience and observation of the reader, or they will not. If they do, I hope that they will help motivate a rethinking of some of the methods employed by yeshivahs to achieve their goals.

The Typical Morning Talmud Class in Yeshivah

Most yeshivah Gemara classes are structured similarly. The morning study session begins between 8:30 and 9:00 AM, and ends at lunch time, about 12:30. The overwhelming majority of the time is dedicated to Talmud, although some students might spend the first half-hour or so studying other material. In general, the morning schedule is divided into two parts: the *seder* and the *shi'ur*. Commonly, the *seder* occupies some two to three hours, while *shi'ur* takes up the last hour or so before lunch. During *seder*, the students learn in a *havruta* format, working in pairs over relatively short passages of text. Students are given direction through the use of *mar'eh mekomot*: a list of passages in the Talmud or traditional commentaries that the students are to prepare. A morning's material might consist of half a page of Gemara with Rashi's commentary, a paragraph of *Tosafot* or another medieval commentary, a few paragraphs from Rambam's code, with perhaps a page or so of a more recent commentary. Although the text itself is quite short, it is complex enough and written compactly enough to occupy students, theoretically, for the entire morning. Teachers often understand that

---

[7] But see the appendix below, for some brief comments on women's programs.

much of the material they assign is beyond the students' ability, particularly at the beginning of the year.

Rebbeim identify a number of obstacles to the most effective use of *seder* time.[8] First, students often lack adequate skills even to translate the texts. Second, even when students can translate the text in question, they often lack the critical tools to process the information. Students may understand what the text says, but not understand *why* it says what it says, or why it does not say something else. Third, it is not always immediately obvious how different commentaries relate to the primary sources, and certainly not how the different sources work together in constructing a systematic *sugya*. Students might read and translate the sources without understanding how they relate to the bigger picture. Most teachers find written or oral ways of guiding students through material that they are not capable of understanding or processing on their own. Teachers are generally present during *seder* and circulate from *havruta* to *havruta*, offering guidance and assistance. These methods do not solve the problems entirely, however. The students with whom I spoke still found that much of the material was beyond their grasp, at least until it was explained in *shi'ur*.

After the students prepare the sources during *seder*, the class gathers for *shi'ur*, a more frontal lecture. The teacher reads or summarizes the *mar'eh mekomot*, while raising questions about them. The teacher organizes the disparate sources into a coherent whole. Different commentaries might be grouped together, emphasizing their shared approach to a certain aspect of the *sugya*. Passages from the Talmud and commentaries that might appear to be disconnected are linked in a way that indicates certain conceptual similarities. In general, the lecture (or series of lectures) culminates in a *hiddush*, a creative analysis of the sources that serves to answer the questions raised during class. This *hiddush* is viewed as the pinnacle of the study, the deepest understanding possible for the *rebbe* and students.

More often than not, the *shi'ur* is a relatively formal lecture. The teacher speaks out loud, asking questions, explaining the Gemara, and leading the lecture towards its climax – the *hiddush*. The teacher tries to tie together all of the assigned sources, linking them in a chain of argument. *Rebbeim* often ask the students leading questions, hoping to guide them toward independent thinking. Even then, the lecture retains its defined structure. The teacher has a pre-planned direction, and questions are designed primarily to help the students predict the next step in the teacher's prepared argument.

---

[8] I refer only to problems involving analysis of text, not to problems of motivation, attendance, and discipline.

A Skills-Oriented Talmud Curriculum

A small minority of *rebbeim* employ an alternative to the standard class. We will refer to this method as a skills-oriented approach. This course of study places much greater emphasis on transmitting skills and independence to students. Although these classes share the basic *seder-shi'ur* structure, they differ from the standard classes in certain critical ways. In general, the skills-oriented curriculum moves at a slower pace, covering less text but demanding that students do the work almost entirely on their own. Lists of *mar'eh mekomot* are shorter and less elaborate, emphasizing the Gemara itself and placing less stress on commentaries, particularly more obscure commentaries. These classes work intensely to define method, making sure that students understand what they are doing and why they are doing it. *Shi'ur* summarizes what students could or should have been able to do on their own, primarily checking to make sure that they did it right, rather than describing something new. Hence, the *hiddush* and the lecture in general are seen as much less central. I would like to expand on six ways in which the skills-oriented curriculum differs from the standard one.

1. In the standard curriculum, the emphasis is on *lomdus* (abstract Talmudic analysis) and *hiddush*, even though students may not have read or translated the sources carefully or precisely. There is less focus on close, systematic text analysis and more focus on the conceptual ideas that underlie an argument or a position. In contrast, the text-oriented courses emphasize translation, grammar, and precise understanding of the words on the pages as a prerequisite for understanding the more abstract ideas that those words represent. Furthermore, because of the text-based concern with methodology, skills-oriented classes accentuate the aspects of Gemara study that take place between translation and *lomdus*. For the most part, the students and teachers I interviewed had very little to say about what happens between reading and dealing with abstract issues. There is, however, a vast amount of work – unpacking, for lack of a better term – that must happen before any reasonable *lomdus* analysis can take place. This includes understanding the text of the Gemara as precisely as possible and identifying ambiguities in it. Further, it includes identifying questions on the Gemara, questions that the *rishonim* are likely to deal with, and thinking about possible answers. It means understanding, as precisely as possible, every case in the Gemara (or at least identifying possible understandings), or every question or answer in the Gemara's text. This also includes identifying why Rashi comments wherever he comments and distinguishing where Rashi merely translates from where he adds information that other *rishonim*

might dispute. Obviously, there are different methods, and each *rebbe* works out for himself how he views the best way to do rigorous analysis of Gemara. However one chooses to define the exact steps that should be followed in studying Talmud, a failure to take those steps creates a danger that students will arrive at incorrect, simplistic, or imprecise understandings of the Gemara.

2. In standard classes, students are often asked to prepare sources even though they do not have the text or analytical skills to do so properly. The teacher explains these sources to the students during class. In the skills-oriented class, students are given sources and assignments that they are capable of working through on their own or that are only slightly more difficult than that. Consequently, the material becomes more difficult over the course of the year. If *shi'ur* includes information that students cannot acquire on their own, it is de-emphasized and covered briefly.

3. Standard classes are often spotty in their presentation of a complete methodological system. Only certain aspects of the method are made explicit, generally those associated with *lomdus* or with the development of *hiddush*. Teachers will present ideas during class, without explaining what method they used to arrive at that conclusion. The skills-oriented curriculum tries to be systematic, and self-consciously tries to develop a systematic method of learning. Each *sugya*, in its entirety, is treated in a relatively predictable, step-by-step, way. When students complete step one (perhaps reading and translating the Gemara), they will know to proceed to step two (perhaps charting the basic arguments and opinions in their notebooks). From there students will proceed to step three (perhaps preparing a list of questions on the Gemara). Teachers will avoid explaining content without also dealing with method.

4. The standard curriculum is more *shi'ur* oriented. The goal of the *seder* time is to prepare for the *shi'ur*, where the *hiddush* and the *lomdus* occur. This helps explain the emphasis on difficult sources, which are necessary for *shi'ur*, but too difficult for students. In contrast, the skills-oriented curriculum emphasizes the *seder* rather than the *shi'ur*. *Shi'ur* generally clarifies what the students understood on their own during *seder*, assuring them that they understood it correctly, or correcting them if they did not.

5. The standard curriculum moves more quickly than the skills-oriented class. In the standard program, less time is spent on any given text or on a *sugya* in general. The skills-based curriculum covers less ground, placing greater emphasis on a more thorough and precise understanding of the material that is covered.

6. In the standard curriculum, students struggle to stay one step ahead of the teacher. Students try to predict what the *rebbe* is going to say in class. This is done either during *seder,* by attempting to figure out how the teacher is going to interpret and link the different sources, or during class, when the *rebbe* asks leading questions hoping to get the students to predict what he is going to say next. In the skills-oriented curriculum, students try to stay one step ahead of the *sugya,* rather than the teacher. That is to say, students try to anticipate the questions that the Gemara is going to raise about the Mishnah, to anticipate the next step of the Talmud's argument, to antici-pate the problems the *rishonim* will raise and the answers they are likely to give. The relatively slow pace makes it easier to do so in a systematic way. Consequently, the standard curriculum may include many obscure sources that logically connect to the teacher's thought patterns, though they may not be the most basic texts relating to the issue at hand. In contrast, the skills-oriented curriculum focuses on the basics, emphasizing the text of the Gemara itself and the most essential commentaries.

This is not meant to place any given *shi'ur* or teacher firmly into one category or the other. It is meant to generalize about overall approaches, while allowing for individual differences in any given classroom. In general, most curricula contain aspects of both models, although the majority closely resemble the standard curriculum. For our purposes, these distinc-tions help clarify how the skills-oriented curriculum is designed to create student independence in Talmud study.

Yeshivahs and Resocialization

It might seem obvious to some that student independence ought to be the primary goal of a Gemara *shi'ur.* If this were the case, the skills-oriented curriculum would be vastly superior to the standard one in virtually every respect. Yet in practice it seems that the standard *shi'ur* is much more common, even though these courses often leave students without adequate ability to learn on their own. Why do schools offer these advanced classes, when students often lack the most basic textual and analytical skills? It seems to me that we may gain insight into this and other aspects of life in contemporary yeshivahs if we examine these institutions through sociologi-cal glasses rather than talmudic ones. Many of the peculiarities of the stan-dard curriculum can be explained if we view the classes not as attempts to develop student independence in Talmud study but as part of an educa-tional system that is deeply committed to socializing students into the kind of Orthodoxy with which the yeshivahs identify.

Contemporary yeshivahs, unlike the Lithuanian yeshivahs of old, do not expect to turn out graduates who are comfortable in rabbinic literature, who are capable of issuing halakhic rulings, or serving as rabbis[9] or teachers. If Lithuanian yeshivahs housed students for several years, perhaps even a decade or more,[10] contemporary yeshivahs almost never have any Diaspora students who remain beyond the second year. Indeed, most yeshivahs do not offer rabbinical ordination programs at all. While a fair percentage of yeshivah alumni, if not a majority, will attend Yeshiva University, and pursue three more years of part-time yeshivah study, few will continue in full time yeshivah alternatives for a long period of time, and fewer still will continue for rabbinic ordination. Contemporary yeshivahs, then, do not serve to teach prospective rabbis or educators, but, rather, a grass-roots group of educated and dedicated laymen.[11]

In order to develop these dedicated laymen, yeshivahs attempt to resocialize their students out of American Modern Orthodoxy, of which yeshivahs are usually very critical. Modern Orthodox standards, according to many yeshivahs, fall short of basic halakhic requirements, let alone the religious ideal, particularly in the areas of relationships between the sexes, modesty in dress, the value of Torah study, commitment to *halakhah* and rabbinic authority, and in resisting absorption of the negative aspects of general culture. The typical yeshivah student, from the yeshivah's perspective, grew up in just such a Modern Orthodox home, attended a Modern Orthodox high school with an inadequate environment, and has largely absorbed flawed Modern Orthodox values. Over the course of the year in Israel, the student is to be resocialized into more acceptable religious standards. Some schools hope to move students out of the Modern Orthodox

---

[9] Lithuanian yeshivahs were not consciously designed to train rabbis, though there was a tacit understanding that many graduates would work as rabbis after leaving yeshivah and yeshivahs would allow students to study for the rabbinate. Among students, particularly the younger ones who did not have to support a family, studying for the rabbinate was often viewed as an inferior kind of study. See Immanuel Etkes, "Talmudic Scholarship and the Rabbinate in Lithuanian Jewry During the Nineteenth Century," in his *The Gaon of Vilna: The Man and His Image* (Berkeley: Univ. of California, 2002), pp. 209–231.

[10] Lithuanian yeshivah students often divided their time among many yeshivahs, spending a few years in each.

[11] Informal observers indicate that they have met with a measure of success. Increasingly, Modern Orthodoxy has become a more Torah-educated, more halakhically committed community in the United States; this is an aspect of what may be considered a communal shift to the "right." See Chaim I. Waxman, "The Haredization of American Orthodox Jewry," *Jerusalem Letter / Viewpoints* #376 (Feb. 15, 1998), pp. 3–5. Many attribute some of these trends to the influence of the yeshivahs on Orthodox laymen.

camp entirely, into a *haredi* approach. Others hope to move them from a flawed Modern Orthodoxy into a more ideal one. These differences notwithstanding, most programs share a negative evaluation of much of contemporary Modern Orthodoxy, and hope to educate better alumni.

Yeshivahs use many methods to resocialize students. They isolate students in relatively closed institutions, far away from the "inadequate" home environment. A proper religious atmosphere holds sway in this isolated environment.[12] The yeshivah emphasizes its values constantly, in *musar* (religious ethics) lectures, *divrei Torah*, and informal conversations between students and staff. As the year progresses, and more students become more "*frum*" (religiously committed), peer pressure helps motivate students to participate more actively in the yeshivah's program.[13] Social standing relative to the staff can depend, at least in part, on proper religious behavior and adequate study habits. Informal rewards and praise are given to students who participate actively in the religious and educational aspects of yeshivah life. Students who complete a major unit of study celebrate a *siyyum*, in which they gain public recognition for their accomplishment. There is little formal punishment, but informal and formal deterrents against inappropriate behavior abound. The informal deterrents, which are probably the most effective, are manifest in the absence of many of the rewards: lack of attention and praise from staff, as well as peer pressure. A student who does not attend classes, does not study, does not attend prayer services, or does not live up to the yeshivah's standards in other areas may get a stern lecture, or even be expelled if the behavior continues for long enough.

The yeshivah succeeds most thoroughly when the student begins to identify himself as a member of the yeshivah community. Modern Jews in general, and American Jews in particular, often develop strong Jewish commitments when they participate in small communities that create a sense of meaning and belonging for the participants.[14] If the students enjoy themselves in yeshivah, then the yeshivah can do just that. It creates a warm, relatively intimate Jewish environment, in which meaning and community are imbibed each day. The transformed yeshivah student comes to

---

[12] Modern Orthodox yeshivah programs are, however, considerably less isolationist than many *haredi* yeshivahs. On the relationship between social isolation and a yeshivah's educational agenda, see my "Haredi Isolation" and Stampfer, "*Ha-Penimiah.*"

[13] Sometimes, however, there can be a backlash against second-year students, who seem to preach too much to less "religious" students.

[14] See Arnold Eisen, *Taking Hold of Torah: Jewish Commitment and Community in America* (Bloomington and Indianapolis: Indiana Univ. Press, 1997). Many of Eisen's suggestions for creating community could be productively adapted by Orthodoxy.

identify himself as the kind of Jew who belongs in the yeshivah's community and who lives up to its values. The student who enjoys his time in yeshivah is more likely to emerge firmly committed to halakhic observance, to Torah study as a lifelong value, to separation between the sexes, to the value of living in Israel, etc. He is more likely to oppose the potentially corrupting influences of aspects of contemporary Western culture as well as what yeshivahs see as the compromises that the Modern Orthodox community has made in its religious life.

Personal identification with the yeshivah and its values is often manifest in ways other than changed attitudes and renewed commitment to *halakhah*. Resocialized students may begin to dress differently. Some will don the yeshivah-style black hat, wear a suit jacket to prayers, or simply stop wearing shorts and T-shirts. Students may adopt "yeshivish" jargon, saying "*mistama*" instead of "probably," for example.[15] Together with the books that they need for their studies, students may buy stacks of advanced *sefarim* that they would not understand, even were they to open them. While these outward behaviors are not mandated by Jewish law, and do not seem to have any direct relationship to religious values, they indicate, both to the student himself and to others, identification with the "yeshivish" community.[16]

Whatever the teachers' attitudes toward these outward changes, the schools do hope that students will come to identify with the yeshivah and maintain that identity as they enter college and the workplace. Students are more likely to do so if they enjoy the yeshivah environment. Yeshivahs have a variety of methods to insure that students enjoy themselves: regular hikes and field trips; on-campus sports facilities; Shabbat and holiday programs in yeshivah, which include singing, dancing, and extra food; and invitations to teachers' homes during weekends and vacations. Certainly, the academic aspects of the curriculum, which take up the lion's share of the time, must also be enjoyable.

A skills-oriented Talmud curriculum would frustrate students, as well as the yeshivah's hope to keep students motivated and satisfied. The yeshivah's broader social goals cannot allow such frustration. A student who enjoys the experience of Torah study, even if he never gains textual competence himself, is more likely to adopt the new "yeshivish" identity than one

---

[15] For a somewhat humorous explication of this jargon, see Chaim M. Weiser, *Frumspeak: The First Dictionary of Yeshivish* (Northvale, NJ: Aronson, 1995).

[16] Of course, problems ensue when students adopt these outward signs of identification without internalizing the yeshivah community's more significant religious values.

who does not enjoy his learning experience. Students who lack text skills may be able to think abstractly, or at least appreciate a sharp idea. Students will feel challenged by the *lomdus* and will feel a sense of accomplishment in arriving at a *hiddush,* whether or not they can actually read the page of Talmud being discussed. Ensuring that students enjoy their time in yeshivah and feel a sense of accomplishment helps further the yeshivah's larger socio-religious goals, even if it hurts the student's ability to understand and analyze a *sugya.* There is little social benefit in emphasizing the frustrating aspects of a skills-oriented education, even though such a program might create greater academic independence. Educated laymen need not become competent in Talmud study, as long as they set aside regular time for learning – which often means attending a lecture taught by somebody else – and as long as they respect the minority that does study Gemara at a high level.

A Latent Function of the Standard Talmud Curriculum

The changing population of yeshivahs provides the impetus for these socio-religious goals. The Eastern European yeshivah catered to the cream of the intellectual crop. A student would attend a yeshivah only if he were motivated and intellectually talented enough to handle the grueling schedule. The student had to jump many hurdles in the educational system before he made it to the yeshivah. The system was designed to filter out any student who could not meet the rigorous yeshivah standards, so that society could be sure that yeshivah graduates, i.e. the future rabbis, would be genuine scholars.[17] This is no longer the case. In fact, the opposite is true. Orthodox yeshivah high school students attend yeshivah in Israel almost as a matter of course, and their high schools encourage this. The year in Israel is viewed as a critical stage in the process of ensuring the observance of the next generation of Orthodox laymen, a kind of "finishing school" for yeshivah high school graduates. There is no longer any expectation that graduates will be scholars, per se. After all, Talmud is, and always has been, an enterprise of the spiritual-intellectual elite. Independent Talmud study appeals to certain kinds of personalities and intelligences. It is cognitive, text-oriented, and intellectually challenging. It takes several years to gain basic competence, and decades to master. At the outset, many current students lack the intellectual skills, the interest, the temperament, or the study habits to gain independent competence in Gemara. They may be religiously dedicated students, extraordinarily talented in many ways, but they lack the particular talents and interests necessary for Gemara. Eastern European

---

[17] Stampfer, "Heder."

yeshivahs did not teach basic skills, because students already possessed them; contemporary yeshivahs do not teach basic skills, because most students will never acquire them.[18]

In the Lithuanian environment, where students were serious about their studies from the outset, the emphasis was on independent work. Attendance in *shi'ur* was voluntary; students attended only if they wanted to. Students did not necessarily use their time in the *beit midrash* to prepare for *shi'ur*; they simply learned on their own.[19] The contemporary yeshivah emphasizes *shi'ur* because students could not learn on their own even if they wanted to. Contemporary yeshivahs cannot afford to emphasize text skills, because most students will be unwilling to tolerate the frustrations associated with the skills-oriented curriculum. The average student will simply be frustrated and bored.

In order to move toward student resocialization, the Talmud curriculum must also exude authenticity. Students often feel that their high school Torah education was coerced and formal. Students were forced to attend high school, and did precisely defined homework assignments, which were graded and included in their transcripts and college applications. This is not *Torah li-shemah* (for its own sake), but school. In contrast, yeshivah education is informal and voluntary. Students attend school out of choice, and there is little manifest discipline for most issues, including simply cutting class. Assignments are vague (read these sources, and prepare for class), not written, almost never graded, and only indirectly affect any college transcripts. This creates an image of authentic *Torah li-shemah*. Students are invigorated by doing something the right way, by participating in Torah study at the highest level. They can come to feel a sense of belonging to the historical community of yeshivahs, with their tradition of pure Torah study.

Emphasis on *lomdus* maximizes that sense of authenticity and continuity with the past. In large part due to the prevailing influence of Rabbi Joseph

---

[18] Similar frustrations developed in other contexts in which advanced yeshivah education became a universal norm. For example, neither contemporary Israeli mitnagdic *haredi* youth, nor students from the old *yishuv* in Jerusalem, had a legitimate option other than yeshivah study, which created considerable tension. On the old *yishuv*, see Menahem Friedman, *Hevrah be-Mashber Legitimatziah: Ha-Yishuv ha-Yashan ha-Ashkenazi, 1900–1917* (Jerusalem: Mosad Bialik, 2001), pp. 51ff. I am not familiar with serious research on the frustrations of contemporary *haredi* yeshivah students in Israel.

[19] Stampfer, *Ha-Yeshivah*, pp. 91–95. Stampfer points out that students in Lithuanian yeshivahs did not study in a *havruta* format (ibid., pp. 146–147) and has speculated that the *havruta* system became widespread in the twentieth century in order to assist the less intellectually gifted students who began to attend yeshivahs as they became less elite institutions. (Stampfer voiced this speculation at a seminar for the ATID Fellows, September 1999.)

B. Soloveitchik on American Modern Orthodoxy, Brisker style *lomdus*, and the Lithuanian tradition it represents, is simply identified, in the popular perception, with real learning. A student who arrives at a *hiddush*, at an abstract *shoresh mahloket* (root of a dispute), at a *hilluk* (analytical distinction), feels that he is out of high school, that he is doing things properly.[20] He feels attached to the great yeshivahs like Volozhin and to everything they represent in his mind. From a functional perspective, it does not matter that no "authentic" *talmid hakham* (talmudic scholar) would develop any conceptual generalizations without having read the *Tosafot* properly, or that most contemporary yeshivah students would never have been accepted to an Eastern European yeshivah.

This perception of authenticity would be minimized in a skills-oriented curriculum. A student who must memorize lists of terms, struggle to "break his teeth" over a difficult term in Rashi, or "map out" the outline of the *sugya* in his notebook will feel that he is involved in remedial Gemara. "This is not the way they studied in the great yeshivahs," he might think to himself. Indeed, he would be absolutely correct, even though remedial Gemara might be just what he needs in order to gain the textual and analytical skills that he lacks.

In short, contemporary yeshivahs create a "virtual Volozhin," an illusion that students are participating in the kind of rigorous Torah study that was practiced in the great yeshivahs of the past, even though contemporary students often cannot read the page. The contemporary student feels like he is participating in that Eastern European Jewish world, which is idealized and romanticized in so much of contemporary Orthodox collective memory. It does not matter that the sense of continuity with the past, is, to at least some degree, imagined. A selective perception of history bridges the gap between the past and the present and helps to create social and ideological cohesion in the contemporary "yeshivish" collective.[21]

---

[20] R. Yehiel Ya'akov Weinberg made a similar point when he said, "It is true that Rabbi Hayim [Brisker] brought a new type of logical *pilpul* into the *yeshivot*. Anyone can have a grasp of logic, and therefore all yeshivah students can come up with novel insights in this fashion. This is not so with regard to the approach of the Shakh and Rabbi Akiva Eiger, concerning which one needs to have great erudition in order to be a little sharp-witted [*harif*]. Therefore, since all yeshivah students want to be 'creators' [of such insights] they prefer Rabbi Hayim to all the sages who preceded him." Quoted in Marc B. Shapiro, *Between the Yeshiva World and Modern Orthodoxy: The Life and Works of Rabbi Yechiel Jacob Weinberg* (London and Portland: Valentine Mitchell Co., 1999), p. 195.

[21] On the way in which idealized images of the past serve to create contemporary social cohesion, see Malcolm Chase and Christopher Shaw, "The Dimensions of Nostalgia," in *The Imagined Past: History and Nostalgia*, ed. Malcolm Chase and Christopher Shaw (Manchester and New York: Manchester University Press, 1989), pp. 10–11. Cf. Bene-

Of course, a minority of students genuinely understand the basics of studying Talmud. These students' academic needs are best served by the advanced level of the *shi'ur*. They do not require remedial Gemara. These students help contribute to the sense of authenticity in the classroom. They ask sharp questions, identify where the *rebbe*'s ideas are likely to lead, challenge the teacher's understanding, and generally create a dialogue between the class and the teacher.[22] The weaker students feel that they are witnessing the exciting back-and-forth of Torah study, even if they do not appreciate (or even understand) the kinds of issues that are bandied about.

The emphasis on Gemara in these yeshivahs itself stems, at least in part, from the drive for authenticity. Contemporary Orthodox collective perception, under the pervasive influence of the mitnagdic Lithuanian approach, views Talmud not only as Torah study, but as *the* Torah study. While many students might benefit from greater emphasis on *Tanakh*, *halakhah*, philosophy, or *musar* in their curriculum, such a modified curriculum would be hard to sell.[23] Students would perceive it – wrongly, I believe – as a kind of "cop out," as an inferior program for people who cannot handle more serious Talmud study. This perception would likely continue, no matter how rigorous and serious the alternative curriculum. Such a program would have trouble providing a sense of authenticity.[24]

The emphasis on *shi'ur* in the standard curriculum, and the fact that students are not necessarily expected to understand everything they read in *seder*, can help further the yeshivah's socio-religious goals in another way, by

---

dict Anderson's reflections on the role of remembering in the creation of nations, in his *Imagined Communities: Reflections on the Origin and Spread of Nationalism* (London and New York: Verso, 1991), chap. 5. The construction of an idealized Eastern European past, and a partially imagined sense of continuity with that past, are undoubtedly more important in *haredi* yeshivahs than in Modern Orthodox ones.

[22] On the function of students' questions during *shi`ur* in Lithuanian yeshivahs, see Stampfer, *Ha-Yeshivah*, pp. 105ff.

[23] This, it seems to me, is an issue that proponents of radical change in Orthodox curricula need to take into account. Will students perceive the new curriculum as authentic?

[24] This perception is much less dominant in Israel, where Gemara is frequently disliked by high school and even yeshivah students. See S. Weiser and M. Bar Lev, "Teaching of Talmud in the Yeshiva High School: Difficulties and Dangers" (Hebrew), *Nir ha-Midrashiah* 8 (1990): 233–256. By now, there is generally talk of a "crisis" in the study of Gemara in Israeli yeshivah high schools. See, for example, the symposium on the topic, *"Talmud Akhshav," Meimad* 17 (Aug. 1999): 16–20 and R. Aharon Lichtenstein, "Teaching Gemara in Yeshiva High Schools" (Hebrew), *Shanah be-Shanah* (5761): 315–327. Even if my analysis of the social function of Gemara in programs for American students is accurate, the situation in Israel is much different. It will be interesting to see how curriculum will change if and when this popular American equation of Gemara with "real" Torah study changes as well.

providing opportunities for students to rethink their attitudes toward Orthodoxy.[25] The standard curriculum affords students opportunities to do things other than study Talmud. The basic issues in the *sugya* will be laid out clearly during class, so they will still be able to follow the discussion even if they do not use their *seder* time to prepare. They can — and very often do — use much of their time in *seder* to discuss things far removed from the *sugya* at hand. This does not contribute much when students discuss basketball playoffs. But there is also very constructive *"battalah"* (wasted time). Students may use *seder* as a time to process many of the new ideas and stimulants that they experience in yeshivah. Educators may prefer that this processing time occur in the *beit midrash*. First, the generally serious atmosphere in the *beit midrash* helps the students draw the "right" conclusions. Second, if these discussions take place during *seder*, the *rebbeim* may know about them and be able to participate in the conversation. Teachers often encourage and participate in student conversation about religious outlook, though the students "should" be studying a *Tosafot*. This kind of "constructive *battalah*" occurs more easily in a standard class than in a skills-oriented one. Since the skills-oriented class focuses on the student's own work, and since the class time depends on student participation, a group of students who spent their *seder* time discussing *hashkafah* (religious outlook) are more likely to fall behind than in a more typical lecture class.

The specific role of the *rebbe* in yeshivahs can also mitigate the desire to educate toward independence. A close and intimate relationship between staff and students provides a crucial venue through which to accomplish the socio-religious transformation that the yeshivahs work toward. Students look for "a *rebbe*," somebody whom they can turn to for advice, assistance, and even authority, during their transition from what yeshivahs see as a problematic Modern Orthodoxy to a more ideal one. On the one hand, the *rebbe* is a friend, a confidant, and even a "buddy." On the other hand, the *rebbe* is an authority, someone to respect, fear, or awe. Students look up to the *rebbe* as an authority on issues of religious outlook, on Jewish law, and even on personal problems. The source of the *rebbe*'s charisma rests, first and foremost, on his superior competence in Torah. The teacher who uses an obscure commentary to discover a *hiddush* at the end of a complex class impresses the group with his insight. When method is not discussed explicitly, students do not understand how the teacher arrived at his conclusions or how he found his sources; mystery enhances the *rebbe*'s charisma. Furthermore, the contemporary "yeshivish" community places great emphasis

---

[25] I would like to thank R. Menachem Leibtag, who raised this issue.

on rabbinic authority, often in conscious opposition to the modern emphasis on individual autonomy. This goes beyond a narrow acceptance of the heteronomously binding halakhah. *Haredi* ideologies like *da'at Torah*, which in some versions can grant the Torah scholar virtually unlimited authority over all aspects of a Jew's life, generally appear in less extreme forms in Modern Orthodox contexts. The spirit of submission permeates contemporary Orthodoxy, particularly in the yeshivahs.[26] Education, however, can be a subversive enterprise when it grants students independence. Knowledge and authority become democratized when students are independent, when the teacher's method is explicated clearly, and when the student can envision himself with the same talents as his *rebbe*.[27]

There is also an economic aspect in the need to emphasize the satisfactory aspect of Talmud rather than the difficult legwork. Lithuanian yeshivahs earned their money by international fund raising. Students and their parents were not an important source of funds, since students paid no tuition and were, in fact, granted a stipend to cover their basic living costs.[28] There was little financial incentive for the yeshivah to attract more students, though yeshivahs were eager to teach Torah and improve their reputations by attracting more and better students. In contrast, one-year yeshivah programs depend on tuition, on stipends from Israel's Ministry of Religions, and on donations from parents. Contemporary yeshivahs have a great many expenses: large staffs and a low staff/student ratio; formal programming and classes that can run as late as midnight; dormitories and food for students; extra-curricular programming; trips, tours, and *shabbatonim* that help break up the monotony of yeshivah life. The more students the yeshivah can attract, the easier it is for the institution to balance its budget. Furthermore, the happier the students are, the more likely it is that their parents will feel motivated to donate to the school. A student who enjoys the yeshivah will report to his younger friends and to his parents, making the ye-

---

[26] While Lawrence Kaplan identifies submission as a *haredi* value, it is gradually extending its influence in the Modern Orthodox community as well. See his "Hazon Ish: Haredi Critic of Traditional Orthodoxy," in *The Uses of Tradition: Jewish Continuity in the Modern Era*, ed. Jack Wertheimer (New York: Jewish Theological Seminary, 1992), pp. 145–174, and Waxman, "Haredization."

[27] This image of the *rebbe*-student relationship certainly does not apply to all students. Teachers often identify students whom they view as destined for careers as rabbis or educators. They will likely push them to attend yeshivah and *kolel* for an extended period. The system retains its basic form when there is some movement between the class of leaders and the class of followers. But the ethic of submission might be somewhat compromised if too many students became too independent.

[28] On fund raising, see Stampfer, *Ha-Yeshivah*, pp. 40–43. On student stipends, and the power they granted the yeshivah administration over the students, see pp. 114ff.

shivah's future recruitment more effective and its fund-raising more lucrative. Furthermore, individual teachers are motivated to try to attract large classes. It is not easy to earn a living as a teacher in yeshivahs, and many teachers work in several institutions simultaneously, patching together enough work to make ends meet. Students have some independence in choosing their teachers, and a teacher who attracts a large class will earn more teaching hours in a single institution and, consequently, a more comfortable living.

Marketing a Skills-Oriented Curriculum

Despite all of these important advantages of the standard approach, there is a price to be paid for the focus on nostalgia and enjoyment. This approach may keep students "happier" while in yeshivah, but they will eventually leave. Students who return to universities in the Diaspora inevitably undergo a post-yeshivah letdown.[29] What do the students take with them when they leave that can help sustain them religiously over the course of their lives? What long-term influence will the yeshivah experience continue to have on alumni? I fear that mere memories of learning experiences that seemed authentic, without acquisition of the skills to learn independently, will have less staying power than educators would like. Many alumni will feel frustrated if they leave yeshivah with a desire to learn but without the ability to do so to their satisfaction. The identity and commitment that students adopt in Israel may fade, or disappear entirely, over time.

Learning to learn Gemara independently is a long and difficult task. Probably, the majority of Orthodox Jews will never acquire the necessary skills to do so. A small minority either have the skills when they enter yeshivah or acquire them there. There remains a sizeable group of students who have the natural talents to learn to study on their own, but fail to acquire the skills through the standard curriculum. It seems to me that a skills-oriented program should be marketed heavily to that segment of the yeshivah population. The skills they will acquire will allow them to participate continually in Torah study and help support their long-term commitment to high religious standards, and, indeed, make them more ideal laymen.

I am not suggesting that all, or even most, students be fed a strictly skills-oriented curriculum, certainly not at the beginning of the year. Most students lack the enthusiasm and dedication to Torah study, particularly early on. Many gain this dedication gradually over the course of the year, in

---

[29] See Dodi Tobin's contribution to this volume, and Berger, "Year of Study," chap. 5.

part because the social aspects of the standard curriculum inspire them. Once the students are inspired, however, they may continue in standard classes, without realizing that they are not acquiring the skills they will need later on, skills that more of them would acquire in a skills-oriented class. How can we direct the right students into skills-oriented classes without frustrating them and damaging their motivation and inspiration? How can we convince students to sacrifice the instant gratification of the standard curriculum for the long-term goals of the skills-oriented curriculum?

I do not have adequate answers to these questions, but I think it is important to develop effective means of marketing a skills-oriented curriculum to the right students. When I spoke to teachers of skills-oriented classes, they said that they had trouble marketing their product to students, for many of the reasons discussed above. Students were reluctant to attend, as they felt frustrated by the work, and believed that attending what was perceived as a lower-level class damaged their self-esteem. The few schools that emphasize skills-oriented curricula attract a higher percentage of post-college students: a self-selected group of more mature, more patient students, with a more focused sense of what they want to accomplish. Teachers of a skills-oriented curriculum in more mainstream programs have trouble attracting students. They hope that a group of the more mature students will be willing to put up with the frustration and lack of instant gratification for the sake of long-term goals. The class becomes a self-selected group of students who feel that they need to learn the basics.

Yeshivahs must find the proper balance between skills-oriented and standard classes. I am not, as should be clear, advocating the elimination of standard classes for any students. The "illusion of Volozhin" is important for student motivation and development, and exposure to advanced *lomdus* can help teach students what they have to strive for in the future. I am suggesting that teachers, administrators, and staff should confront frankly their emphasis on advanced classes and on *lomdus*. In the scheme of things, yeshivahs should urge more students to spend more of their day working on skills.

This undoubtedly will create some frustrations, so I urge yeshivahs to work on skills in relatively small doses, particularly early on. Still, yeshivahs can do a great deal to alleviate the self-esteem problems. Skills-based classes must not be presented by anybody as remedial Gemara. On the contrary! They should be presented as a high-level class; as classes for mature students who have a long-term vision of independence in Torah study; as classes for people who realize that they need to work on basics in addition to *lomdus*. Instead of feeling insecure, the student should be made to feel proud of his maturity, vision, and willingness to delay gratification. This can help offset the loss that is incurred by implicitly questioning the illusion of "learning as it used to be." Once the students understand that they do not measure up in their preparation and training to the students of the elite European yeshivahs, some will realize that in order for them to learn "authentically" in the long run they must do some remedial work now.

To overcome frustration, teachers must not ignore the aspect of positive reinforcement and short-term gratification. Preparing assignments that are just hard enough to be challenging, but easy enough to be doable, can serve that goal. The skills-oriented curriculum focuses on method and makes explicit the steps involved in analyzing and breaking down a *sugya* from beginning to end. If students have a defined assignment, which they are capable of doing when they work hard, and if they are made to realize that they have, in fact, done good work, then they can gain a short-term sense of accomplishment. Furthermore, students who persevere in a skills-oriented class are likely to gain a sense of long-term accomplishment as well, to look back at themselves after several months of work and be able to identify clearly what they are capable of doing now that they were not capable of doing before.

If a skills-oriented curriculum were marketed more successfully to a greater percentage of the population, it might help make the next generation of Orthodox laymen better able to understand Torah at a higher level and to participate more fully in Jews' eternal commitment to Torah study.

Concluding Note: Some Brief Thoughts on Women's Torah Study

Thus far, I have deliberately addressed only men's programs because I am more familiar with them than with women's programs, and because women's programs are structured differently from men's. In addition, Lithuanian yeshivas were exclusively male institutions, such that today's women's programs are not modeled directly after them. Still, with some hesitancy, I would like to make a few comments on women's learning as well, with the hope that they may inspire some thought and research on the part of people more familiar than I with the intricacies of women's Torah study.

Orthodox women's learning has advanced dramatically in the past several generations. Lacking the model of the Lithuanian yeshivah, a model that inspires but also confines the men's programs, women's seminaries have a more diverse curriculum, do not focus primarily on Talmud, and are freer to improvise. They can adopt alternative curricula, attempt experimental pedagogic techniques, and teach more diverse disciplines, like Jewish thought, *Tanakh*, or *halakhah*. Women's programs generally (though not universally) spend less time in *havruta* learning in the *beit midrash*, and more time in frontal lectures. Furthermore, because women are formally exempt from aspects of the halakhic obligation of Torah study, and because of some of the ideological complexities regarding the role of women in Orthodoxy in general, some women's programs do not see the acquisition of independent learning skills as central to their goals. Consequently, many aspects of the tension between skills and enjoyment are not as relevant to women's seminaries, and the "Virtual Volozhin" model is considerably less central to women's learning than it is to men's. Indeed, many women's programs do not teach Talmud at all. To make the discussion even more complex, the women's programs themselves are much more diverse than the men's programs – both in their overall religious outlooks, and in their curricula and educational approaches. It is much more difficult to generalize about women's programs than about men's yeshivahs.

Yet, the women's programs share many of the same socio-religious goals as the men's yeshivahs. They are concerned, no less than the men's programs, with ensuring that the young women enjoy their year in Israel in general, and their experience of Torah study in particular, with the hope that this will inspire them to move beyond the proclaimed faults of Modern Orthodoxy and adopt stricter, at times "yeshivish," standards and identities. Women's programs use some of the same techniques as the men's institutions to accomplish their socio-religious goals – relative social isolation in intensely religious environments[30]; enjoyable extra-curricular activities and field trips; close, personal relations between students and staff; etc.

Indeed, my sense is – and I say this with some caution – that the "Virtual Volozhin" model is not entirely absent from the women's programs. While they are not directly inspired by the model of the Eastern European yeshivahs, they may be indirectly influenced, both because male teachers and administrators in women's programs are inevitably yeshivah graduates, and because some aspects of women's learning are modeled on the contemporary men's programs. When women are taught Talmud, some classes simply admit that the young women know very little of Talmud study. These classes are able to break free of the "Virtual Volozhin" model by starting with the basics. In consequence, they suffer from many of the same frustrations that come with the men's text-oriented classes. But other women's Talmud classes focus on higher levels of *lomdus*, which helps

---

[30] Women's schools, however, are generally less isolated than some of the men's institutions.

maintain student motivation, but does not do enough to provide the students with the textual and analytical skills they lack. A related phenomenon may exist in other areas of study, like *Tanakh* or *halakhah*. Again, some teachers understand that many students arrive in Israel lacking basic learning skills, and they accommodate them by beginning with the basics. Others, however, focus on the conclusions derived from study methods that students cannot imitate. Instead of learning how to study Rashi's commentary on *Humash* carefully, methodically, and independently, some students are told what the teacher's conclusions were when he or she compared Rashi to the *midrash* upon which his commentary was based. Instead of learning how to unpack a *Beit Yosef* or read a *teshuvah* (responsum), students receive "cut-and-pasted" source sheets, which do the legwork for them and include only the simple, readable, bottom line of an obscure source.[31] This may, indeed, impress students and maintain a fast moving pace in class, which can keep students excited, happy, and motivated, with all the advantages that engenders. But, I fear, it may not do enough to prepare them for the ongoing task of life-long Torah learning.[32]

---

[31] At least in the area of *halakhah*, another motivation for pre-digesting the sources for the students may be the legitimate desire that they cover ground and know the practical *halakhah*.

[32] I would like to thank all of those who read and commented on earlier drafts of this paper: R. Dr. Eliezer and Marilyn Finkelman, Dr. Kimmy Caplan, Noam Davidovitz, R. Efraim Levitz, R. Moshe Lichtman, David Polsky, Dr. Shaul Stampfer, Prof. Chaim Waxman, Eitan Zeryiker, and Yael Ziegler. Needless to say, I take full responsibility for any errors. In addition, I would like to thank ATID, whose generous fellowship helped support this research, conducted during the 1999–2000 academic year.

THE POST-HIGH SCHOOL YEAR IN ISRAEL: PARENT-CHILD RELATIONSHIPS AND RELIGIOUS GROWTH

DODI F. TOBIN

A YEAR OF INTENSIVE TORAH STUDY in a yeshivah program in Israel is considered the culmination of a Modern Orthodox day school education. For so many students it is a year of intense personal growth, in which students strengthen their Jewish identification, deepen their relationship to the Jewish people, fortify their affiliation with the State of Israel, and commit themselves to Torah study and *mitzvah* observance throughout their adult lives. These programs benefit not only the students, but their families and communities as well. Parents, who continue to send their children to Israel in increasing numbers year after year, are often proud of their children's' personal, intellectual, and religious growth. Diaspora high schools are encouraged by the ways the Israel programs cement the values of Torah and *mitzvot*, which the high schools have worked so hard to instill in their students. Diaspora communities are enriched by the return of more mature, more educated, and more committed youth. The year in Israel is, no doubt, one of the critical factors in the growth of committed Modern Orthodoxy in America in recent decades.

One recent study undertook to examine in a systematic way the success of the year in Israel. Analysis of data gathered from hundreds of yeshivah program students indicated that many became more observant of *mitzvot* over the course of the year, including increased prayer and fasting, modest dress, commitment to Torah study, and rejection of activities such as seeing R-rated movies.[1] These results support what virtually every observer of Or-

---

[1] Shalom Z. Berger, "A Year of Study in an Israeli Yeshiva Program: Before and After," (D.Ed. thesis, Yeshiva University, 1997), summarized as "The Impact of One-Year Israel Study on American Day School Graduates" *Ten Da'at*, 12 (1999): 5–14.

thodox education understands: the year in Israel is a critical factor in the formation of religious commitment among Orthodox young adults.

But every period of growth comes with tensions and challenges. Personal change always entails stresses and conflicts, at both the individual and interpersonal levels. This study focuses on one example of those tensions: the potential conflict between parents and child that develops as the student changes in Israel, conflict that may increase when the young adult returns home. Anecdotal evidence suggests that while most parents may desire and expect their child to undergo a rich Jewish experience during study in Israel, not all parents are happy with the idea that their child may return home more stringently observant. We all have heard of individual parents who are wary about what will happen to their child in yeshivah, such as a mother who expressed fear of sending her son, lest he return home and find her kashrut unacceptable. I am also aware of a recent situation in a Modern Orthodox school, in which a group of parents of high school seniors lobbied the rest of the parent body not to send their children to Israel for the year, lest they become too religious.

What, I wondered, made these parents fearful of their children becoming more religious? What did they find threatening in becoming more observant? Moreover, what did it mean for the child to embark on the experience with the knowledge that his parents disapprove of him becoming more *mitzvah*-observant?

I have communicated with educators, parents, and students, and have reviewed recent literature, in an attempt to understand the phenomenon of increased observance and how it affected and was affected by the parent-child relationship. The assertions I make are based upon the themes that emerged in these communications. I also make recommendations that may serve to decrease the potential for parent-child conflict surrounding increased observance, throughout the year of study and thereafter.[2]

Obviously, there are many variables at play that influence the student's increased observance and its manifestations, as well as how parents react to

---

[2] This essay is based upon research completed as an ATID Fellow during the 1999–2000 academic year. Information gathering included interviews and correspondence with parents, Israel-program guidance counselors in Jewish high schools, prominent Jewish educators, and educators in various Israel programs. In addition, students attending a yeshivah program over the course of that year, as well as recent yeshivah program alumni, completed a written survey. Although the target populations were North American students and their parents, I believe my findings and recommendations are applicable to the many students from other Diaspora countries who study in Israel (though they represent a smaller percentage of the Jewish populations of those countries).

those changes. These variables include the yeshivah program and high school attended by the student; his or her community of origin; and the goals, attitudes, fears, and expectations of both parents and students regarding the year in Israel. In this essay, I write about the apprehension of some parents that their children will become, or have become, too observant. This is not to dismiss the parents who are *hoping* their children will become more religious. Indeed, the schools and many parents look to the yeshivah programs as the "last best hope" that the child will not leave religion. In order to present a survey of some of the considerations in the interplay of these variables and the year in Israel, I have oversimplified some of my presentation, for which I ask the reader's forgiveness. In reality, each student and family must independently evaluate the important experience of Torah study in Israel.

Intensified *Mitzvah* Observance in *Shanah Alef* (First-Year) Students
The Effects of Maturity and Environment

To understand the phenomenon of increased observance in yeshivah students, it is important to recognize that a particular combination of circumstances common to many participants predisposes them to changes over the course of their year in Israel. Specifically, the students are engaged in a developmental process of separating and individuating from their parents as they move into young adulthood. This process involves moving from dependence on parents to increased independence from them.[3] Many students at this age embark on a journey to find out who they are and what they believe in, and they will often consciously seek out authority figures or values that differ from those of their parents or communities of origin. These students may also make changes in their dress and appearance as an external manifestation of their identity struggles. Their drive to separate and individuate from their parents is a natural and healthy part of the growth process.

In addition, the environment of many yeshivahs in Israel serves as a catalyst for change. Yeshivah students are immersed in a unique spiritual environment that most have not been exposed to before. In contrast to many prominent Modern Orthodox communities in America, where spiri-

---

[3] Kenneth Rice, "Separation-Individuation and Adjustment to College: A Longitudinal Study," *Journal of Counseling Psychology* 39:2 (1992): 203–213.

tuality goes hand in hand with an emphasis on material wealth,[4] most yeshivahs in Israel emphasize Torah learning as the primary focus in life, deemphasizing the material. The modest surroundings of the yeshivah dormitory and the personal examples of piety offered by the faculty create a sacred atmosphere that may have a considerable impact upon the student's religious outlook and behavior.

When you place a high school graduate who is striving for identity and independence within the intensely spiritual environment of a yeshivah far from home, the probability that he will be influenced religiously is considerable. Were these graduates to go off to college instead of *shanah alef*, they would be similarly likely to undergo changes as well, though not necessarily of a religious nature. They might become vegans, activists, feminists, and so on. The point is that alterations in values and behavior is par for the course for an older adolescent, and the direction his transformation takes will depend in part upon the milieu he finds himself in.

The Impact of Family Relationships

The direction that a student's religious development will take during her year in Israel will depend upon a complex set of factors, unique to each student. These factors include but are not limited to the *hashkafah* and intensity of the yeshivah program she is attending, the quality of her previous schooling, the religious and secular culture she grew up in, and her family relationships.

With regard to the specific influence of family, current research on college adjustment suggests that students who grow up in a household where there are warm, healthy family relationships are more likely to be well-adjusted socially, academically, and psychologically and to hold religious values and beliefs that are similar to those of their parents. Conversely, students who grow up in a home in which family relationships are conflicted, and where parents are authoritarian or harsh, are more likely to experience

---

[4] This is reflected in one journalist's description of a Modern Orthodox community in New York, in which "huge houses are being torn down to build even huger ones," and where "they walk to their Orthodox synagogues on the Sabbath, where men and women are separated in prayer. But as the adults worship, their sons and daughters, in the temple lobby, trade Pokemon cards." Obviously these observations would not hold true for every Modern Orthodox community throughout the Diaspora, but for the yeshivah student, the contrast between his home society and that of the yeshivah is usually quite stark. See Jane Gross, "Young Orthodox Jews Blend Word and World" *The New York Times*, September 16, 1999.

maladjustment, depression, or other emotional problems and to reject their parents' religious outlook.[5]

In applying these findings to Israel program students, who are similar to college freshmen in terms of age, developmental stage, and first-time separation from home, we can speculate that those students who have a conflicted relationship with their parents may be more likely to encounter difficulty adjusting to the yeshivah experience than those who enjoy a warm relationship with their parents. Equally, students coming from a conflicted home environment may be more likely to markedly diverge from the religious stance of their parents, as compared to students coming from warm family environments.

In concurrence with this proposition, one veteran Jewish educator shared with me his observation that many of the students who become "fanatically" religious, whom he termed "turnaround kids," come from troubled homes.[6] Indeed, mental health professionals can verify that a young adult may use religious issues to express general anger toward his parents and that a religious persona can be adopted as a cover for other, unaddressed conflicts in the family. An essential way to determine whether this is in fact the case is to listen closely for hostility when the student discusses his religious life. The more hostility he expresses, the more likely it is that his religious behavior is being compelled by underlying conflict. [7]

The Impact of Modern Technology

Today, cellular phones have enabled yeshivah students to be in contact with their parents in a way that was unimaginable a few years ago, and the ease of air travel and prevalence of lower fares mean students will likely see their parents at least once during the course of their year. Therefore, in comparison to decades past, parents are much more present in the student's life on a daily basis, though physically they may be thousands of miles away. The frequency of this parent-child communication can have both positive and negative consequences.

---

[5] K. Rice, "Separation-Individuation"; Maureen Kenny & Gail Donaldson, "The Relationship of Parental Attachment and Psychological Separation to the Adjustment of First-Year College Women," *Journal of College Student Development* 33:5 (1992): 431–438.

[6] All sources quoted in this essay remain anonymous, for reasons of confidentiality.

[7] Miriam Schacter, "Familial Dissonance as a Result of Influences of the Post-High School Israel Yeshiva Programs," (Presentation to Edah Conference, February 1999, New York). Schacter's presentation has helped shape a number of my observations in this essay.

One educator described the positive effects of the visiting parents, who generally stay longer than regular tourists, and whose experience is more spiritual because they are included by their children in classes, *havrutot, shabbatonim*, and social life. Moreover, parents are impressed to see their children experiencing Judaism in such a positive, meaningful way.

With regard to frequent telephone contact, parents feel it serves an important purpose. They are relieved to be able to speak to their children often, as it makes the distance more bearable and allows them to keep their fingers on the pulses of their children's lives.[8] Many students also report that frequent contact with parents leads to a deeper and more mature relationship with them.

At the same time, some educators have observed a negative consequence of the ease and frequency with which students and parents are able to speak to each other, namely, that parents can become too involved and influential in their children's day-to-day lives. One educator shared a situation in which a student was not pleased with the roommate he was assigned. Rather than the student himself working it out, he had his parents immediately telephone the school to complain. In other instances, parents are consulted by their children to determine which classes to take or where to go for Shabbat. Furthermore, cellular phones enable parents to repeatedly share their views and attitudes throughout the year. If the parents frequently communicate their fear or disapproval of their child becoming "more religious," the aspiring student may inhibit her own yearning for religious growth. Accordingly, these educators contend that today's students are less autonomous than students who attended Israel programs ten years ago.

Parental Discomfort with the Student's Increased Observance

While there is no way to verify the proportion of parents who may be ambivalent or fearful about their children becoming more observant while in Israel, anecdotal evidence clearly suggests that such parents do, in fact, exist. For instance, one mother of a yeshivah alumnus shared with me her sentiment that, "We want them to learn more, but to a certain degree...we want them to come home the same way." One educator described to me an airport scene in which a parent left her child with the parting words: "I bet-

---

[8] I undertook this research prior to the onset of the "Second Intifada" in the fall of 2000. Once Israel began to endure the wave of terror attacks, the cell phone took on tremendous importance, such that as of this writing I presume most educators and parents alike appreciate the necessity that students have and use cell phones as often as needed.

ter get you back just the way that I am sending you!" Another told me of an informal network of parents in America who warn each other about how their children will become more religious while in Israel.

What causes a parent to be disappointed or even fearful about her child's religious changes, and is the fear justified? The answer is, it depends. In some cases, a parent's unwarranted disapproving stance toward a child is caused by the parent's own personal issues or inner conflict. For instance, there are parents who may be concerned that the child will be critical of their religious stance and reject them. This is particularly true if the parents are not actively involved with their own spirituality, or are insecure about the decisions they have made about their own levels of observance. A child returning home with newfound religious fervor challenges such a parent to revisit his or her own life choices, a process that may cause anxiety. The parent may well deal with this anxiety by reacting disapprovingly toward the child.

Alternatively, a parent may be envious of a child's opportunity to learn Torah in a way the parent never could and may therefore harbor feelings of resentment. Other parents may not have successfully individuated from their own parents, such that when they observe the independence their children have and gain while in Israel, they feel threatened or resentful. Still others may resent that the change in the child's religious practice has curtailed favorite family activities. If the child refuses to go to the family's favorite mixed beach or will only eat in restaurants that are *mehadrin*, or if he has decided he no longer kisses women, including aunts and close family friends, a parent may feel offended.

The foregoing rationales see the parent's fear or disapproval as emanating from the parent's own emotional issues or needs. The child, in these cases, is the passive recipient of the parents' negativity. On the other hand, there are situations in which the child is an active participant in bringing about reprimand. This is particularly the case where a student returns home with a "holier than thou" attitude and arrogantly conveys to his parents that their religious outlook and observance are inferior to his. In this kind of situation, it is instructive to examine why the child has a superior attitude to begin with. This arrogance may reflect a deeper conflict between parent and child, or it may stem from the student's low self-esteem. Then again, it may echo a mindset promoted by one of the student's teachers, or by the program itself.

The concern of some Modern Orthodox parents about the "right wing" influence of particular yeshivah program on their children is not completely without basis. In general, Modern Orthodox parents tend to send their children to yeshivah programs that promote a Religious Zionist *hashkafah*, but the programs vary in their specific religious outlooks. One parent I spoke to complained about a certain "survival guide" that had been given to their son by his yeshivah program just before his return to America. This booklet maintained that university life was spiritually dangerous, recommended that students adopt *yeshivish* dress and hat, disregard involvement in extracurricular activities because they are "*mevattel*" (a waste of) Torah learning time, and discount the importance of expanding one's resume. Overall, the tone of the booklet seemed to suggest to students that returning to their homes in America put their spiritual lives in peril and, further, that certain ideals venerated by the Modern Orthodox community, such as secular culture and professional development, were of little value.[9]

Furthermore, some yeshivah programs actively promote Yeshiva University over secular colleges, and this has influenced many students to switch from Ivy League or other prestigious universities. At the same time, some post-high school programs discourage even Yeshiva University as insufficiently religious and encourage students to attend local colleges so that they can spend more time studying in a nearby right-wing yeshivah. The desire of the student to switch colleges in order to place himself in an environment more conducive to Torah learning and *mitzvah* observance is unsettling for some parents.

This leads us to another major source of parental distress: a radical religious change. For the Modern Orthodox parent, radical change often means the child has become "Ultra-Orthodox." Parents of these children are often concerned about the child's stability and ultimate self-sufficiency. In other words, they worry that their son will not want to pursue a degree or profession, and will choose a *kollel* lifestyle, (which will leave him financially dependent), or they fear their daughter will abandon secular pursuits and marry a *kollel* student. One prominent Modern Orthodox educator maintains that when Modern Orthodox parents see their child come home with a black hat, they feel they have "lost control" of their child.

Given that some parents are uncomfortable with their children becoming more religious while in Israel, it is not surprising that conflict arises between these parents and children around the question of staying a second year in yeshivah (*shanah bet*). One educator relayed his observation that while many of the yeshivahs promote a second year of study, many parents

---

[9] An educator informed me that the yeshivah program recognized that the booklet misstated its position and no longer distributes it.

are shocked to find out their child wishes to stay in Israel another year. In these cases, parent-child conflict is virtually guaranteed.

Parent-Child Relationships: The Students' Perspective

Although there exist parents who are uncomfortable with their child's increased observance for reasons personal, emotional, or ideological, the continued popularity of yeshivah study in Israel attests that a majority of parents are generally satisfied with their children's religious growth and experience. This is further borne out by the fact that many students I interviewed described the improvement in their relationships with their parents over the course of the year. Several students attributed this to their own maturation and to a deeper appreciation of their parents that came with living away from home. Students also cited that learning the Jewish laws about respecting one's parents positively influenced how they related to them. The perspectives of these students seem to verify that many may be gaining exactly what was hoped for – maturity and positive religious growth. It also suggests that students are leaving Israel with a dedication to further nurturing their relationships with their parents.

Returning Home

Research has found that students studying abroad, not necessarily in Israel, often undergo changes in lifestyle and values while living within the new culture, and it is not uncommon for these students to have short-term difficulties adapting upon their return home.[10] Adjustment difficulties and personal conflict come about as the students become aware of changes in themselves and in others, and in the differences between the cultures they have studied in and those they have returned to.[11]

This may be no less true for students who have gone abroad to study at a yeshivah in Israel. Many students expect to encounter at least some adjustment difficulties upon returning home. Their reasons include difficulties in finding time and partners for Torah study; re-entering a culture whose values they do not share; explaining to others about new religious attitudes or practices; and having to leave the "utopian" environment of the yeshivah. Some students pointed out that while their readjustment to American culture would be difficult, readjustment to their family would not.

---

[10] Jolene Koester, "Communication and the Intercultural Reentry: A Course Proposal," *Communication Education* 33:3 (1984): 251–256.

[11] Robert A. Raschio, "College Students' Perceptions of Reverse Culture Shock and Reentry Adjustments," *Journal of College Student Personnel* 28:2 (March 1987): 156–162.

Other students predicted that religious issues would in fact be a source of conflict between them and their parents upon their return home. This may lead some students to defer or reduce this anticipated stress of readjustment to home by actions such as staying for a second year or switching colleges in order to be in what they consider a more religious environment.

While returning students may expect their parents and friends to be receptive to discussions about their experiences abroad, research suggests that this is often not the case. Rather, it is usually those who have been through similar experiences themselves who in the end provide the support, validation, and empathy the returning student needs. For this reason, returning students will often seek out friends who have studied abroad themselves. And it would be reasonable to expect that parents who had themselves studied in Israel will be more understanding and accepting of their children's overall religious changes than parents who never had that opportunity.

Research also indicates that those overseas students who are most successful in adapting to the foreign culture may be those who experience the greatest difficulty readjusting to home. Applied to Israel program students, this finding suggests that those who most identify with and internalize the values of the yeshivah environment may have the most difficulty readjusting to home. Studies also show that the better the returning student is prepared for the difficulties she may face, the easier her readjustment will be.[12] The parents of these students have the same need for preparation.

Recommendations

In preparation for the high school graduate's year in Israel, it is incumbent upon all those involved in the experience to consider how they can contribute to fostering understanding, respect, and *shalom bayit* (domestic harmony) between students and parents. The following suggestions may help each group in that effort.

Preparing the Parents

According to one prominent Jewish educator, parents often do not know what to expect of their child's year in Israel, and they blame changes they are unhappy with upon the yeshivah or seminary their child attended. Therefore, it is important that parents gain a clear sense of the yeshivah's religious outlook and of what their child's yeshivah experience will be like. Israel program fairs in American yeshivah high schools are routine, but they

---

[12] J. Koester, "Communication," pp. 251–53.

may not provide parents adequate information about what takes place in the yeshivah program or sufficient connection to the program staff. Recently, some schools have begun holding parlor meetings in private homes in the Diaspora. In this more intimate forum, parents can ask their questions, discuss the yeshivah program's mission statement, and encounter one or more of the program's senior staff.

In general, parents should help their child choose a school that meets the child's own specific needs, in the same way that they help him choose a university. Further, if a child does not wish to go to Israel for the year, parents should not to push him, as coercion is generally unsuccessful. For many, study in Israel is an invaluable opportunity to fortify religious attitudes, practices, and enthusiasm before beginning college, but others may not be ready to enroll in a yeshivah program immediately following high school. For these young adults, "junior year abroad" may be an opportune time to go, for they generally will be more emotionally and intellectually mature and will have already adapted to living away from home. The result may be a more powerful and meaningful yeshivah experience.

Once the students have commenced their year in Israel, parents should be informed and educated about what their children may be experiencing, from a developmental and a religious perspective. One vehicle for doing so could be an evening for parents of children currently in Israel, sponsored by the Jewish high school, in which a counselor[13] and a Jewish educator are available to address relevant issues. Parents could be given the opportunity to ask questions and air concerns. During this session, parents could be made aware of the possibility that their child may become more observant while in Israel, and should be helped to appreciate the positive aspects of these changes. Further, parents can be reminded of the importance of healthy communication with their children throughout and beyond the year in Israel.

A parents' session might also be useful in anticipation of the year's conclusion. The aim of this session would be to prepare the parents for the adjustment difficulties their child may encounter when she re-enters their home. These young adults have grown and changed, and they will be struggling to integrate their new personas into their old environment. Parents should be encouraged to support and validate their children wherever possible.

---

[13] Counselors in this case could be the high school guidance counselor, or even a mental health professional such as a social worker or psychologist who is familiar with the Israel yeshivah experience.

Throughout the year, yeshivah program administrators should be sure to send informative e-mails to parents on a consistent basis. This would help forge a trusting relationship between the yeshivah program and the parents, sensitize parents to their child's experiences, and, ultimately, bring parents and children closer together.

Parents can gain the greatest appreciation for their child's experience by encountering it firsthand. To the extent it is not disruptive to the program, parents who visit in Israel during the year should spend some substantial time with their child learning in the yeshivah. Yeshivah programs may wish to consider ways to open the yeshivah experience to parents in a more formal way, as in a special learning program or a *shabbaton* for students and parents. If parents are not able to visit Israel, yeshivah programs might consider organizing sessions in various Diaspora communities, where parents can meet and learn with one of their child's teachers.

Preparing the Students

Returning home can be a positive growing opportunity for the student if she is prepared to deal with the inner conflict she may experience when she re-enters her Diaspora community. Her adjustment to home will be most successful if she is trusting, patient, and able to reflect upon the nature of her inner discord.[14] Examples of the way *shanah alef* programs today prepare their students for this event include informal individual meetings between students and teachers or a formal evening during which students can ask questions of responsive staff members or hear a "*musar shmooz*" on the topic. Quite often, these evenings are optional.

One question regarding these preparatory efforts is whether they have the proper focus. One educator expressed his concern that some yeshivah programs are emphasizing halakhic dilemmas that students may encounter in the Diaspora, while neglecting less sharply defined or ethical issues, such as respectful communication with one's parents. Interestingly, the study that found an increase in ritual *mitzvah* observance for a majority of post-high school students in Israel did not find a similar increase in the students' ethical (*bein adam le-havero*) behavior.[15] While this finding may reflect the students' high expectations of themselves, such that they rated themselves low in ethical behavior because they did not feel they were as virtuous as they should be, it could also reflect the possibility that some yeshivahs may not be concentrating enough upon interpersonal and moral issues.

---

[14] R. Raschio, "College Students' Perceptions."

[15] S. Berger, "Impact of One-Year Israel Study."

As students return to their parents' homes and communities, they may encounter behaviors, practices, or values that they do not agree with. Students must be shown how to respond to these situations appropriately. Yeshivah program staff can and should view the return home as an educational opportunity and, as the end of year approaches, dedicate significant time to preparing students for their return home. At these designated times, which may be during or after class, students can be prepared for the possibility that some parents and friends may have negative reactions to their religious growth. Through guided discussions, students may come to appreciate the nature of those reactions and learn how to respond in a mature and respectful manner.

Like all returning overseas students, students returning from yeshivah programs in Israel need opportunities to feel supported and validated if they are to adjust well to their home culture. To that end, the yeshivah programs, or an on-campus Jewish group serving post-Israel students, might consider organizing a "debriefing" session or a *shabbaton* early in the year, where students can reconnect with peers and discuss adjustment issues. This would be particularly important for a student at a university with a small Orthodox community, where there are fewer peers who appreciate his Israel experience and a wider discrepancy between the religious community he has entered and the yeshivah environment he has left.

Conclusion

For most Jewish high school graduates, the year in Israel provides a wonderful opportunity for personal exploration and religious growth. The normal young adult desire for independence and identity, coupled with the spiritual environment of the yeshivah, commonly results in religious intensification among yeshivah students. For many of these young adults, increased observance is a result of mature and authentic religious growth, while for others it may reflect rebellion against parents. While many parents consider their child's increased observance as a desired and wonderful outcome, there are those parents who will react negatively, for reasons ranging from their own inner struggle with religiosity to concern about their child's self-sufficiency and professional development. To reduce the potential for parent-child conflict during this exciting, intense, and potentially transformational year, and to ease the student's readjustment to home, parents and students must appreciate each other's perspective. To the extent that parents are familiar with the nature of their child's experience, to the extent that students have been imbued with the importance of maintaining *shalom bayit,* and to the extent that yeshivah programs respond to parents' needs and prepare students accordingly, the outcome of the Israel experience will be positive.

The post-high school year in Israel is a vital component of a Diaspora Jewish education, occurring at a decisive crossroads in a young person's life. The success of the experience is reflected in the many students who return home more mature in their attitudes and relationships and more committed to the ideals of Torah study, *mitzvah* observance, and Zionism throughout their lives. Therefore, it is incumbent upon all those who promote the Israel yeshivah experience to regularly evaluate it, in order to ensure its continued success.

CONTRIBUTORS

Rabbi Hayyim Angel is Associate Rabbi of Congregation Shearith Israel of New York and teaches *Tanakh* at Yeshiva University.

Steve Bailey, Ph.D., is Director of a four-year Judaic Studies curriculum development project at Moriah College in Sydney, Australia. He was co-founder and educational director of an experimental Jewish High School in Los Angeles that pioneered the Kohlbergian "Just Community" model. Dr. Bailey has written two books; the latest is a co-authored work entitled, *Curriculum: Real Teachers in Focus – A Study in Jewish Education*.

Rabbi Yitzchak Blau, currently a *rebbe* at Yeshivat HaMivtar and formerly at the Yeshivah of Flatbush High School, has published articles in *The Torah u-Madda Journal, Tradition* and *Ten Da'at*.

Rabbi Chaim Brovender, President of ATID, is Rosh Yeshivah of Yeshivat HaMivtar in Efrat.

Erica Brown is scholar-in-residence for the Jewish Federation of Greater Washington and is director of its Leadership Institute. She is the author of the forthcoming *Sacred Canvas: The Hebrew Bible through the Eyes of the Artist*.

Rabbi Shalom Carmy teaches Jewish Studies and philosophy at Yeshiva University and is Consulting Editor of *Tradition*. He is editor, most recently, of *Modern Scholarship in the Study of Torah: Contributions and Limitations*.

Dr. Yoel Finkelman, a Senior Educational Researcher at ATID and a graduate of the ATID Fellows, has taught at several one-year programs in Israel. His doctoral dissertation, entitled "Religion and Public Life in 20th Century American Jewish Thought," was recently completed for the Department of Jewish Thought at the Hebrew University of Jerusalem.

Rabbi Asher Friedman, formerly an ATID Fellow, is a *musmakh* of the Rabbi Isaac Elchanan Theological Seminary and is completing an M.A. in Jewish Philosophy at the Bernard Revel Graduate School. Asher teaches at Yeshivat Lev HaTorah, an innovative post-high school men's yeshivah, in Ramat Beit Shemesh, Israel.

Dr. Beverly Gribetz is principal of the Evelina de Rothschild Secondary School for religious girls in Jerusalem and has been teaching Talmud for nearly thirty years. Dr. Gribetz is a member of the board and faculty of ATID.

Rabbi Dr. Norman Lamm, chancellor of Yeshiva University and Rosh Yeshivah of its affiliated Rabbi Isaac Elchanan Theological Seminary, was President of Yeshiva University from 1976–2003.

Rabbi Aharon Lichtenstein is co-Rosh Yeshivah of Yeshivat Har Etzion in Alon Shevut, Israel, and a *maggid shi'ur* at the Gruss Center of Yeshivat Rabbeinu Yitzhak Elchanan in Jerusalem. A collection of his essays was recently published as *Leaves of Faith: The World of Jewish Learning.*

Gilla Ratzersdorfer Rosen is Rosh Beit Midrash of the Israeli program at Midreshet Lindenbaum and works at developing curriculum for adults in Bible, *midrash*, and Talmud at Beit Kenesset Yakar in Jerusalem. She holds an M.A. in Comparative Literature from Manchester University and is certified as a *yo'etzet halakhah* (halakhic advisor) from Nishmat.

Rabbi Gidon Rothstein is the Gruss Scholar in Residence at NYU Law School, and has taught Talmud and *Tanakh* at The Frisch School in Paramus, NJ. He is a *musmakh* of Yeshiva University with a Ph.D. from Harvard University in Jewish History and Literature.

Rabbi Doniel Schreiber teaches at Yeshivat Har Etzion in Alon Shevut, Israel, and is Director of its Overseas Student Program. He has an M.S. in Medieval Jewish History from the Bernard Revel Graduate School and rabbinic ordination from the Rabbi Isaac Elchanan Theological Seminary.

Rabbi Moshe Simkovich is the founding Head of School of Stern Hebrew High School in Philadelphia and teaches at the University of Pennsylvania Hillel. He previously taught at Maimonides School and at Ma'ayan, in Boston; served as Orthodox Adviser at Brandeis University Hillel; and was Rabbi of Congregation Shaarei Tefilla.

Dr. Dodi F. Tobin, an ATID Fellows graduate, has a Ph.D. in Clinical Psychology from Fairleigh Dickinson University. She is the Director of Social Services for the Nefesh B'Nefesh Foundation, and previously served as the Director of Student Affairs at Pardes Institute of Jewish Studies.

Yael Unterman has taught and lectured in a wide range of frameworks including Pardes, MaTaN and the Israel Defense Forces officers' course. She appears nationally in the educational play about Jewish stereotyping, "The Four Faces," and is currently writing a biography of Nehama Leibowitz *z"l*.

Rabbi Avraham Walfish holds a Ph.D. in rabbinic literature from the Hebrew University. He is an instructor at the Herzog Teacher's Training College at Yeshivat Har Etzion, and at the Teko'a Yeshivah.

Yael Wieselberg holds a degree in English Literature from Cambridge University and has taught *midrash* at seminaries in Jerusalem. A graduate of the ATID Fellows, she is currently completing a doctorate on Maharal in the department of Jewish Thought at the Hebrew University.

Dr. Joel B. Wolowelsky is Dean of the Faculty at the Yeshivah of Flatbush and a member of ATID's advisory board. He is associate editor of *Tradition* and of the series *MeOtzar HoRav: Selected Writings of Rabbi Joseph B. Soloveitchik* and the author of *Women, Jewish Law and Modernity*.

ABOUT THE EDITORS

Rabbi Jeffrey Saks is the founding director of ATID. He received ordination and an M.A. from Yeshiva University, NY, and was previously the director of Yeshivat HaMivtar in Efrat. He was a participant in the Jerusalem Fellows program for senior educators, and has published articles in *Tradition*, *The Torah U-Madda Journal*, and the *Journal of Jewish Education*.

Prof. Susan Handelman, a member of ATID's faculty and academic board, is Professor of English literature at Bar-Ilan University and for many years taught literature and Jewish studies at the University of Maryland. Her books include *The Slayers of Moses: The Emergence of Rabbinic Interpretation in Modern Literary Theory* and *Fragments of Redemption: Jewish Thought and Literary Theory in Scholem, Benjamin and Levinas*. She recently co-edited *Torah of the Mothers: Contemporary Jewish Women Read Classical Jewish Texts*.

לז"נ הילדים

נשמה חיה
כ"ה - כ"ז באדר א' תש"ס

יונה
כ"ח בסיון תשס"ג